KV-171-562

Contents

4

Mazda 323 Hatchback 1300 three-door

Mazda 323 Hatchback 1500 GT three-door five-speed

Mazda 323 Owners Workshop Manual

John S Mead

Models covered

Mazda 323 Hatchback, Saloon and Estate front-wheel-drive,
including GT versions. 1071 cc, 1296 cc and 1490 cc

Does not cover 1.6i or Turbo 4X4 models

(1033-3N1)

ABCDE
FGHIJ
KLMNO
P

Haynes Publishing Group
Sparkford Nr Yeovil
Somerset BA22 7JJ England

Haynes Publications, Inc
861 Lawrence Drive
Newbury Park
California 91320 USA

Acknowledgements

Thanks are due to Guy's Automobile Engineers of Sturminster Newton, Dorset for the provision of technical information. The Champion Sparking Plug Company supplied the illustrations showing various spark plug conditions, and Sykes-Pickavant Limited provided some of the workshop tools. Special thanks are also due to the staff at Sparkford who assisted in the production of this manual.

© **Haynes Publishing Group 1985, 1987**

A book in the **Haynes Owners Workshop Manual Series**

Printed by J. H. Haynes & Co. Ltd, Sparkford, Nr Yeovil, Somerset BA22 7JJ, England

ISBN 1 85010 315 1

British Library Cataloguing in Publication Data
Mead, John S.
    Mazda 323 (front-wheel-drive) owner's workshop
    manual. – (Owner's Workshop Manual).
    1. Mazda automobile
    I. Title   II. Series
    629.28'722   TL215.M39
    ISBN 1-85010-315-1

About this manual

Its aim

The aim of this manual is to help you get the best value from your vehicle. It can do so in several ways. It can help you decide what work must be done (even should you choose to get it done by a garage), provide information on routine maintenance and servicing, and give a logical course of action and diagnosis when random faults occur. However, it is hoped that you will use the manual by tackling the work yourself. On simpler jobs it may even be quicker than booking the car into a garage and going there twice, to leave and collect it. Perhaps most important, a lot of money can be saved by avoiding the costs a garage must charge to cover its labour and overheads.

The manual has drawings and descriptions to show the function of the various components so that their layout can be understood. Then the tasks are described and photographed in a step-by-step sequence so that even a novice can do the work.

Its arrangement

The manual is divided into thirteen Chapters, each covering a logical sub-division of the vehicle. The Chapters are each divided into Sections, numbered with single figures, eg 5; and the Sections into paragraphs (or sub-sections), with decimal numbers following on from the Section they are in, eg 5.1, 5.2, 5.3 etc.

It is freely illustrated, especially in those parts where there is a detailed sequence of operations to be carried out. There are two forms of illustration: figures and photographs. The figures are numbered in sequence with decimal numbers, according to their position in the Chapter – eg Fig. 6.4 is the fourth drawing/illustration in Chapter 6. Photographs carry the same number (either individually or in related groups) as the Section or sub-section to which they relate.

There is an alphabetical index at the back of the manual as well as a contents list at the front. Each Chapter is also preceded by its own individual contents list.

References to the 'left' or 'right' of the vehicle are in the sense of a person in the driver's seat facing forwards.

Unless otherwise stated, nuts and bolts are removed by turning anti-clockwise, and tightened by turning clockwise.

Vehicle manufacturers continually make changes to specifications and recommendations, and these, when notified, are incorporated into our manuals at the earliest opportunity.

Whilst every care is taken to ensure that the information in this manual is correct, no liability can be accepted by the authors or publishers for loss, damage or injury caused by any errors in, or omissions from, the information given.

Introduction to the Mazda 323

Introduced into the UK in the spring of 1981 the Mazda 323 quickly established itself as a leading contender in the small to medium car market and soon became the most popular Japanese car in its class in Europe.

The cars feature front-wheel-drive from a transverse engine/transmission arrangement with independent front and rear suspension, dual circuit brakes and four- or five-speed manual or three-speed automatic transmission.

The model range includes three- or five-door Hatchback or four-door Notchback Saloon versions with a choice of 1100, 1300 or 1500 cc engines and a top of the range 1500 GT twin carburettor sports model. In May 1986, a 1500 cc Estate model was introduced, and details of this and other later models will be found in the Supplement of the end of this manual.

All cars in the range have been designed with the emphasis on economical motoring, with a high standard of handling, performance and comfort.

General dimensions, weights and capacities

Dimensions

Turning circle (between kerbs)	9703 mm (382 in)
Wheelbase	2365 mm (93.1 in)
Overall length:	
Hatchback models	3955 mm (155.8 in)
Saloon models	4155 mm (163.7 in)
Overall width	1630 mm (64.2 in)
Overall height	1375 mm (54.1 in)
Ground clearance	154.9 mm (6.1 in)
Track:	
Front	1390 mm (54.7 in)
Rear	1395 mm (54.9 in)

Weights

Kerb weight (approximate)	851 kg (1872 lb)

Capacities

Engine oil (refill with filter change)	3.7 litres (6.5 Imp pints)
Manual transmission	3.2 litres (5.6 Imp pints)
Automatic transmission	5.7 litres (10 Imp pints)
Cooling system	5.5 litres (9.7 Imp pints)
Fuel tank	42 litres (9.2 Imp gallons)

Jacking and towing

Jacking

To raise the car to change a wheel ensure that it is located on firm level ground, then apply the handbrake securely. On cars equipped with manual transmission engage reverse gear, if automatic transmission is fitted place the selector lever in the park (P) position. Chock the wheel diagonally opposite the one to be changed at both the front and the rear of the tyre. Remove the spare wheel, jack handle, jack and wheel brace from the luggage compartment. Remove the plastic wheel trim, where fitted, by inserting the end of the wheel brace between trim and wheel and release with a twisting action. Slacken each of the wheel nuts by one turn. Engage the jack head with the front or rear jacking point nearest the wheel to be changed then raise the car until the tyre is clear of the ground. Remove the wheel nuts, lift off the wheel and fit the spare wheel. Screw the spare nuts back on by hand initially and then lightly tighten them using the brace. Lower the car to the ground and tighten the nuts fully. Refit the wheel trim and stow the wheel and tools in the luggage compartment. Finally, remove the chocks.

When jacking up the car to carry out repair and maintenance tasks, position the jack as follows.

If the front of the car is to be raised, position the jack head under the towing hook on the front crossmember. When the car is raised, supplement the jack with axle stands positioned under the side jacking points.

If the rear of the car is to be raised, position the jack head centrally under the rear crossmember. When the car is raised, supplement the jack with axle stands positioned alongside the jack under the crossmember or under the rear jacking points. Never work under, around or near a raised car unless it is adequately supported in at least two places with axle stands or suitable sturdy blocks.

Towing

The car may be towed for breakdown recovery purposes only using the towing hook on the front crossmember. This hook is intended for traction loads only and must not be used for lifting the car either directly or indirectly. If automatic transmission is fitted the car should only be towed at slow speed for a short distance. If a greater distance must be covered or if there is any possibility of a fault in the transmission the car must be towed with the front wheels lifted. The hook at the rear of the car is a transporter anchorage point only and should not be used to tow another vehicle.

HATCHBACK

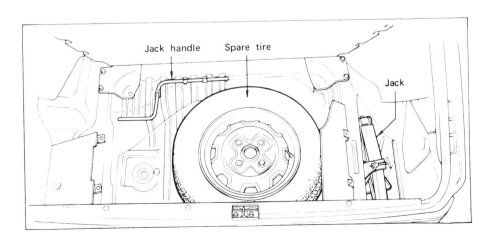

Jack, tool kit and spare wheel locations

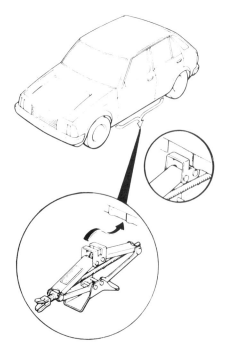

Front and rear side jacking points

Raising the front of the car using the front crossmember
jacking point

Front axle stand positions

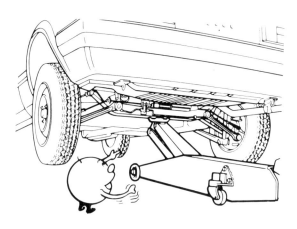

Raising the rear of the car using the rear crossmember
jacking point

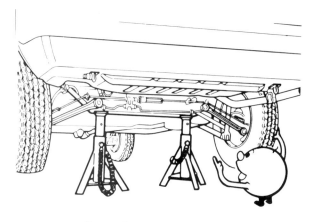

Rear axle stand positions

Buying spare parts
and vehicle identification numbers

Buying spare parts

Spare parts are available from many sources, for example Mazda garages, other garages and accessory shops, and motor factors. Our advice regarding spare part sources is as follows.

Officially appointed Mazda garages – This is the best source of parts which are peculiar to your car and are not generally available (eg complete cylinder heads, internal gearbox components, badges, interior trim etc). It is also the only place at which you should buy parts if your vehicle is still under warranty – non Mazda components may invalidate the warranty. To be sure of obtaining the correct parts it will always be necessary to give the storeman your car's vehicle identification number, and if possible, to take the 'old' part along for positive identification. Many parts are available under a factory exchange scheme – any parts returned should always be clean. It obviously makes good sense to go straight to the specialists on your car for this type of part for they are best equipped to supply you.

Other dealers and accessory shops – These are often very good places to buy materials and components needed for the maintenance of your car (eg oil filters, spark plugs, bulbs, drivebelts, oils and grease, touch-up paint, filler paste etc). They also sell general accessories, usually have convenient opening hours, charge lower prices and can often be found not far from home.

Motor factors – Good factors will stock all of the more important components which wear out relatively quickly (eg clutch components, pistons, valves, exhaust systems, brake pipes/seals and pads etc). Motor factors will often provide new or reconditioned components on a part exchange basis – this can save a considerable amount of money.

Vehicle identification numbers

Modifications are a continuing and unpublicised process in vehicle manufacture, quite apart from major model changes. Spare parts manuals and lists are compiled upon a numerical basis, the individual vehicle numbers being essential to correct identification of the component required.

When ordering spare parts, always give as much information as possible. Quote the car model, year of manufacture, body and engine numbers as appropriate.

The vehicle identification number (VIN) is stamped on a plate attached to the right-hand side of the engine compartment bulkhead.

The engine number is stamped on the upper rear edge of the cylinder block below the distributor.

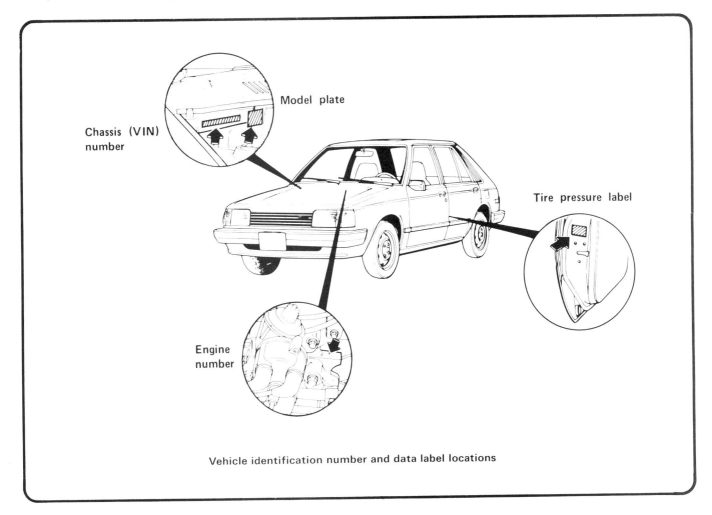

Vehicle identification number and data label locations

General repair procedures

Whenever servicing, repair or overhaul work is carried out on the car or its components, it is necessary to observe the following procedures and instructions. This will assist in carrying out the operation efficiently and to a professional standard of workmanship.

Joint mating faces and gaskets

Where a gasket is used between the mating faces of two components, ensure that it is renewed on reassembly, and fit it dry unless otherwise stated in the repair procedure. Make sure that the mating faces are clean and dry with all traces of old gasket removed. When cleaning a joint face, use a tool which is not likely to score or damage the face, and remove any burrs or nicks with an oilstone or fine file.

Make sure that tapped holes are cleaned with a pipe cleaner, and keep them free of jointing compound if this is being used unless specifically instructed otherwise.

Ensure that all orifices, channels or pipes are clear and blow through them, preferably using compressed air.

Oil seals

Whenever an oil seal is removed from its working location, either individually or as part of an assembly, it should be renewed.

The very fine sealing lip of the seal is easily damaged and will not seal if the surface it contacts is not completely clean and free from scratches, nicks or grooves. If the original sealing surface of the component cannot be restored, the component should be renewed.

Protect the lips of the seal from any surface which may damage them in the course of fitting. Use tape or a conical sleeve where possible. Lubricate the seal lips with oil before fitting and, on dual lipped seals, fill the space between the lips with grease.

Unless otherwise stated, oil seals must be fitted with their sealing lips toward the lubricant to be sealed.

Use a tubular drift or block of wood of the appropriate size to install the seal and, if the seal housing is shouldered, drive the seal down to the shoulder. If the seal housing is unshouldered, the seal should be fitted with its face flush with the housing top face.

Screw threads and fastenings

Always ensure that a blind tapped hole is completely free from oil, grease, water or other fluid before installing the bolt or stud. Failure to do this could cause the housing to crack due to the hydraulic action of the bolt or stud as it is screwed in.

When tightening a castellated nut to accept a split pin, tighten the nut to the specified torque, where applicable, and then tighten further to the next split pin hole. Never slacken the nut to align a split pin hole unless stated in the repair procedure.

When checking or retightening a nut or bolt to a specified torque setting, slacken the nut or bolt by a quarter of a turn, and then retighten to the specified setting.

Locknuts, locktabs and washers

Any fastening which will rotate against a component or housing in the course of tightening should always have a washer between it and the relevant component or housing.

Spring or split washers should always be renewed when they are used to lock a critical component such as a big-end bearing retaining nut or bolt.

Locktabs which are folded over to retain a nut or bolt should always be renewed.

Self-locking nuts can be reused in non-critical areas, providing resistance can be felt when the locking portion passes over the bolt or stud thread.

Split pins must always be replaced with new ones of the correct size for the hole.

Special tools

Some repair procedures in this manual entail the use of special tools such as a press, two or three-legged pullers, spring compressors etc. Wherever possible, suitable readily available alternatives to the manufacturer's special tools are described, and are shown in use. In some instances, where no alternative is possible, it has been necessary to resort to the use of a manufacturer's tool and this has been done for reasons of safety as well as the efficient completion of the repair operation. Unless you are highly skilled and have a thorough understanding of the procedure described, never attempt to bypass the use of any special tool when the procedure described specifies its use. Not only is there a very great risk of personal injury, but expensive damage could be caused to the components involved.

Tools and working facilities

Introduction

A selection of good tools is a fundamental requirement for anyone contemplating the maintenance and repair of a motor vehicle. For the owner who does not possess any, their purchase will prove a considerable expense, offsetting some of the savings made by doing-it-yourself. However, provided that the tools purchased are of good quality, they will last for many years and prove an extremely worthwhile investment.

To help the average owner to decide which tools are needed to carry out the various tasks detailed in this manual, we have compiled three lists of tools under the following headings: *Maintenance and minor repair*, *Repair and overhaul*, and *Special*. The newcomer to practical mechanics should start off with the *Maintenance and minor repair* tool kit and confine himself to the simpler jobs around the vehicle. Then, as his confidence and experience grow, he can undertake more difficult tasks, buying extra tools as, and when, they are needed. In this way, a *Maintenance and minor repair* tool kit can be built-up into a *Repair and overhaul* tool kit over a considerable period of time without any major cash outlays. The experienced do-it-yourselfer will have a tool kit good enough for most repair and overhaul procedures and will add tools from the *Special* category when he feels the expense is justified by the amount of use to which these tools will be put.

It is obviously not possible to cover the subject of tools fully here. For those who wish to learn more about tools and their use there is a book entitled *How to Choose and Use Car Tools* available from the publishers of this manual.

Maintenance and minor repair tool kit

The tools given in this list should be considered as a minimum requirement if routine maintenance, servicing and minor repair operations are to be undertaken. We recommend the purchase of combination spanners (ring one end, open-ended the other); although more expensive than open-ended ones, they do give the advantages of both types of spanner.

Combination spanners - 10, 11, 12, 13, 14 & 17 mm
Adjustable spanner - 9 inch
Spark plug spanner (with rubber insert)
Spark plug gap adjustment tool
Set of feeler gauges
Brake bleed nipple spanner
Screwdriver - 4 in long x ¼ in dia (flat blade)
Screwdriver - 4 in long x ¼ in dia (cross blade)
Combination pliers - 6 inch
Hacksaw (junior)
Tyre pump
Tyre pressure gauge
Oil can
Fine emery cloth (1 sheet)
Wire brush (small)
Funnel (medium size)

Repair and overhaul tool kit

These tools are virtually essential for anyone undertaking any major repairs to a motor vehicle, and are additional to those given in the *Maintenance and minor repair* list. Included in this list is a comprehensive set of sockets. Although these are expensive they will be found invaluable as they are so versatile - particularly if various drives are included in the set. We recommend the ½ in square-drive type, as this can be used with most proprietary torque wrenches. If you cannot afford a socket set, even bought piecemeal, then inexpensive tubular box spanners are a useful alternative.

The tools in this list will occasionally need to be supplemented by tools from the *Special* list.

Sockets (or box spanners) to cover range in previous list
Reversible ratchet drive (for use with sockets)
Extension piece, 10 inch (for use with sockets)
Universal joint (for use with sockets)
Torque wrench (for use with sockets)
'Mole' wrench - 8 inch
Ball pein hammer
Soft-faced hammer, plastic or rubber
Screwdriver - 6 in long x 56 in dia (flat blade)
Screwdriver - 2 in long x 56 in square (flat blade)
Screwdriver - 1½ in long x ¼ in dia (cross blade)
Screwdriver - 3 in long x ⅛ in dia (electricians)
Pliers - electricians side cutters
Pliers - needle nosed
Pliers - circlip (internal and external)
Cold chisel - ½ inch
Scriber
Scraper
Centre punch
Pin punch
Hacksaw
Valve grinding tool
Steel rule/straight-edge
Allen keys
Selection of files
Wire brush (large)
Axle-stands
Jack (strong trolley or hydraulic type)

Special tools

The tools in this list are those which are not used regularly, are expensive to buy, or which need to be used in accordance with their manufacturers' instructions. Unless relatively difficult mechanical jobs are undertaken frequently, it will not be economic to buy many of these tools. Where this is the case, you could consider clubbing together with friends (or joining a motorists' club) to make a joint purchase, or borrowing the tools against a deposit from a local garage or tool hire specialist.

The following list contains only those tools and instruments freely available to the public, and not those special tools produced by the vehicle manufacturer specifically for its dealer network. You will find occasional references to these manufacturers' special tools in the text of this manual. Generally, an alternative method of doing the job without the vehicle manufacturers' special tool is given. However, sometimes, there is no alternative but to using them. Where this is the case and the relevant tool cannot be bought or borrowed, you will have to entrust the work to a franchised garage.

> *Valve spring compressor*
> *Piston ring compressor*
> *Balljoint separator*
> *Universal hub/bearing puller*
> *Impact screwdriver*
> *Micrometer and/or vernier gauge*
> *Dial gauge*
> *Stroboscopic timing light*
> *Dwell angle meter/tachometer*
> *Universal electrical multi-meter*
> *Cylinder compression gauge*
> *Lifting tackle*
> *Trolley jack*
> *Light with extension lead*

Buying tools

For practically all tools, a tool factor is the best source since he will have a very comprehensive range compared with the average garage or accessory shop. Having said that, accessory shops often offer excellent quality tools at discount prices, so it pays to shop around.

Remember, you don't have to buy the most expensive items on the shelf, but it is always advisable to steer clear of the very cheap tools. There are plenty of good tools around at reasonable prices, so ask the proprietor or manager of the shop for advice before making a purchase.

Care and maintenance of tools

Having purchased a reasonable tool kit, it is necessary to keep the tools in a clean serviceable condition. After use, always wipe off any dirt, grease and metal particles using a clean, dry cloth, before putting the tools away. Never leave them lying around after they have been used. A simple tool rack on the garage or workshop wall, for items such as screwdrivers and pliers is a good idea. Store all normal wrenches and sockets in a metal box. Any measuring instruments, gauges, meters, etc, must be carefully stored where they cannot be damaged or become rusty.

Take a little care when tools are used. Hammer heads inevitably become marked and screwdrivers lose the keen edge on their blades from time to time. A little timely attention with emery cloth or a file will soon restore items like this to a good serviceable finish.

Working facilities

Not to be forgotten when discussing tools, is the workshop itself. If anything more than routine maintenance is to be carried out, some form of suitable working area becomes essential.

It is appreciated that many an owner mechanic is forced by circumstances to remove an engine or similar item, without the benefit of a garage or workshop. Having done this, any repairs should always be done under the cover of a roof.

Wherever possible, any dismantling should be done on a clean, flat workbench or table at a suitable working height.

Any workbench needs a vice: one with a jaw opening of 4 in (100 mm) is suitable for most jobs. As mentioned previously, some clean dry storage space is also required for tools, as well as for lubricants, cleaning fluids, touch-up paints and so on, which become necessary.

Another item which may be required, and which has a much more general usage, is an electric drill with a chuck capacity of at least 56 in (8 mm). This, together with a good range of twist drills, is virtually essential for fitting accessories such as mirrors and reversing lights.

Last, but not least, always keep a supply of old newspapers and clean, lint-free rags available, and try to keep any working area as clean as possible.

Spanner jaw gap comparison table

Jaw gap (in)	Spanner size
0.250	$\frac{1}{4}$ in AF
0.276	7 mm
0.313	$\frac{5}{16}$ in AF
0.315	8 mm
0.344	$\frac{11}{32}$ in AF; $\frac{1}{8}$ in Whitworth
0.354	9 mm
0.375	$\frac{3}{8}$ in AF
0.394	10 mm
0.433	11 mm
0.438	$\frac{7}{16}$ in AF
0.445	$\frac{3}{16}$ in Whitworth; $\frac{1}{4}$ in BSF
0.472	12 mm
0.500	$\frac{1}{2}$ in AF
0.512	13 mm
0.525	$\frac{1}{4}$ in Whitworth; $\frac{5}{16}$ in BSF
0.551	14 mm
0.563	$\frac{9}{16}$ in AF
0.591	15 mm
0.600	$\frac{5}{16}$ in Whitworth; $\frac{3}{8}$ in BSF
0.625	$\frac{5}{8}$ in AF
0.630	16 mm
0.669	17 mm
0.686	$\frac{11}{16}$ in AF
0.709	18 mm
0.710	$\frac{3}{8}$ in Whitworth; $\frac{7}{16}$ in BSF
0.748	19 mm
0.750	$\frac{3}{4}$ in AF
0.813	$\frac{13}{16}$ in AF
0.820	$\frac{7}{16}$ in Whitworth; $\frac{1}{2}$ in BSF
0.866	22 mm
0.875	$\frac{7}{8}$ in AF
0.920	$\frac{1}{2}$ in Whitworth; $\frac{9}{16}$ in BSF
0.938	$\frac{15}{16}$ in AF
0.945	24 mm
1.000	1 in AF
1.010	$\frac{9}{16}$ in Whitworth; $\frac{5}{8}$ in BSF
1.024	26 mm
1.063	$1\frac{1}{16}$ in AF; 27 mm
1.100	$\frac{5}{8}$ in Whitworth; $\frac{11}{16}$ in BSF
1.125	$1\frac{1}{8}$ in AF
1.181	30 mm
1.200	$\frac{11}{16}$ in Whitworth; $\frac{3}{4}$ in BSF
1.250	$1\frac{1}{4}$ in AF
1.260	32 mm
1.300	$\frac{3}{4}$ in Whitworth; $\frac{7}{8}$ in BSF
1.313	$1\frac{5}{16}$ in AF
1.390	$\frac{13}{16}$ in Whitworth; $\frac{15}{16}$ in BSF
1.417	36 mm
1.438	$1\frac{7}{16}$ in AF
1.480	$\frac{7}{8}$ in Whitworth; 1 in BSF
1.500	$1\frac{1}{2}$ in AF
1.575	40 mm; $\frac{15}{16}$ in Whitworth
1.614	41 mm
1.625	$1\frac{5}{8}$ in AF
1.670	1 in Whitworth; $1\frac{1}{8}$ in BSF
1.688	$1\frac{11}{16}$ in AF
1.811	46 mm
1.813	$1\frac{13}{16}$ in AF
1.860	$1\frac{1}{8}$ in Whitworth; $1\frac{1}{4}$ in BSF
1.875	$1\frac{7}{8}$ in AF
1.969	50 mm
2.000	2 in AF
2.050	$1\frac{1}{4}$ in Whitworth; $1\frac{3}{8}$ in BSF
2.165	55 mm
2.362	60 mm

Conversion factors

Length (distance)

Inches (in)	X	25.4	= Millimetres (mm)	X 0.0394	= Inches (in)
Feet (ft)	X	0.305	= Metres (m)	X 3.281	= Feet (ft)
Miles	X	1.609	= Kilometres (km)	X 0.621	= Miles

Volume (capacity)

Cubic inches (cu in; in^3)	X	16.387	= Cubic centimetres (cc; cm^3)	X 0.061	= Cubic inches (cu in; in^3)
Imperial pints (Imp pt)	X	0.568	= Litres (l)	X 1.76	= Imperial pints (Imp pt)
Imperial quarts (Imp qt)	X	1.137	= Litres (l)	X 0.88	= Imperial quarts (Imp qt)
Imperial quarts (Imp qt)	X	1.201	= US quarts (US qt)	X 0.833	= Imperial quarts (Imp qt)
US quarts (US qt)	X	0.946	= Litres (l)	X 1.057	= US quarts (US qt)
Imperial gallons (Imp gal)	X	4.546	= Litres (l)	X 0.22	= Imperial gallons (Imp gal)
Imperial gallons (Imp gal)	X	1.201	= US gallons (US gal)	X 0.833	= Imperial gallons (Imp gal)
US gallons (US gal)	X	3.785	= Litres (l)	X 0.264	= US gallons (US gal)

Mass (weight)

Ounces (oz)	X	28.35	= Grams (g)	X 0.035	= Ounces (oz)
Pounds (lb)	X	0.454	= Kilograms (kg)	X 2.205	= Pounds (lb)

Force

Ounces-force (ozf; oz)	X	0.278	= Newtons (N)	X 3.6	= Ounces-force (ozf; oz)
Pounds-force (lbf; lb)	X	4.448	= Newtons (N)	X 0.225	= Pounds-force (lbf; lb)
Newtons (N)	X	0.1	= Kilograms-force (kgf; kg)	X 9.81	= Newtons (N)

Pressure

Pounds-force per square inch (psi; lbf/in^2; lb/in^2)	X	0.070	= Kilograms-force per square centimetre (kgf/cm^2; kg/cm^2)	X 14.223	= Pounds-force per square inch (psi; lbf/in^2; lb/in^2)
Pounds-force per square inch (psi; lbf/in^2; lb/in^2)	X	0.068	= Atmospheres (atm)	X 14.696	= Pounds-force per square inch (psi; lbf/in^2; lb/in^2)
Pounds-force per square inch (psi; lbf/in^2; lb/in^2)	X	0.069	= Bars	X 14.5	= Pounds-force per square inch (psi; lbf/in^2; lb/in^2)
Pounds-force per square inch (psi; lbf/in^2; lb/in^2)	X	6.895	= Kilopascals (kPa)	X 0.145	= Pounds-force per square inch (psi; lbf/in^2; lb/in^2)
Kilopascals (kPa)	X	0.01	= Kilograms-force per square centimetre (kgf/cm^2; kg/cm^2)	X 98.1	= Kilopascals (kPa)

Torque (moment of force)

Pounds-force inches (lbf in; lb in)	X	1.152	= Kilograms-force centimetre (kgf cm; kg cm)	X 0.868	= Pounds-force inches (lbf in; lb in)
Pounds-force inches (lbf in; lb in)	X	0.113	= Newton metres (Nm)	X 8.85	= Pounds-force inches (lbf in; lb in)
Pounds-force inches (lbf in; lb in)	X	0.083	= Pounds-force feet (lbf ft; lb ft)	X 12	= Pounds-force inches (lbf in; lb in)
Pounds-force feet (lbf ft; lb ft)	X	0.138	= Kilograms-force metres (kgf m; kg m)	X 7.233	= Pounds-force feet (lbf ft; lb ft)
Pounds-force feet (lbf ft; lb ft)	X	1.356	= Newton metres (Nm)	X 0.738	= Pounds-force feet (lbf ft; lb ft)
Newton metres (Nm)	X	0.102	= Kilograms-force metres (kgf m; kg m)	X 9.804	= Newton metres (Nm)

Power

Horsepower (hp)	X	745.7	= Watts (W)	X 0.0013	= Horsepower (hp)

Velocity (speed)

Miles per hour (miles/hr; mph)	X	1.609	= Kilometres per hour (km/hr; kph)	X 0.621	= Miles per hour (miles/hr; mph)

Fuel consumption*

Miles per gallon, Imperial (mpg)	X	0.354	= Kilometres per litre (km/l)	X 2.825	= Miles per gallon, Imperial (mpg)
Miles per gallon, US (mpg)	X	0.425	= Kilometres per litre (km/l)	X 2.352	= Miles per gallon, US (mpg)

Temperature

Degrees Fahrenheit $= (°C \times 1.8) + 32$

Degrees Celsius (Degrees Centigrade; °C) $= (°F - 32) \times 0.56$

*It is common practice to convert from miles per gallon (mpg) to litres/100 kilometres (l/100km), where mpg (Imperial) x l/100 km = 282 and mpg (US) x l/100 km = 235

Safety first!

Professional motor mechanics are trained in safe working procedures. However enthusiastic you may be about getting on with the job in hand, do take the time to ensure that your safety is not put at risk. A moment's lack of attention can result in an accident, as can failure to observe certain elementary precautions.

There will always be new ways of having accidents, and the following points do not pretend to be a comprehensive list of all dangers; they are intended rather to make you aware of the risks and to encourage a safety-conscious approach to all work you carry out on your vehicle.

Essential DOs and DON'Ts

DON'T rely on a single jack when working underneath the vehicle. Always use reliable additional means of support, such as axle stands, securely placed under a part of the vehicle that you know will not give way.

DON'T attempt to loosen or tighten high-torque nuts (e.g. wheel hub nuts) while the vehicle is on a jack; it may be pulled off.

DON'T start the engine without first ascertaining that the transmission is in neutral (or 'Park' where applicable) and the parking brake applied.

DON'T suddenly remove the filler cap from a hot cooling system – cover it with a cloth and release the pressure gradually first, or you may get scalded by escaping coolant.

DON'T attempt to drain oil until you are sure it has cooled sufficiently to avoid scalding you.

DON'T grasp any part of the engine, exhaust or catalytic converter without first ascertaining that it is sufficiently cool to avoid burning you.

DON'T allow brake fluid or antifreeze to contact vehicle paintwork.

DON'T syphon toxic liquids such as fuel, brake fluid or antifreeze by mouth, or allow them to remain on your skin.

DON'T inhale dust – it may be injurious to health (see *Asbestos* below).

DON'T allow any spilt oil or grease to remain on the floor – wipe it up straight away, before someone slips on it.

DON'T use ill-fitting spanners or other tools which may slip and cause injury.

DON'T attempt to lift a heavy component which may be beyond your capability – get assistance.

DON'T rush to finish a job, or take unverified short cuts.

DON'T allow children or animals in or around an unattended vehicle.

DO wear eye protection when using power tools such as drill, sander, bench grinder etc, and when working under the vehicle.

DO use a barrier cream on your hands prior to undertaking dirty jobs – it will protect your skin from infection as well as making the dirt easier to remove afterwards; but make sure your hands aren't left slippery.

DO keep loose clothing (cuffs, tie etc) and long hair well out of the way of moving mechanical parts.

DO remove rings, wristwatch etc, before working on the vehicle – especially the electrical system.

DO ensure that any lifting tackle used has a safe working load rating adequate for the job.

DO keep your work area tidy – it is only too easy to fall over articles left lying around.

DO get someone to check periodically that all is well, when working alone on the vehicle.

DO carry out work in a logical sequence and check that everything is correctly assembled and tightened afterwards.

DO remember that your vehicle's safety affects that of yourself and others. If in doubt on any point, get specialist advice.

IF, in spite of following these precautions, you are unfortunate enough to injure yourself, seek medical attention as soon as possible.

Asbestos

Certain friction, insulating, sealing, and other products – such as brake linings, brake bands, clutch linings, torque converters, gaskets, etc – contain asbestos. *Extreme care must be taken to avoid inhalation of dust from such products since it is hazardous to health.* If in doubt, assume that they *do* contain asbestos.

Fire

Remember at all times that petrol (gasoline) is highly flammable. Never smoke, or have any kind of naked flame around, when working on the vehicle. But the risk does not end there – a spark caused by an electrical short-circuit, by two metal surfaces contacting each other, by careless use of tools, or even by static electricity built up in your body under certain conditions, can ignite petrol vapour, which in a confined space is highly explosive.

Always disconnect the battery earth (ground) terminal before working on any part of the fuel or electrical system, and never risk spilling fuel on to a hot engine or exhaust.

It is recommended that a fire extinguisher of a type suitable for fuel and electrical fires is kept handy in the garage or workplace at all times. Never try to extinguish a fuel or electrical fire with water.

Fumes

Certain fumes are highly toxic and can quickly cause unconsciousness and even death if inhaled to any extent. Petrol (gasoline) vapour comes into this category, as do the vapours from certain solvents such as trichloroethylene. Any draining or pouring of such volatile fluids should be done in a well ventilated area.

When using cleaning fluids and solvents, read the instructions carefully. Never use materials from unmarked containers – they may give off poisonous vapours.

Never run the engine of a motor vehicle in an enclosed space such as a garage. Exhaust fumes contain carbon monoxide which is extremely poisonous; if you need to run the engine, always do so in the open air or at least have the rear of the vehicle outside the workplace.

If you are fortunate enough to have the use of an inspection pit, never drain or pour petrol, and never run the engine, while the vehicle is standing over it; the fumes, being heavier than air, will concentrate in the pit with possibly lethal results.

The battery

Never cause a spark, or allow a naked light, near the vehicle's battery. It will normally be giving off a certain amount of hydrogen gas, which is highly explosive.

Always disconnect the battery earth (ground) terminal before working on the fuel or electrical systems.

If possible, loosen the filler plugs or cover when charging the battery from an external source. Do not charge at an excessive rate or the battery may burst.

Take care when topping up and when carrying the battery. The acid electrolyte, even when diluted, is very corrosive and should not be allowed to contact the eyes or skin.

If you ever need to prepare electrolyte yourself, always add the acid slowly to the water, and never the other way round. Protect against splashes by wearing rubber gloves and goggles.

When jump starting a car using a booster battery, for negative earth (ground) vehicles, connect the jump leads in the following sequence: First connect one jump lead between the positive (+) terminals of the two batteries. Then connect the other jump lead first to the negative (–) terminal of the booster battery, and then to a good earthing (ground) point on the vehicle to be started, at least 18 in (45 cm) from the battery if possible. Ensure that hands and jump leads are clear of any moving parts, and that the two vehicles do not touch. Disconnect the leads in the reverse order.

Mains electricity

When using an electric power tool, inspection light etc, which works from the mains, always ensure that the appliance is correctly connected to its plug and that, where necessary, it is properly earthed (grounded). Do not use such appliances in damp conditions and, again, beware of creating a spark or applying excessive heat in the vicinity of fuel or fuel vapour.

Ignition HT voltage

A severe electric shock can result from touching certain parts of the ignition system, such as the HT leads, when the engine is running or being cranked, particularly if components are damp or the insulation is defective. Where an electronic ignition system is fitted, the HT voltage is much higher and could prove fatal.

Routine maintenance

For additional information, see Supplement at end of manual

Maintenance is essential for ensuring safety, and desirable for the purpose of getting the best in terms of performance and economy from your car. Over the years the need for periodic lubrication has been greatly reduced if not totally eliminated. This has unfortunately tended to lead some owners to think that, because no such action is required, the items either no longer exist, or will last forever. This is certainly not the case; it is essential to carry out regular visual examination as comprehensively as possible in order to spot any possible defects at an early stage before they develop into major expensive repairs.

The following service schedules are a list of the maintenance requirements and the intervals at which they should be carried out, as recommended by the manufacturers. Where applicable these procedures are covered in greater detail throughout this manual, near the beginning of each Chapter.

Engine and underbonnet component locations (air cleaner removed for clarity)

1	Vehicle identification number	5 Fuel filter	9 Radiator filler cap	13 Oil filler cap
2	Carburettor	6 Cooling system expansion tank	10 Air cleaner hot air stove	14 Brake fluid reservoir
3	Fuel pump	7 Ignition coil	11 Engine oil dipstick	15 Alternator
4	Distributor	8 Battery	12 Washer reservoir	16 Clutch adjuster

Front underbody view (engine undertrays removed for clarity)

1 Front towing hook
2 Front crossmember
3 Front lower suspension arm
4 Transmission drain plug
5 Tie-rod outer balljoint
6 Steering gear tie-rod
7 Lower suspension arm front mounting
   bracket

8 Lower suspension arm rear mounting
9 Exhaust rubber mounting
10 Gearchange rod
11 Exhaust intermediate pipe
12 Gearchange remote control housing
13 Exhaust system flexible joint

14 Driveshaft vibration damper
15 Balljoint retaining nuts
16 Engine oil drain plug
17 Exhaust front pipe
18 Bottom hose
19 Radiator drain plug

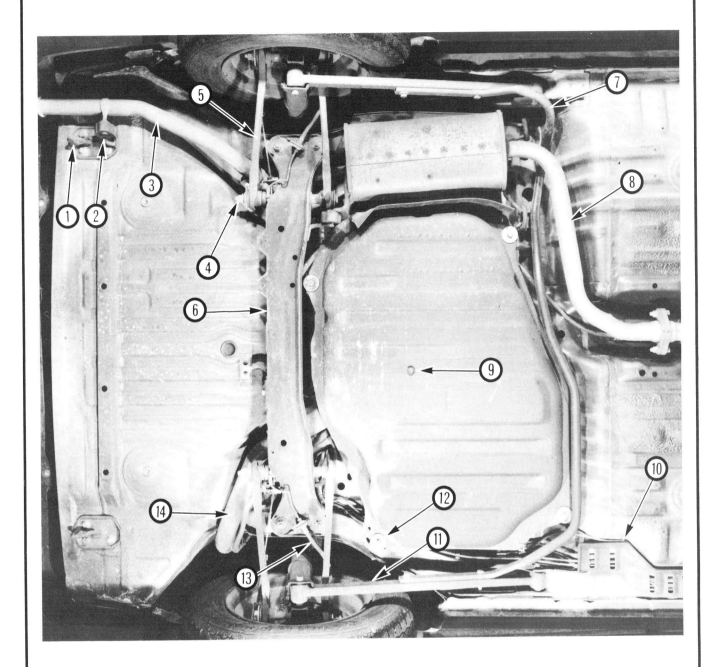

Rear underbody view

1 Anchorage hook	5 Lateral link	10 Fuel and fluid pipe plastic cover
2 Exhaust rear mounting	6 Rear crossmember	11 Trailing arm
3 Exhaust tailpipe	7 Rear anti-roll bar	12 Fuel tank mounting
4 Lateral link retaining nut and toe	8 Exhaust rear section	13 Rear brake hose
setting adjustment point	9 Fuel tank drain plug	14 Fuel tank filler and vent hoses

Every 250 miles (400 km) or weekly – whichever comes first

Engine, cooling system and brakes:
Check the engine oil level and top up if necessary (Chapter 1, Section 2)
Check the water level in the radiator or, on later models the expansion tank, and top up if necessary (Chapter 2, Section 2)
Check the brake fluid level in the master cylinder reservoir and top up if necessary (Chapter 9, Section2)

Battery, lights and wipers:
Check the operation of all interior and exterior lights, wipers and washers (Section 3)
Check and if necessary top up the washer reservoir (Section 3)
Check and if necessary top up the battery (Section 3)

Tyres:
Check the tyre pressures (Chapter 10, Section 27)
Visually examine the tyres for wear or tread damage (Chapter 10, Section 27)

General:
Clean the windscreen and if necessary the windows
Clean the headlight and rear light lenses

Every 6000 miles (10 000 km) or 6 months – whichever comes first

Engine (Chapter 1):
Renew the engine oil and filter (Section 2)
Adjust the valve clearances (Section 42)

Cooling system (Chapter 2):
Check the water level and top up if necessary (Section 2)
Check the drivebelt condition and renew it or adjust its tension (Section 13)

Fuel and exhaust system (Chapter 3):
Clean the air cleaner element (Section 2)
Set the air cleaner temperature control according to season (Section 2)
Adjust the carburettor idle speed and mixture settings (Section 9)

Ignition system (Chapter 4):
Clean the distributor cap and examine the segments (Section 2)
Check and adjust the contact breaker points (where fitted) (Sections 3 and 4)
Remove, clean, regap and test the spark plugs (Section 11)
Check and if necessary adjust the ignition timing (Section 9)

Clutch (Chapter 5):
Check and if necessary adjust the clutch pedal height and free play (Section 2)

Manual transmission (Chapter 6):
Check and if necessary top up transmission lubricant (Section 2)

Driveshafts (Chapter 8):
Check the condition of the constant velocity joint rubber boots (Section 2)

Braking system (Chapter 9):
Check and if necessary top up the brake fluid in the master cylinder reservoir (Section 2)
Check the front disc pad thickness (Section 4)
Check and if necessary adjust the brake pedal height and free play (Section 3)
Check the handbrake operation (Section 15)

Suspension and steering (Chapter 10):
Check the condition of all balljoint and steering gear rubber boots (Section 2)

Check all the steering and suspension components for wear or excess free play (Section 2)
Check the tyres for damage, tread depth and uneven wear (Section 27)
Check the tightness of the wheel nuts (Section 27)

Every 12 000 miles (20 000 km) or 12 months – whichever occurs first

In addition to all the items in the 6000 mile (10 000 km) service, carry out the following:

Engine (Chapter 1):
Visually check the engine for oil leaks and for the security and condition of all related components and attachments (Section 2)

Cooling system (Chapter 2):
Check the hoses, hose clips and visible joint gaskets for leaks and any signs of corrosion or deterioration (Section 2)

Fuel and exhaust system (Chapter 3):
Visually inspect the fuel tank and fuel pipes for leaks and security (Section 2)
Renew the fuel filter (Section 2)
Check the operation of the accelerator and choke control linkage and lubricate the linkage (Section 2)
Check the carburettor vacuum diaphragm and secondary fuel cut-off system adjustment (Sections 10 and 11)
Check the condition of the exhaust system and mountings (Section 2)

Ignition system (Chapter 4):
Clean the distributor cap, HT lead and related wiring and check the leads and wiring for security (Section 2)

Manual transmission (Chapter 6):
Visually check the transmission joint faces and oil seals for leaks (Section 2)

Automatic transmission (Chapter 7):
Check and if necessary top up the transmission fluid (Section 3)
Check transmission joint faces and oil seals for leaks (Section 2)

Driveshaft (Chapter 8):
Check the condition of the driveshafts, driveshaft joints and rubber boots (Sections 2, 4 and 5)

Braking system (Chapter 9)
Check the front disc pads and rear brake shoes for the condition and thickness of the friction material (Sections 4 and 7)
Visually inspect all brake pipes, hoses and unions for corrosion, chafing, leakage and security (Section 13)
Check the operation of the vacuum servo unit (Section 20)
Lubricate the handbrake exposed cables and linkage (Section 17)

Suspension and steering (Chapter 10):
Check the operation of the shock absorbers and inspect for fluid leakage (Section 2)
Check the front and rear wheel toe setting (Section 26)

Bodywork (Chapter 11):
Carefully inspect the paintwork for damage and the bodywork for condition (Section 2)
Check the condition of the underseal (Section 2)
Lubricate all locks and hinges (not the steering lock) (Section 6)

Electrical system (Chapter 12):
Check the operation of all electrical equipment and accessories (Section 3)
Check the condition and security of all accessible wiring connectors, harnesses and retaining clips (Section 3)
Check the headlight aim (Section 26)
Check the battery condition (Sections 3 and 5)

Check the security of the battery terminals and smear with petroleum jelly (Section 3)

Road test:
Check the function of all instruments and electrical equipment
Check the operation of the seat belts
Check for any abnormalities in the steering, suspension handling or road feel
Check the performance of the engine, clutch and transmission
Check the performance of the braking system

Every 24 000 miles (40 000 km) or 24 months – whichever occurs first

In addition to all the items in the 12 000 mile (20 000 km) service, carry out the following

Engine (Chapter 1):
Check the torque of the cylinder head bolts (Section 4)

Cooling system (Chapter 2):
Drain and flush the system and refill with fresh antifreeze (Sections 3, 4 and 5)

Fuel and exhaust system (Chapter 3):
Renew the air cleaner element (Sections 2 and 3)

Manual transmission (Chapter 6):
Renew the transmission lubricant (Section 3)

Braking system (Chapter 9):
Renew the brake fluid (Section 14)

Suspension and steering (Chapter 10):
Pack the front and rear hub bearings with fresh grease (Sections 4 and 11)

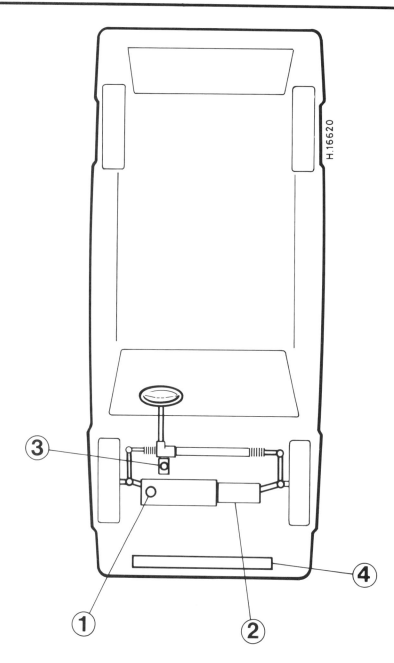

H.16620

Recommended lubricants and fluids

Component or system	Lubricant type or specification
Engine (1)	SAE 10W/40 multigrade engine oil (or multigrade engine oil with a viscosity rating suitable for the environmental temperature in which the vehicle is operated – see owners handbook)

Manual transmission (2)
    Up to approximately September 1981
    From approximately September 1981 onward
	Type F automatic transmission fluid
	SAE 80 or SAE 90 gear oil

Automatic transmission (2)	Type F automatic transmission fluid
Brake fluid reservoir (3)	Hydraulic fluid to SAE J1703a, DOT-3 or DOT-4
Cooling system (4)	Ethylene Glycol antifreeze
General greasing	NLG1 No 2 Multi-purpose lithium based grease

Fault diagnosis

Introduction

The vehicle owner who does his or her own maintenance according to the recommended schedules should not have to use this section of the manual very often. Modern component reliability is such that, provided those items subject to wear or deterioration are inspected or renewed at the specified intervals, sudden failure is comparatively rare. Faults do not usually just happen as a result of sudden failure, but develop over a period of time. Major mechanical failures in particular are usually preceded by characteristic symptoms over hundreds or even thousands of miles. Those components which do occasionally fail without warning are often small and easily carried in the vehicle.

With any fault finding, the first step is to decide where to begin investigations. Sometimes this is obvious, but on other occasions a little detective work will be necessary. The owner who makes half a dozen haphazard adjustments or replacements may be successful in curing a fault (or its symptoms), but he will be none the wiser if the fault recurs and he may well have spent more time and money than was necessary. A calm and logical approach will be found to be more satisfactory in the long run. Always take into account any warning signs or abnormalities that may have been noticed in the period preceding the fault – power loss, high or low gauge readings, unusual noises or smells, etc – and remember that failure of components such as fuses or spark plugs may only be pointers to some underlying fault.

The pages which follow here are intended to help in cases of failure to start or breakdown on the road. There is also a Fault Diagnosis Section at the end of each Chapter which should be consulted if the preliminary checks prove unfruitful. Whatever the fault, certain basic principles apply. These are as follows:

Verify the fault. This is simply a matter of being sure that you know what the symptoms are before starting work. This is particularly important if you are investigating a fault for someone else who may not have described it very accurately.

Don't overlook the obvious. For example, if the vehicle won't start, is there petrol in the tank? (Don't take anyone else's word on this particular point, and don't trust the fuel gauge either!) If an electrical fault is indicated, look for loose or broken wires before digging out the test gear.

Cure the disease, not the symptom. Substituting a flat battery with a fully charged one will get you off the hard shoulder, but if the underlying cause is not attended to, the new battery will go the same way. Similarly, changing oil-fouled spark plugs for a new set will get you moving again, but remember that the reason for the fouling (if it wasn't simply an incorrect grade of plug) will have to be established and corrected.

Don't take anything for granted. Particularly, don't forget that a 'new' component may itself be defective (especially if it's been rattling round in the boot for months), and don't leave components out of a fault diagnosis sequence just because they are new or recently fitted. When you do finally diagnose a difficult fault, you'll probably realise that all the evidence was there from the start.

Electrical faults

Electrical faults can be more puzzling than straightforward mechanical failures, but they are no less susceptible to logical analysis if the basic principles of operation are understood. Vehicle electrical wiring exists in extremely unfavourable conditions – heat, vibration and chemical attack – and the first things to look for are loose or corroded connections and broken or chafed wires, especially where the wires pass through holes in the bodywork or are subject to vibration.

All metal-bodied vehicles in current production have one pole of the battery 'earthed', ie connected to the vehicle bodywork, and in nearly all modern vehicles it is the negative (–) terminal. The various electrical components – motors, bulb holders etc – are also connected to earth, either by means of a lead or directly by their mountings. Electric current flows through the component and then back to the battery via the bodywork. If the component mounting is loose or corroded, or if a good path back to the battery is not available, the circuit will be incomplete and malfunction will result. The engine and/or gearbox are also earthed by means of flexible metal straps to the body or subframe; if these straps are loose or missing, starter motor, generator and ignition trouble may result.

Assuming the earth return to be satisfactory, electrical faults will be due either to component malfunction or to defects in the current supply. Individual components are dealt with in Chapter 12. If supply wires are broken or cracked internally this results in an open-circuit, and the easiest way to check for this is to bypass the suspect wire temporarily with a length of wire having a crocodile clip or suitable connector at each end. Alternatively, a 12V test lamp can be used to verify the presence of supply voltage at various points along the wire and the break can be thus isolated.

If a bare portion of a live wire touches the bodywork or other earthed metal part, the electricity will take the low-resistance path thus

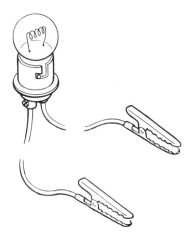

A simple test lamp is useful for checking electrical circuits

carried. Experience and available space will modify the list below, but the following may save having to call on professional assistance:

Spark plugs, clean and correctly gapped
HT lead and plug cap – long enough to reach the plug furthest from the distributor
Distributor rotor, condenser and contact breaker points (where applicable)
Drivebelt(s) – emergency type may suffice
Spare fuses
Set of principal light bulbs
Tin of radiator sealer and hose bandage
Exhaust bandage
Roll of insulating tape
Length of soft iron wire
Length of electrical flex
Torch or inspection lamp (can double as test lamp)
Battery jump leads
Tow-rope
Ignition waterproofing aerosol
Litre of engine oil
Sealed can of hydraulic fluid
Emergency windscreen
'Jubilee' clips
Tube of filler paste

If spare fuel is carried, a can designed for the purpose should be used to minimise risks of leakage and collision damage. A first aid kit and a warning triangle, whilst not at present compulsory in the UK, are obviously sensible items to carry in addition to the above.

When touring abroad it may be advisable to carry additional spares which, even if you cannot fit them yourself, could save having to wait while parts are obtained. The items below may be worth considering:

Clutch and throttle cables
Cylinder head gasket
Tyre valve core

One of the motoring organisations will be able to advise on availability of fuel etc in foreign countries.

formed back to the battery: this is known as a short-circuit. Hopefully a short-circuit will blow a fuse, but otherwise it may cause burning of the insulation (and possibly further short-circuits) or even a fire. This is why it is inadvisable to bypass persistently blowing fuses with silver foil or wire.

Spares and tool kit

Most vehicles are supplied only with sufficient tools for wheel changing; the *Maintenance and minor repair* tool kit detailed in *Tools and working facilities,* with the addition of a hammer, is probably sufficient for those repairs that most motorists would consider attempting at the roadside. In addition a few items which can be fitted without too much trouble in the event of a breakdown should be

Carrying a few spares may save a long walk!

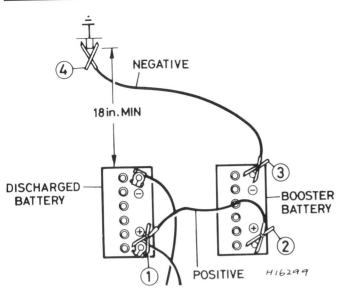

Jump start lead connections for negative earth vehicles –
connect leads in order shown

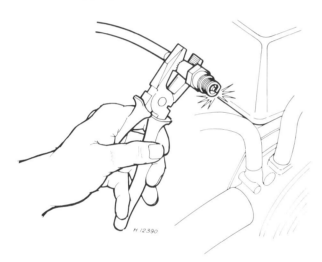

Crank engine and check for spark. Note use of insulated
tool to hold lead

Engine will not start

Engine fails to turn when starter operated

Flat battery (recharge, use jump leads, or push start)
Battery terminals loose or corroded
Battery earth to body defective
Engine earth strap loose or broken
Starter motor (or solenoid) wiring loose or broken
Automatic transmission selector in wrong position, or inhibitor switch faulty
Ignition/starter switch faulty
Major mechanical failure (seizure)
Starter or solenoid internal fault (see Chapter 12)

Starter motor turns engine slowly

Partially discharged battery (recharge, use jump leads, or push start)
Battery terminals loose or corroded
Battery earth to body defective
Engine earth strap loose
Starter motor (or solenoid) wiring loose
Starter motor internal fault (see Chapter 12)

Starter motor spins without turning engine

Flat battery
Starter motor pinion sticking on sleeve
Flywheel gear teeth damaged or worn
Starter motor mounting bolts loose

Engine turns normally but fails to start

Damp or dirty HT leads and distributor cap (crank engine and check for spark)
Dirty or incorrectly gapped distributor points (if applicable)
No fuel in tank (check for delivery at carburettor)
Excessive choke (hot engine) or insufficient choke (cold engine)
Fouled or incorrectly gapped spark plugs (remove, clean and regap)
Other ignition system fault (see Chapter 4)
Other fuel system fault (see Chapter 3)
Poor compression (see Chapter 1)
Major mechanical failure (eg camshaft drive)

Engine fires but will not run

Insufficient choke (cold engine)
Air leaks at carburettor or inlet manifold
Fuel starvation (see Chapter 3)
Ballast resistor defective, or other ignition fault (see Chapter 4)

Engine cuts out and will not restart

Engine cuts out suddenly – ignition fault

Loose or disconnected LT wires
Wet HT leads or distributor cap (after traversing water splash)
Coil or condenser failure (check for spark)
Other ignition fault (see Chapter 4)

Engine misfires before cutting out – fuel fault

Fuel tank empty
Fuel pump defective or filter blocked (check for delivery)
Fuel tank filler vent blocked (suction will be evident on releasing cap)
Carburettor needle valve sticking
Carburettor jets blocked (fuel contaminated)
Other fuel system fault (see Chapter 3)

Engine cuts out – other causes

Serious overheating
Major mechanical failure (eg camshaft drive)

Engine overheats

Ignition (no-charge) warning light illuminated

Slack or broken drivebelt – retension or renew (Chapter 2)

Ignition warning light not illuminated

Coolant loss due to internal or external leakage (see Chapter 2)
Thermostat defective
Low oil level
Brakes binding
Radiator clogged externally or internally
Electric cooling fan not operating correctly
Engine waterways clogged
Ignition timing incorrect or automatic advance malfunctioning
Mixture too weak

Note: Do not add cold water to an overheated engine or damage may result

Low engine oil pressure

Gauge reads low or warning light illuminated with engine running

Oil level low or incorrect grade
Defective gauge or sender unit

Wire to sender unit earthed
Engine overheating
Oil filter clogged or bypass valve defective
Oil pressure relief valve defective
Oil pick-up strainer clogged
Oil pump worn or mountings loose
Worn main or big-end bearings

Note: *Low oil pressure in a high-mileage engine at tickover is not necessarily a cause for concern. Sudden pressure loss at speed is far more significant. In any event, check the gauge or warning light sender before condemning the engine.*

Engine noises

Pre-ignition (pinking) on acceleration

Incorrect grade of fuel
Ignition timing incorrect
Distributor faulty or worn
Worn or maladjusted carburettor
Excessive carbon build-up in engine

Whistling or wheezing noises

Leaking vacuum hose
Leaking carburettor or manifold gasket
Blowing head gasket

Tapping or rattling

Incorrect valve clearances
Worn valve gear
Worn timing chain or belt
Broken piston ring (ticking noise)

Knocking or thumping

Unintentional mechanical contact (eg fan blades)
Worn drivebelt
Peripheral component fault (generator, water pump etc)
Worn big-end bearings (regular heavy knocking, perhaps less under load)
Worn main bearings (rumbling and knocking, perhaps worsening under load)
Piston slap (most noticeable when cold)

Chapter 1 Engine

For modifications, and information applicable to later models, see Supplement at end of manual.

Contents

Specifications

1100 cc engine
General

Type	Four cylinder in-line overhead camshaft
Designation	E1
Bore	70.0 mm (2.75 in)
Stroke	69.6 mm (2.74 in)
Capacity	1071 cc
Compression ratio	9.2:1
Firing order	1 – 3 – 4 – 2 (No 1 cylinder at crankshaft pulley end)

Crankshaft

Number of main bearings	5
Main bearing journal diameter	49.938 to 49.956 mm (1.967 to 1.968 in)
Main bearing journal maximum permissible ovality	0.05 mm (0.002 in)
Crankpin journal diameter	39.940 to 39.956 mm (1.573 to 1.574 in)
Crankpin journal maximum permissible ovality	0.05 mm (0.002 in)
Bearing undersizes available	0.25 mm, 0.50 mm, 0.75 mm (0.010 in, 0.020 in, 0.030 in)
Crankshaft endfloat:	
Standard	0.10 to 0.15 mm (0.004 to 0.006 in)
Limit	0.30 mm (0.012 in)

Cylinder block and pistons

Maximum cylinder block face distortion	0.15 mm (0.006 in)
Piston diameter	69.944 to 69.964 mm (2.755 to 2.756 in)
Piston to bore clearance:	
Standard	0.036 to 0.075 mm (0.0014 to 0.0030 in)
Limit	0.15 mm (0.006 in)
Piston oversizes available	0.25 mm, 0.050 mm, 0.75 mm, 1.0 mm (0.010 in, 0.020 in, 0.030 in, 0.040 in)
Piston ring thickness:	
Top ring	1.17 to 1.19 mm (0.0460 to 0.0468 in)
Second ring	1.47 to 1.49 mm (0.0579 to 0.0587 in)
Piston ring to groove clearance:	
Top and second rings	0.03 to 0.07 mm (0.0011 to 0.0027 in)
Limit	0.15 mm (0.006 in)
Piston ring end gap:	
Top and second rings	0.20 to 0.40 mm (0.0078 to 0.0157 in)
Oil control ring	0.30 to 0.90 mm (0.0118 to 0.0354 in)
Limit	0.15 mm (0.006 in)
Gudgeon pin diameter	19.976 to 19.988 mm (0.787 to 0.7875 in)
Gudgeon pin fit in piston	Hand push fit
Gudgeon pin fit in connecting rod	Interference

Camshaft

Camshaft journal diameter:	
Front and rear	41.949 to 41.965 mm (1.6527 to 1.6534 in)
Centre	41.919 to 41.935 mm (1.6516 to 1.6522 in)
Maximum permissible journal running clearance	0.15 mm (0.006 in)
Camshaft endfloat:	
Standard	0.2 to 0.18 mm (0.001 to 0.007 in)
Limit	0.20 mm (0.008 in)
Cam lobe lift height:	
Standard	44.119 mm (1.7382 in)
Limit	43.919 mm (1.7304 in)

Valves

Seat angle	45°
Head diameter:	
Inlet	35.95 to 36.05 mm (1.416 to 1.420 in)
Exhaust	30.95 to 31.05 mm (1.219 to 1.223 in)
Valve stem diameter:	
Inlet:	
Standard	8.030 to 8.045 mm (0.316 to 0.317 in)
Limit	7.980 mm (0.314 in)
Exhaust:	
Standard	8.025 to 8.045 mm (0.316 to 0.317 in)
Limit	7.975 mm (0.314 in)
Valve stem to guide clearance:	
Standard	0.018 to 0.053 mm (0.0007 to 0.0020 in)
Limit	0.20 mm (0.008 in)
Valve spring free length:	
Standard	43.3 mm (1.70 in)
Limit	42.0 mm (1.65 in)
Valve clearances (warm engine – measured between valve stem and rocker):	
Inlet	0.25 mm (0.010 in)
Exhaust	0.30 mm (0.012 in)
Valve timing:	
Inlet opens	15° BTDC
Inlet closes	44° ABDC
Exhaust opens	53° BBDC
Exhaust closes	6° ATDC

Rocker gear

Rocker shaft diameter	18.959 to 18.980 mm (0.7469 to 0.7478 in)
Rocker arm to shaft clearance:	
Standard	0.020 to 0.074 mm (0.0008 to 0.003 in)
Limit	0.10 mm (0.004 in)

Cylinder head

Height	90.5 mm (3.565 in)
Maximum permissible warp	0.15 mm (0.006 in)
Grinding limit	0.20 mm (0.008 in)

Lubrication system

Maximum oil pump outer rotor to body clearance	0.35 mm (0.014 in)
Maximum rotor lobe clearance	0.25 mm (0.0098 in)
Maximum rotor endfloat	0.15 mm (0.006 in)
Oil pressure at 3000 rpm	3.5 to 4.5 bar (50 to 64 lbf/in²)

1300 cc engine

The engine specification is identical to the 1100 cc unit except for the following differences

General

Designation	E3
Bore	77.0 mm (3.03 in)
Capacity	1296 cc

Cylinder block and pistons

Piston diameter	76.944 to 76.964 mm (3.0315 to 3.0323 in)
Piston oversizes available	0.25 mm (0.010 in)

Camshaft

Cam lobe lift height:	
Standard	44.114 mm (1.7380 in)
Limit	43.914 mm (1.7302 in)

Valves

Valve timing:	
Inlet opens	15° BTDC
Inlet closes	58° ABDC
Exhaust opens	58° BBDC
Exhaust closes	15° ATDC

1500 cc engine

The engine specification is identical to the 1300 cc unit except for the following differences

General

Designation	E5
Bore	77.0 mm (3.03 in)
Stroke	80.0 mm (3.15 in)
Capacity	1490 cc
Compression ratio:	
1500 models	9.0:1
1500 GT models	10.0:1

Cylinder block and pistons

Piston diameter	76.954 to 76.974 mm (3.0319 to 3.0327 in)
Piston to bore clearance:	
Standard	0.026 to 0.065 mm (0.0010 to 0.0025 in)
Limit	0.15 mm (0.006 in)
Piston oversizes available	0.50 mm (0.020 in)

Camshaft

Cam lobe lift height:	
1500 models:	
Standard	44.114 mm (1.7380 in)
Limit	43.914 mm (1.7302 in)
1500 GT models:	
Standard	44.719 mm (1.7619 in)
Limit	44.519 mm (1.7540 in)

Valves

Valve spring free length – 1500 GT models:	
Inner spring	
Standard	36.8 mm (1.45 in)
Limit	35.7 mm (1.44 in)
Outer spring:	
Standard	40.3 mm (1.58 in)
Limit	39.1 mm (1.54 in)
Valve timing:	
1500 models:	
Inlet opens	15° BTDC
Inlet closes	58° ABDC
Exhaust opens	58° BBDC
Exhaust closes	15° ATDC
1500 GT models:	
Inlet opens	16° BTDC
Inlet closes	59° ABDC
Exhaust opens	59° BBDC
Exhaust closes	16° ATDC

All engines

Torque wrench settings

	Nm	lbf ft
Cylinder head bolts	78 to 82	57 to 60
Main bearing cap bolts	66 to 71	48 to 52
Big-end cap nuts	30 to 35	22 to 26
Camshaft sprocket nut	70 to 80	51 to 59
Crankshaft pulley bolt	110 to 120	81 to 88
Flywheel bolts	88 to 90	65 to 66
Sump bolts	7 to 12	5 to 9
Timing cover bolts	19 to 31	14 to 23
Oil pump bolts	19 to 31	14 to 23
Engine-to-transmission bolts:		
12 mm bolt	65 to 95	47 to 69
14 mm bolt	90 to 120	65 to 87
Engine/transmission mounting to bracket nuts	32 to 47	23 to 34
Transmission front mounting (early models)	19 to 26	14 to 19
Lower arm balljoint pinch-bolt	44 to 55	33 to 40
Roadwheel nuts	90 to 110	65 to 80

1 General description

The engine is of four-cylinder, in-line overhead camshaft type mounted transversely at the front of the car and available in 1071 cc, 1296 cc and 1490 cc versions. Apart from the cylinder bore diameter, crankshaft stroke and minor detail differences, all three engine types are virtually identical in design and construction.

The crankshaft is supported within the cast iron cylinder block on five shell type main bearings. Thrust washers are fitted at the rear main bearing to control crankshaft endfloat.

The connecting rods are attached to the crankshaft by horizontally

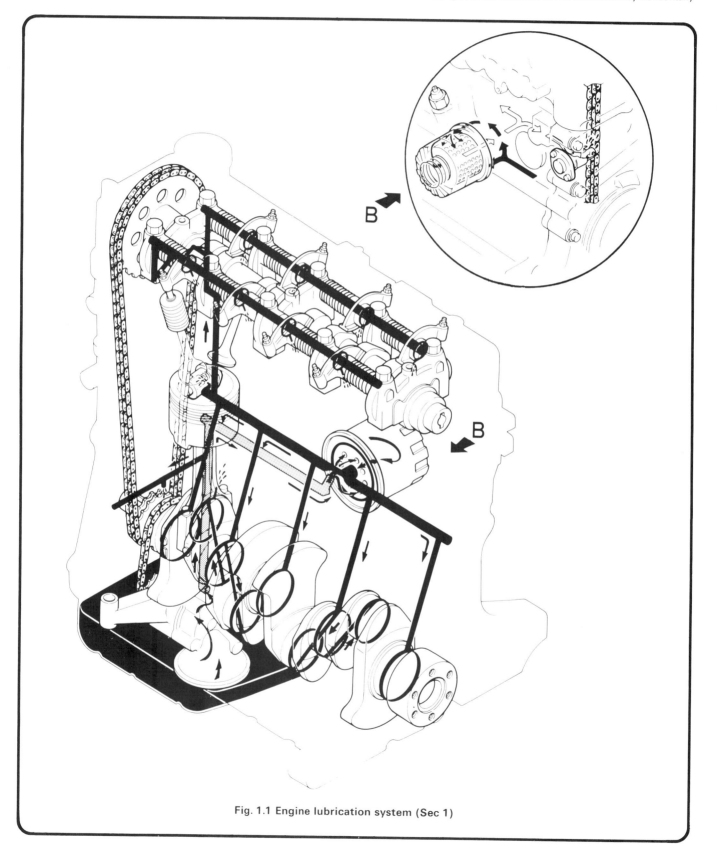

Fig. 1.1 Engine lubrication system (Sec 1)

split shell type big-end bearings, and to the pistons by interference fit gudgeon pins. The aluminium alloy pistons are of the slipper type and each is fitted with two compression rings and a three-piece oil control ring.

The camshaft is chain driven from the crankshaft and is carried in half bearings machined directly in the aluminium cylinder head. The inclined inlet and exhaust valves are actuated by rocker arms located in a rocker shaft assembly, the pedestals of which form the camshaft bearing upper halves.

Lubrication is by a rotor type oil pump, chain driven from the crankshaft and located in the crankcase. Engine oil is fed through an externally mounted full-flow filter to the engine oil gallery, and then to the crankshaft, camshaft and rocker shaft bearings. A pressure relief valve is incorporated in the oil pump.

A semi-closed crankcase ventilation system is employed and crankcase gases are drawn from the rocker cover via hoses to the air cleaner and inlet manifold.

2 Maintenance and inspection

1   At the intervals specified in Routine Maintenance at the beginning of this Manual, carry out the following maintenance operations on the engine.
2   Place a suitable container beneath the oil drain plug on the sump. Unscrew the plug and allow the oil to drain (photo). Refit and tighten the plug after draining.

Fig. 1.2 Oil filter removal tool in use (Sec 2)

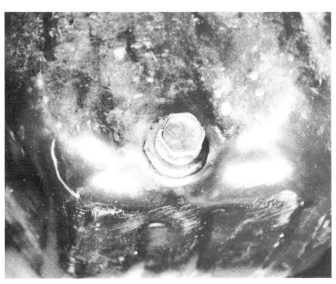

2.2 Engine oil drain plug location

2.5 Lubricate the seal before fitting a new filter

3   Move the container to the rear of the engine, under the oil filter.
4   Using a strap wrench or filter removal tool, slacken the filter and then unscrew it from the engine and discard.
5   Wipe the filter mating face on the cylinder block with a rag and then lubricate the seal of a new filter using clean engine oil (photo).
6   Screw the filter into position and tighten it by hand only. *Do not use any tools.*
7   Refill the engine using the correct grade of oil through the filler on the rocker cover (photo). Fill until the level reaches the F mark on the dipstick.
8   Start the engine, check for leaks around the filter seal then switch off and recheck the level.
9   Visually check the engine joint faces, gaskets and seals for any sign of oil or water leaks. Pay particular attention to the areas around the rocker cover, cylinder head, timing cover and sump joint faces. Rectify any leaks by referring to the appropriate Sections of this Chapter.
10 Also, at the intervals specified, retorque the cylinder head retaining bolts and adjust the valve clearances as described in Sections 41 and 42 respectively.

2.7 Fill the engine with oil through the filler on the rocker cover

3 Major operations possible with the engine in the car

The following operations can be carried out without having to remove the engine from the car:

(a) *Removal and refitting of the cylinder head, camshaft and rocker gear assembly*
(b) *Removal and refitting of the timing cover, chain and gears*
(c) *Removal and refitting of the sump*
(d) *Removal and refitting of the oil pump*
(e) *Removal and refitting of the piston and connecting rod assemblies*
(f) *Removal and refitting of the engine mountings*

4 Major operations requiring engine removal

The following operations can only be carried out after removal of the engine from the car:

(a) *Removal and refitting of the crankshaft and main bearings*
(b) *Removal and refitting of the flywheel or torque converter drive plate*
(c) *Removal and refitting of the crankshaft rear oil seal*

5 Methods of engine removal

The engine is removed upwards and out of the engine compartment in unit with the transmission, or on its own if the transmission is removed first. Owing to the limited space available in the engine compartment, it is not possible to remove the engine leaving the transmission in place in the car.

6 Engine – removal with manual or automatic transmission

1 Disconnect the battery negative terminal then remove the bonnet as described in Chapter 11.
2 Drain the cooling system as described in Chapter 2.
3 Drain the engine oil as described in Section 2 of this Chapter, then drain the manual transmission lubricant or automatic transmission fluid as described in Chapters 6 or 7 respectively.
4 Remove the air cleaner as described in Chapter 3.
5 Disconnect the fuel feed and return hoses from the fuel pump (photo). Plug the hose ends after removal.
6 Disconnect the brake servo vacuum hose at the inlet manifold.
7 Pull off the spark plug and ignition coil HT leads then remove the distributor cap and leads (photo).
8 Make a note of the LT wiring connections at the ignition coil and disconnect them (photo).
9 Disconnect the earth link wire at the connector (photo) then remove the main engine earth cable at the transmission bracket.
10 On manual transmission models disconnect the clutch cable at the transmission as described in Chapter 5.
11 Disconnect the top hose at the radiator and thermostat housing and remove the hose.
12 Disconnect the leads at the cooling fan switch and temperature gauge sender (photo) and remove the cable clips.
13 Disconnect the heater hoses at the bypass pipe and inlet manifold (photos).
14 Undo the retaining bolt and withdraw the speedometer cable and gear from the transmission. Plug the transmission orifice to prevent dirt entry.
15 Refer to Chapter 3 if necessary, and disconnect the accelerator and choke cables at the carburettor.
16 Disconnect the carburettor fuel cut-off valve solenoid wiring at the connector.
17 On automatic transmission models, disconnect and plug the fluid pipes at the transmission.
18 Firmly apply the handbrake, chock the rear wheels and slacken the front wheel nuts. Jack up the front of the car and support it on axle stands. Remove the front roadwheels.

6.5 Fuel feed and return hose connections (arrowed)

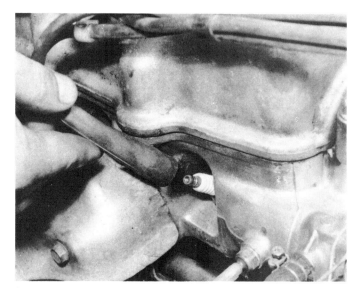
6.7 Remove the distributor cap and leads

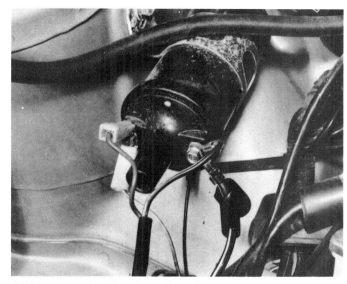
6.8 Disconnect the LT wiring at the coil

6.9 Disconnect the earth link wire

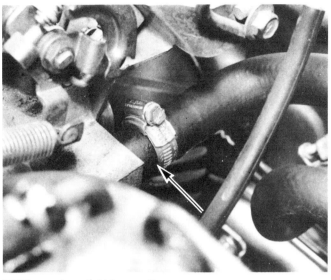

6.13B ... and manifold (arrowed)

6.12 Disconnect the leads at the fan switch, gauge sender and cable clip (arrowed)

19 Remove the engine undertray retaining bolts and lift away the undertrays.
20 Disconnect the bottom hose at the radiator and water pump and remove the hose.
21 Undo the nuts securing the exhaust front pipe to the manifold and the bolt securing the pipe to the bracket at the front of the engine. Separate the pipe from the manifold flange and recover the gasket.
22 Undo and remove the pinch-bolt securing the lower suspension arm balljoint to the swivel hub.
23 Using a long stout bar, lever the lower suspension arm down to release the balljoint shank from the swivel hub.
24 Pull the swivel hub outwards firmly, to release the driveshaft inner constant velocity joint from the transmission. Support the driveshaft at its inner end to avoid damaging the transmission oil seal as the constant velocity joint is withdrawn.
25 Make a note of the wiring connections at the rear of the alternator and starter motor solenoid and disconnect them.
26 Disconnect the lead at the oil pressure switch (photo).
27 Disconnect the reversing light switch wires at the connector and release the wiring from the transmission cable clips.

6.13A Disconnect the heater hoses at the bypass pipe ...

6.26 Disconnect the lead at the oil pressure switch

28 On automatic transmission models disconnect the starter inhibitor switch, neutral switch and kickdown solenoid wiring connectors then disconnect the vacuum hose from the diaphragm.

29 Disconnect the automatic transmission selector linkage front selector rod and counter rod at the transmission.

30 Disconnect the manual transmission gearchange rod by undoing the nut and bolt securing the rod to the transmission shift rod (photo). Undo the nut and washers and withdraw the remote control housing extension bar from the stud on the transmission.

31 Attach a suitable hoist or crane to the engine using chains or rope slings or preferably by attaching the chains or ropes to the engine lifting brackets. Raise the hoist to just take the weight of the engine.

32 Undo the nuts securing the engine/transmission rubber mountings to the transmission brackets (photo).

33 Undo the nut and through-bolt securing the right-hand mounting to the body bracket (photo).

34 On early models remove the additional mounting from the front face of the transmission.

35 Check that all pipes, cable, cable clips, hoses or other attachments have been removed and positioned well clear of the engine and transmission.

6.33 ... and the right-hand mounting nut and through-bolt (arrowed)

6.30 Undo and remove the gearchange rod nut and retaining bolt

6.36 Removing the engine and transmission assembly

36 Lift the engine and transmission slightly and release the front and rear mountings from the transmission brackets. Continue lifting the unit carefully out of the engine compartment (photo). As soon as the engine is high enough, move the hoist backwards, swing the engine and transmission over the front body panel and lower the unit to the ground.

7 Engine – separation from manual or automatic transmission

Manual transmission

1 Undo the three bolts securing the starter motor and remove the motor.

2 Support the transmission on blocks or with a jack.

3 Undo all the bolts securing the transmission to the engine, ease the clutch housing off the engine locating dowels and withdraw the transmission squarely off the engine (photo).

Automatic transmission

4 Undo the three bolts securing the starter motor and remove the motor.

6.32 Undo the engine/transmission retaining nuts (arrowed) ...

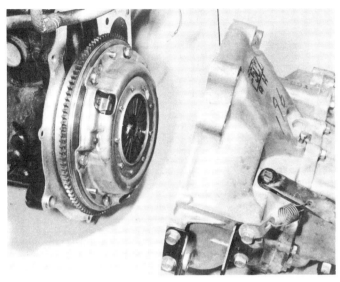

7.3 Separating the engine from the transmission

5 Undo the retaining bolts and lift off the cover plate to gain access to the torque converter.
6 Undo the bolts securing the torque converter to the driveplate.
7 Support the transmission on blocks or with a jack.
8 Undo all the bolts securing the transmission to the engine, ease the torque converter housing off the engine locating dowels and withdraw the transmission squarely off the engine. As the transmission is removed, hold the torque converter in place and make sure it stays on the transmission.

8 Engine dismantling – general

1 If possible, mount the engine on a stand for the dismantling procedure, but failing this support it in an upright position with blocks of wood placed under each side of the sump or crankcase.
2 Drain the oil into a suitable container before cleaning the engine or major dismantling, if this has not already been done.
3 Cleanliness is most important, and if the engine is dirty it should be cleaned with paraffin or a suitable solvent while keeping it in an upright position.
4 Avoid working with the engine directly on a concrete floor, as grit presents a real source of trouble.
5 As parts are removed, clean them in a paraffin bath. However, do not immerse parts with internal oilways in paraffin as it is difficult to remove, usually requiring a high pressure hose. Clean oilways with nylon pipe cleaners.
6 It is advisable to have suitable containers to hold small items, as this will help when reassembling the engine and also prevent possible losses.
7 Always obtain complete sets of gaskets when the engine is being dismantled, but retain the old gaskets with a view to using them as a pattern to make a replacement if a new one is not available.
8 When possible, refit nuts, bolts and washers in their location after being removed, as this helps to protect the threads and will also be helpful when reassembling the engine.
9 Retain unserviceable components in order to compare them with the new parts supplied.
10 The operations described in this Chapter are a step by step sequence, assuming that the engine is to be completely dismantled for major overhaul or repair. Where an operation can be carried out with the engine in the car, the dismantling necessary to gain access to the component concerned is described separately.

9 Ancillary components – removal

1 With the engine separated from the transmission, the externally mounted ancillary components, as given in the following list can be removed. In most cases removal is straightforward and the procedure will be obvious on inspection. If necessary however, further information will be found in the relevant Chapters.

Distributor (Chapter 4)
Inlet manifold and carburettor – photo (Chapter 3)
Exhaust manifold – photos (Chapter 3)
Oil pressure switch – photo
Oil filter (Section 2 of this Chapter)
Alternator – photo (Chapter 12)
Front engine mounting bracket – photo (Section 18 of this Chapter)
Water pump and bypass pipe – photos (Chapter 2)
Thermostat housing and thermostat (Chapter 2)
Fuel pump (Chapter 3)
Clutch assembly (Chapter 5)

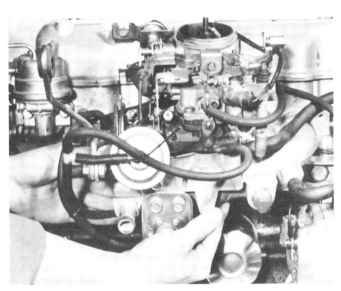

9.1A Remove the inlet manifold and carburettor ...

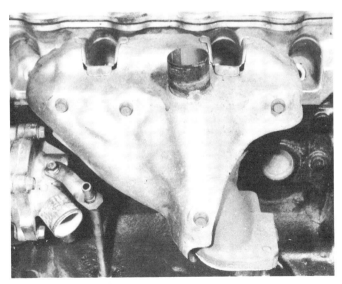

9.1B ... exhaust manifold stove ...

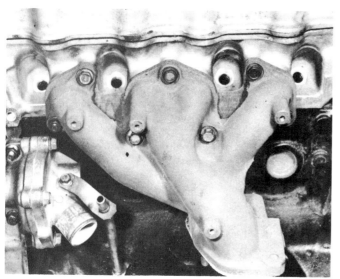

9.1C ... exhaust manifold ...

9.1D ... oil pressure switch ...

9.1E ... alternator ...

9.1F ... front engine mounting bracket bolts (arrowed) ...

9.1G ... bypass hose and pipe ...

9.1H ... water pump

10 Cylinder head, camshaft and rocker gear assembly – removal

1   If the engine has been removed from the car, proceed to paragraph 16. If the engine is in the car, proceed as follows.
2   Disconnect the battery negative terminal.
3   Refer to Chapter 2 and drain the cooling system.
4   Refer to Chapter 4 and remove the distributor.
5   Refer to Chapter 3 and remove the air cleaner and exhaust manifold.
6   Refer to Chapter 12 and remove the alternator.
7   Disconnect the radiator top hose at the thermostat housing (photo).
8   Disconnect the wiring at the temperature gauge sender and cooling fan thermostatic switch (photo). Release the wires from the cable clip on the thermostat housing.
9   Disconnect the bypass hose at the outlet adjacent to the thermostat housing (photo).
10   Disconnect the earth link wire at the connector (photo).
11   Disconnect the brake servo vacuum hose at the inlet manifold (photo).
12   Disconnect the fuel feed, supply and return hoses at the fuel pump

10.9 Disconnect the bypass hose

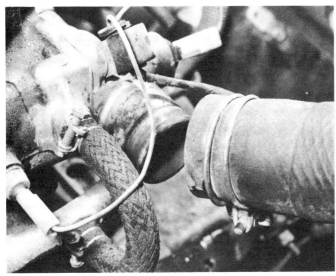
10.7 Disconnect the radiator top hose

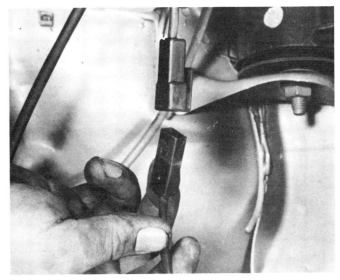
10.10 Disconnect the earth link wire

10.8 Disconnect the temperature gauge and fan switch wiring

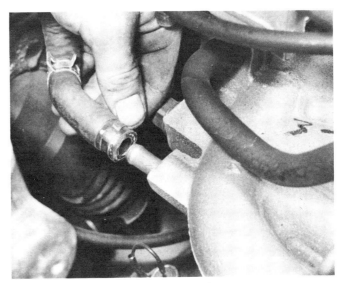
10.11 Disconnect the brake servo vacuum hose

then undo the two bolts and remove the pump. Recover the gaskets and insulator block.

13 Disconnect the heater hose at the inlet manifold.

14 Refer to Chapter 3 if necessary and disconnect the accelerator and choke cables at the carburettor.

15 Disconnect the carburettor fuel cut-off valve solenoid wiring at the connector.

16 Detach the engine breather hose then undo the three bolts and lift off the rocker cover (photo). Remove the half-round rubber sealing grommet from the end of the cylinder head.

17 Observe the camshaft sprocket and note the position of the timing mark and the bright link on the chain (photo). With the engine at TDC with No 1 cylinder on compression, the timing mark and bright link should be at approximately the 3 o'clock position as shown.

18 Using string or wire secure the timing chain to the sprocket so that the chain to sprocket relationship is not lost.

19 Undo the small bolt located just in front of the camshaft sprocket taking care not to drop the bolt in the engine as it is removed (photo). For safety place some rags below the sprocket in case the bolt is dropped.

20 Undo the nut and washer securing the camshaft sprocket to the camshaft. Insert a stout screwdriver through one of the holes in the sprocket to prevent it turning as the nut is undone.

21 At the rear of the engine beneath the engine mounting bracket, undo the two bolts securing the timing chain tensioner to the cylinder

10.19 Undo the cylinder head front retaining bolts (arrowed)

block. Withdraw the tensioner to relieve the tension on the chain. Note that the tensioner cannot be completely removed at this stage owing to interference with the engine mounting bracket.

22 Slacken all the rocker gear and cylinder head retaining bolts half a turn at a time in the order shown in the photo. When the tension has been relieved, remove all the bolts.

23 Hold the two end rocker pedestals together and lift the rocker gear off as an assembly (photo).

24 Move the camshaft rearwards to release it from the sprocket then remove it from the cylinder head (photos).

25 Release the cylinder head from its locating dowels by tapping it upwards using a hide or plastic mallet. When the head is free lift it off the engine complete with inlet manifold and carburettor (photo). Recover the cylinder head gasket.

26 Support the engine under the sump using a jack and interposed block of wood.

27 Undo the nut and through-bolt securing the right-hand engine mounting to the body bracket and the two bolts securing the mounting bracket to the engine. Remove the mounting assembly (photo).

28 The timing chain tensioner can now be withdrawn from its location (photo). Recover the gasket from the tensioner or cylinder block.

10.16 Remove the rocker cover

10.17 Camshaft sprocket timing mark and bright link (arrowed)

10.22 Cylinder head bolt slackening sequence

10.23 Lift off the rocker gear assembly

10.24A Release the camshaft from the sprocket ...

10.24B ... then remove the camshaft

10.25 Remove the cylinder head complete with inlet manifold and carburettor

10.27 Remove the right-hand engine mounting assembly ...

10.28 ... then withdraw the tensioner

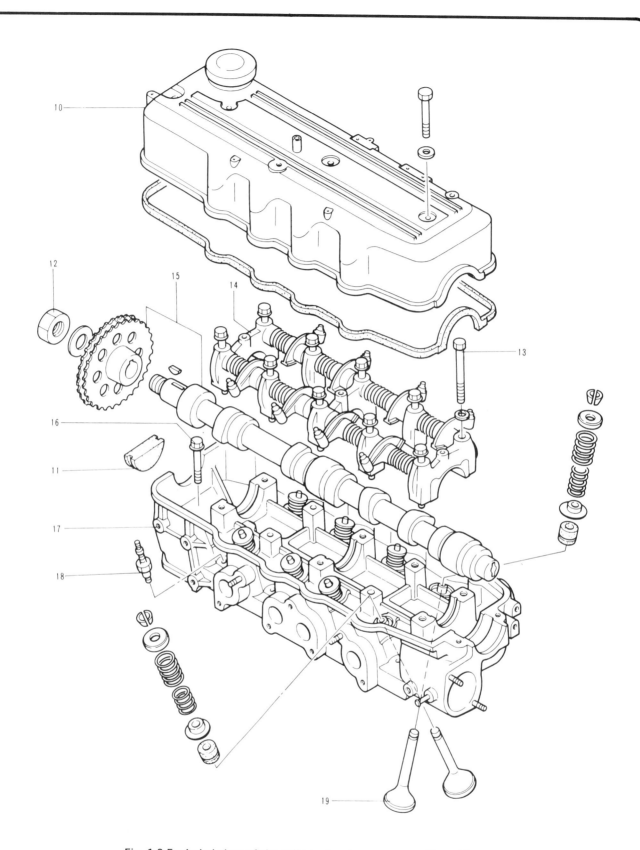

Fig. 1.3 Exploded view of the cylinder head components (Secs 10 and 11)

10 Rocker cover
11 Sealing grommet
12 Sprocket retaining nut

13 Cylinder head bolt
14 Rocker gear
15 Camshaft and sprocket

16 Cylinder head front retaining
   bolt
17 Cylinder head

18 Spark plug
19 Inlet valve

11 Cylinder head – dismantling

1   If the inlet manifold is still in place, refer to Chapter 3 if necessary and remove it from the cylinder head.

2   Remove each valve in turn from the cylinder head by compressing the valve spring with a spring compressor tool until the two halves of the collets can be removed. Release the compressor and remove the spring cap, spring, and spring seat.

3   If, when the spring compressor is screwed down, the valve spring cap refuses to free, do not continue to screw down, but gently tap the top of the tool directly over the cap with a light hammer. At the same time hold the spring compressor firmly in position with one hand to avoid it jumping off.

4   It is essential that the valves are kept in their correct sequence unless they are so badly worn that they are to be renewed. Punch eight holes in a sheet of stiff card and number them No 1 inlet, No 1 exhaust, No 2 inlet, No 2 exhaust etc. As each valve is removed from the cylinder head insert it into its respective hole in the card. Note that No 1 cylinder is nearest to the crankshaft pulley.

5   When all the valves are removed lift off the oil seals from the top of each valve guide.

12 Sump – removal

1   If the engine is in the car first carry out the following operations:

   (a) Drain the engine oil
   (b) Remove the engine undertrays
   (c) Remove the exhaust front pipe

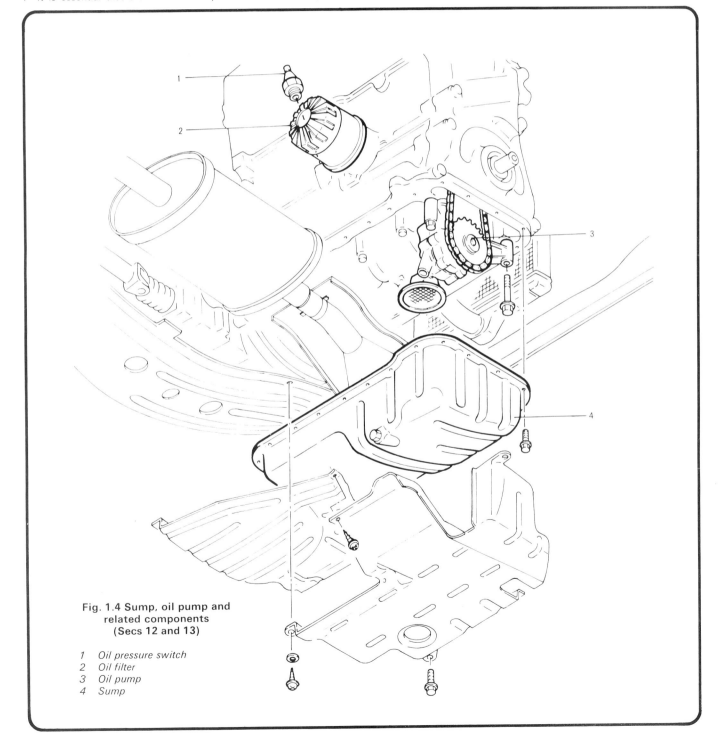

Fig. 1.4 Sump, oil pump and related components (Secs 12 and 13)

1   Oil pressure switch
2   Oil filter
3   Oil pump
4   Sump

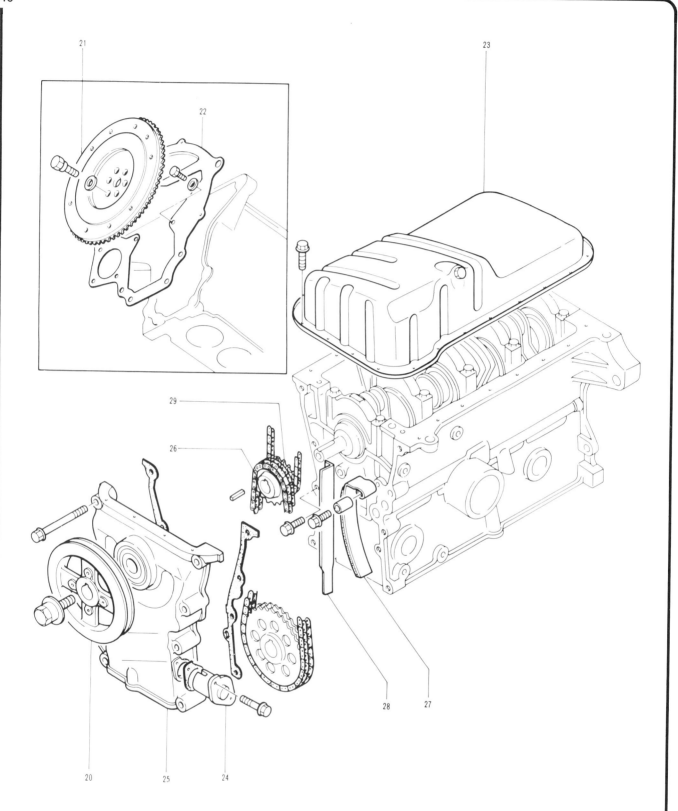

Fig. 1.5 Timing gear, flywheel and sump assemblies (Secs 12, 14 and 16)

20 Crankshaft pulley
21 Flywheel
22 Rear cover

23 Sump
24 Timing chain tensioner
25 Timing cover

26 Sprocket and chain
27 Tensioner arm

28 Chain guide
29 Oil pump drive sprocket

2   Undo and remove the bolts securing the sump to the crankcase. Tap the sump with a hide or plastic mallet to break the seal between sump flange and crankcase and remove the sump.

13 Oil pump – removal

1   If the engine is in the car, first remove the sump as described in the previous Section.
2   Undo the two pump retaining bolts and ease the pump off its crankcase location.
3   Disengage the sprocket from the chain and remove the oil pump.

14 Timing cover, gears and chain – removal

1   If the engine is in the car, first carry out the following operations:

(a) *Remove the side cover from under the right-hand side wheel arch*
(b) *Remove the cylinder head, camshaft and rocker gear assembly*
(c) *Remove the sump*

2   Using a socket and bar undo and remove the crankshaft pulley retaining bolt. Prevent the crankshaft from turning during this operation by placing a block of wood between the crankcase and one of the crankshaft webs.
3   Withdraw the pulley from the crankshaft.
4   Undo the retaining bolts and remove the timing cover from the crankcase. Support the camshaft sprocket and timing chain to prevent them dropping down as the timing cover is removed.
5   Undo the retaining bolt and distance collar, then withdraw the timing chain tensioner arm from the crankcase.
6   Undo the two bolts and remove the chain guide.
7   Slip the chain off the crankshaft sprocket and remove it complete with camshaft sprocket.
8   Withdraw the crankshaft sprocket and, if still in place, the oil pump drive chain. If the crankshaft sprocket is to be removed and the engine is in the car, first remove the oil pump as described in Section 13.
9   Recover the Woodruff key from the crankshaft groove and store it safely.

15 Pistons and connecting rods – removal

1   If the engine is in the car, first carry out the following operations:

(a) *Remove the sump*
(b) *For easier access remove the oil pump*
(c) *Remove the cylinder head, camshaft and rocker gear assembly (not necessary if only the big-end bearings are to be removed)*

2   Rotate the crankshaft so that No 1 big-end cap (nearest to the crankshaft pulley) is at the lowest point of its travel. If the big-end cap and rod are not already numbered, mark them with a centre punch in relation to the cylinder they operate in i.e. one dot for No 1, two dots for No 2 etc. Mark both the cap and rod in this way on the same side.
3   Undo and remove the big-end bearing cap retaining nuts and withdraw the cap, complete with shell bearing from the connecting rod. If only the bearing shells are being attended to, push the connecting rod up and off the crankpin and remove the upper bearing shell. Keep the bearing shells and cap together in their correct sequence if the shells are to be refitted.
4   Push the connecting rod up and remove the piston and rod from the cylinder. Keep the big-end cap together with its rod so they do not become interchanged with any of the other assemblies.
5   Now repeat these operations on the remaining three piston and connecting rod assemblies.

16 Flywheel or torque converter driveplate – removal

1   Lock the crankshaft using a strip of angle iron between the ring gear teeth and one of the locating dowels on the cylinder block flange. Alternatively use a block of wood between the crankcase and one of the crankshaft webs.
2   Mark the flywheel or driveplate in relation to the crankshaft, undo the retaining bolts and withdraw the unit.
3   If required, undo the two bolts and lift off the engine rear plate.

17 Crankshaft and main bearings – removal

1   Identification numbers and an arrow should be visible on each main bearing cap. The caps are numbered 1 to 5 with No 1 being nearest to the crankshaft pulley and with the arrows also pointing this way. If no marks are visible stamp them with a centre punch as was done for the connecting rods and also mark them in such a way as to indicate their fitted direction.
2   Undo and remove the main bearing cap retaining bolts and withdraw the caps complete with bearing shells. To remove the rear (No 5) cap, refit two of the sump retaining bolts to the cap and using two screwdrivers engaged under the bolt heads, lever the cap out of its location (photo). Recover the side oil seal strips from each side of the cap and the two crankshaft thrustwasher lower halves.
3   Carefully lift the crankshaft out of the crankcase and slip the oil seal off the end boss.
4   Remove the thrustwasher upper halves from the rear main bearing, then remove the bearing shell upper halves. Place each shell with its respective bearing cap.

17.2 Using two screwdrivers to release the rear main bearing cap

18 Engine/transmission mountings – renewal

Front and rear mountings
1   Apply the handbrake, chock the rear wheels and jack up the front of the car. Securely support the car on axle stands.
2   Remove the engine undertrays.
3   Place jack and interposed block of wood beneath the end of the transmission and take the weight of the engine and transmission on the jack.
4   Undo the nuts securing the mountings to the transmission brackets.
5   From under the car undo the three nuts and one bolt securing the crossmember to the underbody.
6   Lower the crossmember at the rear to disengage the rear mounting, then disengage the front mounting and remove the crossmember from under the car.

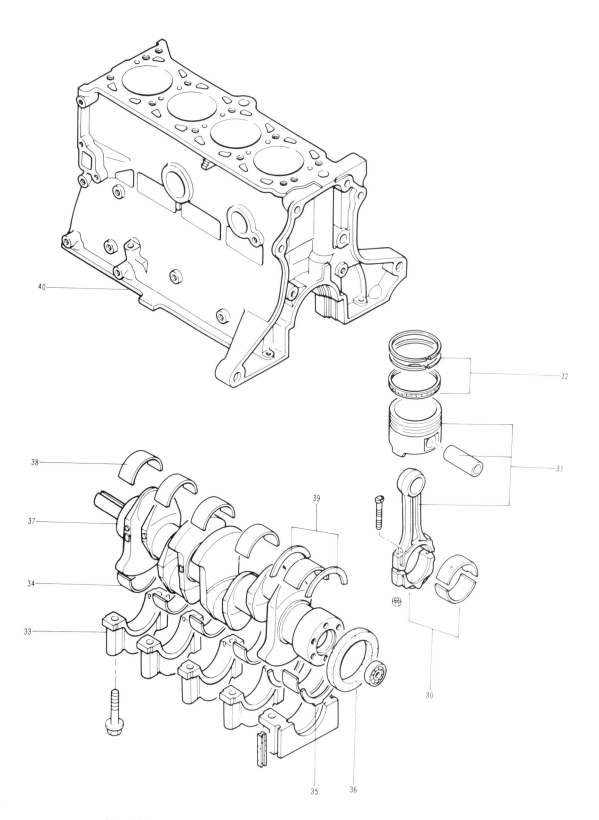

Fig. 1.6 Crankshaft, piston and bearing assemblies (Secs 15 and 17)

30 Connecting rod and big-end bearings
31 Piston and connecting rod assembly
32 Piston rings
33 Main bearing caps
34 Main bearing shells
35 Thrust washers
36 Crankshaft rear oil seal
37 Crankshaft
38 Main bearing shells
39 Thrust washers
40 Cylinder block

7   Remove the mountings from the crossmember after undoing the retaining nuts.

8   Refitting is the reverse sequence of removal.

Right-hand mounting

9   Carry out the operations described in paragraphs 1 to 3, but position the jack under the engine sump.

10 Remove the alternator adjusting arm bolt from the arm.

11 Slacken the three nuts securing the mounting to the engine bracket.

12 Undo the nut and through-bolt securing the mounting to the chassis bracket and the two bolts securing the mounting bracket to the engine. Remove the mounting assembly.

13 Refitting is the reverse sequence of removal, but do not tighten the three mounting to engine bracket nuts until the mounting is in place and centralised on the engine and chassis bracket. Adjust the drivebelt tension as described in Chapter 2 after fitting.

19 Examination and renovation – general

With the engine completely stripped, clean all the components and examine them for wear. Each part should be checked, and where necessary, renewed or renovated as described in the following Sections. Renew main and big-end shell bearings as a matter of course, unless you know that they have had little wear and are in perfect condition.

20 Oil pump – examination and renovation

1   Undo the retaining bolts and lift off the pump cover (photo).

2   Extract the retaining split pin and withdraw the pressure relief valve cap, spring and plunger (photos).

3   Withdraw the outer rotor from the pump body.

4   If the inner rotor is to be removed, it will first be necessary to press off the drive sprocket, but this is only necessary if the inner rotor is to be renewed.

5   Clean the components and carefully examine the rotors, pump body, pump cover and pressure relief valve components for signs of scoring, wear or damage. Renew any worn parts as necessary.

6   If the components appear serviceable, measure the clearance between the rotor lobes, outer rotor and body and between the rotor and cover using feeler gauges (photos). Also check for distortion of the pump cover using a straight-edge (photo).

7   If any of the clearances exceed the specified limits, the pump should be renewed.

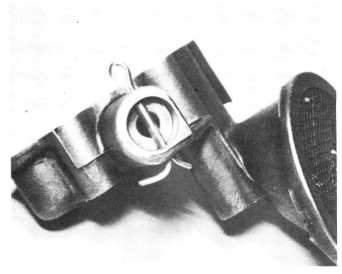

20.2A Extract the retaining split pin ...

20.2B ... then withdraw the pressure relief valve components

20.1 Lift off the oil pump cover

20.6A Checking the pump rotor lobe clearance ...

20.6B ... outer rotor to body clearance ...

20.6C ... and cover distortion

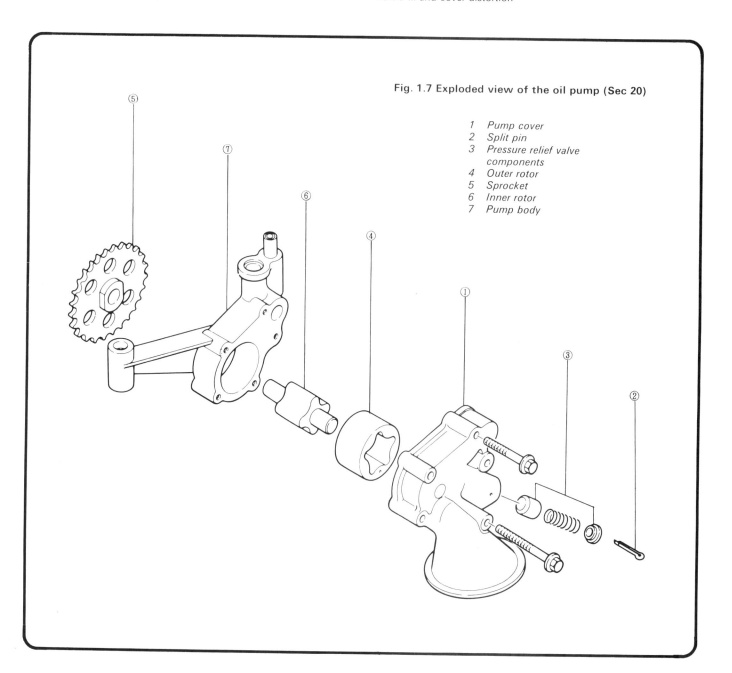

Fig. 1.7 Exploded view of the oil pump (Sec 20)

1 Pump cover
2 Split pin
3 Pressure relief valve
   components
4 Outer rotor
5 Sprocket
6 Inner rotor
7 Pump body

20.8 Assemble the pump with the rotor marks on the same side

8   If the pump is satisfactory reassemble the components in the reverse order of removal, lubricating them thoroughly with engine oil. Ensure that the inner and outer rotor are assembled with the identification marks on the same side (photo). If the sprocket was removed, press it onto the inner rotor until it is flush with the rotor shaft. Be sure to secure the pressure relief valve components using a new split pin.

21 Crankshaft and main bearings – examination and renovation

1   Examine the bearing surfaces of the crankshaft for scratches or scoring and, using a micrometer, check each journal and crankpin for ovality (photo). Where this is found to be outside the specified limits the crankshaft will have to be reground and undersize bearings fitted.
2   Crankshaft regrinding should be carried out by a suitable engineering works, who will normally supply the matching undersize main and big-end shell bearings.
3   If the crankshaft is in a satisfactory condition new bearing shells and thrustwashers should be obtained as a matter of course.

21.1 Checking the crankshaft journal diameters

22 Cylinder block and crankcase – examination and renovation

1   The cylinder bores must be examined for taper, ovality, scoring and scratches. Start by examining the top of the bores; if these are worn, a slight ridge will be found which marks the top of the piston ring travel. If the wear is excessive, the engine will have had a high oil consumption rate accompanied by blue smoke from the exhaust.
2   If available, use an inside dial gauge to measure the bore diameter just below the ridge and compare it with the diameter at the bottom of the bore, which is not subject to wear. If the difference is more than 0.152 mm (0.006 in), the cylinders will normally require boring with new oversize pistons fitted.
3   Provided the cylinder bore wear does not exceed this amount, special oil control rings and pistons can be fitted to restore compression and stop the engine burning oil.
4   If new pistons are being fitted to old bores, it is essential to roughen the bore walls slightly with fine glasspaper to enable the new piston rings to bed in properly.
5   Thoroughly examine the crankcase and cylinder block for cracks and damage, and use a piece of wire to probe all oilways and waterways to ensure they are unobstructed.
6   Using a straight-edge and feeler gauges check for distortion of the block mating face. If the block is distorted beyond the specified limit, it must be machined until flat.

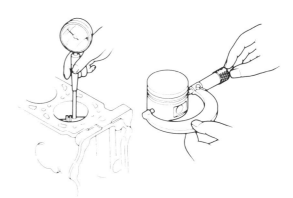

Fig. 1.8 Checking cylinder bore and piston diameters
(Sec 22)

23 Piston and connecting rod assemblies – examination and renovation

1   Examine the pistons for ovality, scoring and scratches, and for wear of the piston ring grooves.
2   If the pistons or connecting rods are to be renewed it is necessary to have this work carried out by a Mazda dealer or suitable engineering works who will have the necessary tooling to remove and refit the interference fit gudgeon pins.
3   If new rings are to be fitted to the original pistons, expand the old rings over the top of the pistons. The use of two or three old feeler blades will be helpful in preventing the rings dropping into empty grooves. Note that the oil control ring is in three sections.
4   Ensure that the ring grooves in the piston are free of carbon by cleaning them using an old ring. Break the ring in half to do this.
5   Before fitting the new rings to the piston insert them into the cylinder bore and use a feeler gauge to check that the end gaps are within the specified limits. Also check the ring to groove clearance in the piston using feeler gauges.
6   When fitting the rings to the piston make sure that the letter R or the word TOP on the two compression rings is toward the top of the piston. After fitting, space the ring grooves as shown in Fig. 1.11.

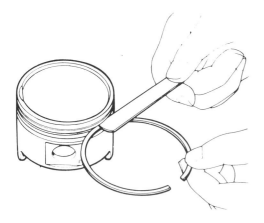

Fig. 1.9 Checking piston ring to groove clearance (Sec 23)

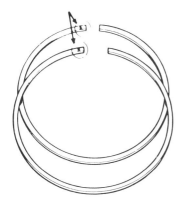

Fig. 1.10 Piston ring R marking stamped on top face
(Sec 23)

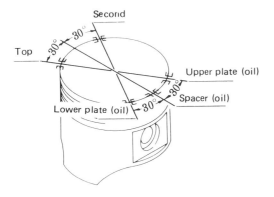

Fig. 1.11 Piston ring gap spacing (Sec 23)

24 Camshaft – examination and renovation

1   Examine the camshaft bearing surfaces, cam lobes and eccentric for wear ridges, pitting, scoring or chipping. Renew the camshaft if any of these conditions are apparent.
2   Using a micrometer check the lift height of each cam lobe and check the journal diameters. Renew the camshaft if any of the dimensions are outside the specified limits.
3   Examine the camshaft bearing surfaces in the cylinder head and rocker shaft pedestals for wear, pitting or scoring. If any of the bearing surfaces show significant signs of wear or damage it will be necessary to renew the cylinder head assembly complete with pedestals. Neither the cylinder head nor any of the pedestals are available separately.

25 Timing cover, gears and chain – examination and renovation

1   Examine all the teeth on the camshaft and crankshaft sprockets. If these are 'hooked' in appearance, renew the sprockets.
2   Examine the timing chain for wear ridges on the rollers or looseness of the rivets or side plates. If it has been in operation for a considerable time, or if when held horizontally (rollers vertical) it takes on a deeply bowed appearance, renew the chain.
3   Check the tensioner for obvious signs of wear or damage. Check for free movement and spring return action of the plunger and ratchet. Renew the tensioner if it is suspect.
4   Prior to refitting, set the tensioner in the retracted position by pushing the plunger in and engaging the catch over the plunger peg (photos). When the engine is started, the action of the chain causes the plunger to move in slightly, releasing the catch.

25.4A Push the tensioner plunger in ...

25.4B ... and engage the catch over the plunger peg (arrowed)

25.5A Hook out the old timing cover oil seal ...

26.3 Checking the rocker shaft diameter

25.5B ... and carefully tap in a new seal

26.4 Correct fitted positions of the rocker gear components

5 Check the timing cover for cracks or damage and renew it if necessary. Renew the oil seal in the timing cover by hooking it out with a screwdriver, then carefully tapping in a new seal until it is flush with the cover face (photo). Lubricate the seal lips with engine oil.

26 Rocker gear – examination and renovation

1 Dismantle the rocker gear by sliding the pedestals, springs and rockers off the rocker shafts, but keeping all the parts in strict order of removal. Note the fitted direction of the rockers and note the arrows on the pedestals which point towards the timing chain end of the engine.
2 Check the rockers for wear on their internal diameter and on the contact pad and adjusting stud.
3 Check the shafts for distortion and wear particularly at the rocker contact areas. Check the shaft diameter at the rocker contact areas and at the pedestal locations to determine the extent of any wear (photo). Renew any worn parts as necessary.
4 Reassemble the rocker gear components ensuring that the bolt holes in the shafts and pedestals are aligned and observe the correct direction of fitting of the parts (photo).

27 Flywheel or torque converter driveplate – examination and renovation

1 Examine the flywheel for scoring of the clutch face and for wear or chipping of the ring gear teeth. If the clutch face is scored, the flywheel should be renewed. If the ring gear is worn or damaged it may be renewed separately, but this is a job best left to a Mazda dealer or engineering works. The temperature to which the ring gear must be heated for installation is critical and if not done accurately, the hardness of the teeth will be destroyed.
2 Check the torque converter driveplate carefully for signs of distortion or any hairline cracks around the bolt holes or radiating outwards from the centre.

28 Cylinder head – decarbonizing, examination and renovation

1 Decarbonizing will normally only be required at comparatively high mileages. However, if persistent 'pinking' occurs and performance has

deteriorated even though the engine adjustments are correct, decarbonizing and valve grinding may be required.

2 With the cylinder head removed, use a scraper to remove the carbon from the combustion chambers and ports. Remove all traces of gasket from the cylinder head surface, then wash it thoroughly with paraffin.

3 Use a straight-edge and feeler blade to check that the cylinder head surface is not distorted (photo). If it is, it must be resurfaced by a suitably equipped engineering works.

4 If the engine is still in the car, clean the piston crowns and cylinder bore upper edges, but make sure that no carbon drops between the pistons and bores. To do this, locate two of the pistons at the top of their bores and seal off the remaining bores with paper and masking tape. Press a little grease between the two pistons and their bores to collect any carbon dust; this can be wiped away when the piston is lowered. To prevent carbon build-up, polish the piston crown with metal polish, but remove all traces of polish afterwards.

5 Scrape away all carbon from the valve head and stem using a scraper and emery cloth.

6 Using a micrometer check the valve stem diameter (photo) and renew the valve if the stem diameter is less than specified. If the valve is satisfactory insert it into its respective guide in the cylinder head and check the valve stem to guide clearance by rocking the valve. This can

only be checked accurately using a dial gauge, but it should be fairly obvious if wear is excessive. If the guides are worn they should be renewed by driving them out, away from the combustion chamber side using a hammer and suitable mandrel. Install the new guide, from the camshaft side of the head and drive it home until the clip on the guide contacts the cylinder head.

7 Examine the heads of the valves for pitting and burning, especially the exhaust valve heads. Renew any valve which is badly burnt. Examine the valve seats at the same time. If the pitting is very slight, it can be removed by grinding the valve heads and seats together with coarse, then fine, grinding paste.

8 Where excessive pitting has occurred, the valve seats must be recut by a suitably equipped engineering works. This will also be necessary if the valve guides have been renewed.

9 Valve grinding is carried out as follows. Place the cylinder head upside down on a bench with a block of wood at each end to give clearance for the valve stems.

10 Smear a trace of coarse carborundum paste on the seat face and press a suction grinding tool onto the valve head. With a semi-rotary action grind the valve head to its seat, lifting the valve occasionally to redistribute the grinding paste. When a dull matt even surface is produced on both the valve seat and the valve, wipe off the paste and repeat the process with fine carborundum paste. A light spring placed under the valve head will greatly ease this operation. When a smooth unbroken ring of light grey matt finish is produced on both the valve and seat, the grinding operation is complete.

11 Check the valve springs for cracks, damage or any signs of distortion. Measure the valve spring free length using vernier calipers and renew all the springs if any are not of the specified length (photo).

12 All the cylinder head components should be thoroughly cleaned in paraffin, or a suitable solvent, to remove all traces of carbon and grinding paste from the previous operations. Do this twice if necessary then dry the parts with a lint-free rag.

28.3 Checking the cylinder head for distortion

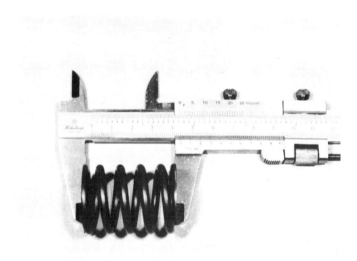

28.11 Checking the valve spring free length

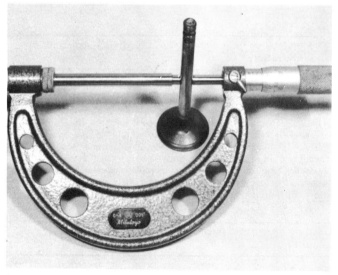

28.6 Checking the valve stem diameter

29 Engine reassembly – general

1 To ensure maximum life with minimum trouble from a rebuilt engine, not only must everything be correctly assembled, but it must also be spotlessly clean. All oilways must be clear, and locking washers and spring washers must be fitted where indicated. Oil all bearings and other working surfaces thoroughly with engine oil during assembly.

2 Before assembly begins, renew any bolts or studs with damaged threads.

3 Gather together a torque wrench, oil can, clean rags and a set of engine gaskets and oil seals, together with a new oil filter.

30 Crankshaft and main bearings – refitting

1 Clean the back of the bearing shells and the bearing recesses in both the cylinder block and main bearing caps.

2 Fit the bearing shells to the main bearing caps and cylinder block recesses ensuring that the tag of the bearing shell engages with the notch in the cap or cylinder block (photo).

3 Using a little grease, stick the thrustwasher upper halves (without the locating tags) to each side of the rear main bearing journal. Ensure that the oilway grooves on each thrustwasher face outwards (photo).

4 Liberally lubricate each bearing shell in the cylinder block and lower the crankshaft into position (photos).

5 Lubricate the lips of a new crankshaft oil seal and carefully slip it over the end of the crankshaft (photo). Do this very carefully as the seal lips are easily damaged.

6 Using grease stick the thrustwasher lower halves (with the locating tags) to each side of the rear main bearing cap. Ensure that the oilway grooves on each thrustwasher face outwards (photo).

7 Fit the bearing caps in their numbered or previously noted locations so that the bearing shell locating notched in the cap and block are both on the same side (photo).

8 Fit the main bearing cap retaining bolts and tighten them so that they are moderately tight. Check that the crankshaft is free to turn then tighten each bolt to the specified torque (photo). Check that the crankshaft still turns freely without any tight spots.

9 Check the crankshaft endfloat using feeler gauges inserted between the thrustwasher and the side of the rear bearing journal. If

30.2 Fit the main bearing shells

30.3 Fit the thrust washer with their oilway grooves outwards

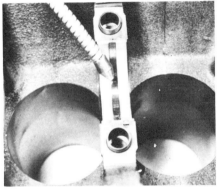

30.4A Lubricate the bearing shells ...

30.4B ... then lower the crankshaft into place

30.5 Slip the oil seal over the end of the crankshaft

30.6 Fit the thrust washer with the oilway grooves outwards

30.7 Fit the main bearing caps

30.8 Tighten the cap retaining bolts to the specified torque

new thrustwashers have been fitted, the endfloat should be in accordance with the dimension given in the Specifications. If the original thrustwashers have been refitted and the endfloat is excessive, new thrustwashers must be fitted.

10 Lubricate the rear bearing cap side seal strips with a little grease and push them fully into their grooves in the bearing cap (photo). Ensure that the seal holes are at 90° to the crankshaft centre line.

31.4B Inserting the piston and connecting rod into the bore

30.10 Fit the new bearing cap side seal strips

5 Compress the piston rings using a ring compressor and with No 1 crankpin journal at its lowest point, tap the piston into the cylinder with the aid of a wooden hammer handle (photo).

6 Guide the connecting rod onto the journal then fit the big-end cap so that the bearing shell notches are both on the same side (photos).

7 Fit the bearing cap retaining nuts and tighten them to the specified torque (photo).

8 Check that the crankshaft is free to turn then repeat the procedure given in paragraphs 4 to 7 on the remaining piston and connecting rod assemblies in turn.

9 If the engine is in the car refit the items listed at the beginning of Section 15.

31 Pistons and connecting rods – refitting

1 Clean the backs of the bearing shells and the recesses in the connecting rods and big-end caps.

2 Press the bearing shells into the rods and caps ensuring that the tag on the bearing shell engages with the notch in the rod and cap.

3 Liberally lubricate the cylinder bores, pistons, bearing shells and crankshaft journals.

4 With the F mark on the side of the piston facing the crankshaft pulley end of the engine, insert No 1 piston into its bore (photos).

32 Oil pump – refitting

1 Locate the Woodruff key into the crankshaft groove with the chamfered end of the key towards No 1 main bearing cap (photo).

2 Slide the oil pump drive sprocket onto the crankshaft with the greater projecting boss away from No 1 main bearing cap.

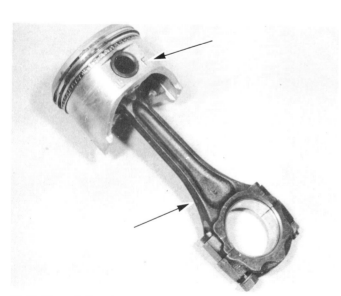

31.4A Piston F (front) mark and connecting rod oil squirt hole relationship (arrowed)

31.5 Compress the rings and tap the piston down the bore

31.6A Fit the big-end cap ...

32.1 Locate the Woodruff key in the crankshaft groove

31.6B ... with the bearing shell notches (arrowed) on the same side

32.3 Engage the sprocket with the chain and fit the pump

31.7 Tighten the big-end nuts to the specified torque

3   Engage the chain with the drive sprocket and driven sprocket then place the pump in position (photo).
4   Refit the pump retaining bolts and tighten to the specified torque.
5   If the engine is in the car, refit the sump.

33 Timing cover gears and chain – refitting

1   Engage the crankshaft and camshaft sprockets with the timing chain so that the timing marks on the sprockets are aligned with the bright links in the chain (photo).
2   Position the crankshaft so that No 1 piston is at TDC and the crankshaft procket Woodruff key is facing the top of the cylinder block.
3   Hold the sprockets and chain together in the correct position and slide the crankshaft sprocket onto the crankshaft (photo).
4   Refit the chain tensioner arm, distance collar and retaining bolt followed by the chain guide and two retaining bolts (photo). Tighten the bolts securely.
5   Apply jointing compound to the timing cover gasket strips and position them on the cylinder block face.

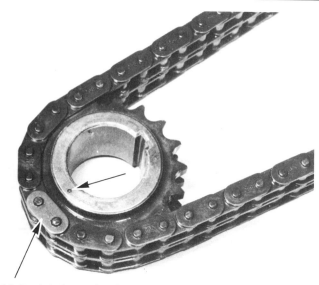

33.1A Crankshaft sprocket timing mark and chain bright link aligned (arrows)

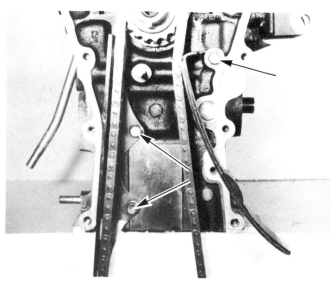

33.4 Chain tensioner arm and chain guide retaining bolts (arrowed)

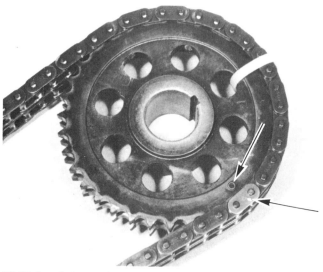

33.1B Camshaft sprocket timing mark and chain bright link aligned (arrows)

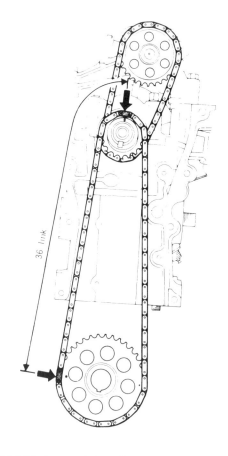

Fig. 1.12 Timing mark location and arrangement on sprockets and chain (Sec 33)

33.3 Fit the sprocket and chain to the crankshaft

6 Refit the timing cover and retaining bolts and progressively tighten the bolts in a diagonal sequence to the specified torque (photo).
7 Slide the crankshaft pulley into place, refit the retaining bolt and tighten it to the specified torque (photo). Prevent the crankshaft turning by placing a block of wood between the crankcase and one of the crankshaft webs.
8 If the engine is in the car refit the items listed at the beginning of Section 14.

33.6 Fit the timing cover and secure with the retaining bolts

34.3 Refit the sump using a new gasket

33.7 Tighten the sprocket retaining bolt to the specified torque

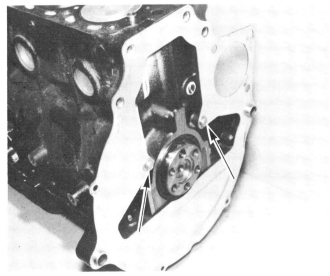

35.1 Refit the rear cover and retaining bolts (arrowed)

34 Sump – refitting

1   Ensure that the sump and cylinder block mating faces are perfectly clean and dry with all traces of old gasket removed. If the ends of the timing cover gaskets are protruding onto the sump face, trim them off flush using a sharp knife.
2   Apply jointing compound to a new sump gasket and lay the gasket on the cylinder block face.
3   Position the sump on the gasket and refit the retaining bolts (photo). Tighten the bolts progressively in a diagonal sequence to the specified torque.
4   If the engine is in the car, refit the items listed at the beginning of Section 12.

35 Flywheel or torque converter driveplate – refitting

1   If removed place the rear cover in position and secure with the two retaining bolts tightened securely (photo).

2   Clean the mating faces then fit the flywheel or driveplate making sure that any previously made marks are aligned.
3   Fit the retaining bolts and tighten them in a diagonal sequence to the specified torque (photo). Lock the crankshaft during this operation with a strip of angle iron (photo).

36 Cylinder head – reassembly

1   Fit new valve stem oil seals over each of the valve guides and tap them into position using a small diameter tube or socket (photo).
2   Lubricate the stems of the valves and insert them into their original locations. If new valves are being fitted, insert them into the locations to which they have been ground (photo).
3   Working on the first valve, fit the spring seat to the cylinder head followed by the valve spring and spring cap (photos).
4   Compress the valve spring assembly and locate the collets in the recess in the valve stem (photo). Note that the collets are different for the inlet and exhaust valves (Fig. 1.13). Make sure that the right ones are being used for the valve concerned.

35.3A Tighten the flywheel retaining bolts ...

35.3B ... with the ring gear locked using a strip of angle iron

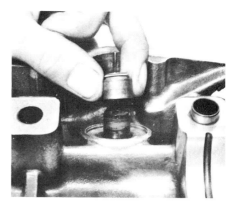

36.1 Fit the valve stem oil seals

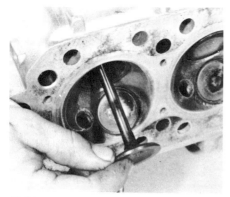

36.2 Insert the valve into its guide

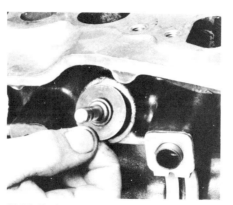

36.3A Fit the valve spring seat ...

36.3B ... followed by the spring ...

36.3C ... and spring cap

36.4 Compress the spring and fit the collets

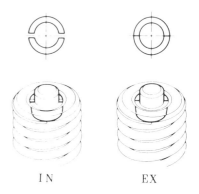

IN   EX

Fig. 1.13 Inlet and exhaust valve collet identification (Sec 36)

5   If the engine is in the car, refer to Chapter 3 and refit the inlet manifold.

37 Cylinder head, camshaft and rocker gear assembly – refitting

1   Make sure that the faces of the cylinder head and cylinder block are spotlessly clean, then lay a new cylinder head gasket on the block face.
2   Carefully lower the cylinder head onto the gasket and fit the small front retaining bolt finger tight only at this stage (photos).
3   Thoroughly lubricate the camshaft bearing journals in the cylinder head.

4   Engage the camshaft with the sprocket, push the sprocket fully into place and lay the camshaft in its bearings (photos).
5   Make sure that the engine is still at TDC and that the timing mark on the camshaft sprocket is at approximately the 3 o'clock position.
6   Lubricate the camshaft bearing journals, then lower the rocker gear into place, ensuring that the arrows on the pedestals are all pointing towards the crankshaft pulley end of the engine (photo).
7   Align the pedestal and rocker shaft holes then refit the cylinder head retaining bolts.
8   Tighten the bolts to the specified torque in two stages in the sequence shown (photo).
9   Now tighten the small front retaining bolt securely.
10 Refit the camshaft sprocket retaining washer and nut, lock the

37.2A Carefully lower the cylinder head onto the gasket ...

37.2B ... and fit the small front retaining bolt

37.4A Engage the camshaft with the sprocket ...

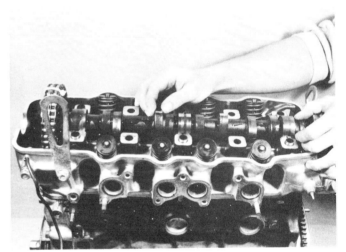

37.4B ... then locate the camshaft in its bearings

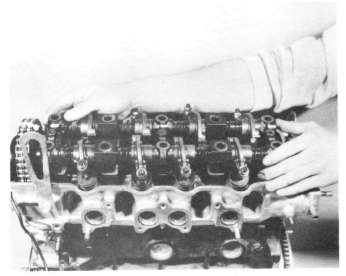

37.6 Fit the rocker gear assembly over the camshaft

37.8 Cylinder head bolt tightening sequence

37.10 Refit the sprocket retaining nut and washer

37.11 Check the camshaft endfloat

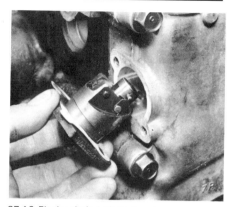

37.12 Fit the timing chain tensioner

sprocket with a screwdriver through one of the sprocket holes then tighten the nut to the specified torque (photo).

11 Check the camshaft endfloat by measuring the clearance between the sprocket and thrust plate using feeler gauges (photo). Renew the thrust plate if the clearance is more than specified.

12 Apply jointing compound to a new timing chain tensioner gasket. Place the tensioner in position on the timing cover and secure with the retaining bolts tightened securely (photo).

13 The valve clearances should now be adjusted using the procedure described in Section 42.

14 If the engine is in the car, refit the controls, cables and services using the reverse of the removal procedure described in Section 10, but bearing in mind the following points:

(a) Refit accelerator and choke cables as described in Chapter 3
(b) Refit the alternator, exhaust manifold, air cleaner and distributor as described in the relevant Chapters of this Manual
(c) Refill the cooling system as described in Chapter 2

38 Ancillary components – refitting

Refer to Section 9 and refit the listed components with reference to the Chapters indicated.

39 Engine – attachment to manual or automatic transmission

Refer to Section 7 and attach the engine using the reverse of the removal procedure. Apply a trace of molybdenum disulphide grease to the transmission primary shaft before fitting.

40 Engine – refitting with manual or automatic transmission

Refitting the engine and transmission assembly is a reverse of the removal procedures contained in Section 6. In addition bear in mind the following points:

(a) Ensure that all the engine/transmission mountings are not strained, twisted or in tension when fitted. Slacken the retaining bolts and reposition where necessary
(b) Refit the accelerator and choke cables as described in Chapter 3 and the clutch cable as described in Chapter 5

(c) Refill the engine and transmission with the specified lubricant as described in Chapters 1, 6 or 7 as applicable
(d) Refill the cooling system as described in Chapter 2

41 Engine – adjustments after major overhaul

1 With the engine and transmission refitted to the car, make a final check to ensure that everything has been reconnected and that no rags or tools have been left in the engine compartment.

2 Make sure that the oil and water levels are topped up and then start the engine; this may take a little longer than usual as the fuel pump and carburettor float chamber may be empty.

3 As soon as the engine starts, watch for the oil pressure light to go out and check for any oil, fuel or water leaks. Don't be alarmed if there are some odd smells and smoke from parts getting hot and burning off oil deposits.

4 If new pistons, rings or crankshaft bearings have been fitted the engine must be run-in for the first 600 miles (1000 km). Do not exceed 45 mph (72 kph), operate the engine at full throttle or allow it to labour in any gear.

5 After the run-in period the cylinder head bolts should be retightened. With the engine cold remove the air cleaner and rocker cover then retorque the bolts in the sequence shown in photo 37.8. Slacken each bolt in sequence half a turn then retighten it to the specified torque before moving on to the next bolt. On completion adjust the valve clearances as described in Section 42.

42 Valve clearances – adjustment

1 If the engine is in the car first remove the air cleaner and disconnect the accelerator cable at the carburettor and rocker cover using the procedures given in Chapter 3. Release the spark plug HT leads, fuel hose and breather hose from the rocker cover, then undo the three bolts and remove the cover. Recover the gasket and rubber sealing grommet from the end of the cylinder head.

2 With No 1 spark plug removed, place your finger over the plug hole and turn the crankshaft until compression can be felt building up in the cylinder. Continue turning the crankshaft until the timing marks on the crankshaft pulley and timing cover are aligned and the engine is at TDC with No 1 cylinder on compression (photo).

3 With the engine in this position the following four valves can be adjusted:

No 1 cylinder exhaust
No 1 cylinder inlet
No 2 cylinder inlet
No 3 cylinder exhaust

4 To adjust the clearances insert a feeler blade of the correct thickness for the valve to be adjusted (see Specifications) between the valve stem and the rocker adjusting screw (photo). Slacken the

42.2 Valve clearance adjustment with the engine at the TDC position for No 1 cylinder

42.6A Fit the rubber sealing grommet with the word OUT facing outwards ...

42.4 Checking a valve clearance

42.6B ... then locate a new gasket on the rocker cover

adjusting screw locknut and turn the screw as necessary until the feeler blade is a firm sliding fit. Tighten the locknut and recheck the adjustment, then repeat the procedure on the remaining three valves in the first group.

5   Turn the crankshaft one complete turn so that the engine is once again at TDC, but this time with No 1 cyliinder on its exhaust stroke. With the engine in this position the remaining four valves can be adjusted as follows.

   No 2 cylinder exhaust
   No 4 cylinder exhaust
   No 3 cylinder inlet
   No 4 cylinder inlet

6   After adjustment refit the rubber sealing grommet to the end of the cylinder head with the word OUT facing outwards (photo). Check the condition of the rocker cover gasket and renew it if necessary (photo).

7   Refit the rocker cover and tighten the three retaining bolts to the specified torque (photo).

8   If the engine is in the car refit the cable clips and hoses to the rocker cover, then refit the accelerator cable and air cleaner as described in Chapter 3.

42.7 Refit the rocker cover to the cylinder head

43 Fault diagnosis – engine

Symptom	Reason(s)
Engine fails to start	Discharged battery
	Loose battery connection
	Loose or broken ignition leads
	Moisture on spark plugs, distributor cap, or HT leads
	Incorrect spark plug gaps
	Cracked distributor cap or rotor arm
	Other ignition system fault
	Dirt or water in carburettor
	Empty fuel tank
	Faulty fuel pump
	Other fuel system fault
	Faulty starter motor
	Low cylinder compressions
Engine idles erratically	Inlet manifold air leak
	Leaking cylinder head gasket
	Worn rocker arms, timing chain, or sprockets
	Worn camshaft lobes
	Faulty fuel pump
	Incorrect valve clearances
	Loose crankcase ventilation hoses
	Carburettor adjustment incorrect
	Uneven cylinder compressions
Engine misfires	Spark plugs worn or incorrectly gapped
	Dirt or water in carburettor
	Carburettor adjustment incorrect
	Burnt out valve
	Leaking cylinder head gasket
	Distributor cap cracked
	Incorrect valve clearances
	Uneven cylinder compressions
	Worn carburettor
Engine stalls	Carburettor adjustment incorrect
	Inlet manifold air leak
	Ignition timing incorrect
Excessive oil consumption	Worn pistons, cylinder bores or piston rings
	Valve guides and valve stem seals worn
	Major gasket or oil seal leakage
Engine backfires	Carburettor adjustment incorrect
	Ignition timing incorrect
	Incorrect valve clearances
	Inlet manifold air leak
	Sticking valve

Chapter 2 Cooling system

For modifications, and information applicable to later models, see Supplement at end of manual

Contents

Specifications

System type .... Pressurized, pump-assisted thermo-syphon with front mounted radiator and electric cooling fan

System pressure .... 0.9 bar ± 0.1 bar (13 lbf/in² ± 1.4 lbf/in²)

System capacity (with heater) .... 5.5 litres (9.7 Imp pints)

Thermostat
Type .... Wax
Start to open temperature .... 88°C ± 1.5°C (191°F ± 2.7°F)
Fully open temperature .... 100°C (212°F)
Lift height .... 8.0 mm (0.315 in) minimum

Radiator cooling fan
Fan motor current consumption:
    270.0 mm (10.6 in) diameter fan .... 9.5 amp (maximum)
    250.0 mm (9.8 in) diameter fan .... 6.5 amp (maximum)

Drivebelt
Deflection:
    New belt .... 12.0 to 13.0 mm (0.4 to 0.5 in)
    Used belt .... 13.0 to 14.0 mm (0.5 to 0.55 in)

Antifreeze properties and quantities
33% antifreeze (by volume):
    Commences freezing .... –19°C (–2°F)
    Frozen solid .... –36°C (–33°F)

	Antifreeze	Water
Quantities (system refill)	1.8 litres (3.2 Imp pints)	3.7 litres (6.5 Imp pints)

50% antifreeze (by volume):
    Commences freezing .... –36°C (–33°F)
    Frozen solid .... –48°C (–53°F)

	Antifreeze	Water
Quantities (system refill)	2.75 litres (4.8 Imp pints)	2.75 litres (4.8 Imp pints)

Torque wrench settings

	Nm	lbf ft
Cooling fan temperature switch	30 to 40	22 to 29
Temperature gauge transmitter	5 to 10	4 to 7
Thermostat housing	19 to 31	14 to 22
Water pump	19 to 31	14 to 22

1 General description

The cooling system is of the pressurized, pump-assisted thermo-syphon type. The system consists of the radiator, water pump, thermostat, electric cooling fan and on later models, radiator expansion tank.

The system functions as follows, cold coolant in the bottom of the radiator passes through the hose to the water pump where it is pumped around the cylinder block and head passages. After cooling the cylinder bores, combustion surfaces and valve seats the coolant reaches the underside of the thermostat which is initially closed and is diverted through a bypass hose and pipe back to the water pump. An additional outlet on the cylinder block also allows coolant to circulate around the heater. When the engine is cold the thermostat remains closed and the coolant only circulates around the engine and heater. When the coolant reaches a predetermined temperature the thermostat opens and the coolant passes through the top hose to the radiator. As the coolant circulates around the radiator it is cooled by the inrush of air when the car is in forward motion. Air flow is supplemented by the action of the electric cooling fan when necessary. The coolant, now cool, reaches the bottom of the radiator where the cycle is repeated.

The electric cooling fan mounted behind the radiator is controlled by a thermostatic switch located in the thermostat housing. At a predetermined coolant temperature the switch contacts close thus actuating the fan through a relay.

On later models a radiator expansion tank is incorporated in the system. As the coolant temperature increases expansion takes place and a small quantity of the coolant is displaced into the expansion tank. The coolant is returned to the radiator when the system cools.

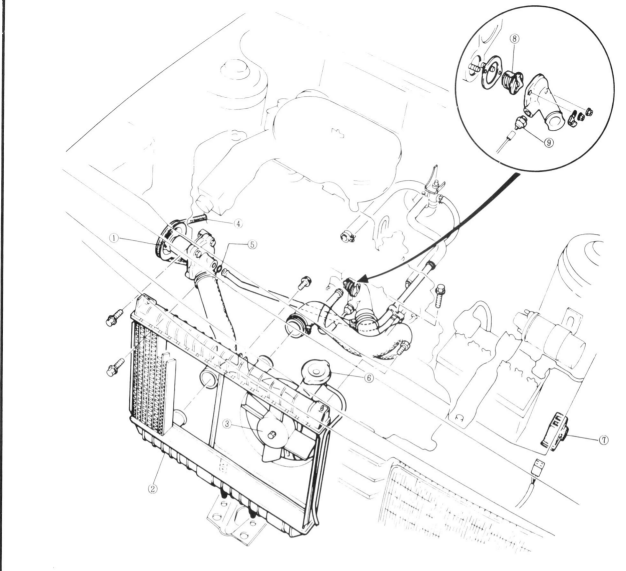

Fig. 2.1 Cooling system component layout (Sec 1)

1	Water pump	4	Drivebelt	7	Cooling fan relay
2	Radiator	5	Bypass pipe O-ring	8	Thermostat
3	Cooling fan	6	Radiator pressure cap	9	Cooling fan temperature switch

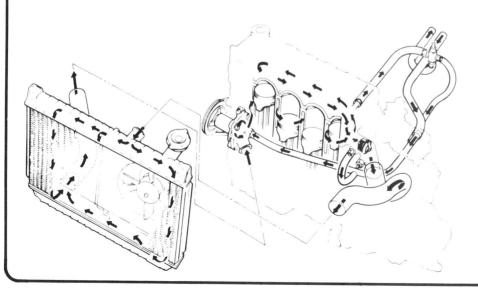

Fig. 2.2 Cooling system coolant flow diagram (Sec 1)

2 Maintenance and inspection

1 Check the coolant level in the system weekly and, if necessary, top up with a 50% water and antifreeze mixture. On models without a cooling system expansion tank, top up the radiator until the level is just above the gauge in the radiator filler neck. On later models equipped with an expansion tank, top up the tank until the level is between the low and full marks (photos).

2 At the service intervals given in Routine Maintenance at the beginning of this Manual, carefully inspect all the hoses, hose clips and visible joint gaskets for cracks, corrosion, deterioration or leakage. Renew any hoses and clips that are suspect and also renew any gaskets if necessary. Check the rubber seal on the radiator pressure cap and renew the cap if the seal shows any sign of deterioration.

3 At the same service interval check the condition of the water pump and alternator drivebelt and renew it if there is any sign of cracking or fraying. Check and adjust the drivebelt tension as described in Section 13.

4 At the service intervals indicated, drain, flush and refill the cooling system, using fresh antifreeze as described in Sections 3, 4, and 5 respectively.

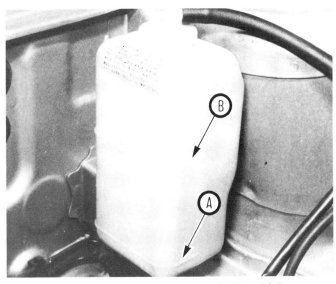

2.1C ... until the level is between the low mark (A) and full mark (B)

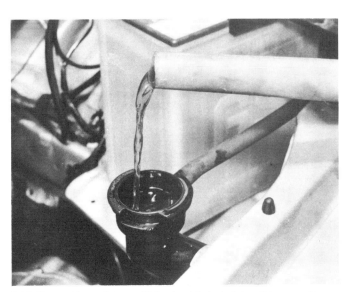

2.1A Top up the radiator until the level is just above the gauge in the filler neck

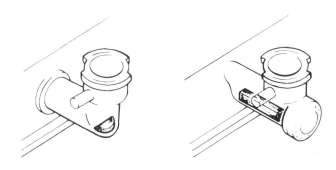

Fig. 2.3 Radiator coolant level gauges (Sec 2)

Left – 1500 cc models
Right – 1100 cc and 1300 cc models

3 Cooling system – draining

1 It is preferable to drain the cooling system when the engine is cold. If the engine is hot, the pressure in the system must be released before draining. Place a cloth over the pressure cap on the radiator and slowly turn the cap anti-clockwise until it reaches its stop.

2 Wait until the pressure has escaped then press the cap downwards and turn it further in an anti-clockwise direction. Release the downward pressure on the cap very slowly and, after making sure that all the pressure in the system has been released, remove the cap.

3 Move the heater control inside the car to the maximum heat position.

4 Place a suitable container beneath the radiator drain plug, unscrew the plug and allow the coolant to drain (photo). On vehicles manufactured before June 1981 a cylinder block drain plug is also provided and is located on the front facing side of the cylinder block, towards the flywheel end. Place a second container beneath the engine, unscrew the cylinder block drain plug and allow the remainder of the coolant to drain.

5 If the system is to be flushed after draining, proceed to the next Section, otherwise refit the drain plug(s).

2.1B On later models top up the expansion tank ...

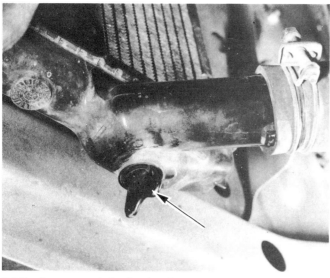

3.4 Cooling system drain plug location

4 Cooling system – flushing

1 With time the cooling system may gradually lose its efficiency as the radiator core becomes choked with rust, scale deposits from the water and other sediment.

2 To flush the system first drain the coolant as described in the previous Section.

3 Remove the filler cap from the radiator, if still in place, and insert a hose into the filler neck. Allow water to circulate through the radiator until it runs clear from the drain plug orifice.

4 In severe cases of contamination the radiator should be reverse flushed. To do this remove the radiator from the car as described in Section 7, invert it and insert a hose in the bottom outlet. Continue flushing until clean water runs from the top outlet. Refit the radiator on completion.

5 To flush the engine disconnect the heater hose at the thermostat housing and insert the flushing hose into the heater hose. Allow water to circulate through the engine until it runs clear from the radiator drain plug orifice.

6 The use of chemical cleaners should only be necessary as a last resort. The regular renewal of antifreeze should prevent the contamination of the system.

5 Cooling system – filling

1 Ensure that all drain plugs and hoses removed for draining and flushing have been refitted and are secure.

2 On all models fill the system through the radiator filler neck with the appropriate mixture of water and antifreeze (see Section 6), until the coolant is just above the gauge in the filler neck. Fill the system slowly to allow all trapped air to escape.

3 When the system is full, start the engine and allow it to idle with the radiator cap removed. Add coolant if necessary to maintain the correct level.

4 When the engine reaches normal operating temperature depress the accelerator two or three times then finally top up the radiator if necessary.

5 Switch off the engine and refit the radiator cap. On models equipped with an expansion tank, add coolant to the tank until the level is between the low and full marks on the side of the tank, then refit the filler cap.

6 Antifreeze mixture

1 The antifreeze should be renewed at regular intervals (see Routine Maintenance). This is necessary not only to maintain the antifreeze properties, but also to prevent corrosion which would otherwise occur as the corrosion inhibitors become progressively less effective.

2 Always use an ethylene glycol based antifreeze which is suitable for use in mixed metal cooling systems.

3 Before adding antifreeze the cooling system should be completely drained and flushed, and all hoses checked for condition and security.

4 The quantity of antifreeze and levels of protection are indicated in the Specifications.

5 After filling with antifreeze, a label should be attached to the radiator stating the type and concentration of antifreeze used and the date installed. Any subsequent topping-up should be made with the same type of antifreeze.

6 Do not use engine antifreeze in the screen washer system, as it will cause damage to the vehicle paintwork. Screen wash antifreeze is available from most motor accessory shops.

7 Radiator – removal, inspection, cleaning and refitting

1 Disconnect the battery negative terminal.

2 Refer to Section 3 and drain the cooling system.

3 Disconnect the radiator cooling fan wiring at the cable connector and at the temperature switch in the thermostat housing (photos).

4 Slacken the retaining clips and detach the radiator top and bottom hoses. Detach the expansion tank hose at the radiator filler neck on later models (photo).

5 Undo the four bolts and lift away the radiator and cooling fan assembly.

6 Undo the two upper retaining bolts then lift the radiator up and out of its location (photos).

7 Radiator repair is best left to a specialist, but minor leaks may be sealed using a proprietary coolant additive. Clean the radiator matrix of flies and small leaves with a soft brush, or by hosing.

8 Reverse flush the radiator as described in Section 4, renew the top and bottom hoses and clips if they are damaged or have deteriorated.

9 Refitting the radiator is the reverse sequence of removal, but ensure that the lower mounting lugs engage fully in their locations. Fill the cooling system as described in Section 5 after fitting.

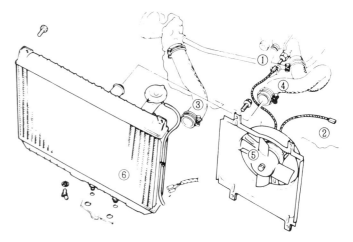

Fig. 2.4 Radiator and cooling fan attachments (Sec 7)

1 Cooling fan wiring at temperature switch	3 Bottom hose
	4 Top hose
2 Cooling fan wiring cable connector	5 Cooling fan assembly
	6 Radiator

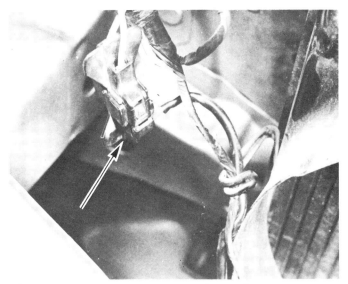

7.3A Cooling fan wiring cable connector (arrowed)

7.6A Undo the radiator upper retaining bolts (arrowed) ...

7.3B Cooling fan temperature switch wiring connector (A) and radiator top hose connection (B)

7.6B ... and lift out the radiator

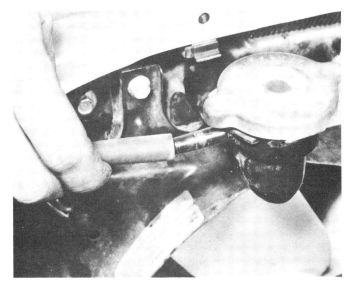

7.4 Detach the expansion tank hose at the filler neck

8 Thermostat – removal, testing and refitting

1 Disconnect the battery negative terminal.
2 Refer to Section 3 and drain the cooling system.
3 Slacken the retaining clip and detach the radiator top hose at the thermostat housing.
4 Disconnect the electrical lead at the cooling fan temperature switch.
5 Undo the two nuts securing the thermostat housing to the cylinder head noting the position of the clip under the outer nut (photo).
6 Withdraw the housing and gasket then lift out the thermostat (photo).
7 To test whether the unit is serviceable, suspend it on a string in a saucepan of cold water together with a thermometer. Heat the water and note the temperature at which the thermostat begins to open. Continue heating the water until the thermostat is fully open, note the temperature then remove it from the water. Before the thermostat begins to close again, measure the lift height which is the distance from the open valve in the centre of the unit to the sealing flange. Compare the figures obtained with those given in the Specifications.
8 If the thermostat does not start to open or fully open at the specified

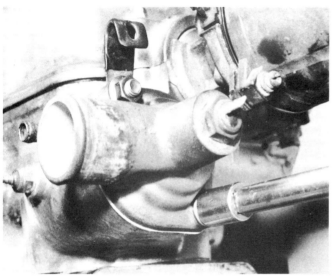

8.5 Undo the thermostat housing retaining bolts

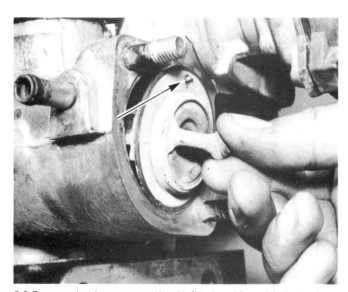

8.6 Remove the thermostat noting its fitted position with jiggle pin (arrowed) uppermost

Fig. 2.6 Testing the thermostat (Sec 8)

temperatures, does not attain the specified lift height or does not fully close when cold, then it must be discarded and a new unit fitted. Under no circumstances should the car be used without a thermostat, as uneven cooling of the cylinder walls and head passages may occur, causing distortion and possible seizure of the engine internal components.

9   To refit the thermostat first clean away all traces of old gasket from the cylinder head and thermostat housing mating faces, using a scraper.

10 Locate the thermostat in its seating in the cylinder head with the 'jiggle pin' uppermost.

11 Apply jointing compound to both sides of a new gasket, then position the gasket carefully over the cylinder head studs.

12 Fit the thermostat housing and secure with the two nuts tigthened to the specified torque.

13 Refit the radiator hose and the electrical lead then reconnect the battery negative terminal.

14 Refer to Section 5 and fill the cooling system.

9   Water pump – removal and refitting

Note: *Water pump failure is indicated by coolant leaking from the gland at the front of the pump or by rough and noisy operation. This is usually accompanied by excessive play of the pump spindle which can*

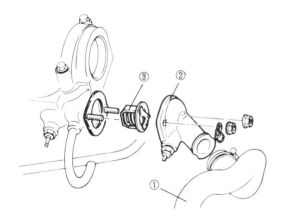

Fig. 2.5 Thermostat removal (Sec 8)

1   Top hose   3   Thermostat
2   Thermostat housing

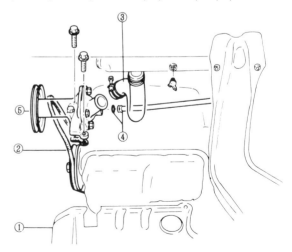

Fig. 2.7 Water pump attachments (Sec 9)

1   Undertray   4   Bypass pipe and O-ring
2   Drivebelt   5   Water pump
3   Bottom hose

be checked by moving the pulley from side to side. Although water pump overhaul is possible, internal parts being available separately, this work entails the use of a number of special tools including a workshop press, and should be left to a Mazda dealer. It may however be less expensive to obtain a complete exchange unit.

1 Disconnect the battery negative terminal.

2 Drain the cooling system as described in Section 3 then remove the drivebelt as described in Section 13.

3 Jack up the front of the car and securely support it on axle stands.

4 Undo the retaining bolts and lift away the undertray to provide access to the pump.

5 Slacken the hose clip and detach the radiator bottom hose from the pump outlet.

6 Undo the bypass pipe support bracket retaining bolts (photo) then withdraw it from the pump using a side to side twisting action. Remove the O-ring seal from the pipe.

7 Undo the nut and two bolts securing the pump to the cylinder block and the bolt securing the engine oil dipstick tube to the pump body (photo). Withdraw the pump from its location.

8 Clean the mating faces of the pump and cylinder block ensuring that all traces of old gasket are removed.

9 Apply jointing compound to both sides of a new gasket and place it in position over the stud in the cylinder block (photo). Smear rubber

9.9A Place a new water pump gasket in position on the cylinder block ...

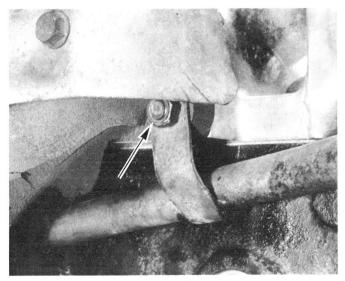

9.6 Bypass pipe support bracket attachment at exhaust manifold stud (arrowed)

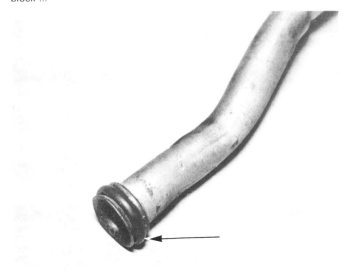

9.9B ... and fit a new O-ring to the bypass pipe

9.7 Water pump retaining nut and bolts (A) and dipstick tube attachment (B)

9.11 Push the bypass pipe (arrowed) firmly into its pump location

grease over a new bypass pipe O-ring and place the O-ring over the end of the pipe (photo).
10 Fit the pump to the cylinder block and secure with the two bolts and nut tightened to the specified torque.
11 Push the bypass pipe firmly into the pump then secure the pipe support brackets (photo).
12 Fit the radiator bottom hose and the undertray.
13 Lower the car to the ground and refit the drivebelt as described in Section 13.
14 Reconnect the battery negative terminal then fill the cooling system as described in Section 5.

10 Cooling fan assembly – removal and refitting

1   Disconnect the battery negative terminal.
2   Disconnect the cooling fan wiring at the cable connector and at the temperature switch in the thermostat housing.
3   Undo the four retaining bolts and withdraw the cooling fan assembly from the radiator.
4   If the motor is to be removed, undo the retaining nut and washers and withdraw the fan from the motor spindle.
5   Undo the three bolts and remove the motor from the shroud.
6   Refitting is the reverse sequence of removal.

11 Cooling fan motor – testing

1   Disconnect the fan motor wiring plug and connect an ammeter between the plug horizontal terminal and the battery positive terminal (Fig. 2.8).
2   Using a suitable lengh of wire connect the plug vertical terminal to the battery negative terminal.
3   The motor should run normally and the current consumption should not exceed the figure given in the Specifications.
4   If the current consumption is excessive or if the motor does not run at all then the motor is faulty and must be renewed.

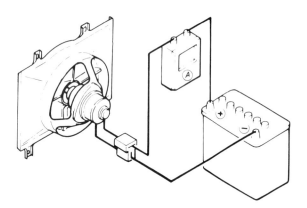

Fig. 2.8 Testing the cooling fan motor (Sec 11)

12 Cooling fan temperature switch – testing, removal and refitting

1   If the operation of the cooling fan is suspect, switch on the ignition and disconnect the wire at the temperature switch in the thermostat housing. The fan should now run. If it does not, check the appropriate fuses, wiring and wiring connectors then test the motor itself as described in the previous Section. If these checks do not highlight the problem, remove and test the temperature switch as follows.
2   Drain the cooling system as described in Section 3.
3   Unscrew the temperature switch from its location in the thermostat housing.
4   Refer to Fig. 2.9 and suspend the switch in a saucepan or suitable

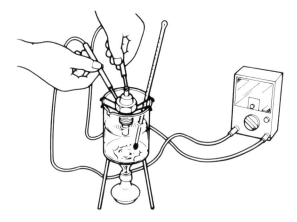

Fig. 2.9 Testing the cooling fan temperature switch (Sec 12)

vessel together with a thermometer. Fill the vessel with water so that the switch probe is completely submerged. Connect an ohmmeter between the switch terminal and switch body.
5   Heat the water and note the operation of the switch which should be:

Open circuit at temperatures above 97°C (207°F) i.e. no reading on the ohmmeter
Closed circuit at temperatures below 90°C (194°F) i.e. full scale deflection on the ohmmeter

6   If the switch does not function as described it is faulty and should be renewed.
7   Refitting the switch is the reverse sequence of removal. Refill the cooling system as described in Section 5 after fitting.

13 Drivebelt – removal, refitting and adjustment

1   To remove the drivebelt slacken the alternator pivot mounting bolt and the adjusting arm bolt, then move the alternator towards the engine. Slip the drivebelt off the pulleys and remove it (photos).
2   Fit the new drivebelt over the pulleys then lever the alternator away from the engine to achieve the correct tension. The tension is correct when the drivebelt deflects by the amount given in the Specifications under moderate finger pressure midway between the alternator and water pump pulleys (photo). The alternator must only be levered at the drive end bracket.
3   Hold the alternator in this position and tighten the adjusting arm bolt followed by the pivot mounting bolt.

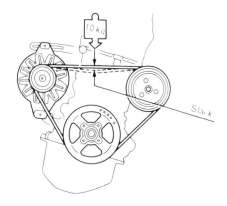

Fig. 2.10 Drivebelt adjustment tension checking point (Sec 13)

13.1A Alternator pivot mounting bolt (arrowed) ...

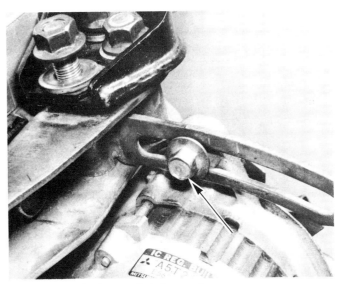

13.1B ... and adjusting arm bolt (arrowed)

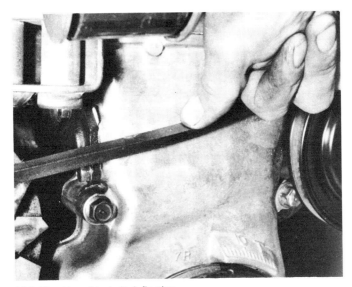

13.2 Checking drivebelt deflection

Fault diagnosis overleaf

14 Fault diagnosis – cooling system

Symptom	Reason(s)
Overheating	Low coolant level (this may be the result of overheating for other reasons) Drivebelt slipping or broken Radiator blockage (internal or external), or grille restricted Thermostat defective Ignition timing incorrect or distributor defective – automatic advance inoperative Carburettor maladjustment Faulty cooling fan, temperature switch or relay Blown cylinder head gasket (combustion gases in coolant) Water pump defective Expansion tank or radiator pressure cap faulty Brakes binding
Overcooling	Thermostat missing, defective or wrong heat range
Water loss – external	Loose hose clips Perished or cracked hoses Radiator core leaking Heater matrix leaking Expansion tank or radiator pressure cap leaking Boiling due to overheating Water pump or thermostat housing leaking Core plug leaking
Water loss – internal	Cylinder head gasket blown Cylinder head cracked or warped Cylinder block cracked
Corrosion	Infrequent draining and flushing Incorrect antifreeze mixture or inappropriate type Combustion gases contaminating coolant

Chapter 3 Fuel and exhaust systems

For modifications, and information applicable to later models, see Supplement at end of manual

Contents

Specifications

General

System type	Centrally mounted fuel tank, mechanically operated fuel pump, single or twin dual throat downdraught carburettors
Fuel tank capacity	42 litre (9.2 Imp gal)
Fuel octane rating:	
All models except 1500 GT	92 RON (2-star)
1500 GT	98 RON (4-star)

Fuel pump

Type	Mechanical, operated by camshaft
Delivery pressure	0.20 to 0.27 bar (2.8 to 3.8 lbf/in²)

Carburettor
1100 models

Type	Hitachi dual throat downdraught
Throat diameter:	
Primary	26 mm (1.02 in)
Secondary	30 mm (1.18 in)
Main jet:	
Primary	90
Secondary	145
Main air bleed:	
Primary	60
Secondary	100
Slow-running jet:	
Primary	48
Secondary	120
Slow air bleed:	
Primary	
No 1	150
No 2	110
Secondary	190
Power jet	40

1300 and 1500 models except 1500GT

Type	Hitachi dual throat downdraught
Throat diameter:	
Primary	26 mm (1.02 in)
Secondary	30 mm (1.18 in)
Main jet:	
Primary	106
Secondary	160
Main air bleed:	
Primary	80
Secondary	100
Slow running jet:	
Primary	48
Secondary	130
Slow air bleed:	
Primary:	
No 1	170
No 2	110
Secondary	130
Power jet	40

1500 GT models

Type	Twin Hitachi dual throat downdraught
Throat diameter:	
Primary	26 mm (1.02 in)
Secondary	30 mm (1.18 in)
Main jet:	
Primary	90
Secondary	135
Main air bleed:	
Primary	60
Secondary	80
Slow running jet:	
Primary	46
Secondary	130
Slow air bleed:	
Primary	
No 1	170
No 2	100
Secondary	150
Power jet	40

Carburettor adjustment data

Choke vacuum diaphragm adjustment clearance:	
1100, 1300 and 1500 models	1.35 to 1.65 mm (0.053 to 0.065 in)
1500 GT	1.45 to 1.75 mm (0.057 to 0.069 in)
Secondary fuel cut-off valve clearance	2.0 mm (0.078 in)
Float height	11.0 mm (0.43 in)
Float opening clearance	1.3 to 1.7 mm (0.05 to 0.06 in)
Fast idle clearance:	
1100, 1300 and 1500 models	1.1 mm (0.043 in)
1500 GT	0.6 mm (0.024 in)
Idle speed:	
All manual transmission models except 1500 GT	800 to 900 rpm
1500 GT	850 to 950 rpm
Automatic transmission models (selector in D range)	700 to 800 rpm
CO mixture	1.5 to 2.5%

Torque wrench settings

	Nm	lbf ft
Inlet manifold to cylinder head	19 to 26	14 to 19
Exhaust manifold to cylinder head	19 to 23	14 to 17

1 General description

The fuel system consists of a centrally mounted fuel tank, mechanical fuel pump and a dual throat downdraught carburettor. Twin caburettors are used on 1500 GT models.

The mechanical fuel pump is operated by an eccentric on the camshaft and is mounted on the rear facing side of the cylinder head. A disposable in-line filter is located in the fuel supply line between the tank and the pump.

The air cleaner contains a paper filter element and incorporates a manually operated two position air temperature control valve. The valve allows warm air from the exhaust manifold stove or cold air from the air cleaner intake spout to enter the air cleaner according to the position of the flap valve.

The carburettor(s) are mounted on a cast aluminium inlet manifold which is water heated to improve fuel atomization, particularly when the engine is cold. Carburettor throttle actuation is by cable and mixture enrichment for cold starting is by a manually operated choke control on all models.

The exhaust system consists of four sections secured by flange joints or push fit with clamps, and a cast iron exhaust manifold. A spring loaded semi ball and socket joint is used to connect the exhaust front pipe to the front silencer thus catering for engine and exhaust

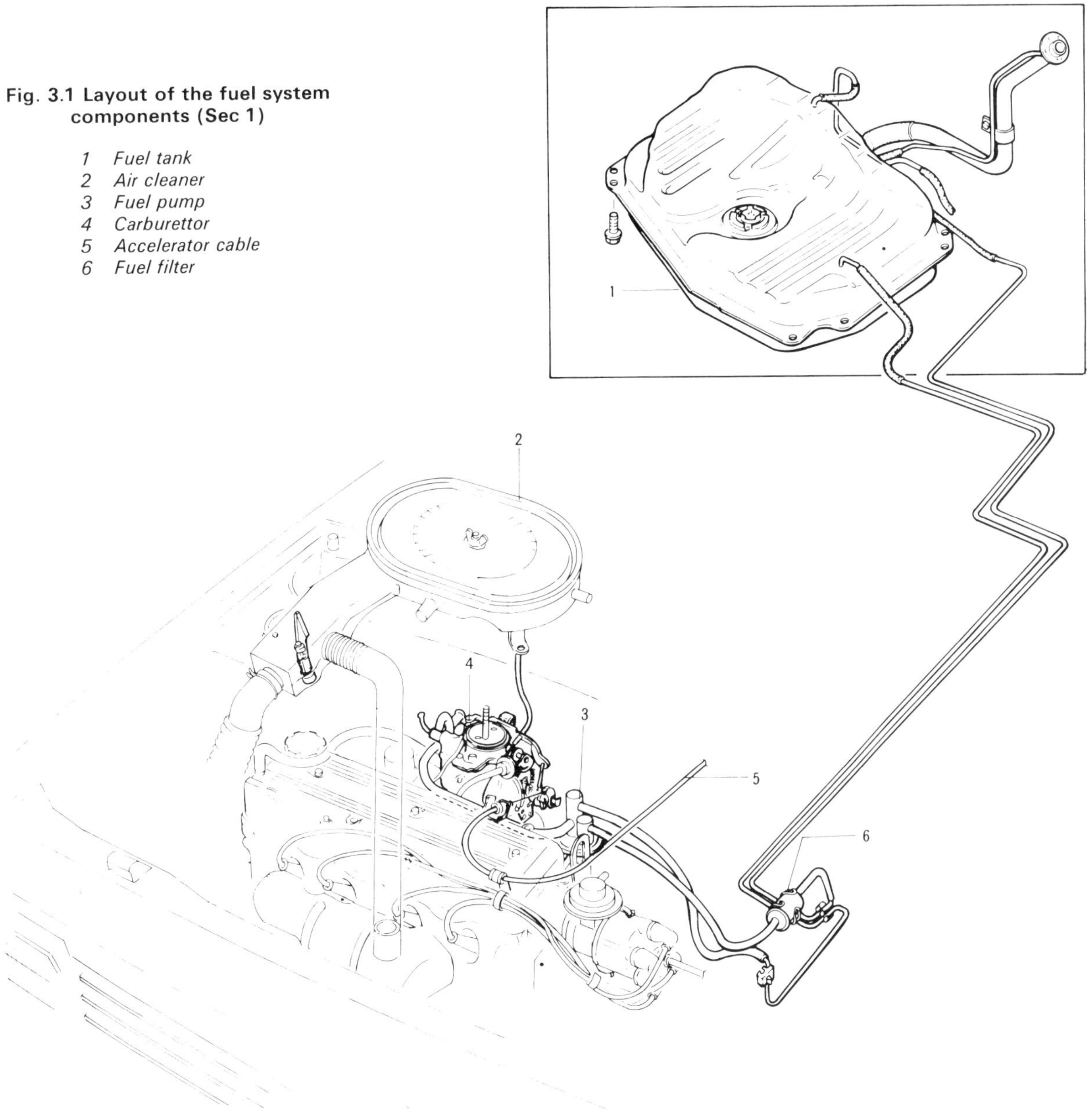

Fig. 3.1 Layout of the fuel system components (Sec 1)

1 Fuel tank
2 Air cleaner
3 Fuel pump
4 Carburettor
5 Accelerator cable
6 Fuel filter

system movement. The system is suspended throughout its length on rubber ring or block type mountings.

Warning: *Many of the procedures in this Chapter entail the removal of fuel pipes and connections which may result in some fuel spillage. Before carrying out any operation on the fuel system refer to the precautions given in Safety First! at the beginning of this Manual and follow them implicitly. Petrol is a highly dangerous and volatile liquid and the precautions necessary when handling it cannot be overstressed.*

2 Maintenance and inspection

1 At the intervals given in Routine Maintenance at the beginning of this Manual the following checks and adjustments should be carried out on the fuel and exhaust system components.

2 With the car over a pit, raised on a vehicle lift or securely supported on axle stands, carefully inspect the underbody fuel pipes, hoses and unions for signs of chafing, leaks and corrosion. Renew any pipes that

are severely pitted with corrosion or in any way damaged. Renew any hoses that show signs of cracking or other deterioration.

3 Check the fuel tank for leaks or for signs of damage or corrosion. Check the tank mountings, and the filler and breather hoses for security.

4 Check the exhaust system visually for corrosion, damage, or obvious signs of leaks. Check the security of all the joints and carefully examine the mounting rubber rings for cracks or deterioration. Renew any of the mountings or parts of the system as necessary with reference to Section 16. Any minor leaks can be sealed with a proprietary exhaust repair kit.

5 Lower the car and check the condition and security of all fuel system fittings and attachments within the engine compartment.

6 Remove the air cleaner element and clean it by blowing through with compressed air from inside to out. Renew the element at the specified intervals or sooner if it is excessively dirty.

7 Set the air temperature control flap in the air cleaner to the winter or summer position according to season.

8 Renew the in line fuel filter at the intervals specified by releasing the hose clips, disconnecting the hoses and slipping the filter out of its

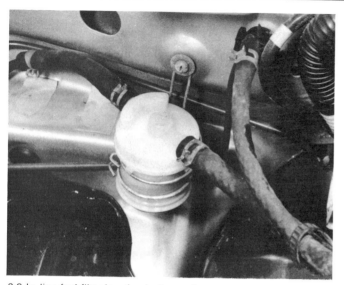

2.8 In-line fuel filter location in the engine compartment

retaining bracket (photo). Fit the new filter ensuring that the arrow stamped on the filter body faces the direction of fuel flow.

9 Check the operation of the accelerator and choke control linkage and lubricate the linkage, cables and accelerator pedal pivot with a few drops of engine oil.

10 Adjust the carburettor idle speed and mixture settings as described in Section 9. Also check the adjustment of the choke vacuum diaphragm and secondary fuel cut-off system as described in Sections 10 and 11 respectively.

3 Air cleaner and element – removal and refitting

1 To remove the air cleaner filter element, unscrew the wing nut then release the wire clips securing the top cover to the air cleaner body. Lift off the cover and remove the filter element (photo).

2 Wipe out the inside of the air cleaner body and clean the element by blowing through it with compressed air, from inside to outside. Renew the element if it has exceeded its service life or if it is excessively dirty.

3.1 Air cleaner filter element renewal

3 Place the element in position, refit the top cover and secure with the wire clips and the wing nut.

4 To remove the complete air cleaner assembly, disconnect the breather hose at the rocker cover and the air cleaner warm air intake duct at the exhaust manifold stove.

5 Undo the bolts securing the air cleaner to the rocker cover and rear support bracket.

6 Undo the top cover wing nut and remove the air cleaner assembly from the engine (photo).

7 Refitting is the reverse sequence of removal.

3.6 Removing the air cleaner assembly from the engine

4 Fuel pump – removal, testing and refitting

Note: *Refer to the warning note in Section 1 before proceeding.*

1 The mechanical fuel pump is located at the rear left-hand side of the cylinder block. The pump is of sealed construction and in the event of faulty operation must be renewed as a complete unit.

2 To remove the pump first disconnect the battery negative terminal.

3 Note the location of the fuel inlet, outlet and return hoses at the pump then, using pliers, release the retaining clips and disconnect the three hoses (photo). Plug the hose ends with a metal rod or old bolt after removal.

4 Undo the two pump retaining bolts then withdraw the pump, insulating block and washers from the cylinder head (photo).

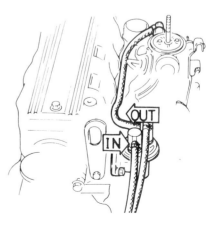

Fig. 3.2 Fuel pump hose connections (Sec 4)

4.3 Disconnect the fuel inlet, outlet and return hoses at the pump

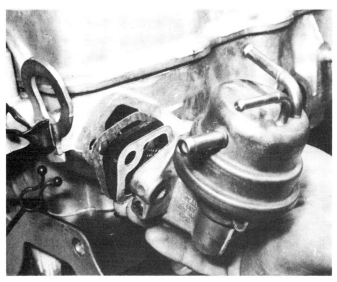

4.6 Note the arrangement of gaskets and insulator block when refitting the fuel pump

4.4 Fuel pump removal

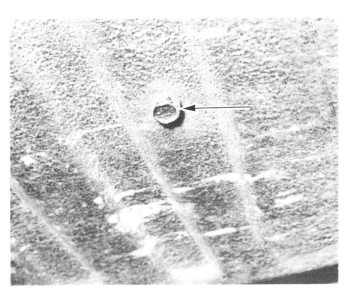

5.2 Fuel tank drain plug (arrowed)

5   To test the pump operation refit the fuel inlet and return hoses and hold a wad of rag near the outlet. Operate the pump lever by hand and if the pump is in a satisfactory condition a strong jet of fuel should be ejected from the pump outlet as the lever is released. If this is not the case, check for a constriction in the fuel line or a blocked filter. If the fuel line is not blocked then the pump is faulty and must be renewed.
6   Before refitting the pump, clean all traces of old gasket from the pump flange, insulating block and cylinder head face. Use a new gasket on each side of the insulator block (photo) and refit the pump using the reverse sequence of removal.

5 Fuel tank – removal, servicing and refitting

Note: *Refer to the warning note in Section 1 before proceeding.*
1   Disconnect the battery negative terminal.
2   Place a suitable receptacle beneath the tank, unscrew the drain plug (photo) and allow the fuel to drain. Refit the plug after draining.

On early models which do not incorporate a fuel tank drain plug it will be necessary to syphon or hand pump the fuel from the tank.
3   From inside the car tip up or remove the rear seat to gain access to the fuel tank.
4   Undo the four bolts, lift off the cover and disconnect the wires and, where fitted, the fuel pipe at the fuel gauge sender unit.
5   Jack up the rear of the car and support it on axle stands.
6   Disconnect the accessible filler and breather pipes and release any cable or pipe retaining clips on the tank sides (photo).
7   Support the tank on a jack with interposed block of wood then undo the four retaining bolts.
8   Slowly lower the jack and tank. As access improves, disconnect any remaining breather pipes then remove the tank from under the car.
9   If the tank is contaminated with sediment or water, remove the sender unit as described in Section 7, and swill the tank out with clean fuel. If the tank is damaged or leaks, it should be repaired by a specialist or, alternatively, renewed. *Do not under any circumstances solder or weld the tank.*
10   Refitting is the reverse sequence of removal.

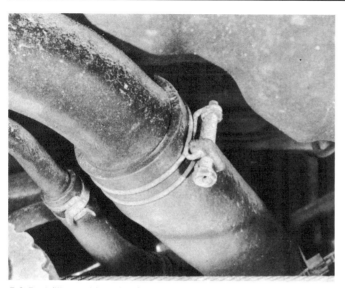

5.6 Fuel filler and breather hoses

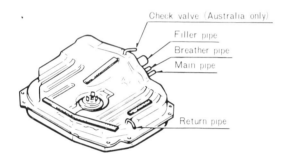

Fig. 3.3 Fuel and breather pipe connections at the fuel tank
(Sec 5)

Check valve (Australia only)
Filler pipe
Breather pipe
Main pipe
Return pipe

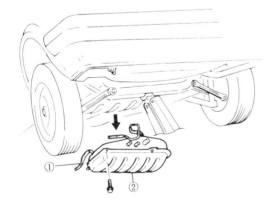

Fig. 3.4 Fuel tank removal (Sec 5)

1   Hose connections   2   Fuel tank

6   Fuel gauge sender unit – removal and refitting

Note: *Refer to the warning note in Section 1 before proceeding.*
1   Disconnect the battery negative terminal.
2   From inside the car tip up or remove the rear seat to gain access to the fuel tank cover on the floor.

3   Undo the four bolts, lift off the cover and disconnect the wires and, where fitted, the fuel pipe at the fuel gauge sender unit.
4   Undo the screws securing the sender unit to the tank then remove the assembly taking care to avoid damaging the float arm. Recover the gasket.
5   Refitting is a reversal of the removal sequence, but use a new gasket if the old one is damaged or shows any sign of deterioration.

7   Accelerator cable – removal and refitting

1   Remove the air cleaner assembly as described in Section 3.
2   Working in the engine compartment disconnect the return spring from the throttle linkage lever.
3   Open the throttle linkage fully by hand and slip the cable end out of the slot on the linkage lever.
4   Slacken the locknuts securing the cable to the bracket on the rocker cover and remove the cable from the bracket.
5   From inside the car remove the cover under the facia.

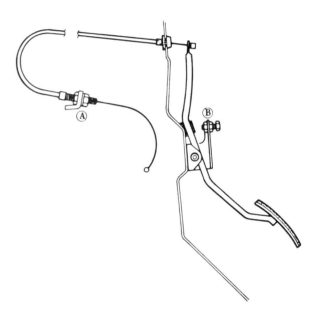

Fig. 3.5 Accelerator cable and pedal arrangement (Sec 7)

A   Cable adjusting locknuts   B   Pedal stop bolt

6   Slip the cable end out of the slot on the accelerator pedal then withdraw the cable through the bulkhead grommet into the engine compartment.
7   Refitting the cable is the reverse sequence of removal. Adjust the cable by means of the locknuts on the rocker cover bracket to provide a small amount of free play with the throttle closed. Depress the accelerator pedal fully and check that the throttle linkage on the carburettor opens fully. If not, adjust the pedal stop bolt (photo) as necessary.

8   Choke cable – removal and refitting

1   Disconnect the battery negative terminal.
2   Remove the air cleaner assembly as described in Section 3.
3   For greater access refer to Chapter 12 and remove the instrument panel.
4   Working in the engine compartment undo the clamp screw (photo) and release the choke outer cable from the carburettor bracket.
5   Close the choke linkage by hand and slip the inner cable end out of the slot on the linkage lever (photo).
6   From inside the car undo the grub screw securing the choke cable knob using a small screwdriver (photo). Withdraw the knob.

7.7 Accelerator pedal stop bolt (arrowed)

8.6 Undo the choke knob grub screw using a small screwdriver

8.4 Choke cable clamp screw (arrowed)

7 Unscrew the knurled retaining ring and push the cable through the facia panel.
8 Working through the instrument panel aperture, pull the cable through the bulkhead grommet and remove it from the car.
9 Refitting is the reverse sequence of removal. Adjust the position of the outer cable in its carburettor bracket clip as necessary so that the choke linkage closes fully when the knob is pulled out and opens fully when it is pushed in.

9 Carburettor – idle speed and mixture adjustment

1 Remove the air cleaner assembly as described in Section 3.
2 Before carrying out the following adjustments, ensure that the valve clearances are correctly set (Chapter 1), that the spark plugs are in good condition and correctly gapped and that, where applicable, the contact breaker points and ignition timing settings are correct (Chapter 4). Ensure that all electrical accessories are switched off and if, during the course of adjustment the radiator cooling fan cuts in, wait until it stops before proceeding.

Single carburettor models
3 Connect a tachometer to the engine in accordance with the manufacturer's instructions. The use of an exhaust gas analyser (CO meter) is also preferable, although not essential. If a CO meter is available this should be connected in accordance with the maker's recommendations.
4 Run the engine until it reaches normal operating temperature then allow it to idle. On models equipped with automatic transmission place the selector lever in the D range. Ensure that the handbrake is firmly applied and the wheels chocked.
5 Turn the throttle adjustment screw (photo) as necessary until the specified idling speed is obtained.
6 Remove the blind cap from the centre of the tamperproof cover over the mixture adjustment screw (Fig. 3.6).
7 Turn the mixture adjustment screw clockwise to weaken the mixture until the engine speed just starts to drop or the tickover becomes lumpy. Now turn the screw slowly anti-clockwise to richen the mixture until the maximum engine speed is obtained consistent with even running. If a CO meter is being used, turn the mixture adjustmenr screw as necessary to obtain the specified CO content.
8 Return the engine idling speed to the specified setting by means of the throttle adjustment screw.
9 Repeat the above procedure a second time then switch off the engine. Refit the blind cap to the tamperproof cover, disconnect the instruments and refit the air cleaner.

8.5 Remove the choke inner cable end (arrowed) from the linkage lever

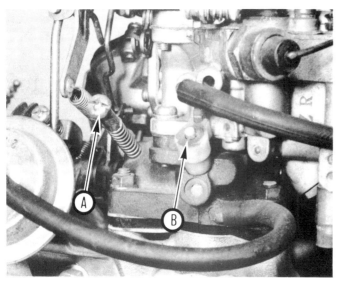

9.5 Carburettor throttle adjustment screw (A) and blind cap over mixture adjustment screw (B)

Fig. 3.6 Removing the blind cap from the carburettor mixture adjustment screw tamperproof cover (Sec 9)

Twin carburettor models

10 Run the engine until it reaches normal operating temperature then switch it off.

11 Disconnect the ball socket of the linkage connecting rod at the throttle shaft lever on the left-hand carburettor (Fig. 3.7).

12 Remove the blind cap from the centre of the tamperproof cover over the mixture adjustment screw on each carburettor (Fig. 3.6).

13 Starting with the left-hand carburettor, back off the throttle adjustment screw (photo 9.5) then screw it in until it just touches the throttle lever. Now screw it in two complete turns. Repeat this operation on the right-hand carburettor.

14 Again starting on the left-hand carburettor screw in the mixture adjustment screw (photo 9.5) until it makes light contact with its seat. Now back the screw off by three complete turns and repeat this operation on the right-hand carburettor also.

15 Connect a tachometer to the engine in accordance with the manufacturer's instructions. The use of an exhaust gas analyser (CO meter) is also preferable, although not essential. If a CO meter is available this should be connected in accordance with the maker's recommendations.

16 Start the engine and turn both throttle adjustment screws by equal amounts until the engine is idling at approximately 850 rpm.

Fig. 3.7 Disconnecting the linkage connecting rod at the throttle shaft lever on twin carburettor models (Sec 9)

17 Using a proprietary balancing meter, in accordance with the manufacturer's instructions, balance the carburettors by altering the throttle adjustment screws until the airflow through both carburettors is the same and the engine is idling at the specified rpm. Depending on the type of meter being used, it may be necessary to remove the air cleaner retaining studs from the intake throat of each carburettor. Once the carburettors are balanced subsequent adjustment of the idling speed must be made by turning both throttle adjustment screws by equal amounts.

18 Turn the mixture adjustment screw on the left-hand carburettor clockwise to weaken the mixture until the engine speed just starts to drop or the tickover becomes lumpy. Now turn the screw slowly anti-clockwise to richen the mixture until the maximum engine speed is obtained consistent with even running. If a CO meter is being used, turn the mixture adjustment screw as necessary to obtain the specified CO content. Repeat this operation on the right-hand carburettor then if necessary return the idling speed to the specified setting using the throttle adjustment screws. It will probably be necessary to repeat the mixture adjustment procedure two or three times until the engine is idling satisfactorily.

19 Make a final check of the carburettor balance then switch off the engine.

20 Refit the linkage connecting rod to the throttle shaft lever. Adjust the length of the rod as necessary so that it does not alter the throttle position as it is fitted.

21 Refit the blind caps to the tamperproof covers, disconnect the instruments and refit the air cleaner.

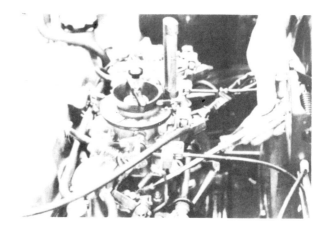

Fig. 3.8 Adjusting the idle speed on twin carburettor models with balancing meter in use (Sec 9)

10 Choke vacuum diaphragm – adjustment

1 Remove the air cleaner as described in Section 3.
2 Start the engine and check that the vacuum diaphragm plunger is pulled fully in with the engine idling. If not, check the condition of the vacuum hoses. If vacuum is present at the hose to diaphragm connection, then the unit is faulty and renewal is necessary. Adjustment is as follows.
3 With the engine switched off, pull the choke knob fully out.
4 Push the vacuum diaphragm plunger in with your finger and, using feeler gauges, check the clearance between the choke flap and the carburettor bore wall (Fig. 3.9). If the clearance is not as given in the Specifications, carefully bend the connecting rod until the specified dimension is obtained.
5 Refit the air cleaner after adjustment.

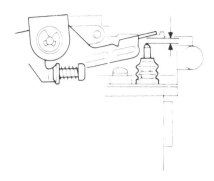

Fig. 3.10 Secondary fuel cut-off system adjusting checking point (Sec 11)

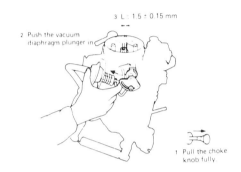

Fig. 3.9 Choke vacuum diaphragm adjustment (Sec 10)

11 Secondary fuel cut-off system – adjustment

1 Remove the air cleaner as described in Section 3.
2 With the throttle linkage at rest measure the clearance between the operating arm and the cut-off valve plunger using feeler gauges (Fig. 3.10).
3 If the clearance is not as given in the Specifications, turn the adjusting screw as necessary until the specified dimension is obtained (photo).
4 Refit the air cleaner after adjustment.

12 Throttle opener system – adjustment

1 Check the engine idle speed and mixture settings as described in Section 9. Leave the tachometer connected.
2 With the engine stopped disconnect the manifold vacuum supply hose at the T-piece connector and also the small vacuum hose from T-piece to throttle opener servo diaphragm, at the servo diaphragm. Now attach the first disconnected hose to the servo diaphragm so that manifold vacuum is supplied directly to the diaphragm.
3 Start the engine and check that the idle speed is now 1400 to 1600 rpm. If adjustment is necessary, turn the adjusting screw on the throttle linkage as necessary (photo).
4 Switch off the engine and return the vacuum hoses to their original positions.
5 The vacuum control valve which controls the operation of the servo diaphragm should also be checked and if necessary adjusted as follows.
6 Using a vacuum gauge, suitable length of vacuum hose and a T-piece, connect the gauge into the vacuum supply line between manifold and control valve as shown in Fig. 3.11.
7 Start the engine, increase the speed to 3000 rpm and quickly release the accelerator. Observe the reading on the vacuum gauge which should initially be high as the accelerator is released, then fall to

11.3 Secondary fuel cut-off system adjustment screw (arrowed)

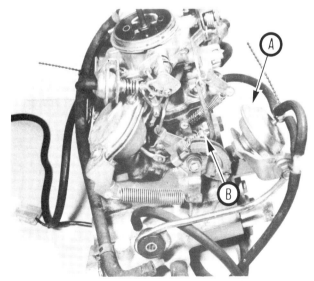

12.3 Throttle opener servo diaphragm (A) and adjustment screw (B)

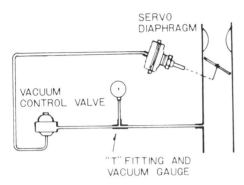

Fig. 3.11 Vacuum gauge connections for vacuum control valve adjustment (Sec 12)

approximately 77.3 to 79.9 kPa (22.8 to 23.6 in Hg). This reading should be maintained for one or two seconds and then fall to a slightly lower steady reading with the engine idling. The critical period is the one to two second intermediate reading and if this is not as specified adjust the vacuum control valve as follows.

8 Remove the rubber cap from the centre of the valve (photo) and turn the adjusting screw as necessary while carrying out the foregoing test. Turning the adjusting screw clockwise will decrease the vacuum and turning it anti-clockwise will increase the vacuum.

9 After adjustment switch off the engine, remove the instruments and reconnect the vacuum hoses in their original positions.

12.8 Vacuum control valve rubber cap (arrowed)

13 Carburettor – removal and refitting

1 Remove the air cleaner assembly as described in Section 3.
2 Disconnect the accelerator and choke cables from the carburettor(s) with reference to Sections 7 and 8 respectively.
3 On twin carburettor models disconnect the ball socket of the linkage connecting rods at the throttle shaft levers on both carburettors.
4 Disconnect the fuel inlet hose and plug its end after removal.

5 Disconnect the fuel cut-off solenoid valve wiring at the connector.
6 Disconnect the relevant vacuum hoses at their carburettor attachments after making a note of their locations.
7 Undo the retaining nuts and lift the carburettor(s) off the inlet manifold. Recover the insulator block and gaskets.
8 Refitting is the reverse sequence of removal, bearing in mind the following points:

(a) *Ensure that all traces of old gasket are removed from the carburettor and inlet manifold mating faces*
(b) *Use new gaskets on either side of the insulator block if the old ones are at all damaged*
(c) *Adjust the idle speed and mixture settings as described in Section 9 after refitting*

14 Carburettor – dismantling and reassembly

1 With the carburettor on the bench, begin dismantling as follows with reference to Fig. 3.12.
2 Using a thin spanner unscrew the secondary fuel cut-off valve lever pivot and withdraw the lever assembly from the side of the carburettor. Turn the lever through 90° and disengage the link rod from the lever slot.
3 Disconnect the return spring, undo the retaining screw and remove the choke cable support bracket.
4 Extract the split pin and cover the small washer securing the choke vacuum diaphragm connecting rod to the choke flap linkage.
5 Disconnect the vacuum hose, undo the two screws and lift off the choke vacuum diaphragm and support bracket.
6 Undo the remaining screw securing the carburettor top cover to the main body. Carefully lift off the top cover, disengage the linkage connecting rod and recover the gasket.
7 Slide out the float pivot pin and remove the float from the top cover.
8 Unscrew the fuel needle valve and withdraw the valve, valve seat and washer from the top cover.
9 Lift the accelerator pump piston out of its location in the main body followed by the spring and accelerator pump inlet ball.
10 Withdraw the accelerator pump discharge weight from its location in the main body.
11 Extract the retaining circlip and remove the rubber boot from the secondary fuel cut-off valve plunger in the main body.
12 Unscrew the cap at the base of the secondary fuel cut-off valve and remove the valve spring and ball.
13 Unscrew the fuel cut-off solenoid valve and remove the valve needle and spring.
14 Unscrew the primary and secondary slow running jets, main air bleed jets and the power jet with reference to Fig. 3.12.
15 Disconnect the linkage return spring at the main diaphragm and extract the split pin securing the diaphragm link rod to the throttle linkage.
16 Undo the retaining screws and withdraw the diaphragm from the main body.
17 Undo the retaining screws and separate the main body from the throttle housing. Recover the insulator block and gaskets.
18 With the carburettor dismantled carefully examine all the parts as follows.
19 Check the top cover, main body and throttle housing for any signs of cracks or damage. Check the operation of the choke flap and throttle valves and check for wear of the spindles or signs of scuffing of the throttle housing bore. Any wear in this area will cause a weakening of the fuel mixture particularly at low speeds.
20 Check the fuel needle valve and seat for damage, wear ridges or corrosion and examine the float for cracks and possible fuel entry.
21 Inspect all the jets and orifices for blockage and blow through them with compressed air. Do not probe with wire or the holes may easily become enlarged.
22 Examine the accelerator pump plunger and cup and the secondary fuel cut-off valve components for signs of distortion or deterioration.
23 Check the operation of the fuel cut-off solenoid valve by connecting it across a 12 volt battery as shown in Fig. 3.13. If the solenoid is functioning correctly the plunger should be pulled into the valve body when the voltage is applied.

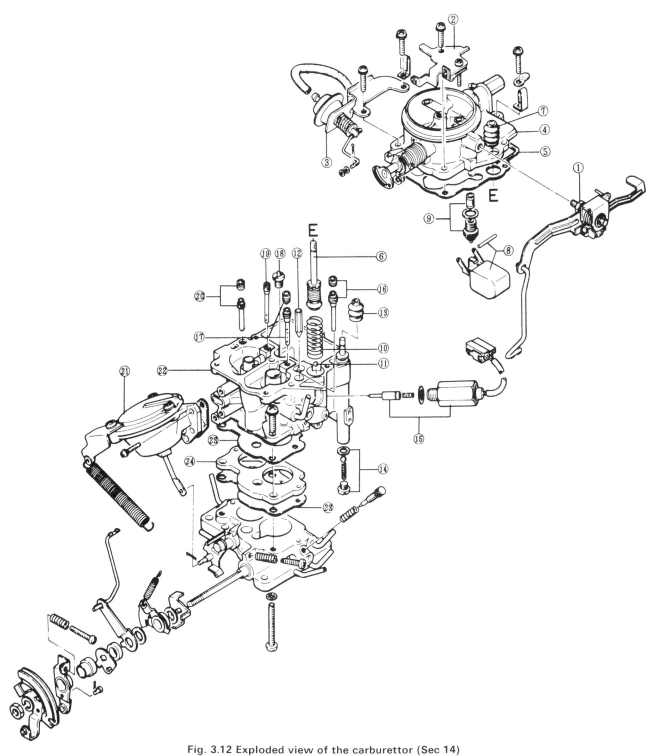

Fig. 3.12 Exploded view of the carburettor (Sec 14)

1 Fuel cut-off valve lever pivot	9 Fuel needle valve
2 Choke cable support bracket	10 Spring
3 Choke vacuum diaphragm	11 Accelerator pump inlet ball
4 Top cover	12 Accelerator pump discharge weight
5 Gasket	13 Rubber boot
6 Accelerator pump piston	14 Secondary fuel cut-off valve cap,
7 Rubber boot	spring and ball
8 Float and pivot pin	15 Fuel cut-off solenoid valve

16 Primary slow running jet
17 Primary main air bleed
18 Power jet
19 Secondary main air bleed
20 Secondary slow running jet
21 Main diaphragm
22 Main body
23 Gasket
24 Insulator block

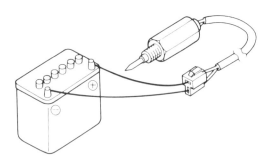

Fig. 3.13 Testing the fuel cut-off solenoid valve (Sec 14)

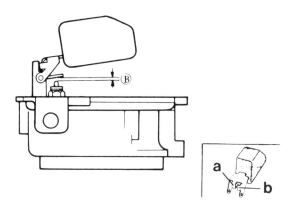

Fig. 3.15 Float opening clearance adjustment (Sec 14)

B   Specified opening clearance   *b   Float stop*
a   Float seat lip

24 Renew any components which are found to be worn, damaged or inoperative and obtain a set of carburettor gaskets which are supplied in the form of a repair kit.
25 Reassemble the carburettor using the reverse of the dismantling sequence and carry out the following adjustments as the work proceeds.

Float height adjustment
26 With the float and fuel needle valve in place, invert the top cover and allow the float to close the needle valve under its own weight. Measure the distance between the float upper face and top cover mating face. This measurement must be taken without the top cover gasket in place (Fig. 3.14). If the measurement differs from the float height dimension given in the Specifications, bend the float seat lip slightly until the correct dimension is obtained.
27 Now lift the float fully and measure the opening clearance from the seat lip to the top of the needle valve (Fig. 3.15). If the measurement differs from the specified opening clearance, carefully bend the float stop as necessary.

Fast idle adjustment
28 With the carburettor assembled operate the choke linkage by hand so that the choke flap is fully closed.
29 Using a drill bit or gauge rod of diameter equal to the specified fast idle clearance, check that the drill bit will just fit between the primary throttle valve and the throttle housing bore (Fig. 3.16). If necessary bend the linkage connecting rod slightly to achieve the specified clearance.

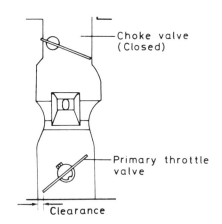

Fig. 3.16 Fast idle clearance checking point (Sec 14)

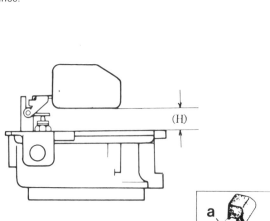

Fig. 3.14 Float height adjustment (Sec 14)

H   Specified float height   *b   Float stop*
a   Float seat lip

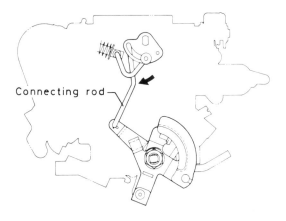

Fig. 3.17 Fast idle adjustment point (Sec 14)

15 Inlet manifold – removal and refitting

1   Drain the cooling system as described in Chapter 2.
2   Remove the carburettor(s) as described in Section 13 of this Chapter.
3   Disconnect the water hose, brake servo vacuum hose and all remaining carburettor vacuum hoses at their manifold connections.
4   Undo the bolts and nuts securing the inlet manifold to the cylinder head and withdraw the manifold off the studs.
5   Clean all traces of old gasket from the cylinder head and manifold mating faces then using a new gasket, refit the manifold using the reverse sequence of removal. Refit the carburettor as described in Section 13, and refill the cooling system as described in Chapter 2.

16 Exhaust system – checking, removal and refitting

1   The exhaust system should be examined for leaks, damage and security at regular intervals (see Routine Maintenance). To do this, apply the handbrake and allow the engine to idle. Lie down on each side of the car in turn, and check the full length of the exhaust system for leaks while an assistant temporarily places a wad of cloth over the end of the tailpipe. If a leak is evident, stop the engine and use a proprietary repair kit to seal it. If the leak is excessive, or damage is evident, renew the section. Check the rubber mountings for deterioration and renew them, if necessary.
2   To remove the complete system or part of the system, jack up the front and/or the rear of the car and support it securely on axle stands. Alternatively drive the front or rear wheels up on ramps.
3   To remove the front pipe and silencer undo the nuts securing the front pipe to the manifold and the bolt securing the front pipe to the engine support bracket (photos). Carefully separate the flange joint and recover the gasket.
4   Undo the two nuts and remove the bolts securing the front silencer to the intermediate pipe. Release the support bracket from the rubber mountings and remove the front pipe and silencer from the car (photo). Recover the gasket.
5   To separate the front silencer undo the nuts and remove the tension springs and bolts at the flexible joint (photo).
6   To remove the intermediate pipe separate the flange joints at each end by removing the nuts, bolts and gaskets, release the rubber mounting rings and remove the pipe (photos).
7   To remove the rear section and tailpipe undo the clamp bolt and slide back the clamp securing the tail pipe to the rear section (photo).

16.3B ... and engine support bracket clamp bolt (arrowed)

16.4 Front silencer flange joint and mountings

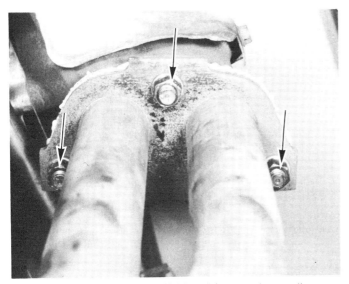

16.3A Exhaust front pipe to manifold retaining nuts (arrowed) ...

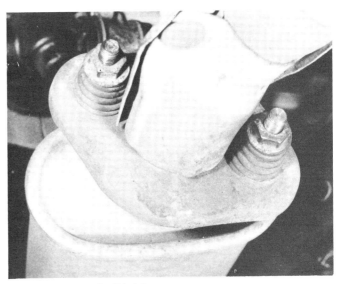

16.5 Front silencer flexible joint

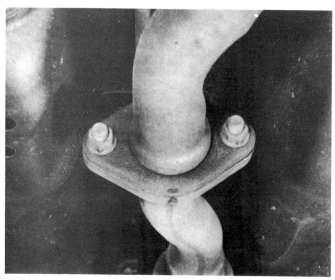

16.6A Intermediate pipe flange joint ...

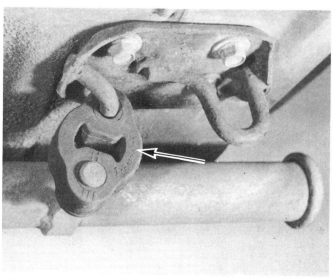

16.7B ... and tailpipe rubber mounting

16.6B ... and rubber mounting rings

16.8 Rear section rubber mounting ring

16.7A Tailpipe to rear section clamp ...

Release the tailpipe from its rubber mounting (photo) then remove it from the rear section using a twisting action. If the tail pipe is corroded in place use liberal amounts of penetrating oil on the tail pipe-to-rear section joint and, if necessary, allow it to soak overnight. Once the tail pipe is free, lift it over the rear crossmember and remove it.

8 Undo the flange joint, release the rubber mounting rings and remove the rear section from the car (photo).

9 Refitting is the reverse sequence of removal using new gaskets at all the flange joints. Use a new sealing ring at the front silencer flexible joint ensuring that it is a snug fit in the joint cup. Clean the cup with emery cloth if necessary to remove any high spots, particularly if creaking of the flexible joint has been experienced. Tighten the joint retaining nuts so that the tension springs are well compressed, but not coil bound.

10 Ensure that all the rubber mountings are seated properly on their brackets and where applicable position the brackets that are adjustable so that there is adequate clearance between the system and underbody.

17 Exhaust manifold – removal and refitting

1   Firmly apply the handbrake, jack up the front of the car and support it on axle stands.

2   From under the car undo the nut securing the exhaust front pipe to the manifold and the bolt securing the front pipe to the engine support bracket. Carefully separate the flange joint and recover the gasket.

3   From within the engine compartment remove the air cleaner warm air duct from the exhaust manifold stove.

4   Undo the four bolts and remove the stove from the manifold (photo).

5   Undo the nuts and bolts securing the manifold to the cylinder head noting the location of the bypass pipe support bracket on the left-hand end stud (photo). Carefully ease the bracket off the stud.

6   Withdraw the manifold from the cylinder head and recover the gasket (photo).

7   Refitting is the reverse sequence of removal. Ensure that the manifold and cylinder head mating faces are clean and always use a new gasket. Tighten the retaining nuts and bolts to the specified torque.

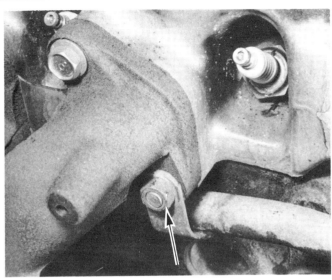

17.5 Bypass pipe support bracket (arrowed) on manifold stud

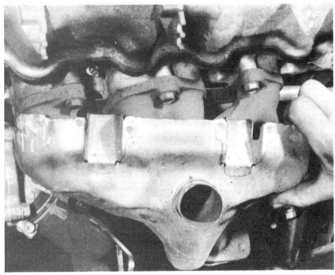

17.4 Removing the exhaust manifold stove

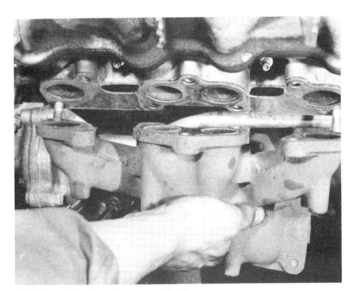

17.6 Removing the exhaust manifold

Fault diagnosis overleaf

18 Fault diagnosis – fuel and exhaust systems

Unsatisfactory engine performance, poor starting and excessive fuel consumption are not necessarily the fault of the fuel system or carburettor. In fact they more commonly occur as a result of ignition and timing faults, particularly on models equipped with conventional contact breaker point ignition systems. Before acting on the following it is necessary to check the ignition system first. Even though a fault may lie in the fuel system it will be difficult to trace unless the ignition system is correct. The faults below, therefore, assume that this has been attended to first.

Symptom	Reason(s)
Engine difficult to start when cold	Choke cable incorrectly adjusted Choke flap not closing Insufficient fuel in float chamber Excessively worn carburettor Fuel pump faulty Blocked carburettor jets or internal passages Faulty fuel cut-off valve
Engine difficult to start when hot	Choke cable incorrectly adjusted Air cleaner element dirty or choked Float chamber flooding Insufficient fuel in float chamber Fuel pump faulty Blocked carburettor jets or internal passages Faulty fuel cut-off valve
Engine will not idle or idles erratically	Air cleaner dirty or choked Choke cable incorrectly adjusted Incorrectly adjusted idle speed or mixture settings Blocked carburettor jets or internal passages Air leaks at carburettor or manifold joint faces Disconnected, perished or leaking vacuum hoses or breather hose Incorrectly adjusted throttle opener system Float chamber flooding Excessively worn carburettor
Engine performance poor accompanied by hesitation, missing or cutting out	Blocked carburettor jets or internal passages Accelerator pump defective Float level low Fuel filter choked Fuel pump faulty Fuel tank vent blocked Fuel pipe restricted Air leaks at carburettor or manifold joint faces Engine internal components worn or out of adjustment
Fuel consumption excessive	Choke cable incorrectly adjusted or linkage sticking Air cleaner dirty or choked Fuel leaking from carburettor, fuel pump, fuel tank or fuel pipes Float chamber flooding
Excessive noise or fumes from exhaust system	Leaking pipe or manifold joints Leaking, corroded or damaged silencers or pipe System in contact with underbody due to broken mounting

Chapter 4 Ignition system

For modifications, and information applicable to later models, see Supplement at end of manual

Contents

Specifications

General

System type:	
Up to December 1981	Conventional contact breaker and coil ignition system
December 1981 onwards	Electronic breakerless High Energy Ignition (H.E.I.) system
Firing order	1 – 3 – 4 – 2
Location of No 1 cylinder	Crankshaft pulley end

Distributor

Contact breaker points gap*	0.45 to 0.55 mm (0.018 to 0.022 in)
Dwell angle*	49° to 55°
Direction of rotor arm rotation	Anti-clockwise (viewed from cap)

Ignition coil

Primary resistance	3.1 ohms
Secondary resistance	10 to 30 Kohms
Ballast resistance*	1.6 ohms

*Conventional ignition systems only

Ignition timing (stroboscopic with vacuum hose connected)

1100 cc models	3° to 5° BTDC at 800 to 900 rpm
1300 cc models	5° to 7° BTDC at 800 to 900 rpm
1500 cc models:	
Manual transmission	5° to 7° BTDC at 800 to 900 rpm
Automatic transmission	5° to 7° BTDC at 700 to 800 rpm (transmission in D range)
1500 GT	5° to 7° BTDC at 850 to 950 rpm
Timing marks	Notch on crankshaft pulley, scale on timing chain cover

Spark plugs and HT leads

Spark plug type	NGK: BPR5ES or BPR6ES; Nippondenso: W16EXR-U or W20EXR-U
Spark plug gap	0.75 to 0.85 mm (0.029 to 0.033 in)
High tension lead resistance	16 Kohms per metre (3.28 ft)

Torque wrench settings

	Nm	lbf ft
Spark plugs	15 to 23	11 to 17

1 General description

Two different types of ignition system are fitted to Mazda 323 models covered by this Manual. Early cars utilize conventional contact breaker point ignition whereas those manufactured after December 1981 are equipped with an electronic High Energy Ignition (H.E.I.) system. The operation of both types is as follows.

In order that the engine can run correctly, it is necessary for an electrical spark to ignite the fuel/air mixture in the combustion chamber at exactly the right moment in relation to engine speed and load. The ignition system is based on feeding low tension voltage from the battery to the coil, where it is converted to high tension voltage. The high tension voltage is powerful enough to jump the spark plug gap in the cylinders many times a second under high compression, providing that the system is in good condition and that all adjustments are correct.

On models equipped with conventional ignition, the system is divided into two circuits, the low tension circuit and the high tension circuit. The low tension (sometimes known as the primary) circuit consists of the battery, lead to the ignition switch, lead from the ignition switch to the low tension or primary coil windings (terminal +) and the lead from the low tension coil windings (terminal −) to the contact breaker points and condenser in the distributor.

The high tension circuit consists of the high tension (sometimes known as the secondary) coil windings, the heavy ignition lead from the centre of the coil to the centre of the distributor cap, the rotor arm, and the spark plug leads and spark plugs.

When the system is in operation, low tension voltage is changed in the coil into high tension voltage by the opening and closing of the breaker points in the low tension circuit. High tension voltage is then fed, via the carbon brush in the centre of the distributor cap, to the rotor arm of the distributor. The rotor arm revolves inside the distributor cap and each time it comes in line with one of the four metal segments in the cap, which are connected to the spark plug leads, the opening and closing of the contact breaker points causes the high tension voltage to build up and jump the gap from the rotor arm to the appropriate metal segment. The voltage then passes via the spark plug lead to the spark plug, where it finally jumps the spark plug gap before going to earth.

On models equipped with electronic ignition the system is also divided into low tension and high tension circuits. The low tension circuit consists of the battery, lead to the ignition switch, lead from the ignition switch to the low tension coil windings and the lead from the low tension coil windings to the igniter and signal generator assembly in the distributor. The layout of the high tension circuit is the same as the conventional ignition system.

When the system is in operation, low tension voltage is changed in the coil into high tension voltage by the action of the igniter in conjunction with the signal rotor, permanent magnet and pick-up coil of the signal generator assembly. As each of the signal rotor teeth pass through the magnetic field around the pick-up coil an electrical signal is sent to the igniter which triggers the coil in the same way as the opening and closing of the contact breaker points in the conventional system. High tension voltage is then fed to the spark plugs as previously described.

On both the conventional and electronic systems, ignition advance is controlled both mechanically and by a vacuum operated system. The mechanical governor mechanism consists of two weights which move out from the distributor shaft as the engine speed rises due to centrifugal force. As they move outwards they rotate the cam relative to the distributor shaft and so advance the spark. The weights are held in

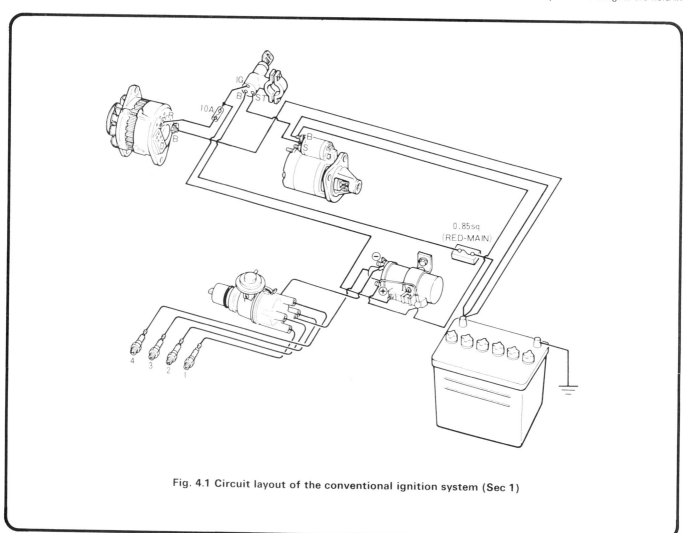

Fig. 4.1 Circuit layout of the conventional ignition system (Sec 1)

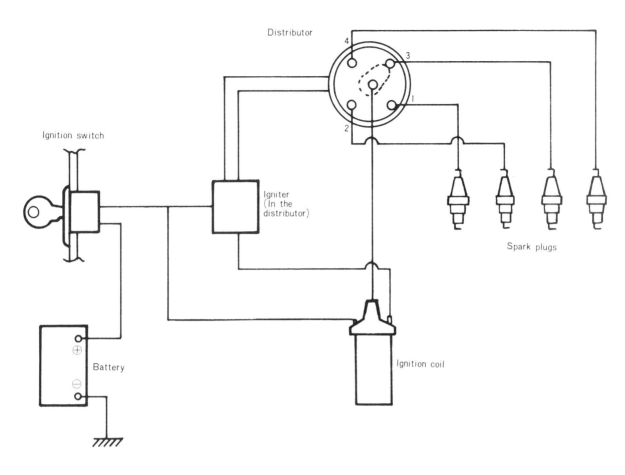

Fig. 4.2 Circuit layout of the electronic ignition system (Sec 1)

position by two light springs and it is the tension of the springs which is largely responsible for correct spark advancement.

The vacuum control consists of a diaphragm, one side of which is connected via a small bore tube to the carburettor, and the other side to the distributor baseplate or signal plate. Depression in the inlet manifold and carburettor, which varies with engine speed and throttle opening, causes the diaphragm to move, so moving the baseplate, and advancing or retarding the spark. A fine degree of control is achieved by a spring in the vacuum assembly.

On conventional systems a ballast resistor is incorporated in the low tension circuit between the ignition switch and coil primary windings. During starting this resistor is bypassed allowing full available battery voltage to be fed to the coil which is of a low voltage type. This ensures that during starting when there is a heavy drain on the battery, sufficient voltage is still available at the coil to produce a powerful spark. During normal running, battery voltage is directed through the ballast resistor before reaching the coil.

Warning: *The voltages produced by the electronic ignition system are considerably higher than those produced by the conventional system. Extreme care must be used when working on the system with the ignition switched on. Persons with surgically implanted cardiac pacemaker devices should keep well clear of the ignition circuits, components and test equipment.*

2 Maintenance and inspection

1   At the intervals specified in Routine Maintenance at the beginning of this Manual, remove the distributor cap and thoroughly clean it inside and out with a dry, lint-free cloth. Examine the four HT lead segments inside the cap. If the segments appear badly burnt or pitted, renew the cap, Make sure that the carbon brush in the centre of the cap

is free to move and that it protrudes slightly from its holder.
2   On models equipped with conventional ignition check the condition of the contact breaker points. Renew the points and/or adjust the gap using the procedures described in Sections 3 and 4.
3   Remove, clean, regap and test the spark plugs as described in Section 11. Renew the plugs in sets of four if any show signs of failure when tested or if, under visial inspection, the end of the centre electrode is rounded off or the earth electrode is at all eroded. At the same time check the spark plug HT leads for any signs of corrosion of the end fittings which if evident should be carefully cleaned away. Wipe the leads clean over their entire length before refitting.
4   When all of the above operations have been carried out, refer to Section 9 and check/adjust the ignition timing.
5   Finally check the condition and security of all leads and wiring associated with the ignition system. Make sure that no chafing is occurring on any of the wires and that all connections are secure, clean and free from corrosion.

3 Contact breaker points (conventional ignition system) – adjustment

1   Spring back the distributor cap retaining clips, lift off the cap and place it to one side.
2   Withdraw the rotor arm from the distributor shaft.
3   Using a screwdriver, gently prise the contact breaker points open to examine the condition of their faces, if they are rough, pitted or dirty they should be renewed as described in the next Section.
4   Assuming that the points are in a satisfactory condition or that they have just been renewed, the gap between the two faces should be measured using feeler gauges, as follows.
5   Turn the crankshaft, using a spanner on the pulley bolt, until the

heel of the contact breaker arm is on the peak of one of the four cam lobes. A feeler blade of thickness equal to the contact breaker points gap as given in the Specifications, should now just slide between the point faces.

6   If the gap varies from this amount slacken the contact breaker point retaining screws and move the fixed point as necessary to achieve the desired gap. The points can be easily moved with a screwdriver inserted through the hole in the breaker point plate and engaged with the corresponding slot in the distributor baseplate.

7   After adjustment tighten the two retaining screws and recheck the gap.

8   Refit the rotor arm and the distributor cap.

9   If a dwell meter is available, a far more accurate method of setting the contact breaker points gap is by measuring and setting the distributor dwell angle.

10 The dwell angle is the number of degrees of distributor cam rotation during which the contact breaker points are closed, ie the period from when the points close after being opened by one cam lobe until they are opened again by the next cam lobe. The advantages of setting the points by this method are that any wear of the distributor shaft or cam lobes is taken into account, and also the inaccuracies of using a feeler gauge are eliminated. In general, a dwell meter should be used in accordance with the manufacturer's instructions. However, the use of one type of meter is outlined as follows:

11 To set the dwell angle, remove the distributor cap and rotor arm and connect one lead of the dwell meter to the '+' terminal on the coil and the other lead to the '−' terminal on the coil.

12 Whilst an assistant turns on the ignition and operates the starter, observe the reading on the dwell meter scale. With the engine turning over on the starter, the reading should be equal to the dwell angle given in the Specifications.

13 If the dwell angle is too small, the contact breaker point gap is too wide, and if the dwell angle is excessive the gap is too small.

14 Adjust the contact breaker points gap, while the engine is cranking, using the method described in paragraphs 6 and 7. When the dwell angle is satisfactory, disconnect the meter then refit the rotor arm and distributor cap.

4   Contact breaker points (conventional ignition system) – removal and refitting

1   Spring back the distributor cap retaining clips, lift off the cap and place it to one side.

2   Withdraw the rotor arm from the distributor shaft.

3   Undo the two screws securing the contact breaker points to the distributor baseplate noting the location of the earth wire under one of the screws.

4   Withdraw the points, undo the LT lead retaining screw noting the arrangement of washer and insulator, then remove the contact breaker point assembly from the distributor.

5   Refit the new points using the reverse of the removal procedure, then refer to Section 3 and adjust the gap or dwell angle.

5   Condenser (conventional ignition system) – removal and refitting

1   The purpose of the condenser (sometimes known as a capacitor) is to prevent excessive arcing of the contact breaker points, and to ensure that a rapid collapse of the magnetic field, created in the coil, and necessary if a healthy spark is to be produced at the plugs, is allowed to occur.

2   The condenser is fitted in parallel with the contact breaker points. If it becomes faulty it will cause ignition failure, as the points will be prevented from cleanly interrupting the low tension circuit.

3   If the engine becomes very difficult to start, or begins to miss after several miles of running, and the contact breaker points show signs of excessive burning, then the condition of the condenser must be suspect. A further test can be made by separating the points by hand, with the ignition switched on. If this is accompanied by an excessively strong flash, it indicates that the condenser has failed.

4   Without special test equipment, the only reliable way to diagnose

condenser trouble is to renew the suspect unit and note if there is any improvement in performance.

5   To remove the condenser from its external location on the side of the distributor, spring back the distributor cap retaining screws, lift off the cap and place it to one side.

6   Undo the screw securing the LT lead to the contact breaker points noting the arrangement of washer and insulator.

7   Detach the LT lead from the coil at the wiring connector.

8   Undo the screw securing the condenser to the distributor, release the LT lead grommet from the distributor rim and remove the condenser from the distributor.

9   Refitting is the reverse sequence of removal.

6   Distributor – removal and refitting

1   Disconnect the battery negative terminal.

2   Pull off the HT lead and remove No 1 spark plug (nearest the crankshaft pulley).

3   Place a finger over the plug hole and turn the crankshaft in the normal direction of rotation (clockwise viewed from the crankshaft pulley end) until pressure is felt in No 1 cylinder. This indicates that the piston is commencing its compression stroke. The crankshaft can be turned with a spanner on the pulley bolt.

4   Continue turning the engine until the notch in the crankshaft pulley is aligned with the T mark on the timing scale just above the pulley (photo). In this position the engine is at Top Dead Centre (TDC) with No 1 cylinder on compression.

5   Make a reference mark on the side of the distributor body, adjacent to the No 1 spark plug HT lead position in the distributor cap. Spring back the clips or remove the two screws and lift off the cap (photo). Check that the metal segment of the rotor arm is pointing towards the reference mark.

6   Make a further reference mark at the base of the distributor body and on the cylinder head (photo).

7   Detach the vacuum advance hose at the distributor vacuum unit and disconnect the distributor wiring at the ignition coil.

8   Undo the bolt securing the distributor clamp to the cylinder head, and withdraw the distributor from the engine (photo).

9   Before refitting, check that the engine is still at the TDC position with No 1 cylinder on compression. If the engine has been turned while the distributor was removed, return it to the correct position as previously described.

10 Lubricate the O-ring seal at the base of the distributor with engine oil then turn the rotor arm until it is pointing towards No 1 spark plug lead position in the cap or towards the reference mark made during removal.

6.4 Crankshaft pulley notch aligned with TDC mark on timing scale

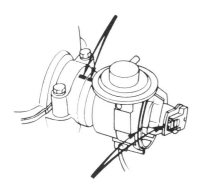

Fig. 4.3 Mark the distributor body and cylinder head prior
to removal (Sec 6)

6.8 Removing the distributor

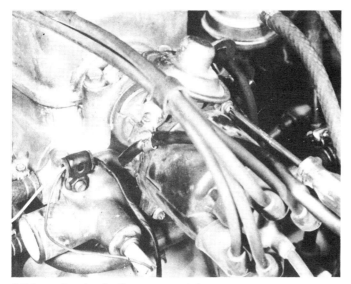

6.5 Removing the distributor cap retaining screws

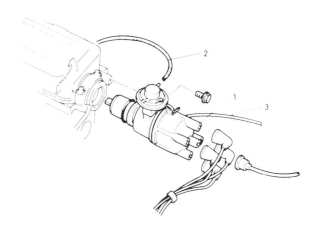

Fig. 4.4 Distributor removal (Sec 6)

1   Distributor cap
2   Vacuum hose
3   LT wiring

11 With the vacuum unit uppermost, insert the distributor into its
location and turn the rotor arm slightly until the distributor shaft
positively engages with the camshaft.
12 Turn the distributor until the alignment marks on the cylinder head
and distributor base, made during removal, are aligned. If a new
distributor is being fitted turn the unit until the rotor arm is pointing
towards the No 1 spark plug lead segment in the cap.
13 Refit the distributor clamp bolt and tighten securely.
14 Reconnect the vacuum advance hose and the wiring at the ignition
coil. Refit No 1 spark plug, distributor cap and HT leads.
15 Reconnect the battery then refer to Section 9 and adjust the
ignition timing.

7 Distributor (conventional ignition system) – dismantling and reassembly

1   Remove the distributor as described in the previous Section.
2   Remove the contact breaker points and condenser from the
distributor as described in Sections 4 and 5 respectively.

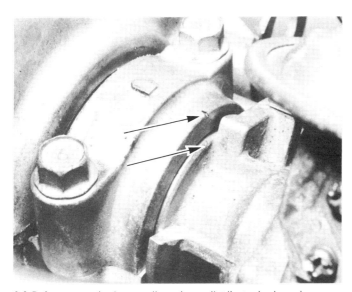

6.6 Reference marks (arrowed) made on distributor body and
cylinder head

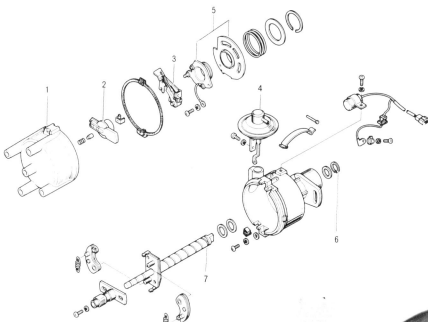

Fig. 4.5 Exploded view of the conventional ignition distributor (Sec 7)

1   Distributor cap
2   Rotor arm
3   Contact breaker points
4   Vacuum unit
5   Baseplate assembly
6   Distributor shaft circlip
7   Distributor shaft

3   Undo the screws securing the vacuum unit to the side of the distributor. Disengage the pullrod from the peg on the baseplate and withdraw the unit from the distributor.

4   Undo the screws securing the baseplate in position and remove the baseplate.

5   At the base of the distributor shaft, extract the circlip and spring washer then withdraw the shaft complete with centrifugal governor, from the distributor. Recover the thrust washers from the shaft.

6   With the distributor dismantled, renew any parts that show signs of wear, or damage, and any that are known to be faulty. Pay close attention to the centrifugal governor, checking for loose or broken springs, wear in the bob weight pivots and play in the distributor shaft. Apply suction to the vacuum unit and check that the pullrod moves in as suction is applied and returns under spring pressure when the suction is released.

7   Reassembly is the reverse of the dismantling sequence, bearing in mind the following points:

     (a)   Lubricate the distributor shaft with engine oil before refitting
     (b)   Adjust the contact breaker points as described in Section 3 after reassembly then refit the distributor as described in Section 6

---

8   Distributor (electronic ignition system) – dismantling and reassembly

---

1   Remove the distributor as described in Section 6.

2   Undo the two screws and lift off the rotor (photo).

3   Undo the small screw on the side of the distributor body and remove the condenser (photo).

4   Undo the retaining bolt and withdraw the centrifugal governor and signal rotor assembly upwards and off the distributor shaft (photos).

5   Undo the two screws and lift off the igniter and signal generator assembly together with the sealing ring (photos).

6   Undo the screw securing the vacuum unit to the distributor body (photo). Disengage the vacuum unit pullrod from the signal plate peg and withdraw the unit (photo).

7   Undo the two screws and remove the signal plate assembly (photos).

8   Undo the screws securing the bearing retainer plate assembly and withdraw the plate (photos).

9   At the base of the distributor , drive out the roll pin and remove the drive key. Extract the retaining circlip and press the distributor shaft and bearing out of the body (photo).

8.2 Undo the two screws (arrowed) and lift off the rotor

8.3 Undo the screw and remove the condenser

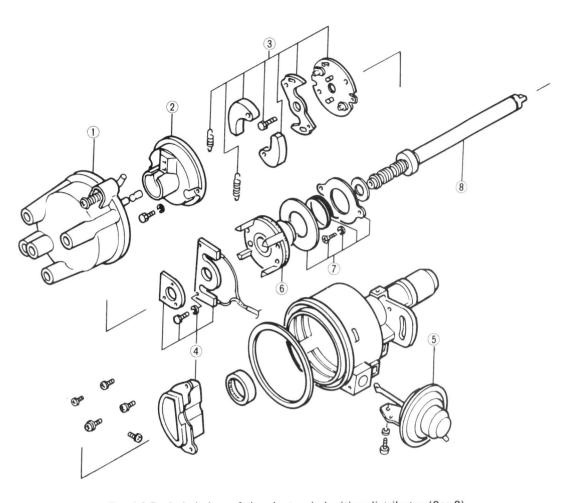

Fig. 4.6 Exploded view of the electronic ignition distributor (Sec 8)

1 Distributor cap
2 Rotor
3 Centrifugal governor assembly
4 Igniter and signal generator assembly
5 Vacuum unit
6 Signal plate
7 Bearing retainer plate assembly
8 Distributor shaft

8.4A Undo the retaining bolt ...

8.4B ... and withdraw the centrifugal governor and signal rotor

8.5A Undo the igniter and signal generator retaining screws ...

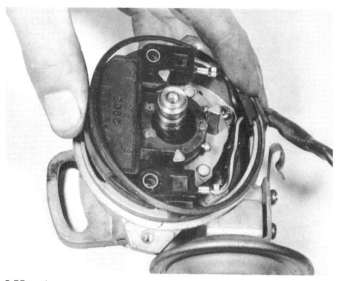

8.5B ... then remove this assembly together with the sealing ring

8.6A Undo the vacuum unit retaining screw (arrowed) ...

8.6B ... disengage the pullrod and remove the vacuum unit

8.7A Undo the two signal plate retaining screws ...

8.7B ... and lift out the assembly

8.8A Remove the bearing retainer plate screws ...

8.8B ... and the retainer plate

10 With the distributor dismantled, renew any parts that show signs of wear, or damage and any that are known to be faulty. Pay close attention to the centrifugal governor mechanism checking for loose or broken springs or wear in the bob weight pivots. Check the operation of the vacuum unit by applying suction to the outlet. As suction is applied the pullrod should move in and stay in this position until the suction is released. If this is not the case renew the vacuum unit.

11 With the new parts obtained as necessary, reassemble the distributor using the reverse of the dismantling sequence.

9 Ignition timing – adjustment

Note: *With modern ignition systems the only suitable way to time the ignition accurately is with a stroboscopic timing light. However, for initial setting up purposes (i.e. after major overhaul, or if the timing has been otherwise completely lost) a basic initial static setting may be used to get the engine started. Once the engine is running, the timing should be accurately set using the timing light.*

1   In order that the engine can run efficiently, it is necessary for a spark to occur at the spark plug and ignite the fuel/air mixture at the instant just before the piston on the compression stroke reaches the top of its travel. The precise instant at which the spark occurs is determined by the ignition timing, and this is quoted in degrees before top-dead-centre (BTDC).

2   If the timing is being checked as a maintenance or servicing procedure, refer to paragraph 11. If the distributor has been dismantled or renewed, or if its position on the engine has been altered, obtain an initial static setting as follows.

Static setting

3   Pull off the HT lead and remove No 1 spark plug (nearest the crankshaft pulley).

4   Place a finger over the plug hole and turn the engine in the normal direction of rotation (clockwise from the crankshaft pulley end) until pressure is felt in No 1 cylinder. This indicates that the piston is commencing its compression stroke. The engine can be turned with a socket and bar on the crankshaft pulley bolt.

5   Continue turning the engine until the notch in the crankshaft pulley is aligned with the appropriate mark on the timing scale. The scale is located on the front of the engine just above the crankshaft pulley. The T on the scale indicates top-dead-centre (TDC) and the marks to the left of T are in increments of 2° BTDC. The marks to the right of T are in increments of 2° ATDC (photo).

6   Remove the distributor cap and check that the rotor arm is pointing towards No 1 spark plug HT lead segment in the cap.

7   On models with conventional ignition lift off the rotor arm then slacken the bolt securing the distributor clamp to the cylinder head.

8.9 Drive key and roll pin at the base of the distributor shaft

9.5 Ignition timing scale and crankshaft pulley notch with engine positioned at 6° BTDC

Turn the distributor body anti-clockwise slightly until the contact breaker points are closed then slowly turn the distributor body clockwise until the points just open. Hold the distributor in this position and tighten the clamp bolt.

8   On models with electronic ignition, remove the rotor then slacken the bolt securing the distributor clamp to the cylinder head. Turn the distributor body as necessary until the teeth on the signal rotor are aligned with the arms of the signal plate (photo). Hold the distributor in this position and tighten the clamp bolt.

9   On all models refit the rotor arm and distributor cap, No 1 spark plug and the HT lead.

10 It should now be possible to start and run the engine enabling the timing to be accurately checked with a timing light as follows.

9.8 Signal rotor tooth (A) aligned with signal plate arm (B)

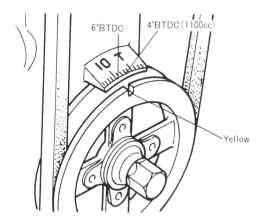

Fig. 4.7 Ignition timing mark arrangement (Sec 9)

Stroboscopic setting

11 Refer to the Specifications for the timing setting applicable to the engine being worked on and then highlight the appropriate mark on the timing scale and the notch in the crankshaft pulley with white chalk (see also paragraph 5).

12 Connect a timing light to the engine in accordance with the manufacturer's instructions (usually between No 1 spark plug and its HT lead).

13 Start the engine and allow it to idle. Point the timing light at the

timing marks and they should appear to be stationary with the crankshaft pulley notch in alignment with the appropriate mark on the scale.

14 If adjustment is necessary (i.e. the pulley notch and timing mark are not aligned) slacken the distributor clamp retaining bolt and turn the distribution body clockwise to advance the timing and anti-clockwise to retard it. Tighten the clamp bolt when the setting is correct.

15 Gradually increase the engine speed while still pointing the timing light at the marks. The pulley notch should appear to advance further, indicating that the centrifugal governor is operating correctly. If the timing marks remain stationary when the engine speed is increased, or if the movement is erratic or jerky, then the distributor should be dismantled for inspection as described in Sections 7 or 8.

16 After adjustment switch off the engine and disconnect the timing light.

10 Ignition coil – general

1   The ignition coil is bolted to the inner valance on the left-hand side of the engine compartment (photo).

2   To remove the coil disconnect the LT leads at the coil positive and negative terminals and the HT lead at the centre terminal.

3   Undo the mounting bracket retaining bolts and remove the coil.

4   Refitting is the reverse sequence of removal.

5   Accurate checking of the coil output requires the use of special test equipment and should be left to a dealer or suitably equipped auto electrician. It is however possible to check the resistance of the primary and secondary coil windings using an ohmmeter as follows. The coil should be at normal operating temperature for these checks.

6   To check the primary resistance, connect the ohmmeter across the coil positive and negative terminals. The resistance should be as given in the Specifications at the beginning of this Chapter.

7   To check the secondary resistance connect one lead from the ohmmeter to the coil negative terminal and the other lead to the centre HT terminal. Again the resistance should be as given in the Specifications.

8   On models with conventional ignition, the resistance of the ballast resistor on the side of the coil can also be checked by connecting the ohmmeter leads to the two resistor terminals.

9   If any of the measured values vary significantly from the figures given in the Specifications, the component concerned should be renewed.

10 If a new coil is to be fitted ensure that it is of the correct type and suitable for use on conventional or electronic ignition systems as applicable. Failure to do so could cause irreparable damage to the coil or, on electronic ignition systems, to the igniter and signal generator assembly in the distributor.

10.1 Ignition coil location in engine compartment

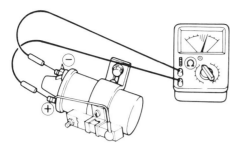

Fig. 4.8 Checking ignition coil primary resistance (Sec 10)

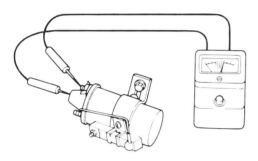

Fig. 4.9 Checking ignition coil secondary resistance (Sec 10)

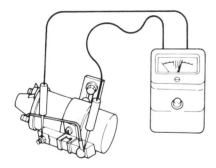

Fig. 4.10 Checking ignition coil ballast resistance (Sec 10)

11 Spark plugs and HT leads – general

1   The correct functioning of the spark plugs is vital for the proper running and efficiency of the engine. The spark plugs should be removed at the intervals given in Routine Maintenance at the beginning of this Manual to allow the following inspection and tests to be carried out.
2   To remove the plugs, first mark the HT leads to ensure correct refitment, and then pull them off the plugs. Using a spark plug spanner, or suitable deep socket and extension bar, unscrew the plugs and remove them from the engine.
3   The condition of the spark plugs will also tell much about the overall condition of the engine.

4   If the insulator nose of the spark plug is clean and white, with no deposits, this is indicative of a weak mixture, or too hot a plug. (A hot plug transfers heat away from the electrode slowly – a cold plug transfers it away quickly.)
5   If the tip and insulator nose are covered with hard black-looking deposits, then this is indicative that the mixture is too rich. Should the plug be black and oily, then it is likely that the engine is fairly worn, as well as the mixture being too rich.
6   If the insulator nose is covered with light tan to greyish brown deposits, then the mixture is correct and it is likely that the engine is in good condition.
7   If there are any traces of long brown tapering stains on the outside of the white portion of the plug, then the plug will have to be renewed, as this shows that there is a faulty joint between the plug body and the insulator, and compression is being lost.
8   Plugs should be cleaned by a sand blasting machine, which will free them from carbon more thoroughly than cleaning by hand. The machine will also test the condition of the plugs under compression. If any of the plugs fail to spark under pressure, if any of the centre electrodes are rounded off, or if the earth electrodes are eroded, then all four spark plugs should be renewed.
9   The spark plug gap is of considerable importance, as, if it is too large or too small, the size of the spark and its efficiency will be seriously impaired. The spark plug gap should be set to the figure given in the Specifications at the beginning of this Chapter.
10   To set it, measure the gap with a feeler gauge, and then bend open, or close, the *outer* plug electrode until the correct gap is achieved. The centre electrode should *never* be bent as this may crack the insulation and cause plug failure, if nothing worse.
11   To refit the plugs, screw them in by hand initially and then fully tighten to the specified torque. If a torque wrench is not available, tighten the plugs until initial resistance is felt as the sealing washer contacts its seat and then tighten by a further eighth of a turn. Refit the HT leads in the correct order, ensuring that they are a tight fit over the plug ends. Periodically wipe the leads clean to reduce the risk of HT leakage by arcing.

12 Fault diagnosis – conventional ignition system

1   By far the majority of breakdown and running troubles are caused by faults in the ignition system either in the low tension or high tension circuits.
2   There are two main symptoms indicating faults. Either the engine will not start or fire, or the engine is difficult to start and misfires. If it is a regular misfire (ie the engine is running on only two or three cylinders), the fault is almost sure to be in the secondary or high tension circuit. If the misfiring is intermittent the fault could be in either the high or low tension circuits. If the car stops suddenly, or will not start at all, it is likely that the fault is in the low tension circuit. Loss of power and overheating, apart from faulty carburation settings, are normally due to faults in the distributor or to incorrect ignition timing.

Engine fails to start
3   If the engine fails to start and the car was running normally when it was last used, first check that there is fuel in the petrol tank. If the engine turns over normally on the starter motor and the battery is evidently well charged, then the fault may be in either the high or low tension circuit. First check the HT circuit.
4   One of the commonest reasons for bad starting is wet or damp spark plug leads and distributor. Remove the distributor cap. If condensation is visible internally dry the cap with a rag and also wipe over the leads. Refit the cap.
5   If the engine still fails to start, check that voltage is reaching the plugs by disconnecting each plug lead in turn at the spark plug end and holding the end of the cable with rubber or an insulated tool about $^1/_4$ in (6 mm) away from the cylinder block. Spin the engine on the starter motor.
6   Sparkling between the end of the cable and the block should be fairly strong with a regular blue spark. If voltage is reaching the plugs, then remove them and regap them. The engine should now start.
7   If there is no spark at the plug leads, take off the HT lead from the centre of the distributor cap and hold it to the block as before. Spin the engine on the starter once more. A rapid succession of blue sparks between the end of the lead and the block indicates that the coil is in

order and that the distributor cap is cracked, the rotor arm is faulty or the carbon brush in the top of the distributor cap is not making good contact with the rotor arm.

8   If there are no sparks from the end of the lead from the coil, check the connections at the coil end of the lead. If it is in order start checking the low tension circuit. Possibly, the points are in bad condition. Clean and reset them as described in this Chapter, Section 3.

9   Use a 12V voltmeter or a 12V bulb and two lengths of wire. With the ignition switch on and the points open, test between the low tension wire to the coil and earth. No reading indicates a break in the supply from the ignition switch. Check the connections at the switch to see if any are loose. Refit them and the engine should run. A reading shows a faulty coil or condenser, or broken lead between the coil and the distributor.

10 Take the condenser wire off the points assembly and with the points open test between the moving point and earth. If there is now a reading then the fault is in the condenser. Fit a new one and the fault is cleared.

11 With no reading from the moving point to earth, take a reading between earth and the distributor terminal of the coil. A reading here shows a broken wire which will need to be replaced between the coil and the distributor. No reading confirms that the coil has failed and must be renewed, after which the engine will run once more. Remember to refit the condenser wire to the points assembly. For these tests it is sufficient to separate the points with a piece of dry paper while testing with the points open.

12 One other fault in this category which can sometimes occur is a failure of the ballast resistor located alongside the ignition coil. The symptoms are that the engine will turn over the starter motor and will start, but as soon as the key is released the engine stops. If this is the case renewal of the ballast resistor should clear the fault. Do not bypass the resistor with ordinary wire, or overheating of the coil will occur.

Engine misfires

13 If the engine misfires regularly run it at a fast idling speed. Pull off each of the plug caps in turn and listen to the note of the engine. Hold the plug cap in a dry cloth or with a rubber glove as additional protection against a shock from the HT supply.

14 No difference in engine running will be noticed when the lead from the defective circuit is removed. Removing the lead from one of the good cylinders will accentuate the misfire.

15 Remove the plug lead from the plug which is not firing and hold it about $1/4$ in (6 mm) away from the block. Restart the engine. If the sparking is fairly strong and regular, the fault must lie in the spark plug.

16 The plug may be loose, the insulation may be cracked, or the points may have burnt away giving too wide a gap for the spark to jump. Worse still, one of the points may have broken off. Either renew the plug or clean it, reset the gap, and then test it.

17 If there is no spark at the end of the plug lead, or if it is weak and intermittent, check the ignition lead from the distributor to the plug. If the insulation is cracked or perished, renew the lead. Check the connections at the distributor cap.

18 If there is still no spark, examine the distributor cap carefully for tracking. This can be recognised by a very thin black line running between two or more electrodes, or between an electrode and some other part of the distributor. These lines are paths which now conduct electricity across the cap thus letting it run to earth. The only answer is a new distributor cap.

19 Apart from the ignition timing being incorrect, other causes of misfiring have already been dealt with under the Section dealing with the failure of the engine to start. To recap, these are that:

   (a)   The coil may be faulty giving an intermittent misfire
   (b)   There may be a damaged wire or loose connection in the low tension circuit
   (c)   The condenser may be faulty
   (d)   There may be a mechanical fault in the distributor (broken driving spindle or contact breaker spring)

20 If the ignition timing is too far retarded, it should be noted that the engine will tend to overheat, and there will be a quite noticeable drop in power. If the engine is overheating and the power is down, and the ignition timing is correct, then the carburettor should be checked, as it is likely that this is where the fault lies.

13 Fault diagnosis – electronic ignition system

Fault diagnosis in the HT circuit of the electronic ignition system is the same as described in the previous Section for conventional systems. If a fault is suspected in the LT circuit special test equipment is needed to diagnose the problem accurately and this work should be left to a Mazda dealer or suitably equipped auto electrician.

Measuring plug gap. A feeler gauge of the correct size (see ignition system specifications) should have a slight 'drag' when slid between the electrodes. Adjust gap if necessary

Adjusting plug gap. The plug gap is adjusted by bending the earth electrode inwards, or outwards, as necessary until the correct clearance is obtained. Note the use of the correct tool

Normal. Grey-brown deposits, lightly coated core nose. Gap increasing by around 0.001 in (0.025 mm) per 1000 miles (1600 km). Plugs ideally suited to engine, and engine in good condition

Carbon fouling. Dry, black, sooty deposits. Will cause weak spark and eventually misfire. Fault: over-rich fuel mixture. Check: carburettor mixture settings, float level and jet sizes; choke operation and cleanliness of air filter. Plugs can be re-used after cleaning

Oil fouling. Wet, oily deposits. Will cause weak spark and eventually misfire. Fault: worn bores/piston rings or valve guides; sometimes occurs (temporarily) during running-in period. Plugs can be re-used after thorough cleaning

Overheating. Electrodes have glazed appearance, core nose very white – few deposits. Fault: plug overheating. Check: plug value, ignition timing, fuel octane rating (too low) and fuel mixture (too weak). Discard plugs and cure fault immediately

Electrode damage. Electrodes burned away; core nose has burned, glazed appearance. Fault: pre-ignition. Check: as for 'Overheating' but may be more severe. Discard plugs and remedy fault before piston or valve damage occurs

Split core nose (may appear initially as a crack). Damage is self-evident, but cracks will only show after cleaning. Fault: pre-ignition or wrong gap-setting technique. Check: ignition timing, cooling system, fuel octane rating (too low) and fuel mixture (too weak). Discard plugs, rectify fault immediately

Chapter 5 Clutch

For modifications, and information applicable to later models, see Supplement at end of manual

Contents

Specifications

Type .... Cable operated single dry plate with diaphragm spring

Driven plate
Diameter:
    1100 cc and 1300 cc models .... 184 mm (7.24 in)
    1500 cc models .... 190 mm (7.48 in)
Minimum lining thickness .... 0.30 mm (0.012 in) above rivet heads
Maximum permissible run-out .... 1.0 mm (0.039 in)

Cover assembly
Maximum permissible pressure plate run-out .... 0.05 mm (0.002 in)

Clutch adjustment
Clutch pedal height .... 225 to 230 mm (8.86 to 9.06 in)
Clutch pedal free play:
    Measured at pedal .... 11 to 17 mm (0.43 to 0.67 in)
    Measured at release lever .... 2 to 3 mm (0.08 to 0.12 in)
Minimum distance from pedal to floor (pedal depressed) .... 80 mm (3.2 in)

Torque wrench settings

	Nm	lbf ft
Clutch cover to flywheel	18 to 27	13 to 20
Release fork to lever retaining bolt	18 to 27	13 to 20

1 General description

All manual transmission models are equipped with a cable operated single plate diaphragm spring clutch. The assembly is enclosed in a pressed steel cover which is bolted to the rear face of the flywheel.

The clutch driven plate is located between the flywheel and the clutch pressure plate and slides on splines on the transmission primary shaft. When the clutch is engaged, the diaphragm spring forces the pressure plate to grip the driven plate against the flywheel and drive is transmitted from the crankshaft, through the driven plate, to the transmission primary shaft. On disengaging the clutch the pressure plate is lifted to release the driven plate with the result that the drive to the transmission is disconnected.

The clutch is operated by a foot pedal suspended under the facia and a cable connected to the clutch release lever mounted on the transmission housing. Depressing the pedal causes the release lever to move the release bearing against the fingers of the diaphragm spring in the pressure plate assembly. The spring is sandwiched between two rings which act as fulcrums. As the centre of the spring is moved in, the periphery moves out to lift the pressure plate and disengage the clutch. The reverse takes place when the pedal is released. Provision is made at both the clutch cable and clutch pedal for adjustment of the clutch operation.

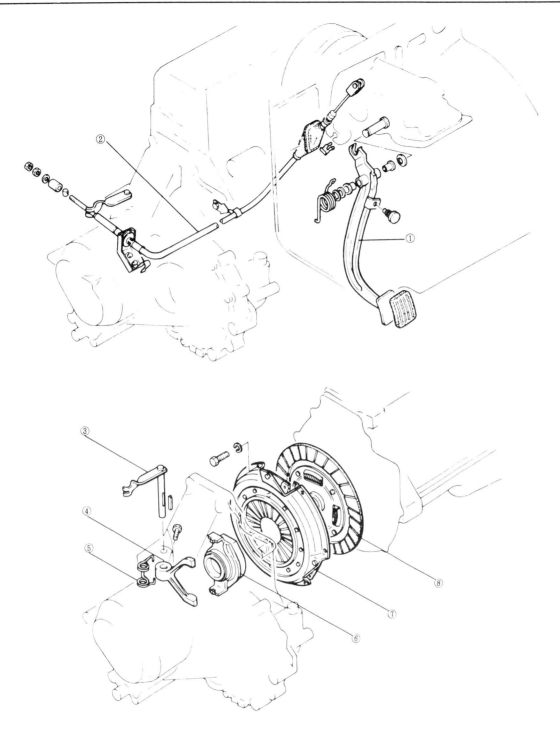

Fig. 5.1 Clutch component layout (Sec 1)

1 Clutch pedal	3 Release lever	5 Return spring (where fitted)	7 Cover assembly
2 Clutch cable	4 Release fork	6 Release bearing	8 Driven plate

2   Clutch – adjustment

1   At the intervals given in Routine Maintenance at the beginning of this manual, check and if necessary adjust the clutch pedal height and free play as described in the following paragraphs. The pedal height should always be checked first, but adjustment will normally only be necessary if the clutch assembly, clutch cable or clutch pedal have

been renewed or in any way disturbed. When the pedal height is correct, the free play can be checked and, if necessary, adjusted.

Clutch pedal height

2   Measure the distance from the centre of the clutch pedal pad upper face to the engine compartment bulkhead (Fig. 5.2). Compare the figure obtained with the clutch pedal height dimension given in the Specifications. Note that the dimension given does not take into

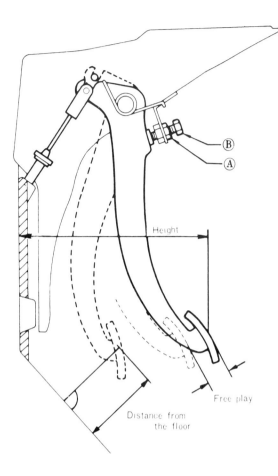

Fig. 5.2 Clutch pedal height and free play details (Sec 2)

A   *Pedal stop locknut*
B   *Pedal stop bolt*

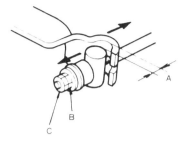

Fig. 5.3 Clutch free play adjustment (Sec 2)

A   *Specified free play at release
    lever*
B   *Adjusting nut*
C   *Locknut*
*Push release lever and pull cable in direction of arrows to check
adjustment*

consideration the thickness of sound deadening material affixed to the
bulkhead and an allowance should be made for this.
3   If adjustment is necessary, remove the cover under the facia,
slacken the pedal stop locknut and turn the pedal stop bolt until the
correct dimension is obtained. Tighten the locknut without altering the
stop bolt position. After adjustment refit the cover under the facia.

Clutch pedal free play
4   From inside the car depress the clutch pedal by hand and measure
the distance from the pedal at rest position until firm resistance is met.
This is the clutch pedal free play and should be as given in the
Specifications.
5   If adjustment is necessary, slacken the locknut at the cable end in
the engine compartment. Now turn the adjusting nut until the distance
from the release lever to the roller on the cable is as specified when the
lever is held and the cable is pulled (Fig. 5.3). Tighten the locknut after
adjustment.
6   Finally, check that when the pedal is depressed fully, the distance
from the centre of the pedal pad upper face to the floor is not less than
the dimension given in the Specifications.

---

3   Clutch cable – removal and refitting

1   Disconnect the battery negative terminal.
2   Working in the engine compartment disconnect the return spring at
the clutch release lever (where fitted).
3   Unscrew the locknut and adjusting nut from the end of the cable
then withdraw the plain washer, damper and roller.

4   Open the cable retaining clip at the rear of the engine and slip the
cable out.
5   Withdraw the cable end from the transmission attachment bracket.
6   From inside the car remove the cover under the facia and
disconnect the cable end from the hook on the pedal.
7   Extract the retaining clip and withdraw the cable from the master
cylinder bracket.
8   Release the rubber boot and pull the cable through into the engine
compartment.
9   Release the cable from the remaining support clips and brackets
and remove it from the engine compartment.
10 Inspect the cable for damage to the rubber boots, for signs of
fraying and for smoothness of operation. Renew the cable if any of
these areas are unsatisfactory.
11 Refitting is the reverse sequence of removal, bearing in mind the
following points:

(a) *Lubricate the clutch pedal hook and the cable roller with
     multi-purpose grease*
(b) *Apply a suitable sealant to the groove of the bulkhead rubber
     grommet before refitting*
(c) *With the cable installed, adjust the clutch pedal height and
     free play as described in Section 2*

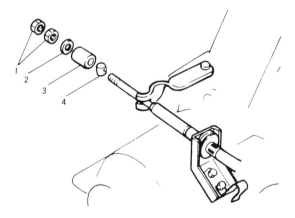

Fig. 5.4 Clutch cable connections at release lever (Sec 3)

1   *Locknut and adjusting nut*
2   *Plain washer*
3   *Damper*
4   *Roller*

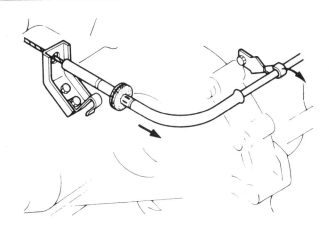

Fig. 5.5 Clutch cable removal at release lever end (Sec 3)

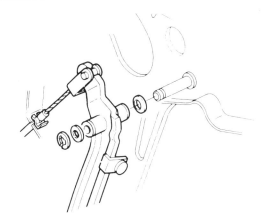

Fig. 5.7 Clutch pedal attachment details (Sec 4)

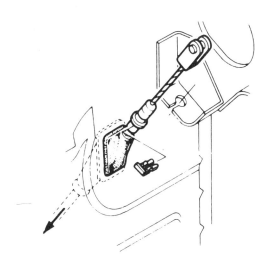

Fig. 5.6 Clutch cable removal at pedal end (Sec 3)

4 Clutch pedal – removal and refitting

1   Disconnect the battery negative terminal then remove the cover under the facia.
2   Release the pedal return spring then extract the retaining clip on the end of the pedal pivot pin.
3   Withdraw the pivot pin from the master cylinder bracket and clutch pedal and recover the washers and return spring.
4   Withdraw the pedal from its location, disconnect the clutch cable and remove the pedal. It may be necessary to slacken the pedal stop bolt to facilitate removal.
5   Check the pedal for twists or distortion and check the pivot pin bushes and pedal pad for wear. Renew any components as necessary.
6   Refitting is the reverse sequence of removal bearing in mind the following points:

   (a) Lubricate the pivot pin bushes and pedal hook with multi-purpose grease
   (b) Ensure that the pedal return spring is correctly located against the pedal and over the edge of the master cylinder bracket
   (c) With the pedal installed, adjust the clutch pedal height and free play as described in Section 2

5 Clutch assembly – removal and refitting

1   Refer to Chapter 6 and remove the transmission.
2   Working in a diagonal sequence, undo the bolts securing the clutch cover assembly to the flywheel. Slacken each bolt a few turns at a time initially until all spring tension is relieved. If necessary hold the crankshaft pulley bolt with a spanner to prevent the flywheel rotating.
3   With all the bolts removed, ease the cover assembly off the flywheel dowels and be prepared to catch the driven plate which will drop out as the cover is removed. Note which way round the driven plate is fitted.
4   With the clutch assembly removed, refer to Section 7 and carry out a careful inspection of the components.
5   It is important that no oil or grease is allowed to come into contact with the friction material of the clutch disc or the pressure plate and flywheel faces. It is advisable to refit the clutch assembly with clean hands and to wipe down the pressure plate and flywheel faces with a clean dry rag before assembly begins.
6   Ensure that the splines of the driven plate are clean then lubricate them very sparingly with molybdenum disulphide grease.
7   Hold the driven plate in position with the side having the longer offset projection of the centre hub facing away from the flywheel (photo).

5.7 Hold the driven plate in position ...

8 Place the cover assembly over the driven plate and engage it with the locating dowels on the flywheel. Refit the retaining bolts and tighten them finger-tight so that the clutch driven plate is gripped, but can still be moved (photo).

9 The driven plate must now be centralised so that when the transmission is refitted, the splines of the primary shaft will pass through the splines in the driven plate hub.

10 Centralisation can be carried out quite easily by inserting a round bar or long screwdriver through the driven plate hub so that the end of the bar rests in the hole in the end of the crankshaft. Using this as a fulcrum, moving the bar sideways or up and down will move the driven plate in whichever direction is necessary to achieve centralisation (photo).

11 Centralisation can be judged by removing the bar and viewing the driven plate hub in relation to the hole in the crankshaft. When the hole in the crankshaft appears exactly in the centre of the driven plate hub, all is correct.

12 An alternative and more accurate method of centralisation is to use a commercially available clutch aligning tool obtainable from most accessory shops.

13 Once the clutch is centralised, progressively tighten the cover bolts, in a diagonal sequence, to the torque setting given in the Specifications.

14 The transmission can now be refitted as described in Chapter 6.

6 Clutch release bearing – removal and refitting

1 Remove the transmission as described in Chapter 6.

2 With the transmission on the bench, disconnect the hooked ends of the return spring from the release fork (where fitted), twist the release lever and slide the bearing off the primary shaft sleeve (photo).

3 If necessary the release lever and fork can be removed after undoing the retaining bolt. Withdraw the release lever upwards then lift out the release fork, key and where fitted, the return spring (photos).

4 With the components removed carry out a careful inspection as described in Section 7 and renew any worn parts as necessary.

5.8 ... then refit the cover assembly

6.2 Slide the release bearing off the primary shaft sleeve

5.10 Using a round bar to centralise the driven plate

6.3A Undo the release fork retaining bolt (arrowed) ...

6.3B ... pull the release lever upward and remove the Woodruff key (arrowed) and fork

5   Refitting is the reverse sequence of removal, bearing in mind the following points:

   (a) Lubricate the inner circumference of the release bearing and the release fork contact area with molybdenum disulphide grease
   (b) If a return spring is fitted ensure that it is correctly located around the release fork

7 Clutch components – inspection

1   With the clutch assembly removed, examine the driven plate friction linings for wear and loose rivets. Also examine the hub for distortion, cracks, broken or weak cushioning springs and worn splines. The surface of the friction linings may be glazed, but as long as the friction material pattern can be clearly seen, this is acceptable. If the friction material is worn down to less than the minimum dimension given in the Specifications above the rivet heads, the driven plate must be renewed. The plate must also be renewed if there is any sign of oil contamination of the friction material caused by a leaking transmission primary shaft oil seal or crankshaft rear oil seal. If oil contamination is evident the cause of the trouble must be rectified immediately, as described in Chapter 1 or Chapter 6.
2   Check the machined faces of the flywheel and pressure plate. If either is grooved or heavily scored, renewal is necessary. If the pressure plate is cracked or split, or if the diaphragm spring is loose, damaged or its pressure suspect, a new unit must be fitted. Minor scratches or discolouration of the pressure plate, flywheel and driven plate faces may be removed by lightly rubbing with medium sandpaper.
3   Check the release bearing for smoothness of operation. There should be no harshness or slackness in it and it should spin freely without tight spots. Check also that the bearing slides freely on the transmission primary shaft sleeve.
4   Inspect the release fork and release lever for any signs of cracks or distortion and check the return spring (where fitted) for signs of fatigue. Renew any of these components if necessary.
5   When considering renewing clutch components individually (ie. driven plate, cover assembly or release bearing) bear in mind that new parts, or parts from different manufacturers do not always bed into old ones satisfactorily. A clutch cover assembly or driven plate renewed separately may sometimes cause judder or snatch. Also a release bearing that may appear sound now, could start to rumble or squeal when operating against the increased pressure of a new diaphragm spring. Although expensive, the clutch cover assembly, driven plate and release bearing should be renewed together wherever possible.

8 Fault diagnosis – clutch

Symptom	Reason(s)
Judder when taking up drive	Loose or worn engine or transmission mountings Oil contamination of driven plate friction linings Excessive wear of driven plate friction linings Broken or weak driven plate cushioning springs Distorted or damaged pressure plate or diaphragm spring Clutch cable binding
Clutch spin (failure to disengage so that gears are difficult to engage)	Incorrect clutch adjustment Driven plate sticking to flywheel face due to corrosion or oil contamination Corrosion of driven plate or primary shaft splines
Clutch slip (increase in engine speed does not result in increase in road speed – particularly on gradients)	Incorrect clutch adjustment Oil contamination of driven plate friction linings Excessive wear of driven plate friction linings Weak or broken diaphragm spring
Noise evident on depressing clutch pedal	Worn or damaged release bearing Damaged or broken diaphragm spring Incorrect clutch adjustment
Noise evident as clutch pedal is released	Broken or weak driven plate cushioning springs Damaged or broken diaphragm Worn transmission bearings or internal components (see Chapter 6)

Chapter 6 Manual transmission

Contents

Specifications

Type .... Four or five forward speeds (all synchromesh) and reverse. Final drive integral with transmission

Gear ratios
1st .... 3.416 : 1
2nd .... 1.842 : 1
3rd .... 1.290 : 1
4th .... 0.918 : 1
5th .... 0.775 : 1
Reverse .... 3.214 : 1

Final drive ratios
1100 models .... 4.388 : 1
1300 models .... 4.105 : 1
1500 models .... 3.850 : 1

Transmission overhaul data
Synchro baulk ring to gear clearance:
    Standard .... 1.5 mm (0.059 in)
    Limit .... 0.8 mm (0.031 in)
Selector fork to synchro sleeve clearance:
    Standard .... 0.2 to 0.458 mm (0.008 to 0.018 in)
    Limit .... 0.5 mm (0.020 in)
Reverse idler gear to engagement lever clearance:
    Standard .... 0.095 to 0.318 mm (0.003 to 0.012 in)
    Limit .... 0.5 mm (0.020 in)
Geartrain running clearances:
    Clearance between 1st gear and pinion:
        Standard .... 0.14 to 0.37 mm (0.005 to 0.014 in)
        Limit .... 0.5 mm (0.020 in)
    Clearance between 2nd gear and thrust washer:
        Standard .... 0.245 to 0.405 mm (0.009 to 0.016 in)
        Limit .... 0.5 mm (0.020 in)
    Clearance between 3rd gear and thrust washer:
        Standard .... 0.095 to 0.38 mm (0.003 to 0.015 in)
        Limit .... 0.5 mm (0.020 in)
    Clearance between 4th gear and bearing inner race:
        Standard .... 0.095 to 0.4 mm (0.003 to 0.16 in)
        Limit .... 0.5 mm (0.020 in)
    Clearance between 5th speed driven gear and sleeve:
        Standard .... 0.15 to 0.287 mm (0.006 to 0.011 in)
        Limit .... 0.5 mm (0.020 in)

Torque wrench settings

	Nm	lbf ft
5th speed driving gear retaining nut	130 to 210	96 to 155
5th speed synchroniser unit retaining nut	130 to 210	96 to 155
End cover retaining bolts	8 to 11	6 to 8
Reverse idler shaft lock bolt	21 to 31	15 to 23
Selector rod guide bolt	9 to 14	7 to 10
Transmission case to clutch housing	18 to 26	13 to 19
Transmission to engine:		
12 mm bolt	65 to 95	47 to 69
14 mm bolt	90 to 120	65 to 87
Crossmember front mounting nuts	61 to 87	44 to 63
Crossmember rear mounting nuts	65 to 91	47 to 66
Engine/transmission mounting to bracket nuts	32 to 47	23 to 34
Number four mounting to transmission bolts	19 to 26	14 to 19
Lower arm balljoint pinch-bolt	44 to 55	33 to 40
Roadwheel nuts	90 to 110	65 to 80

1 General description

The manual transmission is equipped with either four forward and one reverse gear or five forward and one reverse gear, according to model. Baulk ring synchromesh gear engagement is used on all forward gears.

The final drive (differential) unit is integral with the transmission and is located between the clutch housing and transmission case. The transmission and final drive both share the same lubricating oil.

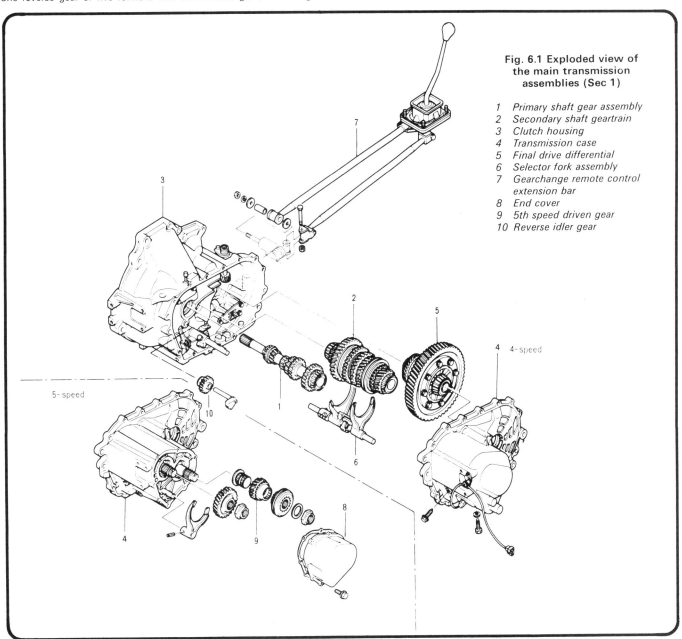

Fig. 6.1 Exploded view of the main transmission assemblies (Sec 1)

1 Primary shaft gear assembly
2 Secondary shaft geartrain
3 Clutch housing
4 Transmission case
5 Final drive differential
6 Selector fork assembly
7 Gearchange remote control extension bar
8 End cover
9 5th speed driven gear
10 Reverse idler gear

Gear selection is by means of a floor mounted lever connected by a remote control housing and gearchange rod to the transmission shift rod.

If transmission overhaul is necessary, due consideration should be given to the costs involved, since it is often more economical to obtain a service exchange, or good secondhand transmission rather than fit new parts to the existing unit.

2 Maintenance and inspection

1   At the intervals specified in Routine Maintenance at the beginning of this Manual, inspect the transmission joint faces and oil seals for any signs of damage, deterioration or oil leakage.
2   At the same service intervals the transmission oil level should be checked as follows. Wipe clean the area around the speedometer cable connection at the clutch housing (photo). Undo the cable retaining bolt and withdraw the cable and gear which acts as the oil level dipstick. Wipe the gear, reinsert it fully, withdraw it once more and observe the level. This should be between the upper edge of the gear teeth and the shoulder of the gear. There is a diagrammatic representation of this cast into the clutch housing above the gear

2.2C Topping up the transmission lubricant

2.2A Speedometer cable and gear at transmission lubricant filler orifice

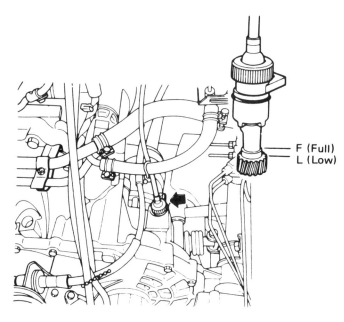

F (Full)
L (Low)

Fig. 6.2 Lubricant level markings on speedometer gear (Sec 2)

orifice (photo). If topping up is necessary, add the specified lubricant through the filler hole until the level is correct (photo), then refit the cable and gear.
3   At the less frequent intervals given in Routine Maintenance drain the transmission and refill with fresh lubricant as described in Section 3.
4   It is also advisable to check for excess free play or wear in the gear linkage joints and rods with reference to Sections 12 and 13.

3 Manual transmission lubricant – draining and refilling

1   Position the car on level ground and place a suitable container beneath the transmission drain plug, which is accessible through a hole in the crossmember.

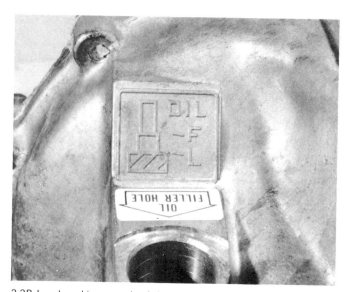

2.2B Level markings on clutch housing

2 Using a socket and extension bar, unscrew the plug and allow the lubricant to drain into the container. Refit the plug after draining.
3 From within the engine compartment, wipe clean the area around the speedometer cable attachment on the clutch housing. Undo the retaining bolt and withdraw the cable and gear.
4 Add the specified type and quantity of lubricant through the speedometer gear orifice until the level is between the upper edge of the gear teeth and the shoulder of the gear. Note that early models utilize automatic transmission fluid as a lubricant whereas later models are filled with gear oil. *Under no circumstances may the two types of lubricants be interchanged.*
5 When the transmission has been filled to the correct level, refit the speedometer cable and gear assembly.

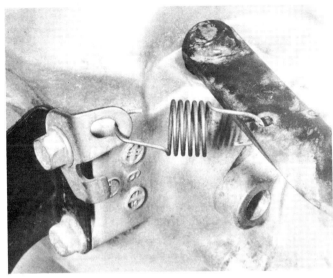

4.4 Disconnect the clutch release lever return spring

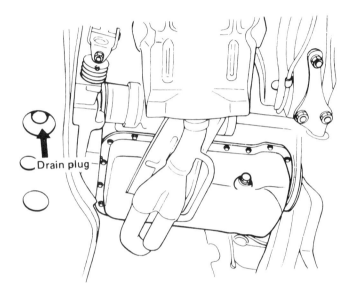

Fig. 6.3 Transmission drain plug location (Sec 3)

4.5 Unscrew the clutch cable locknut and adjusting nut (arrowed)

4 Manual transmission – removal and refitting

1 Disconnect the battery negative terminal.
2 Refer to Section 3 and drain the transmission lubricant.
3 Wipe clean the area around the speedometer cable attachment on the clutch housing. Undo the retaining bolt and withdraw the cable and gear assembly. Plug the orifice with a rag after removal to prevent dirt entry.
4 Where fitted disconnect the return spring at the clutch release lever (photo).
5 Unscrew the locknut and adjusting nut from the end of the cable then withdraw the plain washer, damper and roller (photo).
6 Open the cable retaining clip at the rear of the engine and slip the clutch cable out. Withdraw the cable end from the transmission attachment bracket and place the cable to one side.
7 Undo the bolt securing the earth cable and cable clip to the transmission and remove the cable and clip (photo).
8 Undo the exhaust manifold nut and clutch housing bolt securing the cooling system bypass pipe support brackets and free the pipe.
9 Release all the relevant wiring harnesses and cables, that are likely to impede transmission removal, from their respective cable clips.
10 Disconnect the reversing light switch wiring at the harness connector.
11 Refer to Chapter 12 and remove the starter motor.
12 Slacken the wheel nuts, jack up the front of the car and securely support it on axle stands. Remove the front roadwheels.
13 Where fitted remove the front anti-roll bar as described in Chapter 10.

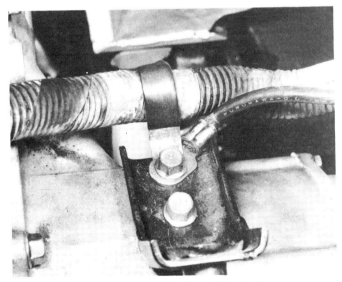

4.7 Undo the earth cable and cable clip retaining bolt

14 Remove the undertray and the left-hand side cover to gain access to the transmission from below.

15 Undo and remove the pinch-bolt securing the lower suspension arm balljoint to the swivel hub.

16 Using a long stout bar, lever the suspension arm down to release the balljoint shank from the swivel hub.

17 Pull the swivel hub outwards firmly to release the driveshaft inner constant velocity joint from the transmission. Support the driveshaft at its inner end to avoid damaging the transmission oil seal as the constant velocity joint is withdrawn.

18 Undo the nut and bolt securing the gearchange rod to the transmission shift rod (photo).

19 Undo the nut and remove the washers securing the remote control housing extension bar to the transmission (photo). Remove the outer washers, slide the bar off the stud and recover the inner washers.

20 Undo the bolts securing the flywheel cover plate to the clutch housing (photo).

21 Place a jack with interposed block of wood beneath the engine sump and take the weight of the engine.

22 Place a second jack and block of wood beneath the transmission.

23 Undo the nuts securing the front and rear engine/transmission mounting rubbers to the transmission brackets (photos).

4.18 Undo the nut and bolt securing the gearchange rod to the shift rod

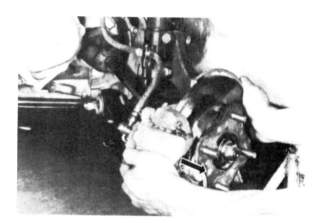

Fig. 6.4 Pull the swivel hub outwards to release the driveshaft inner joint (Sec 4)

4.19 Remove the remote control housing extension bar from the transmission stud

Fig. 6.5 Driveshaft inner constant velocity joint removed from transmission (Sec 4)

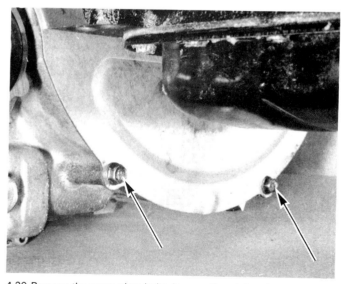

4.20 Remove the cover plate bolts (arrowed) and the plate

4.23A Undo the front mounting nut (arrowed) ...

4.23B ... and rear mounting nut (arrowed)

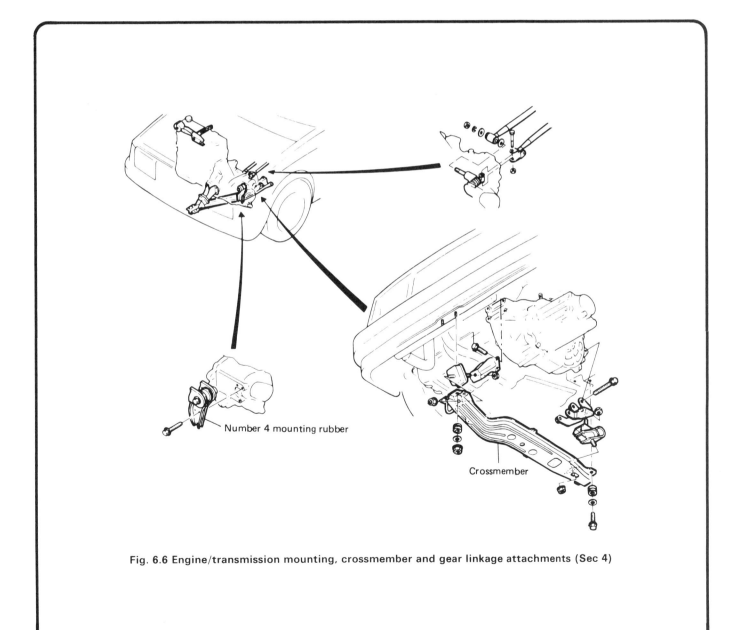

Number 4 mounting rubber

Crossmember

Fig. 6.6 Engine/transmission mounting, crossmember and gear linkage attachments (Sec 4)

24 Undo the three nuts and one bolt securing the crossmember to the underbody and remove the washers (photos).
25 Disengage the mountings from the transmission brackets and remove the crossmember.
26 On early models refer to Fig. 6.6 and undo the bolts securing the number four mounting to the transmission.
27 Undo the bolts securing the transmission clutch housing to the engine.
28 Lower the jacks slightly and withdraw the transmission from the engine. It may initially be tight owing to the locating dowels. Once the transmission is free, lower the jack and remove the unit out from under the car.
29 Refitting the transmission is the reverse sequence of removal bearing in mind the following points:

    (a) *Tighten all nuts and bolts to the specified torque where applicable*
    (b) *Refill the transmission with lubricant as described in Section 3*
    (c) *Adjust the clutch as described in Chapter 5*

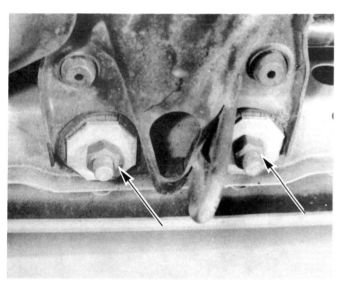

4.24A Undo the crossmember front ...

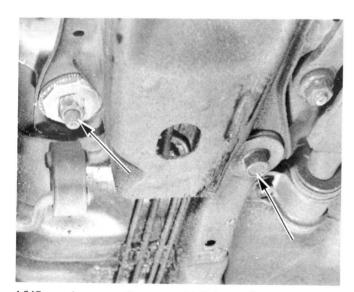

4.24B ... and rear mounting nuts and bolt (arrowed)

5 Transmission overhaul – general

Complete dismantling and overhaul of the transmission, particularly with respect to the differential and the bearings in the clutch housing and transmission case entails the use of a hydraulic press and a number of Mazda special tools. For this reason it is not recommended that a complete overhaul be attempted by the home mechanic. However the transmission can at least be dismantled into its major assemblies, or further if a hydraulic puller with tubes of suitable diameter are available, and the following Sections describe this and the overhaul procedure.

Before starting any repair work, thoroughly clean the exterior of the casings using paraffin or a suitable solvent. Dry the unit with a lint free rag. Make sure that a clean uncluttered working area is available with some small containers and trays handy to store the various parts. Label everything as it is removed.

Before starting reassembly all the components must be spotlessly clean and should be liberally lubricated with the specified lubricant according to transmission type.

Apart from the additional 5th gear and slight differences in the selector mechanism, the four and five-speed transmissions are virtually identical and the following Sections are applicable to both types. Where any slight differences occur, these will be described in the text.

After dismantling, all roll pins, circlips, snap-rings and gaskets must be renewed, regardless of their condition, before reassembling.

6 Manual transmission – dismantling

Note: *If working on the four-speed transmission proceed to paragraph 10. If working on the five-speed unit, proceed as follows.*
1 Undo the bolts securing the end cover to the transmission case and remove the end cover.
2 Using a suitable punch release the staking securing the 5th speed driving gear and 5th speed synchroniser unit retaining nuts to their respective shafts.
3 Using a 4 mm diameter parallel pin-punch, tap out the roll pin securing the 5th speed selector fork to the selector rod.
4 Engage 1st gear by pulling the transmission shift rod outwards then engage 5th gear by moving the 5th gear selector fork.
5 With the geartrain now locked, undo the 5th speed synchroniser unit retaining nut using a 38 mm socket and bar.
6 Lift off the synchoniser unit together with the selector fork as an assembly. Withdraw the fork from the synchroniser and fit the unit back onto the shaft, with 5th gear still engaged.
7 Undo the 5th speed driving gear nut using the 38 mm socket and bar.
8 Remove the 5th speed synchroniser unit once more followed by the driven gear with baulk ring and the gear sleeve.
9 Withdraw the 5th speed driving gear from the primary shaft then return the transmission to neutral.
10 Undo the reversing light switch, reverse idler shaft lock bolt and selector rod guide bolt and remove them from the transmission case.
11 Undo the bolts securing the transmission case to the clutch housing noting the various bolt lengths and the location of the cable clips and brackets.
12 Lift the transmission case upwards and off the shafts, bearings and clutch housing.
13 Remove the magnet from the clutch housing and, on early five-speed models the 5th gear oil passage.
14 Lift up the reverse idler shaft and remove the shaft and gear.
15 Undo the lock bolt and withdraw the 5th/reverse selector rod from the clutch housing and from the engagement lever. With the rod removed, lift out the engagement lever.
16 Using the parallel pin-punch, tap out the roll pin securing the crank lever shaft to the clutch housing. Withdraw the crank lever shaft and crank lever. If necessary turn the transmission shift rod to aid removal of the crank lever.
17 Make sure that the upper face of the selector rod interlock sleeve remains flush with the upper face of the control lever and turn the selector rod anti-clockwise.
18 Move the selector rod upwards and tap out the roll pin securing the control end to the selector rod.

19 Hold the geartrain and move the selector forks and selector rod upwards until the selector rod is free of its location in the clutch housing. Move the selector rod and control end to one side slightly and collect the steel detent ball that will be ejected from the reverse lever shaft.

20 Remove the secondary shaft geartrain, selector forks and rod as an assembly from the clutch housing.

21 Withdraw the detent spring from the centre of the reverse lever shaft.

22 Lift out the primary shaft assembly followed by the final drive differential.

23 Undo the three bolts and remove the guide plate noting the different bolt lengths and the distance spacer arrangement.

24 Tap out the roll pin securing the selector to the shift rod and undo the bolt securing the shift arm to the shift rod.

25 Withdraw the shift rod from the clutch housing and as the rod is pulled out, remove the shift arm, spring, reverse gate and selector.

26 Using pliers extract the roll pin securing the engagement plate

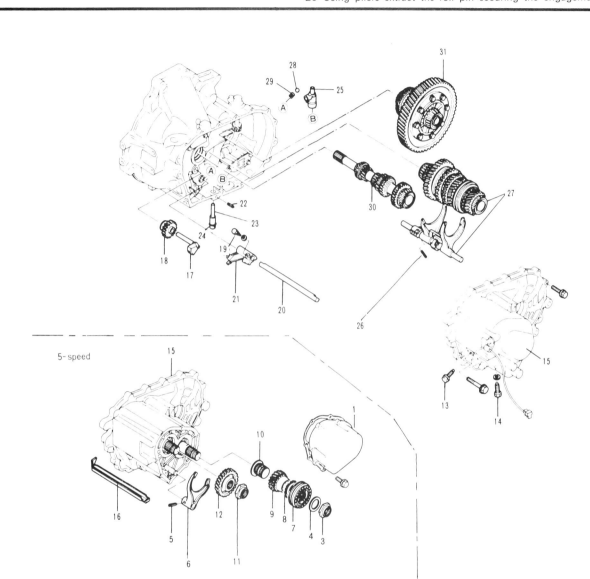

Fig. 6.7 Exploded view of the transmission case and geartrain assemblies (Sec 6)

1   End cover
3   5th speed driven gear retaining nut
4   Washer (where fitted)
5   Roll pin
6   5th speed selector fork
7   5th speed synchroniser unit
8   Baulk ring
9   5th speed driven gear

10 Sleeve
11 5th speed driving gear retaining nut
12 5th speed driving gear
13 Reverse idler shaft lock bolt
14 Selector rod guide bolt
15 Transmission case
16 5th gear oil passage (where fitted)

17 Reverse idler shaft
18 Reverse idler gear
19 Lock bolt
20 5th/reverse selector rod
21 5th/reverse engagement lever
22 Roll pin
23 Crank lever shaft
24 O-ring

25 Crank lever
26 Roll pin
27 Secondary shaft geartrain, selector forks and rod
28 Detent ball
29 Detent spring
30 Primary shaft gear assembly
31 Final drive differential

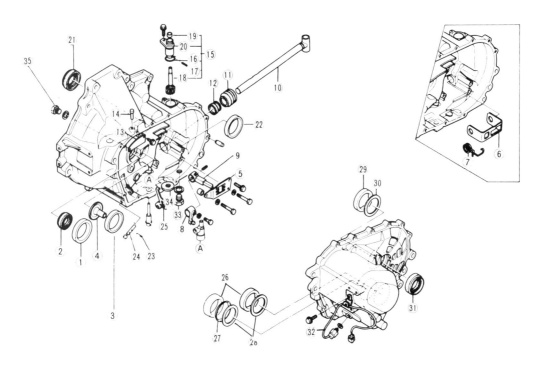

Fig. 6.8 Exploded view of the clutch housing and transmission case components (Sec 6)

1 Primary shaft bearing outer race	9 Selector	18 Driven gear	27 Belville washer
2 Primary shaft oil seal	10 Shift rod	19 Oil seal	28 Adjustment shim
3 Secondary shaft bearing outer race	11 Rubber boot	20 Body	29 Differential bearing outer race
4 Oil funnel	12 Oil seal	21 Differential oil seal	30 Adjustment shim
5 Guide plate	13 Breather cover plate	22 Differential bearing outer race	31 Differential oil seal
6 Reverse gate	14 Breather	23 Roll pin	32 Reversing light switch
7 Spring	15 Speedometer driven gear assembly	24 Reverse lever shaft	33 Drain plug
8 Shift arm	16 O-ring	25 Reverse lever	34 Magnet
	17 Roll pin	26 Bearing outer races	35 Bolt

Fig. 6.9 Removing the 5th speed synchroniser unit and selector fork (Sec 6)

Fig. 6.10 Selector rod and interlock sleeve faces must be flush (upper arrow) to allow selector rod to turn anti-clockwise (lower arrow) (Sec 6)

Fig. 6.11 Removing the control end retaining roll pin (Sec 6)

6.26 Extract the roll pin (arrowed) using pliers

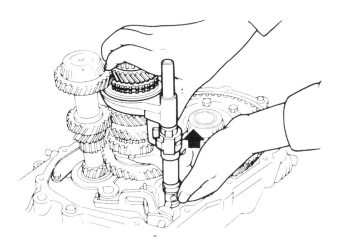

Fig. 6.12 Releasing the selector rod from its location by moving the rod and forks upward (Sec 6)

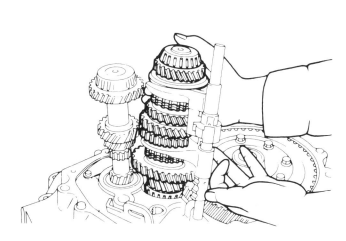

Fig. 6.13 Removing the secondary shaft geartrain and selectors (Sec 6)

(later models only) and reverse lever shaft to the web of the clutch housing (photo).

27 Using a thin rod inserted through the centre of the reverse lever shaft, tap out the shaft end plug from its location in the clutch housing.

28 Withdraw the shaft then lift out the reverse lever and where fitted the engagement plate.

29 On early models undo the retaining bolt and remove the speedometer driven gear assembly if still in place.

7 Secondary shaft geartrain – dismantling and reassembly

1 Remove the secondary shaft geartrain from the transmission as described in the previous Section.

2 Support the geartrain in a vice by securely clamping the pinion teeth between two blocks of wood.

3 Using a hydraulic gear puller with the puller base located under 4th gear, draw off the gear and roller bearing inner race together (photo).

7.3 Using a hydraulic puller to remove 4th gear and the roller bearing

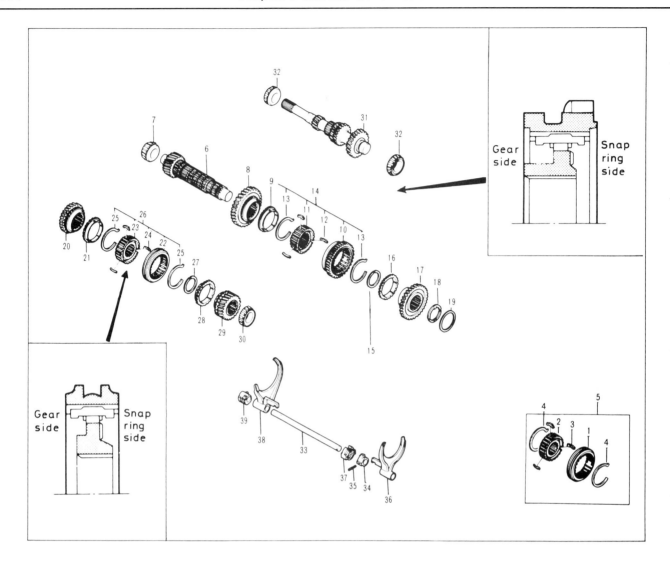

Fig. 6.14 Exploded view of the geartrain and selectors (Sec 7)

1	Sliding sleeve	11	Synchro hub
2	Synchro hub	12	Sliding key
3	Sliding keys	13	Spring
4	Springs	14	1st/2nd synchroniser unit
5	Synchroniser unit	15	Snap-ring
6	Secondary shaft	16	Baulk ring
7	Bearing inner race	17	2nd gear
8	1st gear	18	Thrust washer halves
9	Baulk ring	19	Retaining ring
10	Sliding sleeve	20	3rd gear

21	Baulk ring	31	Primary shaft
22	Sliding sleeve	32	Bearing inner race
23	Synchro hub	33	Selector rod
24	Sliding key	34	Control lever
25	Spring	35	Roll pin
26	3rd/4th synchroniser unit	36	3rd/4th selector fork
27	Snap-ring	37	Interlock sleeve
28	Baulk ring	38	1st/2nd selector fork
29	4th gear	39	Control end
30	Bearing inner race		

4   Lift off the 4th gear baulk ring from the 3rd/4th synchroniser unit.

5   Using circlip pliers extract the synchroniser unit retaining snap-ring.

6   Locate the gear puller base between 3rd gear and 2nd gear and draw off the 3rd/4th synchroniser unit and 3rd gear together.

7   Lift off the retaining ring followed by the two thrust washer halves located above 2nd gear.

8   Lift off 2nd gear followed by the 2nd gear baulk ring.

9   Extract the 1st/2nd synchroniser unit retaining snap ring.

10 Locate the gear puller base beneath 1st gear and draw off the synchroniser unit and 1st gear together.

11 With the geartrain dismantled, examine the gears and synchroniser units as described in Section 8, then proceed with the reassembly as follows.

12 Slide 1st gear down onto the shaft then place the 1st gear baulk ring in position (photos).

13 Fit the 1st/2nd synchroniser unit with the selector fork groove towards 1st gear (photo).

14 Using a tube of suitable diameter in contact with the synchroniser unit hub, drive the assembly fully into position on the shaft (photo). As you do this make sure that the cut-outs on the side of the baulk ring locate over the synchroniser keys.

15 Fit the synchroniser unit retaining snap-ring (photo).

16 Locate the 2nd gear baulk ring over the synchroniser keys then slide 2nd gear onto the shaft (photos).

17 Lay the two thrust washer halves on the face of the 2nd gear ensuring that the half with the peg locates in the slot on the shaft (photo). Lay the retaining ring over the thrust washers (photo).

7.12A Fit 1st gear ...

7.12B ... followed by the baulk ring

7.13 Fit the 1st/2nd synchroniser unit ...

7.14 ... and drive the assembly fully home using a hammer and tube

7.15 Fit the retaining snap-ring to secure the synchroniser unit

7.16A Locate the 2nd gear baulk ring on the synchroniser ...

7.16B ... then slide 2nd gear onto the shaft

7.17A Engage the thrust washer peg with the slot on the shaft ...

7.17B ... then lay the retaining ring over the thrust washers

7.18A Slide 3rd gear onto the shaft ...

7.18B ... followed by the baulk ring

7.19A Fit the 3rd/4th synchroniser unit ...

7.19B ... and drive the assembly fully home ...

7.19C ... then secure with the snap-ring

7.20A Fit the 4th gear baulk ring ...

7.20B ... followed by 4th gear

7.21A Fit the roller bearing inner race ...

7.21B ... and drive it fully home

18 Slide 3rd gear onto the shaft followed by the 3rd gear baulk ring (photos).

19 Fit the 3rd/4th synchroniser unit, drive it into place using hammer and tube as before, then fit the retaining snap-ring (photos).

20 Place the 4th gear baulk ring on the synchroniser unit then slide 4th gear onto the shaft (photos).

21 Fit the roller bearing inner race and drive it fully home using the hammer and tube (photos).

22 With the geartrain assembled check all the gears for free movement and check that the running clearances are as given in the Specifications.

Fig. 6.15 Checking geartrain running clearance (Sec 7)

8 Shafts, gears and synchroniser units – inspection

1 With the transmission dismantled inspect the primary shaft, secondary shaft, reverse idler shaft and all the gears for signs of obvious wear, chipping of the teeth or scoring of the shafts and contact areas of the gears. Any damaged or worn parts will require renewal.

2 Check the condition of the baulk rings by sliding them onto the land of the relevant gears then measuring the clearance between gear and ring (photo). If the clearance is less than specified renew the baulk ring. Renewal is also necessary if there is evidence of wear or chipping of the dog teeth. It is recommended, having dismantled the transmission this far, that all the baulk rings are renewed as a matter of course. The improvement in gear changing action, particularly if the car has covered a considerable mileage, will be well worth the expense.

3 If necessary the synchroniser units can be dismantled for inspection by covering the assembly with a rag and then pushing the hub out of the sliding sleeve, but mark the hub and sleeve on the same side with a dab of paint first to avoid confusion when reassembling. Collect the sliding keys and the springs which will have been ejected into the rag.

4 Check that the hub and sleeve slide over each other easily and that

there is a minimum of backlash or axial rock. Examine the hub bore, end faces and dog teeth of the sliding sleeve, particularly in the sliding key grooves. Renew the complete assembly if wear is obvious. Note that if the car had a tendency to jump out of a particular gear, then a worn synchroniser unit is the most likely cause and the relevant assembly should be renewed.

5 To reassemble the synchroniser units slide the hub into the sleeve with the marks made during dismantling on the same side. Fit the spring wires to each side of the hub then insert the sliding keys, hooking them over the springs. Ensure that the spring ends engage with the hub grooves.

6 Check the condition of all the selector forks, rods and all the parts

of the shift mechanism. Check the selector fork clearance in the synchro sleeve groove using feeler gauges (photo). Renew the fork if the clearance is excessive and any other parts that show signs of wear. **Note:** *If the primary shaft, secondary shaft or any of the bearings on the shafts are renewed it will be necessary to adjust the bearing preloads. This is a complex operation requiring the use of special jigs and fixtures and the advice of a Mazda dealer should be sought before reassembly.*

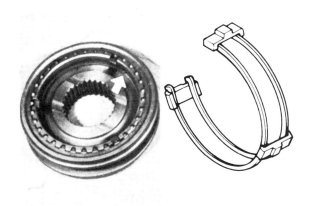

Fig. 6.16 Synchroniser unit sliding key and spring arrangement (Sec 8)

Arrow indicates spring end locating hole in hub

2   If the problem with the differential is purely one of noise, and if the noise is more of a whine than a rumble, the unit may continue working for some considerable time without getting any worse. Again, the help or advice of a dealer is recommended for deciding the course of action to be taken.

10 Clutch housing and transmission case – inspection

1   Examine both the housings for signs of cracks or damage, particularly to the mating faces.
2   Check the condition of the roller bearing outer races looking for any signs of scuffing, pitting or obvious damage. If the bearing inner races on the primary and secondary shafts have been renewed then the outer races must be renewed also. If, however, they are in a satisfactory condition they should be left undisturbed. Mazda special tools are necessary to remove and refit the bearing outer races and if they are renewed it will then be necessary to adjust the bearing preloads. This is a complex operation requiring the use of special jigs and fixtures and the advice of a Mazda dealer should be sought if bearing renewal is necessary.
3   Renew the oil seals in the housings by hooking them out with a screwdriver then carefully tapping in the new seal (photos).

8.2 Measure the baulk ring to gear clearance ...

8.6 ... and selector fork to synchro sleeve clearance using feeler gauges

9   Final drive differential – inspection

1   As described earlier in this Chapter, dismantling and overhaul of the differential are considered beyond the scope of the home mechanic. If the differential assembly is obviously in need of renewal it will be necessary to obtain a complete unit or entrust the work to a dealer, as critical adjustments are required.

10.3A Remove the oil seals by hooking them out with a screwdriver ...

10.3B ... then tap the new seals into place

11.2 Secure the engagement plate and reverse lever shaft with a new roll pin (arrowed)

11 Manual transmission – reassembly

1   Locate the reverse lever and engagement plate in the clutch housing and slide in the reverse lever shaft (photo).
2   Align the holes in the engagement plate, housing web and reverse lever shaft then tap in the retaining roll pin (photo). Leave approximately 6.4 mm (0.25 in) of roll pin protruding above the engagement plate face.
3   Apply sealer around the housing end plug then tap the plug in flush with the housing face (photo).
4   Insert the shift rod into the housing followed by the reverse gate and the selector. Engage the rod with the gate and selector (photo).
5   Locate the spring around the reverse gate then push the shift rod fully home (photo).
6   Refit the guide plate and secure with the retaining bolts. Engage the looped end of the spring around the guide plate retaining bolt distance collar (photo).

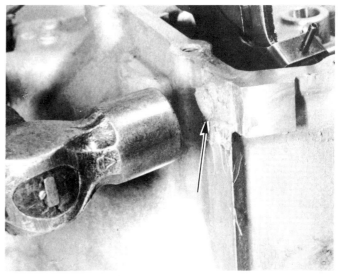

11.3 Tap the end plug (arrowed) into place, flush with the housing

11.1 Fit the reverse lever, engagement plate and reverse lever shaft

11.4 Fit the shift rod, selector and reverse gate

11.5 Locate the spring around the reverse gate

11.7 Slide the shift arm onto the rod and secure with the retaining bolt (arrowed)

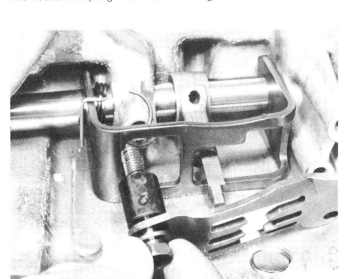

11.6 Refit the guide plate and secure with the retaining bolts

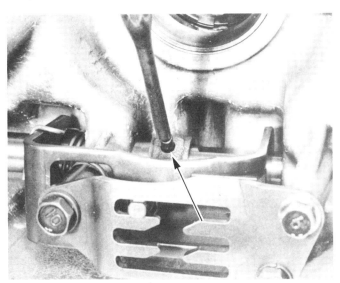

11.8 Tap in a new selector retaining roll pin

7   Slide the shift arm onto the end of the shift rod, align the holes in the arm and rod, and refit the retaining bolt (photo).
8   Align the holes in the selector and shift rod and tap in the retaining roll pin (photo). Leave approximately 3.2 mm (0.125 in) of roll pin protruding above the selector face.
9   Lower the final drive differential into place in the clutch housing (photo).
10 Locate the primary shaft assembly into its bearing in the clutch housing (photo).
11 Refit the detent spring into the centre of the reverse lever shaft (photo).
12 With the selector forks engaged with their respective synchroniser units, refit the secondary shaft geartrain and selectors as an assembly (photo).
13 Hold the geartrain and move the selector forks and selector rod upwards until the selector rod is just free of its location. Move the selector rod and control end to one side slightly and engage the detent ball with the end of the reverse lever shaft (photo).

11.9 Lower the differential into place

11.10 Locate the primary shaft assembly into its bearing

11.13 Engage the detent ball with the reverse lever shaft ...

11.11 Fit the detent spring (arrowed) to the reverse lever shaft

14 Turn the control end clockwise so that the ball engages with one of the detents, then locate the selector rod back into its hole (photo).
15 Return the geartrain to neutral and turn the selector rod so that the hole in the rod and control end are aligned. Ensure that the flat on the upper part of the selector rod is facing outwards (photos).
16 Refit the control end retaining roll pin (photo).
17 Engage the crank lever with the shift arm and control end then slide the crank lever shaft into place (photo).
18 Turn the crank lever shaft until the slots in the shaft and housing are aligned then tap in the retaining roll pin (photo).
19 Refit the 5th/reverse selector rod and engagement lever to the clutch housing (photo). Align the hole in the lever and rod and refit the lock bolt. Ensure that the hole in the rod just above the engagement lever is facing away from the differential.
20 Refit the reverse idler shaft and gear ensuring that the gear engages with the engagement lever and the bolt hole on the shaft is directly in line with the raised projection on the clutch housing mating face (photos).
21 Refit the magnet to its location in the housing (photo) and on early models refit the 5th gear oil passage and speedometer driven gear assembly.

11.12 Fit the secondary shaft geartrain and selectors as an assembly

11.14 ... then turn the control end clockwise to retain the ball

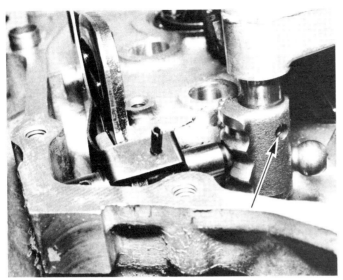

11.15A Align the roll pin hole in the selector rod and control end (arrowed) ...

11.15B ... ensuring that the flat on the rod (arrowed) is facing outwards ...

11.16 ... then fit the retaining roll pin

11.17 Fit the crank lever and crank lever shaft

11.18 Secure the crank lever shaft with a new roll pin (arrowed)

11.19 Fit the 5th/reverse selector rod (A) and engagement lever (B)

22 Apply jointing compound to the mating face of the clutch housing and lower the transmission case into position (photo). Tap the case lightly with a soft-faced mallet, if necessary, until it is fully seated. Refit the case retaining bolts with cable clips and brackets as noted during dismantling.

23 Refit the reversing light switch, reverse idler shaft lock bolt and selector rod guide bolt (photo).

24 The following operations are only applicable to five-speed models.

25 Refit the 5th speed driving gear followed by the driven gear sleeve, 5th speed driven gear, baulk ring and synchroniser unit (photos).

26 Engage 1st gear by moving the shift rod, and 5th gear by pushing down on the synchroniser sleeve.

27 Fit a new 5th speed driving gear retaining nut and tighten the nut to the specified torque (photos).

28 Return the 5th speed synchroniser unit to the neutral position and withdraw it from the shaft.

29 Engage the selector fork with the synchroniser sleeve and selector rod then refit the synchroniser unit once more (photo).

30 Engage 5th gear, fit a new retaining nut and tighten it to the specified torque (photo).

11.20A Fit the reverse idler shaft and gear with the gear engaged with the lever (arrowed) ...

11.20B ... and the shaft bolt hole (A) in line with the projection (B) on the housing

11.22 Fit the transmission case

11.21 Place the magnet in its location

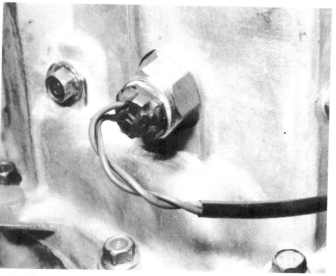

11.23 Fit the reversing light switch

11.25A Fit the 5th speed driving gear followed by ...

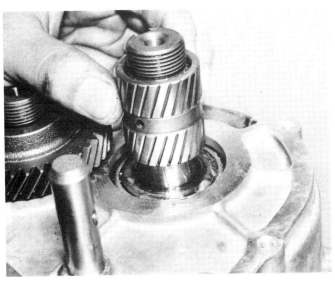

11.25B ... the driven gear sleeve ...

11.25C ... driven gear ...

11.25D ... baulk ring ...

11.25E ... and synchroniser unit

11.27A Fit the driving gear retaining nut ...

11.27B .. and tighten it to the specified torque

11.29 Engage the selector fork with the sleeve and rod

11.30 Tighten the driven gear retaining nut to the specified torque

31 Return the transmission to neutral.
32 Align the fork and selector rod holes and tap in a new retaining roll pin (photo).
33 Stake the retaining nuts into the grooves in their respective shafts using a blunt nosed punch.
34 Place a new gasket on the transmission case and refit the end cover (photos).

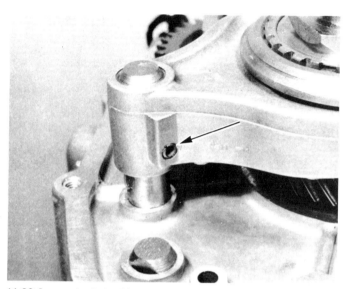

11.32 Secure the fork with a new roll pin (arrowed)

12 Gear lever – removal and refitting

1 Apply the handbrake and chock the rear wheels then jack up the front of the car and support it on axle stands.
2 From under the car undo the nut and remove the through-bolt securing the gear lever to the gearchange rod (photo).
3 From inside the car carefully prise the centre console upper panel out of its locating catches using a screwdriver.
4 Fold back the gear lever rubber boot and release the lever retaining spring using a screwdriver (Fig. 6.19).
5 Withdraw the gear lever from its location in the remote control housing.
6 Examine the gear lever seat components and renew any that show signs of wear or deterioration.
7 Refitting is the reverse sequence to removal, bearing in mind the following points:

(a) *Lubricate the gear lever seat components with multi-purpose grease*
(b) *Ensure that the hooked part of the retaining spring locates properly in the housing groove*

13 Gearchange remote control housing – removal and refitting

1 Remove the gear lever as described in the previous Section.
2 From under the front of the car undo the nut and bolt securing the gearchange rod to the transmission shift rod.
3 Undo the nut and remove the washers securing the remote control housing extension bar to the transmission. Remove the outer washers, slide the bar off the stud and recover the inner washers.
4 From inside the car undo the nuts securing the remote control housing to the underbody and withdraw the unit from under the car.
5 Refitting is the reverse sequence of removal.

11.34A Place a new gasket on the
transmission case ...

11.34B ... and fit the end cover

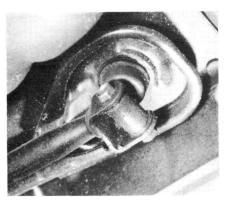

12.2 Undo the nut and bolt securing the
gear lever to the gearchange rod

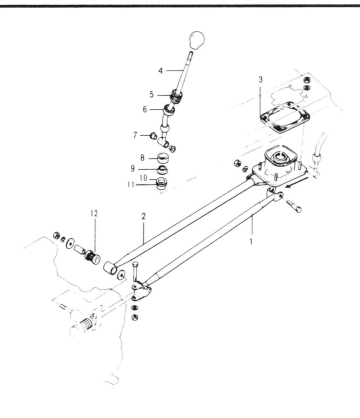

Fig. 6.17 Exploded view of
the gear lever and remote
control housing
(Secs 12 and 13)

1   Gearchange rod
2   Extension bar
3   Insulator
4   Gear lever
5   Lever retaining spring
6   Upper ball seat
7   Bushes
8   Lower ball seat
9   Plate
10 Holder
11 Cup
12 Bush

Fig. 6.18 Prising up the centre console upper panel
(Sec 12)

Fig. 6.19 Releasing the gear lever retaining spring
(Sec 12)

14 Fault diagnosis – manual transmission

Symptom	Reason(s)
Transmission noisy in neutral	Primary shaft bearings worn
Transmission noisy only when moving (in all gears)	Secondary shaft bearings worn Differential bearings worn Wear on differential crown wheel or secondary shaft pinion teeth Incorrect bearing preloads
Transmission noisy in only one gear	Worn, damaged or chipped gear teeth Excessive gear running clearance
Transmission jumps out of gear	Worn synchroniser units Worn selector detent ball and control end or weak spring Worn selector forks
Ineffective synchromesh	Worn synchroniser units or baulk rings
Difficulty in engaging gears	Worn selector forks, selector mechanism or gear linkage Clutch fault (see Chapter 5)

Chapter 7 Automatic transmission

For modifications, and information applicable to later models, see Supplement at end of manual

Contents

Specifications

Type .... F3A three-speed fully automatic

Gear ratios
First 2.84:1
Second 1.54:1
Third 1.00:1
Reverse 2.40:1
Final drive 3.63:1

Torque wrench settings

	Nm	lbf ft
Torque converter to drive plate	35 to 50	25 to 36
Drive plate to crankshaft	83 to 95	60 to 69
Transmission to engine:		
12 mm bolt	65 to 95	47 to 69
14 mm bolt	90 to 120	65 to 87
Oil pan bolts	5 to 8	4 to 6
Starter inhibitor switch	19 to 26	14 to 19
Crossmember front mounting nuts	61 to 87	44 to 63
Crossmember rear mounting bolts	65 to 91	47 to 66
Engine/transmission mounting to crossmember nuts	32 to 47	23 to 34
Engine/transmission mounting to transmission bolts	38 to 53	28 to 38
Number four mounting to transmission bolts	19 to 26	14 to 19
Lower arm balljoint pinch-bolt	44 to 55	33 to 40
Roadwheel nuts	90 to 110	65 to 80

1 General description

Mazda 1500 Automatic models are equipped with a three-speed fully automatic transmission consisting of a torque converter, epicyclic geartrain, hydraulically operated clutches and brakes and incorporating the final drive differential assembly.

The torque converter provides a fluid coupling between the engine and transmission which acts as an automatic clutch and also provides a degree of torque multiplication when accelerating.

The epicyclic geartrain provides either of the three forward or one reverse gear ratios according to which of its component parts are held stationary or allowed to turn. The components of the geartrain are held

or released by brakes and clutches which are activated by hydraulic valves. An oil pump within the transmission provides the necessary hydraulic pressure to operate the brakes and clutches.

Driver control of the transmission is by a six position selector lever which allows fully automatic operation with a hold facility on the first and second gear ratios.

Due to the complexity of the automatic transmission any repair or overhaul work must be left to a Mazda dealer or automatic transmission specialist with the necessary equipment for fault diagnosis and repair. The contents of the following Sections are therefore confined to supplying general information and any service information and instructions that can be used by the owner.

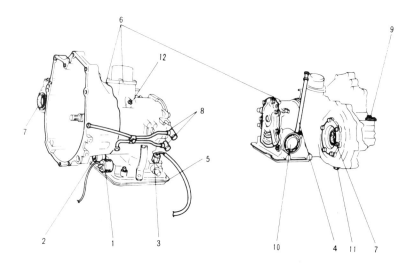

Fig. 7.1 Layout of
transmission external
components (Secs 1 to 9)

1 Kickdown solenoid
2 Vacuum diaphragm
3 Starter inhibitor switch
4 Fluid level/filler tube
5 Oil pan
6 Housing mating faces
7 Side oil seal
8 Fluid pipes
9 Speedometer driven gear
10 Servo retainer
11 Drain plug
12 Fluid pressure test
   connection

2 Maintenance and inspection

1 At the intervals specified in Routine Maintenance at the beginning of this Manual, carefully inspect the transmission joint faces and oil seals for any signs of damage, deterioration or oil leakage. Also check for any excess free play in the selector linkage joints and check the wiring, vacuum hoses and all transmission attachments for security.
2 At the same service intervals check the transmission fluid level using the procedure described in Section 3. Renewal of the automatic transmission fluid is not a service requirement. If, however, when checking the level, the fluid appears thick and discoloured, or smells of burnt oil then the transmission should be drained and filled with fresh fluid as described in Section 4.
3 Carry out a thorough road test ensuring that all gear changes occur smoothly without snatching and without an increase in engine speed between changes. Check that all the gear positions can be engaged with the appropriate movement of the selector lever and with the vehicle at rest, check the operation of the parking pawl when P is selected.

3 Automatic transmission fluid – level checking

1 The automatic transmission fluid level should be checked when the engine is at normal operating temperature, preferably after a short journey.
2 With the car standing on level ground and with the engine running, apply the handbrake and slowly move the selector lever through all gear positions.
3 Return the selector lever to P and with the engine still idling, withdraw the dipstick from the filler tube and wipe it on paper or a non-fluffy cloth.
4 Reinsert the dipstick, withdraw it immediately and observe the fluid level. This should be between the L and F marks on the dipstick.
5 If topping-up is necessary, add the specified fluid, a small amount at a time through the dipstick tube until the level is correct. Use a funnel with a fine mesh screen to avoid spillage and to ensure that any foreign matter is trapped. Take care not to overfill the transmission.
6 After topping-up, recheck the level again, refit the dipstick and switch off the engine.

4 Automatic transmission fluid – draining and refilling

Note: *To avoid the risk of scalding, only drain the fluid when cold or after the vehicle has been standing for some time.*
1 Jack up the front of the car and securely support it on axle stands.
2 Wipe clean the area around the transmission drain plug located at the base of the final drive housing.

Fig. 7.2 Fluid level dipstick location and markings (Sec 3)

3 Place a suitable container beneath the drain plug and, working through the access hole in the crossmember, unscrew the plug and allow the fluid to drain. When all the fluid has drained, refit the plug.
4 If the transmission has been drained to allow a repair operation to be carried out (ie driveshaft removal or transmission removal) then sufficient fluid will have been drained by this method to allow the work to proceed. If the transmission has been drained for fluid renewal then it will also be necessary to drain the small quantity of fluid remaining in the oil pan as follows.
5 Remove the undertray to gain access to the oil pan.
6 Wipe clean the area around the oil pan retaining bolts and joint face.
7 Undo and remove the bolts securing the oil pan to the transmission, but leave one in place, each side, finger tight.
8 Place a suitable container beneath the oil pan and carefully prise the pan downwards to break the gasket seal. Once the pan is free, undo the remaining bolts, lower the pan and tip the fluid into the container.
9 Thoroughly clean the oil pan in paraffin and remove all traces of old gasket from the mating face. Dry the pan with a lint free rag or preferably with compressed air.
10 Clean off all traces of old gasket from the transmission face and make sure that the oil pan and transmission face are spotlessly clean.
11 Apply a small amount of jointing compound to both sides of a new gasket and place the gasket on the oil pan.
12 Refit the oil pan and tighten the bolts progressively and in a diagonal sequence to the specified torque.
13 Refit the undertray and lower the car to the ground.
14 Remove the transmission dipstick from the filler tube and add the specified transmission fluid, a small amount at a time until the level just

starts to register on the dipstick. Use a funnel with a fine mesh screen to avoid spillage and to ensure that any foreign matter is trapped.

15 Continue adding fluid until the level is between the L and F marks on the dipstick.

16 With the selector lever in P (Park), start the engine and allow it to idle.

17 With the hand and footbrake applied, slowly move the selector lever through each gear position then return it to P.

18 With the engine still idling check the fluid level on the dipstick and top up if necessary so that the level is between the L and F marks.

19 Refit the dipstick and drive the car for a short journey until normal engine and transmission operating temperatures are reached.

20 With the car standing on level ground, the engine idling and the transmission in P, make a final check of the fluid level and top up if necessary. Take care not to overfill the transmission.

Fig. 7.3 Transmission fluid drain plug location (arrowed) (Sec 4)

5 Kickdown solenoid – testing

1 A fault in the kickdown solenoid is indicated if the transmission does not downshift under full throttle application, or if the downshift is hesitant or rough.

2 To test the solenoid, jack up the front of the car and support it on axle stands.

3 Disconnect the kickdown solenoid wiring at the snap connector in the wiring (not at the solenoid). Unscrew and remove the solenoid unit from the transmission, but allow for oil spillage (approximately 0.5 litre) as the solenoid is withdrawn. Catch the oil in a suitable container for disposal.

4 Refer to Fig. 7.4 and apply battery voltage to the solenoid as shown. The plunger should operate when the voltage is applied. If this is not the case the unit is faulty and should be renewed.

5 Refitting is the reverse sequence of removal. On completion, top up the transmission fluid level using new fluid of the specified type as described in Section 3.

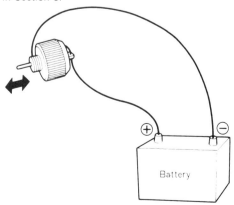

Fig. 7.4 Kickdown solenoid test circuit (Sec 5)

6 Vacuum diaphragm – testing

1 Malfunction of the vacuum diaphragm can cause harsh gear changes and gear changes occurring at higher than normal engine speeds.

2 To test the diaphragm first obtain the transmission fluid as described in Section 4.

3 Disconnect the vacuum hose and remove the diaphragm from the transmission.

4 Apply suction to the diaphragm outlet port and check that the rod moves as suction is applied. If not, the unit is faulty and renewal is ncessary. When obtaining a new unit make sure that the new part is the same as the old; a number of different units are available and each has a different length operating rod.

5 Also make sure that the vacuum hose is in satisfactory condition with no sign of deterioration, cracks or damage.

6 Refit the vacuum diaphragm unit to the transmission, connect the vacuum hose then refill the transmission with fluid, as described in Section 4, after lowering the car to the ground.

7 Starter inhibitor switch – testing

1 If the starter inhibitor switch is operating correctly the engine should only start when the transmission selector lever is in the P or N position and the reversing lights should be illuminated when the selector lever is in the R position.

2 If a fault is suspected, separate the switch wiring connector and check for continuity at connector terminals A and B with the transmission in P and N, and at terminals C and D with the transmission in R (Fig 7.5). If this is not the case, renew the starter inhibitor switch.

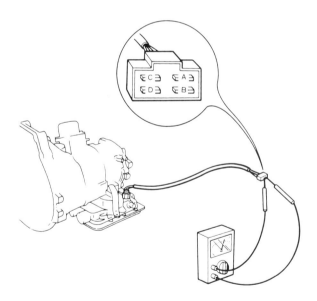

Fig. 7.5 Testing the starter inhibitor switch (Sec 7)

8 Selector linkage – adjustment

1 Move the transmission selector lever through each position, making sure that the movement into each detent is positive and corresponds to the markings on the position plate.

2 The lever should move between D and N without the need to push in the button on the knob. The button must be depressed to move the lever between D and R.

3 If the push button is loose, or if the lever can be moved between D and R without depressing it, then slacken the knob locknut and turn

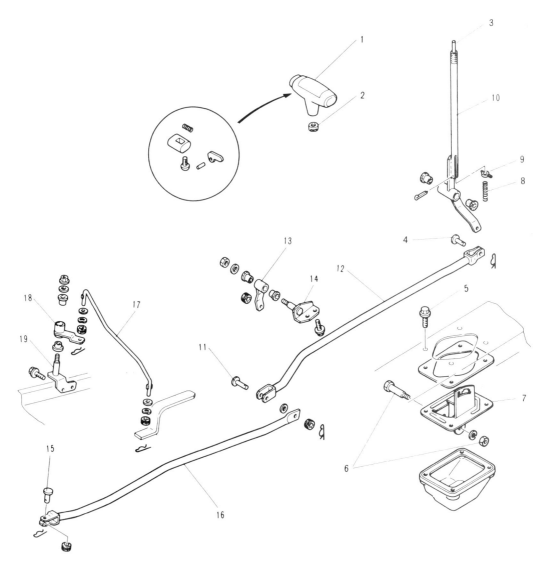

Fig. 7.6 Exploded view of the selector linkage (Sec 8)

1	Selector lever knob	6	Bolt and nut
2	Locknut	7	Selector lever bracket
3	Rod	8	Spring
4	Joint pin	9	Guide pin
5	Bolt	10	Selector lever

11	Joint pin	16	Front selector rod
12	Rear selector lever	17	Counter rod
13	Rear counter lever	18	Front counter lever
14	Rear counter bracket	19	Front counter bracket
15	Joint pin		

the knob until correct operation is restored. Hold the knob in this position and tighten the locknut.

4   If any further adjustment of the selector linkage is necessary this should be left to a Mazda dealer. A number of modifications have been made to the various components of the linkage and different adjustment procedures are used accordingly.

9   Automatic transmission – removal and refitting

1   Disconnect the battery negative terminal.
2   Refer to Section 4 and drain the transmission fluid.
3   Disconnect the speedometer cable and starter inhibitor switch, neutral switch and kickdown solenoid wiring connectors.
4   Disconnect the vacuum hose from the vacuum diaphragm.
5   Slacken the wheel nuts, jack up the front of the car and securely support it on axle stands. Remove the front roadwheels.
6   Where fitted remove the front anti-roll bar as described in Section 9, Chapter 10.

7   Remove the undertray and left-hand side cover to gain access to the transmission from below.
8   Undo and remove the pinch-bolt securing the lower suspension arm balljoint to the swivel hub.
9   Using a long stout bar, lever the lower suspension arm down to release the balljoint shank from the swivel hub.
10 Pull the swivel hub outwards firmly to release the driveshaft inner constant velocity joint from the transmission. Support the driveshaft at its inner end to avoid damaging the transmission oil seal as the constant velocity joint is withdrawn.
11 Disconnect the selector linkage front selector rod and counter rod at the transmission.
12 Support the engine and transmission with suitable jacks and remove the front crossmember and engine/transmission mountings.
13 Disconnect and plug the fluid pipes at the transmission.
14 Refer to Fig. 7.8 and remove the number 4 mounting assembly (early models only).
15 Remove the starter motor as described in Chapter 12 and the end cover.

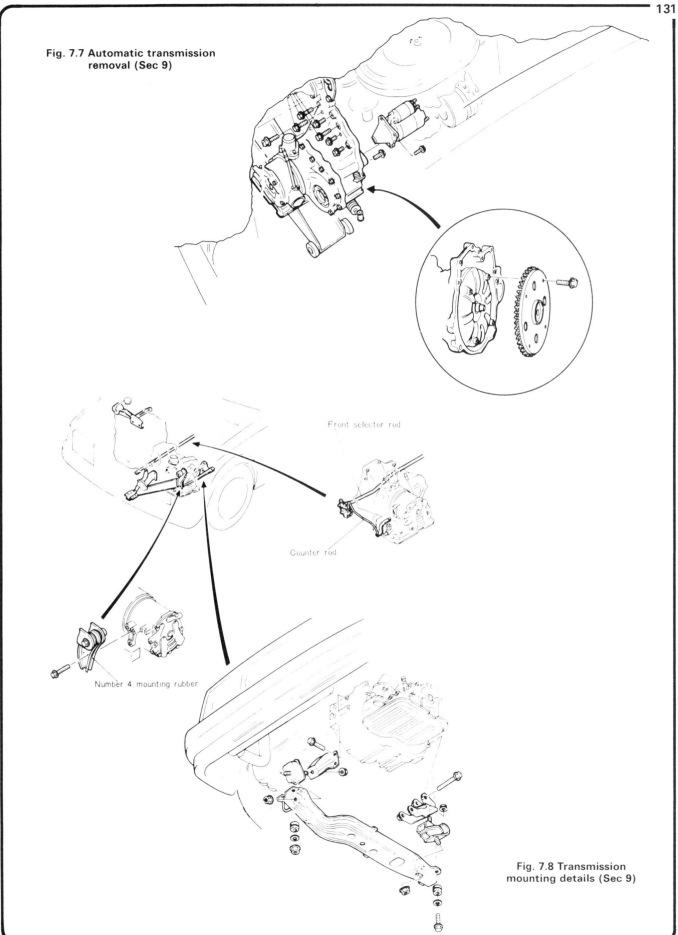

Fig. 7.7 Automatic transmission removal (Sec 9)

Front selector rod

Counter rod

Number 4 mounting rubber

Fig. 7.8 Transmission mounting details (Sec 9)

16 Undo and remove the bolts securing the torque converter to the drive plate.

17 With the engine and transmission well supported on jacks, undo and remove all the bolts securing the transmission to the engine.

18 Separate the transmission from the engine, lower the jack and remove the unit out from under the car. During this operation make sure that the torque converter stays in place on the transmission.

19 Refitting is the reverse sequence of removal bearing in mind the following points.

  (a) Tighten all nuts and bolts to the correct torque setting where specified
  (b) Fill the transmission with fluid as described in Section 4 after refitting

10 Fault diagnosis – automatic transmission

In the event of a fault occurring on the transmission, it is first necessary to determine whether it is of a mechanical or hydraulic nature and to do this the transmission must be in the car. Special test equipment is necessary for this purpose, together with a systematic test procedure, and the work should be entrusted to a suitably equipped Mazda dealer or automatic transmission specialist.

Do not remove the transmission from the car for repair or overhaul until professional fault diagnosis has been carried out.

Chapter 8 Driveshafts

For modifications, and information applicable to later models, see Supplement at end of manual

Contents

Specifications

Type	Unequal length solid steel, splined to inner and outer constant velocity joints

Driveshaft length
Right-hand side	659 mm (25.95 in)
Left-hand side	376 mm (14.80 in)

Driveshaft diameter	25 mm (0.98 in)

Torque wrench settings
	Nm	lbf ft
Driveshaft retaining nut	160 to 240	116 to 174
Anti-roll bar connecting link locknut	12 to 18	9 to 13
Lower arm balljoint pinch-bolt	44 to 55	33 to 40
Roadwheels nuts	90 to 110	65 to 80

1 General description

Drive is transmitted from the differential to the front wheels by means of two unequal length, solid steel driveshafts.

Both driveshafts are fitted with ball and cage type constant velocity joints at each end. The outer joints are splined to accept the driveshaft and wheel hub flange, while the inner joints are splined to accept the driveshaft and differential sun gears. Both the inner and outer constant velocity joints are packed with special grease during manufacture and sealed with a rubber boot.

To eliminate driveshaft induced harmonic vibrations and resonance, a rubber mounted steel damper is attached to the longer right-hand driveshaft.

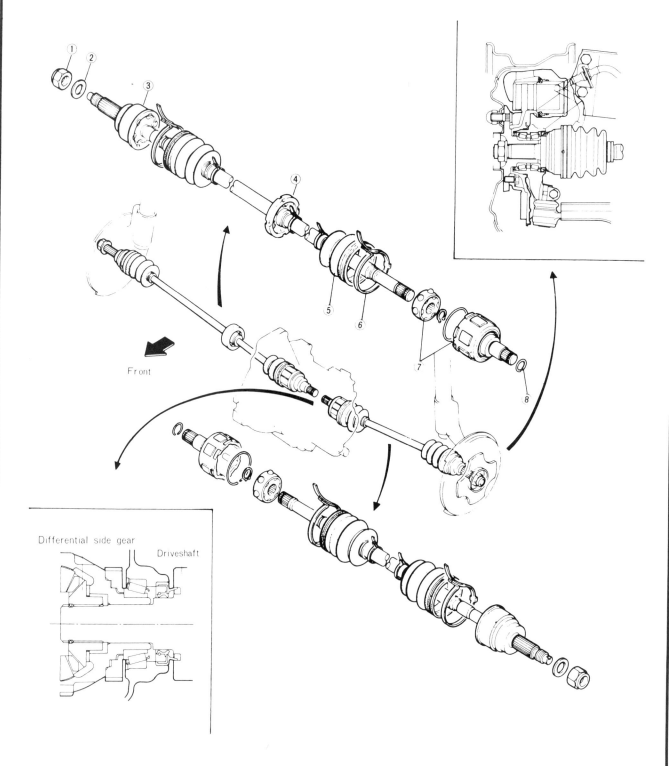

Fig. 8.1 Layout of the driveshaft assemblies and related components (Sec 1)

1	Driveshaft retaining nut	3	Outer constant velocity joint	5	Rubber boot	7 Inner constant velocity joint
2	Thrust washer	4	Vibration damper	6	Retaining clip	assembly
						8 Circlip

Differential side gear

Driveshaft

Front

2 Maintenance and inspection

1   At the intervals given in Routine Maintenance at the beginning of this Manual, carry out a thorough inspection of the driveshafts and joints as follows.
2   Jack up the front of the car and support it securely on axle stands.
3   Slowly rotate the roadwheel and inspect the condition of the outer joint rubber boots (photo). Check for signs of cracking, splits or deterioration of the rubber which may allow the grease to escape and lead to water and grit entry into the joint. Also check the security and condition of the retaining clips. Repeat these checks on the inner constant velocity joints. If any damage or deterioration is found the boots should be renewed as described in Sections 4 or 5.

Fig. 8.2 Releasing the staking on the driveshaft retaining nut (Sec 3)

2.3 Checking the condition of the constant velocity joint rubber boots

3.4 Slacken the driveshaft retaining nut

4   Continue rotating the roadwheel and check for any distortion or damage to the driveshaft. Check for any free play in the joints by first holding the driveshaft and attempting to rotate the wheel. Repeat this check by holding the inner joint and attempting to rotate the driveshaft. Any appreciable movement indicates wear in the joints, wear in the driveshaft splines or loose driveshaft retaining nut.
5   Road test the car and listen for a metallic clicking from the front as the car is driven slowly in a circle with the steering on full lock. If a clicking noise is heard this indicates wear in the outer constant velocity joint caused by excessive clearance between the balls in the joint and the recesses in which they operate. Remove and inspect the joint, as described in Section 4.
6   If vibration, consistent with road speed is felt through the car when accelerating, there is a possibility of wear in the inner constant velocity joint. If so, remove and inspect the joint as described in Section 5.

3 Driveshaft – removal and refitting

1   Chock the rear wheels, firmly apply the handbrake then jack up the front of the car and support it on axle stands. Remove the appropriate front roadwheel.
2   Drain the manual transmission oil or automatic transmission fluid as described in Chapter 6 or 7 respectively.
3   Using a hammer and suitable chisel nosed tool, tap up the staking securing the driveshaft retaining nut to the groove in the constant velocity joint. Note that a new driveshaft retaining nut must be obtained for reassembly.
4   Have an assistant firmly depress the footbrake then using a socket and long bar, slacken, but do not remove, the driveshaft retaining nut (photo).
5   Remove the plastic side cover from under the inner wheel arch (photo).

3.5 Remove the side cover under the wheel arch

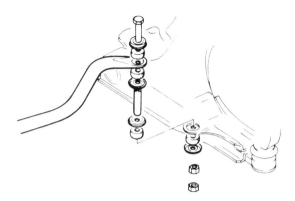

Fig. 8.3 Anti-roll bar connecting link details (Sec 3)

3.8 Lever the lower suspension arm down to release the balljoint shank

6   If an anti-roll bar is fitted, undo the two locknuts and remove the connecting link bolt securing the anti-roll bar to the lower suspension arm. Recover the washers and rubber bush noting their fitted positions.
7   Undo the nut and remove the pinch-bolt securing the lower arm balljoint to the swivel hub (photo).
8   Using a long stout bar, lever the lower suspension arm down to release the balljoint shank from the swivel hub (photo).
9   Pull the swivel hub outwards firmly to release the driveshaft inner constant velocity joint from the transmission. Support the driveshaft at its inner end to avoid damaging the transmission oil seal (photo).
10 Remove the driveshaft retaining nut, pull the swivel hub outwards as far as possible and withdraw the outer constant velocity joint from the hub (photo). Support the driveshaft and remove it from under the wheel arch.
11 Refitting the driveshaft is the reverse sequence of removal bearing in mind the following points:

(a) Apply a smear of multi-purpose grease to the swivel hub and transmission oil seal lips before refitting the driveshaft
(b) Using a new driveshaft retaining nut, tighten it to the specified torque then stake it into the groove on the constant velocity joint using a round nosed tool (photo).
(c) Refill the manual or automatic transmission with the correct type and quantity of lubricant as described in Chapters 6 and 7 respectively

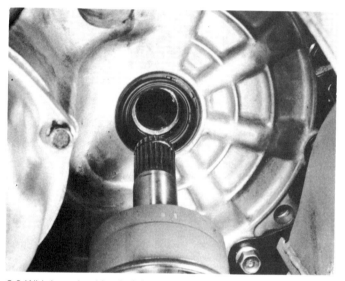

3.9 Withdraw the driveshaft inner constant velocity joint from the transmission

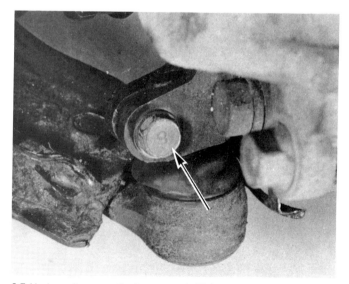

3.7 Undo and remove the lower arm balljoint pinch-bolt (arrowed)

3.10 Withdraw the outer constant velocity joint from the hub

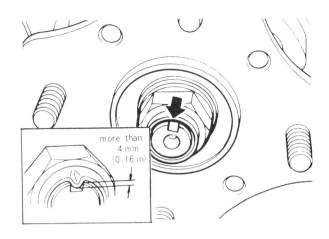

Fig. 8.4 Driveshaft retaining nut staking (Sec 3)

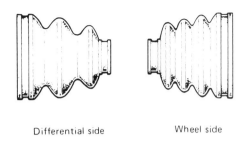

Differential side   Wheel side

Fig. 8.5 Constant velocity joint rubber boot identification
(Sec 4)

8 Inspect the ball tracks on the inner and outer members. If the tracks have widened, the balls will no longer be a tight fit. At the same time check the ball cage windows for wear or for cracking between the balls. Wear in the balls, ball tracks and ball cage windows will lead to the characteristic clicking noise on full lock described previously.
9 If any of the above checks indicate wear in the joint it will be necessary to renew it complete, as the internal parts are not available separately. If the joint is in a satisfactory condition, obtain a repair kit consisting of a new rubber boot, retaining clips, and the correct quantity of grease.
10 To refit the joint first slide the rubber boot together with the small retaining clip onto the shaft taking care not to damage the boot on the driveshaft splines (photo).
11 Ensure that the constant velocity joint retaining circlip is undamaged and correctly located in its groove in the end of the driveshaft (photo). Engage the help of an assistant for the following operations.
12 Position the constant velocity joint over the splines on the driveshaft until it abuts the circlip (photo).
13 Using two small screwdrivers placed either side of the circlip, compress the clip and at the same time have your assistant firmly strike the end of the joint with a hide, or plastic mallet (photos).
14 The joint should slide over the compressed circlip and into position on the shaft. It will probably take several attempts until you achieve success. If the joint does not spring into place the moment it is struck, remove it, reposition the circlip and try again. Do not force the joint, otherwise the circlip will be damaged.

3.11 Stake the new driveshaft retaining nut using a round-nosed tool

4 Outer constant velocity joint – removal, inspection and refitting

1 Remove the driveshaft from the car as described in Section 3.
2 Support the driveshaft in a vice and release the two rubber boot retaining clips by raising the locking tags with a screwdriver and then raising the end of the clips with pliers.
3 Slide the rubber boot down the shaft to expose the outer constant velocity joint.
4 Using a hide or plastic mallet, sharply strike the outer edge of the joint to drive it off the shaft. The outer joint is retained on the driveshaft by an internal circular section circlip and striking the joint in the manner described forces the circlip to contract into a groove, so allowing the joint to slide off.
5 Withdraw the rubber boot from the driveshaft.
6 With the constant velocity joint removed from the driveshaft, thoroughly clean the joint using paraffin, or a suitable solvent, and dry it, preferably using compressed air. Carry out a careful visual inspection of the joint, paying particular attention to the following areas.
7 Move the inner splined driving member from side to side to expose each ball in turn at the top of its track. Examine the balls for cracks, flat spots or signs of surface pitting.

4.10 Fit the rubber boot and clip to the driveshaft

4.11 Ensure that the joint retaining circlip is in place and undamaged

4.12 Position the joint over the splines so that it abuts the circlip

4.13A With the circlip compressed using two screwdrivers ...

4.13B ... strike the joint firmly into position on the driveshaft

4.15 Pack the joint with the grease supplied in the repair kit

4.16 Position the large retaining clip over the joint ...

15 With the joint in position against the retaining collar, pack it thoroughly with the grease supplied in the repair kit. Work the grease well into the ball tracks while twisting the joint, and fill the rubber boot with any excess (photo).

16 Ease the rubber boot over the joint and place the large retaining clip in position (photo). Ensure that the boot locates in the grooves in the driveshaft and constant velocity joint.

17 Using pliers pull the retaining clip tight and fold it over until the end locates between the two raised tags. Hold the clip in this position and bend the tags over to lock the clip (photo). Secure the small retaining clip in the same fashion.

18 The driveshaft can now be refitted to the car as described in Section 3.

Fig. 8.6 Removing the constant velocity joint outer member retaining circlip (Sec 5)

4.17 ... and secure it using pliers

Fig. 8.7 Removing the inner splined driving member retaining circlip (Sec 5)

5 Inner constant velocity joint – removal, inspection and refitting

1 Remove the driveshaft from the car as described in Section 3.
2 Support the driveshaft in a vice and release the two rubber boot retaining clips by raising the locking tags with a screwdriver and then raising the end of the clips with pliers.
3 Slide the rubber boot down the shaft to expose the inner constant velocity joint.
4 Using a screwdriver, release the large circlip securing the outer member in position then remove the outer member (Fig. 8.6).
5 Using circlip pliers, extract the circlip securing the inner splined driving member to the driveshaft. Withdraw the inner member and ball cage assembly as a unit.
6 Remove the rubber boot from the driveshaft.
7 Carry out a careful visual inspection of the joint using the procedure described in Section 4, paragraphs 6 to 9 inclusive.
8 Begin reassembly by sliding the rubber boot together with the small retaining clip onto the shaft, taking care not to damage the boot on the driveshaft splines.
9 Refit the inner splined driving member and ball cage assembly to the driveshaft and secure with the circlip. Ensure that the member is fitted with the balls offset towards the end of the shaft (Fig. 8.9).
10 Pack the inner member, ball cage and outer member thoroughly with the grease supplied in the repair kit.
11 Slide the outer member over the balls and into position then secure it with the larger circlip.
12 Pull the rubber boot up into place ensuring that the boot locates in the grooves in the driveshaft and joint outer member.
13 Locate the large retaining clip over the boot, pull it tight and fold it over so that its end rests between the two raised tags. Hold the clip in

Fig. 8.8 Removing the inner member and ball cage assembly (Sec 5)

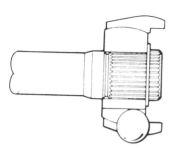

Fig. 8.9 Correct orientation of inner member and ball cage assembly (Sec 5)

this position and lock it by bending over the two raised tags. Secure the small retaining clip in the same fashion.

14 The driveshaft can now be refitted to the car as described in Section 3.

6 Vibration damper – removal and refitting

1 Remove the right-hand driveshaft from the car as described in Section 3, then remove the inner constant velocity joint as described in Section 5.

2 Release the retaining clip and slide the damper off the driveshaft.

3 Renew the damper if it is obviously damaged or distorted or if there is any sign of deterioration of the rubber.

4 Refit the damper with the retaining clip side facing the inner constant velocity joint and positioned as shown in Fig. 8.10.

5 Secure the damper with the retaining clip then refit the inner constant velocity joint as described in Section 5.

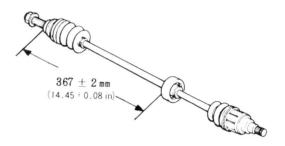

367 ± 2 mm
(14.45 ± 0.08 in)

Fig. 8.10 Vibration damper positioning dimension (Sec 6)

7 Fault diagnosis – driveshafts

Symptom	Reason(s)
Vibration and/or noise on turns	Worn constant velocity outer joint(s)
Vibration when acclerating	Worn constant velocity inner joint(s) Bent or distorted driveshaft
Noise on taking up drive	Worn driveshaft or constant velocity joint splines Loose driveshaft retaining nut Worn constant velocity joints

See also Fault diagnosis – suspension and steering

Chapter 9 Braking system

For modifications, and information applicable to later models, see Supplement at end of manual

Contents

Specifications

System type	Diagonally split dual circuit hydraulic with dual proportioning valve in rear hydraulic circuit. Cable operated handbrake on rear wheels. Servo assistance on all models

Front brakes

Type	Disc with single piston sliding calipers
Disc diameter	227 mm (8.9 in)
Disc thickness	11.0 mm (0.43 in)
Maximum disc run-out	0.1 mm (0.004 in)
Disc pad thickness:	
New	10.0 mm (0.4 in)
Minimum	1.0 mm (0.04 in)

Rear brakes

Type	Single leading shoe drum, self-adjusting
Drum internal diameter	180 mm (7.1 in)
Brake lining thickness:	
New	4.0 mm (0.16 in)
Minimum	1.0 mm (0.04 in)
Wheel cylinder bore diameter	17.46 mm (0.68 in)

General

Brake pedal height	215 to 220 mm (8.47 to 8.66 in)
Brake pedal free play	7.0 to 9.0 mm (0.28 to 0.35 in)
Minimum distance from brake pedal to floor (pedal depressed)	83.0 mm (3.27 in)
Master cylinder bore diameter	20.64 mm (0.81 in)
Vacuum servo unit diameter	178 mm (7.0 in)
Vacuum servo unit output rod clearance	0.1 to 0.5 mm (0.004 to 0.020 in)

Torque wrench settings

	Nm	lbf ft
Brake pedal pivot bolt	20 to 35	15 to 26
Brake caliper slide pins	45 to 55	33 to 41
Brake caliper mounting bracket to swivel hub	56 to 66	41 to 49
Flexible brake hose to caliper	22 to 30	16 to 22
Brake pipe union nuts	13 to 22	10 to 16
Wheel cylinder to backplate	13 to 16	10 to 12
Backplate to stub axle	46 to 68	34 to 50
Vacuum servo to bulkhead	13 to 16	10 to 12
Master cylinder to servo	13 to 16	10 to 12
Roadwheel nuts	90 to 110	65 to 80

1 General description

The braking system is of the servo assisted, dual-circuit hydraulic type with disc brakes at the front and drum brakes at the rear. The arrangement of the hydraulic system is such that each circuit operates one front and one rear brake from a tandem master cylinder. Under normal conditions both circuits operate in unison. However, in the event of hydraulic failure in one circuit, full braking force will still be available at two wheels. A dual proportioning valve is also incorporated in the hydraulic circuit to regulate the pressure applied to the rear brakes and reduce the possibility of the rear wheels locking under heavy braking.

The front disc brakes are actuated by single piston sliding type calipers. At the rear, leading and trailing brake shoes are actuated by twin piston wheel cylinders and are self-adjusting by footbrake application.

The handbrake provides an independent mechanical means of rear brake application.

2 Maintenance and inspection

1 At the intervals given in Routine Maintenance at the beginning of this Manual the following service operations should be carried out on the braking system components.
2 Check the brake hydraulic fluid level and if necessary, top up with the specified fluid to the MAX mark on the reservoir. Any need for frequent topping up indicates a fluid leak somewhere in the system which must be investigated and rectified immediately (photo).
3 Check the front disc pads and the rear brake shoe linings for wear and inspect the condition of the discs and drums. Details will be found in Sections 4 and 7 respectively.
4 Check the condition of the hydraulic pipes and hoses as described in Section 13. At the same time check the condition of the handbrake

cables, lubricate the exposed cables and linkages and if necessary adjust the handbrake as described in Section 15.
5 Renew the brake hydraulic fluid at the specified intervals by draining the system and refilling with fresh fluid as described in Section 14.
6 Check the operation of the vacuum servo unit as described in Section 20, and check the brake pedal height and free play as described in Section 3.

3 Brake pedal height and free play – checking and adjustment

1 At the intervals given in Routine Maintenance at the beginning of this Manual, check and if necessary adjust the brake pedal height and free play as described in the following paragraphs. The pedal height should always be checked first, but adjustment will normally only be necessary if the vacuum servo unit, or brake pedal have been renewed, or in any way disturbed. When the pedal height is correct, the free play can be checked and, if necessary, adjusted.

Brake pedal height
2 Measure the distance from the centre of the brake pedal pad upper face to the engine compartment bulkhead (Fig. 9.1). Compare the

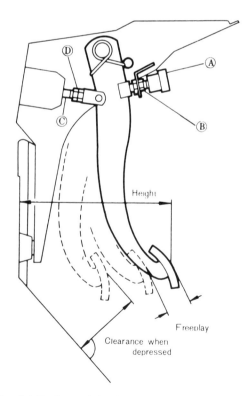

Fig. 9.1 Brake pedal adjustment details (Sec 3)

A Brake light switch
B Brake light switch locknut
C Vacuum servo pushrod
D Vacuum servo pushrod locknut

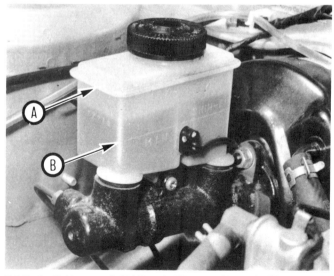

2.2 Brake fluid reservoir MAX mark (A) and MIN mark (B)

figure obtained with the brake pedal height dimension given in the Specifications. Note that the dimension given does not take into consideration the thickness of sound deadening material affixed to the bulkhead and an allowance should be made for this.

3 If adjustment is necessary, remove the cover under the facia and disconnect the wiring at the brake light switch.

4 Slacken the switch locknut and unscrew the switch until it is clear of the pedal (photo).

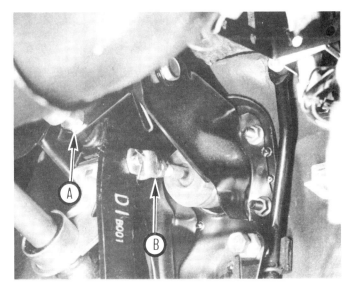

3.4 Brake light switch locknut (A) and vacuum servo pushrod locknut (B)

5 Slacken the vacuum servo pushrod locknut and turn the pushrod as necessary until the correct pedal height is obtained. Hold the pushrod in this position and tighten the locknut.

6 Screw the brake light switch in until it just touches the pedal then screw it in a further half a turn. Tighten the locknut and reconnect the wiring.

Brake pedal free play

7 Depress the brake pedal lightly by hand and measure the distance from the pedal at rest position until resistance is just felt, ie when the servo pushrod just contacts the servo piston. This is the brake pedal free play and should be as given in the Specifications.

8 If adjustment is necessary slacken the vacuum servo pushrod locknut once more and turn the pushrod until the specified free play is obtained. Tighten the locknut after adjustment then refit the cover under the facia.

9 Finally, check that when the pedal is depressed under a load of 60 kg (132.0 lb), the distance from the centre of the pedal pad upper face to the floor is not less than the dimension given in the Specifications. If it is, check that there is no air in the system by bleeding the brakes as described in Section 14. Also check that the rear brake shoes are not excessively worn and that the self-adjusting mechanism is operating correctly.

4 Front disc pads – inspection and renewal

1 Apply the handbrake, slacken the front wheel nuts then jack up the front of the car. Support the car on axle stands and remove the roadwheels.

2 The thickness of the disc pads can now be checked by viewing through the small opening in the front of the caliper body. If the lining on any of the pads is at or below the minimum specified thickness, all four pads must be renewed as a complete set. As a guide, a wear indicator groove is provided on the front edge of the pads which can be seen through the caliper opening. If the groove is not visible, the pad is worn (photo).

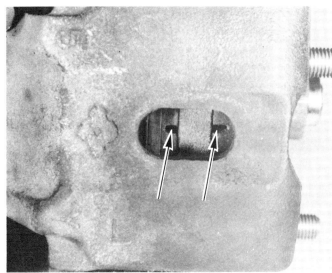

4.2 Wear indicator grooves on disc pads (arrowed) viewed through the caliper opening

3 To remove the pads first release the return spring using a screwdriver and remove it from the top of the caliper body (photo).

4 Unscrew the lower slide pin, pivot the caliper upwards and retain it in this position using string or wire attached to the suspension strut. Remove the shim from the caliper piston (photos).

5 Remove the shim from the outer pad then remove the pad from the mounting bracket (photos).

6 Remove the inner pad from the mounting bracket and recover the spring clips from the top of each pad.

7 Brush the dust and dirt from the caliper, piston, disc and pads, but do not inhale, as it is injurious to health.

8 Inspect the caliper for signs of fluid leaks around the piston, corrosion or other damage. Refer to Section 5 and renew the piston seals or the caliper body if any of these conditions are apparent. Check the condition of the disc using the procedure described in Section 6.

9 To refit the pads first attach the small spring clips then very slightly smear the pad and mounting bracket contact areas with a silicone grease ensuring that no grease is allowed to come into contact with the disc or the pad friction material.

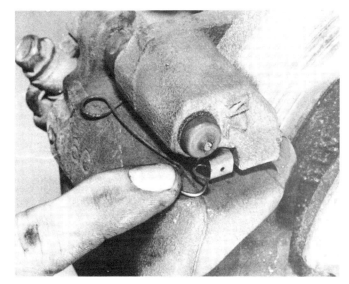

4.3 Remove the disc pad return spring

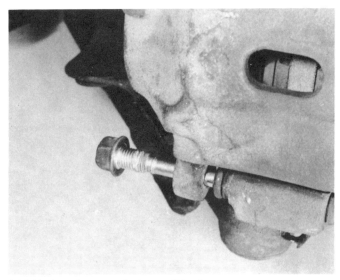

4.4A Undo and remove the lower slide pin ...

4.5B ... then remove the pad

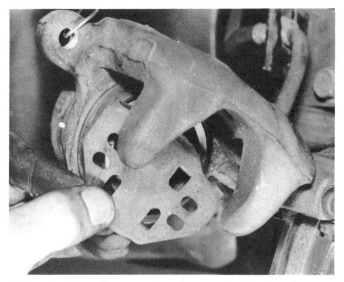

4.4B ... pivot the caliper upwards and remove the shim from the piston

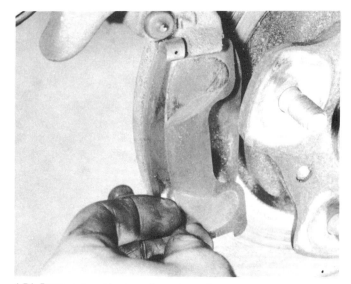

4.5A Remove the shim from the outer pad ...

10 Place the inner and outer pads in position and place the shim against the backing plate of the outer pad.
11 Locate the other shim over the piston then pivot the caliper assembly down over the pads. It may be necessary to ease the piston back into its bore slightly to accommodate the new thicker pads.
12 Refit the lower slide pin and tighten it to the specified torque.
13 Hook the return spring into position over the top of the caliper body.
14 Depress the footbrake two or three times to bring the piston into contact with the pads then refit the roadwheel and lower the car to the ground. Tighten the roadwheel nuts finally with the car on its wheels and check the fluid level in the master cylinder reservoir.

5 Front brake caliper – removal, overhaul and refitting

1 Apply the handbrake and slacken the front wheel retaining nuts. Jack up the front of the car and support it on axle stands. Remove the front roadwheel.
2 Using a screwdriver, hook out the disc pad return spring.
3 Undo and remove the two slide pins and withdraw the caliper leaving the disc pads and mounting bracket still in position. It is not necessary to remove the mounting bracket unless it requires renewal owing to accident damage or severe corrosion.
4 With the flexible hydraulic hose still attached to the caliper body, very slowly depress the brake pedal until the piston has been ejected just over half way out of its bore.
5 Using a brake hose clamp or other similar tool, clamp the brake hose to prevent loss of fluid during subsequent operations.
6 Undo the brake hose-to-caliper union bolt and remove the hose. Plug the end of the hose and the caliper orifice to prevent dirt entry.
7 With the caliper on the bench, wipe away all traces of dust and dirt, but avoid inhaling the dust as it is injurious to health.
8 Remove the shim from the caliper piston noting its fitted position.
9 Withdraw the partially ejected piston from the caliper body and remove the dust cover.
10 Using a suitable blunt instrument, such as a knitting needle, carefully extract the piston seal from the caliper bore.
11 Remove the slide pin bushes by pushing them out with the slide pins.
12 Clean all the parts in methylated spirit, or clean brake fluid, and wipe dry using a lint free cloth. Inspect the piston and caliper bore for signs of damage, scuffing or corrosion and if these conditions are evident, renew the complete caliper body assembly. Also renew the slide pins if they are bent or damaged.
13 If the components are in a satisfactory condition, a repair kit

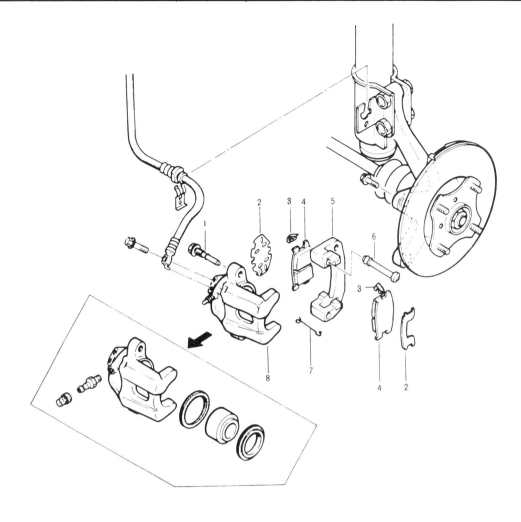

Fig. 9.2 Front disc pad and brake caliper components (Secs 4 and 5)

1   Slide pin
2   Shim
3   Spring clip
4   Disc pad
5   Mounting bracket
6   Slide pin bush
7   Return spring
8   Caliper

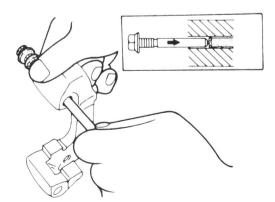

Fig. 9.3 Removing the slide pin bushes from the caliper
using the slide pins (Sec 5)

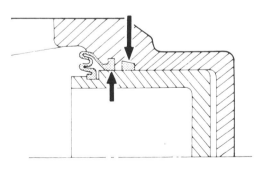

Fig. 9.4 Correct positioning of piston seal and dust cover
in the brake caliper (Sec 5)

consisting of new seals, bushes and special lubricant should be obtained.

14 Thoroughly lubricate the new seals with the special lubricant in the repair kit according to the instructions provided. Lubricate the piston and caliper bore with clean brake fluid.

15 Using the fingers only, carefully fit the new piston seal to the caliper bore.

16 Position the dust cover over the innermost end of the piston so that the caliper bore sealing lip protrudes beyond the base of the piston. Using a blunt instrument, if necessary, engage the sealing lip of the dust cover with the groove in the caliper. Now push the piston into the bore until the other sealing lip of the dust cover can be engaged with the groove in the piston. Having done this, push the piston fully into its bore. Ease the piston out again slightly, and make sure that the cover lip is correctly seating in the piston groove.

17 Fit the slide pin bushes to the caliper body using the slide pins to push them in, then thoroughly lubricate the bushes with the special lubricant.

18 Refit the shim to the caliper piston.

19 Position the caliper over the disc pads then refit the slide pins. Tighten the slide pins to the specified torque.

20 Refit the brake hose to the caliper and tighten the union bolt to the specified torque.

21 Remove the brake hose clamp and bleed the brakes as described in Section 14. If precautions were taken to minimise fluid loss, it should only be necessary to bleed the relevant front brake.

Fig. 9.5 Checking front brake disc run-out using a dial gauge (Sec 6)

6 Front brake disc – inspection

1   Refer to Section 4 and remove the disc pads.

2   Rotate the disc by hand and examine it for deep scoring, grooving or cracks. Light scoring is normal, but if excessive, the disc must be renewed. Any loose scale and rust around the outer edge of the disc can be removed by lightly tapping it with a small hammer while rotating the disc.

3   Using a dial gauge firmly anchored to the swivel hub, check that the disc run-out does not exceed the figure given in the Specifications. The disc thickness should also be checked at various points on the disc surface, using a micrometer. The disc should be renewed if the run-out is excessive or the thickness less than specified.

4   To remove the disc it is first necessary to remove the front swivel hub assembly and details of this procedure will be found in Chapter 10.

Fig. 9.6 Checking front brake disc thickness (Sec 6)

7 Rear brake shoes – inspection and renewal

1   Chock the front wheels and slacken the rear wheel retaining nuts. Jack up the rear of the car and support it on axle stands. Remove the rear roadwheel and make sure that the handbrake is fully released. Remove the hub cap.

2   Using a pointed tool, tap up the staking securing the rear hub retaining nut to the groove in the stub axle. Undo and remove the hub nut (photo).

3   Pull the brake drum and hub assembly squarely off the stub axle while at the same time holding the outer bearing and thrustwasher in place with your thumbs to prevent them dropping out (photo). If it is not possible to remove the assembly owing to the brake shoes binding on the drum, remove the handbrake lever stop at the rear of the backplate using a screwdriver. If the brake shoes are still binding, extract the handbrake cable clevis pin and push the lever up against the backplate. This will increase the clearance between the brake shoes and drum and allow the drum and hub assembly to be removed.

4   With the brake drum assembly removed, brush or wipe the dust from the brake drum, brake shoes and backplate. **Take great care not to inhale the dust, as it is injurious to health.**

5   Measure the brake shoe lining thickness. If it is worn down to the specified minimum amount, renew all four rear brake shoes. The shoes must also be renewed if any are contaminated with brake fluid or grease, or show signs of cracking or glazing. If contamination is evident, the cause must be traced and cured before fitting new brake shoes.

6   If the brake shoes are in a satisfactory condition proceed to paragraph 21. If removal is necessary, proceed as follows.

7   First make a careful note of the location and position of the various springs and linkages as an aid to refitting.

8   Depress the leading brake shoe hold-down spring while supporting the hold-down pin from the rear of the backplate with your finger. Turn the spring through 90° and lift off, then withdraw the hold-down pin.

9   Release the leading shoe from its lower pivot and disconnect the lower return spring. Remove the spring from both brake shoes.

10 Ease the upper end of the leading brake shoe out of its wheel cylinder location and detach it from the quadrant of the self-adjust mechanism. Disconnect the upper return spring and remove the leading shoe.

11 Remove the trailing shoe hold-down spring and pin as described in paragraph 8.

12 Disconnect the anti-rattle spring from the trailing shoe, release the shoe from its pivot locations and remove the shoe.

13 Check for signs of wear on the self-adjust mechanism and make sure that the quadrant and lever move freely on their pivots. The mechanism can be removed from the backplate if necessary after removing the handbrake cable clevis pin.

7.2 Remove the rear hub retaining nut

7.3 Withdraw the drum and hub assembly while holding the bearing and thrust washer

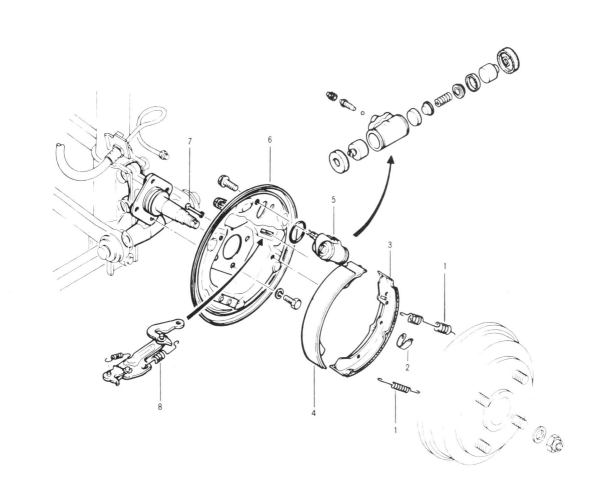

Fig. 9.7 Exploded view of the rear brake assembly (Secs 7 to 10)

1 Return spring	3 Trailing brake shoe	5 Wheel cylinder	7 Hold-down pin
2 Hold-down spring	4 Leading brake shoe	6 Backplate	8 Anti-rattle spring

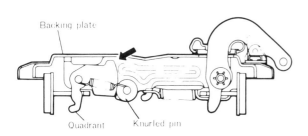

Fig. 9.8 Self-adjust mechanism quadrant (arrowed) set in
the fully retracted position (Sec 7)

7.15 Set the self-adjust mechanism quadrant in the fully retracted
position

14 Before fitting the new brake shoes clean off the brake backplate
with a rag and apply a trace of silicone grease to the brake shoe contact
areas, lower pivots and wheel cylinder pistons (photo).

15 Set the self-adjust mechanism in its fully retracted position by
easing the quadrant away from the knurled pin and turning it so that
touches the backplate (photo).

16 Engage the handbrake lever on the self-adjust mechanism with the
slot on the trailing brake shoe and place the shoe in position on the
backplate.

17 Refit the trailing shoe anti-rattle spring followed by the hold-down
pin and spring (photos).

18 Fit the upper and lower return springs to the trailing shoe then
connect them to the leading shoe (photo).

19 Locate the leading shoe over the self-adjust mechanism quadrant
then engage the shoe with its lower pivot and wheel cylinder piston
(photo).

20 Refit the leading shoe hold-down pin and spring (photo).

21 Tap the brake shoes up or down as necessary so that they are
central on the backplate and make sure that the self-adjust mechanism
is still fully retracted as described in paragraph 15.

22 Refit the brake drum and hub assembly then screw on a new hub
retaining nut.

23 Tighten the hub nut to a torque of 25 to 30 Nm (18 to 22 lbf ft)
while at the same time turning the drum to settle the bearings. Now
slacken the hub nut by one complete turn.

24 Using a spring balance connected to one of the wheel studs on the
brake drum, measure the torque at which the drum just starts to turn.
This should be 0.4 to 1.0 kg (0.9 to 2.2 lbs). Tighten the hub retaining
nut as necessary until the correct starting torque is obtained.

7.17A Refit the trailing shoe anti-rattle spring ...

7.14 Apply a trace of silicone grease to the areas arrowed

7.17B ... followed by the hold-down pin and spring

7.18 Fit the upper and lower return springs to both shoes

7.25 Stake the hub retaining nut using a round-nosed tool

7.19 Locate the leading shoe over the self-adjust mechanism quadrant

25 With the hub correctly adjusted, stake the retaining nut into the stub axle groove using a round nosed tool (photo).
26 Refit the handbrake lever stop or handbrake cable clevis pin if these were removed to facilitate drum removal.
27 Depress the footbrake two or three times and check that the brakes are operating correctly. Also check the operation of the handbrake then refit the roadwheel and hub cap and lower the car to the ground.

8 Rear wheel cylinder – removal and refitting

1 Remove the rear brake shoes as described in Section 7.
2 Using a brake hose clamp or similar tool, clamp the rear flexible brake hose to prevent loss of fluid during subsequent operations.
3 Wipe clean the area around the brake pipe union and wheel cylinder mounting bolts at the rear of the backplate.
4 Unscrew the brake pipe union nut and carefully withdraw the brake pipe from the wheel cylinder. Plug or tape over the end of the pipe to prevent dirt entry (photo).

7.20 Fit the leading shoe hold-down pin and spring

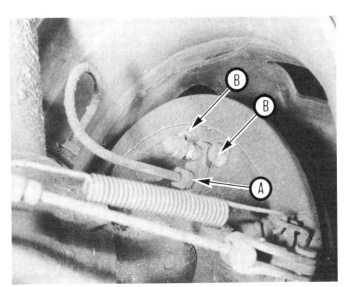
8.4 Brake pipe union nut (A) and wheel cylinder retaining bolts (B)

5 Undo the two retaining bolts and remove the wheel cylinder from the backplate.
6 To refit the wheel cylinder place it in position on the backplate and engage the brake pipe and union nut. Screw in the union nut two or three turns to ensure the thread has started.
7 Refit the wheel cylinder retaining bolts and tighten them to the specified torque. Now fully tighten the brake pipe union nut. Remove the clamp from the flexible brake hose.
8 Refit the brake shoes and the hub and drum assembly as described in Section 7, but do not depress the brake pedal or refit the roadwheel at this stage.
9 Refer to Section 14 and bleed the brake hydraulic system noting that if precautions were taken to minimise fluid loss it should only be necessary to bleed the relevant rear brake.
10 Check that the footbrake and handbrake are operating correctly then refit the roadwheel and lower the car to the ground.

9 Rear wheel cylinder – overhaul

1 Remove the wheel cylinder from the car as described in the previous Section.
2 With the cylinder on the bench, remove the bleed screw and the steel ball from the bleed screw orifice. It may be necessary to tap the cylinder on a block of wood to dislodge the ball.
3 Remove the dust covers and withdraw the pistons from each end of the cylinder.
4 Remove the fluid seals, filling blocks and spring by pushing them out from one end of the wheel cylinder bore.
5 Thoroughly clean all the components in methylated spirit or clean brake fluid and dry with a lint-free rag.
6 Carefully examine the surfaces of the pistons and cylinder bore for wear, score marks, ridges or corrosion and, if evident, renew the complete wheel cylinder. If the pistons and cylinder bore are in a satisfactory condition, obtain a repair kit consisting of new seals and dust covers.
7 Dip the new seals and pistons in clean brake fluid and assemble them wet as follows.
8 Refer to Fig. 9.9 and place the spring in the cylinder bore followed by the two filling blocks, one each side.
9 Insert a fluid seal into each end of the cylinder bore with the flat face of the seals facing outwards.
10 Fit the two pistons followed by the dust covers ensuring that the dust cover lips engage in the groove on the wheel cylinder body.
11 Place the steel ball in the bleed screw orifice and refit the bleed screw.
12 The wheel cylinder can now be refitted as described in the previous Section.

10 Rear brake backplate – removal and refitting

1 Remove the rear brake shoes as described in Section 7, and the rear wheel cylinder as described in Section 8.
2 Disconnect the handbrake cable from the brake shoe self-adjust mechanism by removing the clevis pin.
3 Undo the four retaining bolts and remove the backplate from the stub axle.
4 Examine the backplate for signs of damage, distortion or severe corrosion and renew the backplate if necessary.
5 Refitting is the reverse sequence of removal, but tighten the backplate retaining bolts to the specified torque.

11 Master cylinder – removal and refitting

1 Unscrew the master cylinder reservoir filler cap, place a piece of polythene over the filler neck and refit the cap. This will minimise brake fluid loss during subsequent operations. As an added precaution place absorbent rags beneath the brake pipe unions on the master cylinder.
2 Disconnect the brake fluid level warning light lead at the wiring connector.
3 Wipe clean the area around the brake pipe unions on the side of the master cylinder. Unscrew the two union nuts and carefully withdraw the pipes. Plug or tape over the pipe ends and the orifices in the master cylinder to prevent loss of fluid and dirt entry. Take care not to allow any brake fluid to come into contact with the vehicle paintwork.
4 Undo the two nuts securing the master cylinder to the vacuum servo unit and withdraw the unit from its location.
5 Refitting the master cylinder is the reverse sequence of removal. Tighten the retaining nuts to the specified torque and on completion, bleed the brake hydraulic system as described in Section 14.

12 Master cylinder – overhaul

1 Remove the master cylinder as described in Section 11.
2 Drain and discard the fluid from the master cylinder reservoir, then prepare a clean uncluttered working surface ready for dismantling.
3 Remove the retaining screw then carefully ease the reservoir off the rubber bush seals on the cylinder body.
4 Extract the bush seals from the master cylinder inlet ports.
5 At the base of the cylinder body remove the stopper bolt and O-ring that retain the secondary piston.

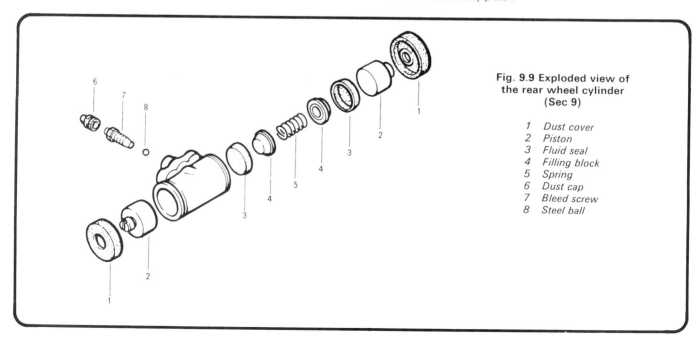

Fig. 9.9 Exploded view of the rear wheel cylinder (Sec 9)

1 Dust cover
2 Piston
3 Fluid seal
4 Filling block
5 Spring
6 Dust cap
7 Bleed screw
8 Steel ball

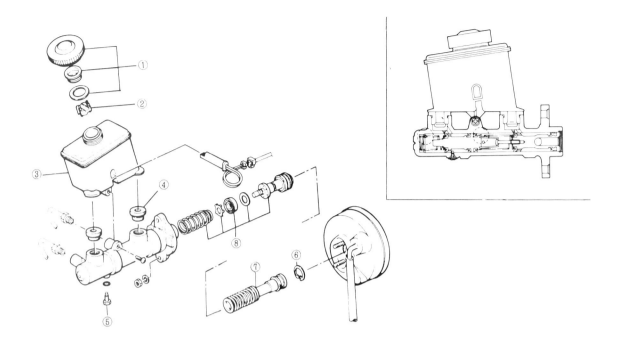

Fig. 9.10 Exploded view of the brake master cylinder (Secs 11 and 12)

1 Reservoir filler cap assembly	3 Reservoir	5 Stopper bolt	7 Primary piston assembly
2 Float	4 Rubber bush seal	6 Primary piston circlip	8 Secondary piston assembly

6   Using circlip pliers, extract the primary piston retaining circlip from the end of the cylinder bore.

7   Withdraw the primary piston assembly followed by the secondary piston assembly. It may be necessary to tap the cylinder body on a block of wood to release the pistons.

8   Note the location and position of the components on the secondary piston then remove the spring, spreader plate, first rubber seal, shims, then the second and third rubber seals.

9   The primary piston should not be dismantled, as parts are not available separately. If the master cylinder is in a serviceable condition, and is to be re-used, a complete new primary piston assembly is included in the repair kit.

10 With the master cylinder completely dismantled, clean all the components in methylated spirit, or clean brake fluid, and dry with a lint-free rag.

11 Carefully examine the cylinder bore and secondary piston for signs of wear, scoring or corrosion, and if evident renew the complete cylinder assembly.

12 If the components are in a satisfactory condition, obtain a repair kit consisting of new seals, springs and primary piston assembly.

13 Lubricate the master cylinder bore, pistons and seals thoroughly in clean brake fluid, and assemble them wet.

14 Using the fingers only fit the new rubber seals, shim, spreader plate and spring to the secondary piston using the reverse of the dismantling sequence and with reference to Figs. 9.10 and 9.11.

15 Insert the secondary piston assembly into the cylinder bore taking care not to turn over the lips of the seals as the piston is inserted.

16 Insert the new primary piston assembly into the cylinder bore again taking care not to turn over the seal lips as they enter the bore.

17 Refit the primary piston retaining circlip and the secondary piston stopper bolt using a new O-ring.

18 Fit the new reservoir bush seals to the inlet ports and push the reservoir firmly into place. Refit the reservoir retaining screw.

19 The master cylinder can now be refitted to the car as described in Section 11.

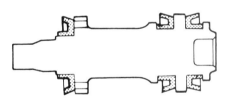

**Fig. 9.11 Secondary piston rubber seal arrangement
(Sec 12)**

13 Hydraulic pipes and hoses – inspection, removal and refitting

1   At intervals given in Routine Maintenance carefully examine all brake pipes, hoses, hose connections and pipe unions.

2   First check for signs of leakage at the pipe unions. Then examine the flexible hoses for signs of cracking, chafing and fraying (photo).

3   The brake pipes must be examined carefully and methodically. They must be cleaned off and checked for signs of dents, corrosion or other damage. Corrosion should be scraped off and, if the depth of pitting is significant, the pipes renewed. This is particularly likely in those areas underneath the vehicle body where the pipes are exposed and unprotected.

4   If any section of pipe or hose is to be removed, first unscrew the master cylinder reservoir filler cap, place a piece of polythene over the filler neck and refit the cap. This will minimise brake fluid loss when the pipe or hose is removed.

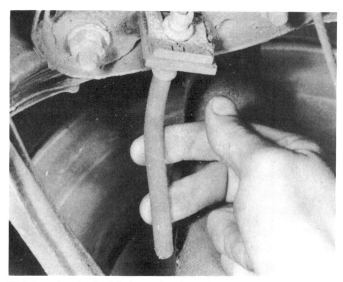

13.2 Examine the flexible hoses for signs of cracking, chafing and fraying

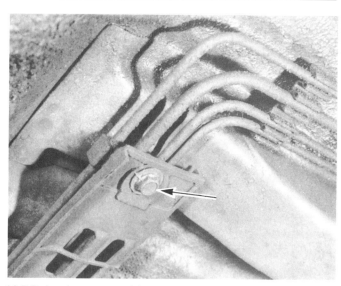

13.5 Brake pipe cover retaining screw (arrowed)

5   Brake pipe removal is usually quite straightforward. The union nuts at each end are undone, the pipe and union pulled out and the centre section of the pipe removed from the body clips. Where the union nuts are exposed to the full force of the weather they can sometimes be quite tight. As only an open-ended spanner can be used, burring of the flats on the nuts is not uncommon when attempting to undo them. For this reason a self-locking wrench is often the only way to separate a stubborn union. To gain access to the pipes under the centre section of the car it will first be necessary to undo the screws and remove the plastic protection covers (photo).

6   To remove a flexible hose, wipe the unions and brackets free of dirt and undo the union nut from the brake pipe end(s).
7   Next extract the hose retaining clip (photo) and lift the end of the hose out of its bracket. If a front hose is being removed, it can now be unscrewed from the brake caliper (photo).
8   Brake pipes can be obtained individually, or in sets, from most accessory shops or garages with the end flares and union nuts in place. The pipe is then bent to shape, using the old pipe as a guide, and is ready for fitting to the car.
9   Refitting the pipes and hoses is a reverse of the removal sequence.

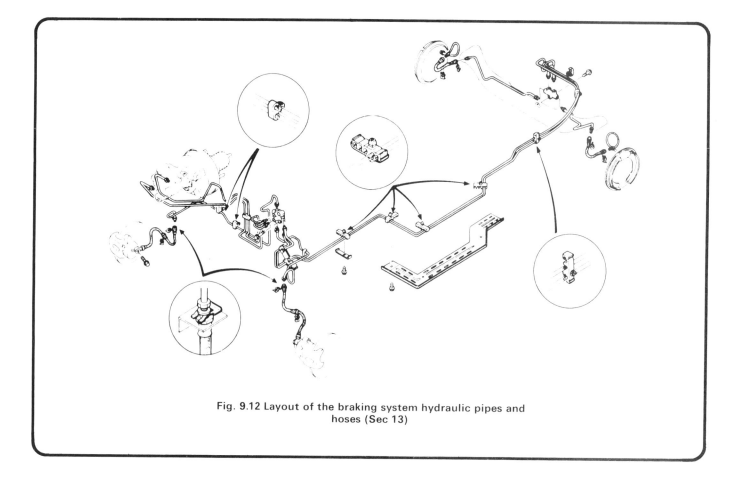

Fig. 9.12 Layout of the braking system hydraulic pipes and hoses (Sec 13)

13.7A Brake hose retaining clip ...

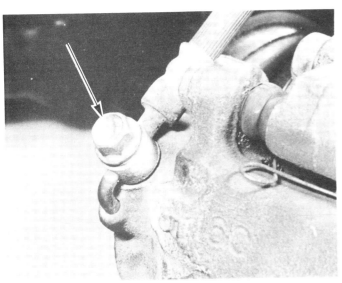

13.7B ... and hose to caliper union bolt (arrowed)

Make sure that the hoses are not kinked when in position and also make sure that the brake pipes are securely supported in their clips. After refitting, remove the polythene from the reservoir and bleed the brake hydraulic system, as described in Section 14.

14 Hydraulic system – bleeding

1   The correct functioning of the brake hydraulic system is only possible after removal of all air from the components and circuit; this is achieved by bleeding the system. Note that only clean unused brake fluid, which has remained unshaken for at least 24 hours, must be used.
2   If there is any possibility of incorrect fluid being used in the system, the brake lines and components must be completely flushed with uncontaminated fluid and new seals fitted to the components.
3   *Never reuse brake fluid which has been bled from the system.*
4   During the procedure, do not allow the level of brake fluid to drop more than halfway down the reservoir.
5   Before starting work, check that all pipes and hoses are secure, unions tight and bleed screws closed. Take great care not to allow brake fluid to come into contact with the car paintwork, otherwise the

finish will be seriously damaged. Wash off any spilled fluid immediately with cold water.
6   There are a number of one-man, do-it-yourself, brake bleeding kits currently available from motor accessory shops. Always follow the instructions supplied with the kit. It is recommended that one of these kits is used wherever possible, as they greatly simplify the bleeding operation and also reduce the risk of expelled air and fluid being drawn back into the system. If one of these kits is not available, it will be necessary to gather together a clean jar and a suitable length of clear plastic tubing which is a tight fit over the bleed screw, and also to engage the help of an assistant.
7   If brake fluid has been lost from the master cylinder due to a leak in the system, ensure that the cause is traced and rectified before proceeding further.
8   If the hydraulic system has only been partially disconnected and suitable precautions were taken to prevent further loss of fluid it should only be necessary to bleed the part of the system being worked on (i.e. at the brake caliper or wheel cylinder nearest to the disconnected pipe or hose).
9   If the complete system is to be bled then it should be done in the following sequence:

    (a) Right-hand front brake caliper
    (b) Left-hand rear wheel cylinder
    (c) Right-hand rear wheel cylinder
    (d) Left-hand front brake caliper

10   To bleed the system, first clean the area around the bleed screw (photo) and fit the bleed tube. If necessary top up the master cylinder reservoir with brake fluid.
11   If the system incorporates a vacuum servo, destroy the vacuum by giving several applications of the brake pedal in quick succession.

14.10 Front brake caliper bleed screw (arrowed)

Bleeding – two man method
12   Gather together a clean jar and a length of rubber or plastic tubing which will be a tight fit on the brake bleed screws.
13   Engage the help of an assistant.
14   Push one end of the bleed tube onto the first bleed screw and immerse the other end in the jar which should contain enough hydraulic fluid to cover the end of the tube.
15   Open the bleed screw one half a turn and have your assistant depress the brake pedal fully then slowly release it. Tighten the bleed screw at the end of each pedal downstroke to obviate any chance of air or fluid being drawn back into the system.
16   Repeat this operation until clean brake fluid, free from air bubbles, can be seen coming through into the jar.
17   Tighten the bleed screw at the end of a pedal downstroke and remove the bleed tube. Bleed the remaining screws in a similar way.

Bleeding – using one-way valve kit

18 There are a number of one-man, one-way brake bleeding kits available from motor accessory shops. It is recommended that one of these kits is used wherever possible as it will greatly simplify the bleeding operation and also reduce the risk of air or fluid being drawn back into the system, quite apart from being able to do the work without the help of an assistant.

19 To use the kit, connect the tube to the bleed screw and open the screw one half turn.

20 Depress the brake pedal fully then slowly release it. The one-way valve in the kit will prevent expelled air from returning at the end of each pedal downstroke. Repeat this operation several times to be sure of ejecting all air from the system. Some kits include a translucent container which can be positioned so that the air bubbles can actually be seen being ejected from the system.

21 Tighten the bleed screw, remove the tube and repeat the operations on the remaining brakes.

22 On completion, depress the brake pedal. If it still feels spongy, repeat the bleeding operations, as air must still be trapped in the system.

Bleeding – using a pressure bleeding kit

23 These kits are available from motor accessory shops and are usually operated by air pressure from the spare tyre.

24 By connecting a pressurised container to the master cylinder fluid reservoir, bleeding is then carried out simply by opening each bleed screw in turn and allowing the fluid to run out, rather like turning on a tap, until no air is visible in the expelled fluid.

25 By using this method, the large reserve of brake fluid provides a safeguard against air being drawn into the master cylinder during bleeding which may occur if the fluid level in the reservoir is not maintained.

26 Pressure bleeding is particularly effective when bleeding 'difficult' systems or when bleeding the complete system at the time of routine fluid renewal.

All methods

27 When bleeding is completed, check and top up the fluid level in the master cylinder reservoir.

28 Check the feel of the brake pedal. If it feels at all spongy, air must still be present in the system and the need for further bleeding is indicated. Failure to bleed satisfactorily after a reasonable repetition of the bleeding operations may be due to worn master cylinder seals.

29 Discard brake fluid which has been expelled. It is almost certain to be contaminated with moisture, air and dirt, making it unsuitable for further use. Clean fluid should always be stored in an airtight container as it is hygroscopic (absorbs moisture readily) which lowers its boiling point and could affect braking performance under severe conditions.

15 Handbrake – adjustment

1 Normal adjustment of the handbrake is automatically achieved by the self-adjust mechanism on the rear brake shoes. However, to provide an initial setting and to provide for stretch in the cable, a facility for manual adjustment is provided at the forward end of the cable.

2 To check whether adjustment is necessary first apply the footbrake firmly two or three times to ensure full movement of the self-adjust mechanism on the rear brake shoes. This is particularly important if the brake drums have recently been removed.

3 Now apply the handbrake in the normal way and count the number of clicks of the ratchet. Under a normal pull (approximately 10 kg – 22 lb) the lever should be applied by between 5 and 9 clicks of the ratchet.

4 If this is not the case, adjustment can be made at the handbrake end of the cable.

5 Using a suitable spanner on the adjusting nut at the end of the cable, turn the nut as necessary until the correct adjustment is obtained.

6 Release the lever and make sure that the car is free to roll and the rear brakes are not binding.

7 Switch on the ignition and check that the warning light on the instrument panel illuminates when the handbrake lever is applied by one click. If not, reposition the warning light switch on the side of the lever by slackening the retaining bolt and moving the switch slightly in

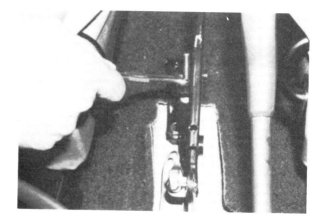

Fig. 9.13 Handbrake cable adjustment (Sec 15)

its elongated slot. Tighten the bolt when the switch is positioned correctly.

8 Refit the centre console as described in Chapter 11 after adjustment.

16 Handbrake lever assembly – removal and refitting

1 Remove the centre console as described in Chapter 11.

2 Unscrew the handbrake cable adjusting nut and withdraw the cable from the lever assembly.

3 Disconnect the warning light switch wiring.

4 Undo the retaining bolts and remove the lever assembly from the car.

5 Refitting is the reverse sequence of removal. Adjust the handbrake cable as described in the previous Section before refitting the centre console.

17 Handbrake cable – removal and refitting

1 Chock the front wheels, jack up the rear of the car and securely support it on axle stands.

2 Refer to Chapter 11 and remove the centre console.

3 Unscrew the handbrake cable adjusting nut and remove the cable from the handbrake lever.

4 From under the rear of the car, disconnect the return spring, extract the split pin then remove the clevis pin securing the cable ends to the levers at the rear of each brake backplate (photo).

5 Undo the two nuts and release the cable compensator assembly from the support bracket on the underbody (photo).

6 Extract the retaining clips and remove the cable guides from the rear crossmember.

7 Undo the cable clip retaining bolts and withdraw the cable assembly from under the car (photo).

8 Refitting is the reverse sequence of removal, bearing in mind the following points.

   (a) Use new split pins to secure the cable to rear brake lever clevis pins
   (b) Lubricate the exposed linkages and cable guides with multi-purpose grease
   (c) Adjust the cable as described in Section 15 before refitting the centre console

18 Footbrake pedal – removal and refitting

1 Remove the cover under the facia to gain access to the pedal mounting.

2 Extract the split pin then remove the clevis pin securing the vacuum servo unit pushrod to the brake pedal (photo).

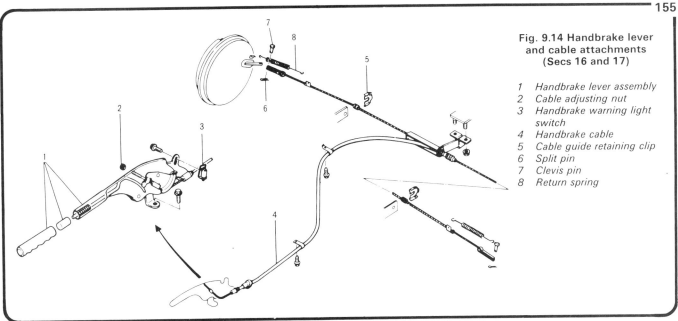

Fig. 9.14 Handbrake lever
and cable attachments
(Secs 16 and 17)

1 Handbrake lever assembly
2 Cable adjusting nut
3 Handbrake warning light
   switch
4 Handbrake cable
5 Cable guide retaining clip
6 Split pin
7 Clevis pin
8 Return spring

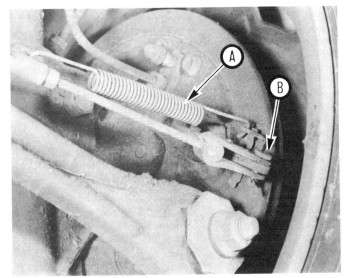

17.4 Handbrake cable return spring (A) and clevis pin (B)

17.5 Cable compensator retaining nuts (arrowed)

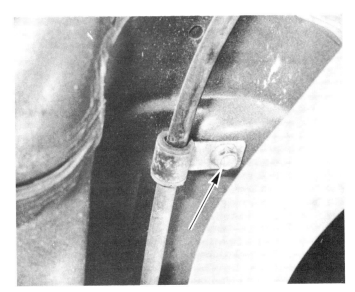

17.7 Cable clip retaining bolt (arrowed)

18.2 Vacuum servo pushrod clevis pin (A) and brake pedal pivot
bolt (B)

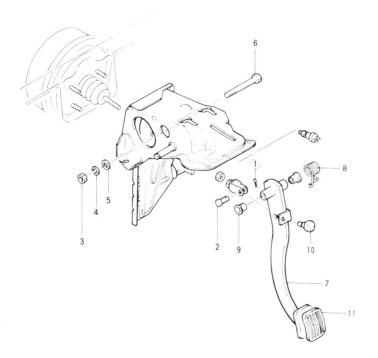

Fig. 9.15 Exploded view of the footbrake pedal components (Sec 18)

1   Split pin
2   Clevis pin
3   Nut
4   Split washer
5   Flat washer
6   Pivot bolt
7   Footbrake pedal
8   Return spring
9   Pivot bushes
10 Return stop
11 Pedal pad

3   Undo the brake pedal pivot bolt retaining nut and recover the washers.
4   Disengage the return spring from the pedal, withdraw the pivot bolt and remove the pedal from under the facia.
5   With the pedal removed, check for wear or damage to the pivot bushes and renew them if necessary.
6   Refitting is the reverse sequence of removal, but lubricate the pivot bushes and clevis pin with multi-purpose grease before fitting. With the pedal installed check and if necessary adjust the pedal height and free play as described in Section 3, before refitting the cover under the facia.

19 Brake light switch – removal, refitting and adjustment

1   Remove the cover under the facia to gain access to the switch.
2   Disconnect the wiring at the switch, unscrew the locknut then unscrew the switch from the brake pedal bracket (photo).
3   When refitting the switch, screw it in until it just touches the brake pedal, then screw it in a further half a turn. Tighten the locknut and reconnect the wiring.
4   Refit the cover under the facia.

20 Vacuum servo unit – general

A vacuum servo unit is fitted into the brake hydraulic circuit in series with the master cylinder, to provide assistance to the driver when the brake pedal is depressed. This reduces the effort required by the driver to operate the brakes under all braking conditions.
The unit operates by vacuum obtained from the inlet manifold and comprises basically a booster diaphragm, control valve, and a non-return valve.
The servo unit and hydraulic master cylinder are connected together so that the servo unit piston rod acts as the master cylinder pushrod. The driver's braking effort is transmitted through another pushrod to the servo unit piston and its built-in control system. The servo unit piston does not fit tightly into the cylinder, but has a strong diaphragm to keep its edges in constant contact with the cylinder wall, so ensuring an airtight seal between the two parts. The forward chamber is held under vacuum conditions created in the inlet manifold of the engine and, during periods when the brake pedal is not in use,

19.2 Brake light switch locknut (arrowed)

the controls open a passage to the rear chamber so placing it under vacuum conditions as well. When the brake pedal is depressed, the vacuum passage to the rear chamber is cut off and the chamber opened to atmospheric pressure. The consequent rush of air pushes the servo piston forward in the vacuum chamber and operates the main pushrod to the master cylinder.
To test the operation of the servo, depress the footbrake several times, hold it down and then start the engine. As the engine starts there should be a noticeable 'give' in the brake pedal. Allow the engine to run for at least two minutes and then switch it off. If the brake pedal is now depressed it should feel normal, but further applications should result in the pedal feeling firmer, with the pedal stroke progressively decreasing with each application. If the servo does not operate as described, remove the vacuum hose from the inlet manifold and servo unit and examine the hose for damage, splits, cracks or general

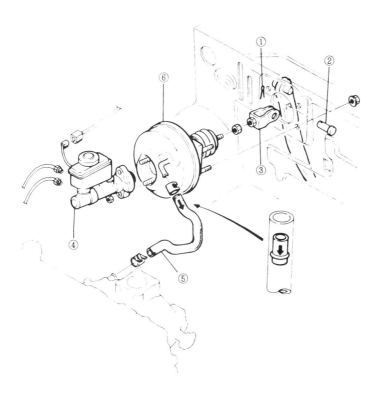

Fig. 9.16 Vacuum servo unit
attachments
(Secs 20 and 21)

1   Split pin
2   Clevis pin
3   Servo pushrod yoke
4   Master cylinder
5   Vacuum hose
6   Vacuum servo unit

deterioration. Make sure that the check valve inside the hose is working correctly by blowing through the hose from the servo end. Air should flow in this direction, but not when blown through from the engine end. Renew the hose and check valve assembly if it is at all suspect. If the servo still fails to operate satisfactorily the fault lies with the servo. Repairs to the servo unit are possible, but special tools are necessary and the work should be entrusted to a suitably equipped Mazda dealer.

21 Vacuum servo unit – removal and refitting

1   Remove the cover under the facia to gain access to the servo pushrod attachment.
2   Extract the split pin and withdraw the clevis pin securing the servo pushrod to the brake pedal.
3   Working in the engine compartment disconnect the vacuum hose at the elbow connection on the servo unit.
4   Refer to Section 11 and remove the brake master cylinder.
5   From under the facia, undo the four nuts securing the servo to the bulkhead and remove the unit from the engine compartment (photo).
6   Before refitting, it is necessary to measure the length of the servo unit output rod and adjust it if necessary using the following procedure.
7   Using a depth gauge, measure the distance from the end of the master cylinder to the bottom of the primary piston bore (Fig. 9.17). Call this dimension A.
8   Now measure the distance from the end of the master cylinder to the edge of the mounting flange (Fig. 9.17). Call this dimension B.
9   On the servo unit measure the distance from the master cylinder mating face to the end of the output rod (Fig. 9.17). Call this dimension C. Calculate the output rod clearance D using the following formula:

$$D = (A-B) - C$$

The output rod clearance D should be as given in the Specifications at the beginning of this Chapter. If adjustment is necessary, slacken the locknut and turn the end of the output rod as necessary until its length

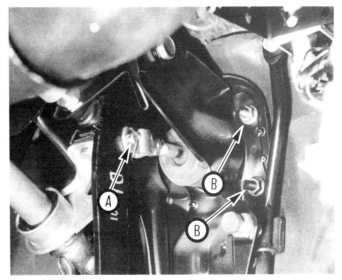

21.5 Vacuum servo pushrod clevis pin (A) and servo unit retaining nuts (B)

is correct to achieve the specified clearance. Tighten the locknut after adjustment.
10 After setting the output rod clearance the servo can be fitted using the reverse of the removal sequence, but bearing in mind the following points.

(a) Tighten the servo mounting nuts to the specified torque
(b) Use a new split pin to secure the servo pushrod clevis pin
(c) Refit the master cylinder as described in Section 11 and bleed the hydraulic system as described in Section 14.

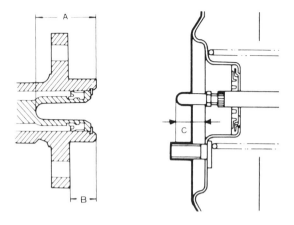

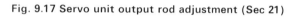

Fig. 9.17 Servo unit output rod adjustment (Sec 21)

A   Master cylinder edge to base of primary piston bore dimension
B   Master cylinder edge to mounting flange dimension
C   Master cylinder mating face on servo to end of output rod
    dimension

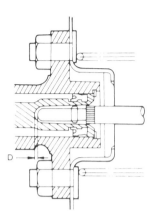

Fig. 9.18 Servo unit output rod clearance (Sec 21)

D   Specified clearance

22 Fault diagnosis – braking system

Symptom	Reason(s)
Excessive pedal travel	Rear brake self-adjust mechanism inoperative Air in hydraulic system Faulty master cylinder
Brake pedal feels spongy	Air in hydraulic system Faulty master cylinder
Judder felt through brake pedal or steering wheel when braking	Excessive run-out or distortion of front discs or rear drums Disc pads or brake linings worn Brake backplate or disc caliper loose Wear in suspension or steering components or mountings (Chapter 10)
Excessive pedal pressure required to stop car	Faulty servo unit, disconnected, damaged or insecure vacuum hose Wheel cylinder(s) or caliper piston seized Disc pads or brake shoe linings worn or contaminated Brake shoes incorrectly fitted Incorrect grade of pads or linings fitted Primary or secondary hydraulic circuit failure
Brakes pull to one side	Disc pads or linings worn or contaminated Wheel cylinder or caliper piston seized Seized rear brake self-adjust mechanism Disc pads or linings renewed on one side only Faulty dual proportioning valve Tyre, steering or suspension defect (Chapter 10)
Brakes binding	Wheel cylinder or caliper piston seized Handbrake incorrectly adjusted Faulty master cylinder
Rear wheels locking under normal braking	Rear brake shoe linings contaminated Faulty dual proportioning valve

Chapter 10 Suspension and steering

For modifications, and information applicable to later models, see Supplement at end of manual

Contents

Specifications

Front suspension

Type	Independent by MacPherson struts with coil springs and integral shock absorbers. Anti-roll bar on 1500 GT models
Coil spring free length	364.5 mm (14.36 in)
Spring wire diameter (maximum)	12.5 mm (0.49 in)
Spring coil diameter	132.5 mm (5.2 in)
Number of spring coils	5.8

Rear suspension

Type	Independent by MacPherson struts with coil springs and integral shock absorbers located by lateral links and trailing arm. Anti-roll bar on all models
Coil spring free length	357.5 mm (14.07 in)
Spring wire diameter (maximum)	11.5 mm (0.45 in)
Spring coil diameter	114 mm (4.49 in)
Number of spring coils	7.05
Rear wheel toe setting	Parallel

Steering

Type	Rack and pinion
Turns lock-to-lock	3.6
Steering wheel diameter	380 mm (14.97 in)
Camber angle	0° 55′
Castor angle	1° 45′
Steering axis inclination	12° 10′
Toe setting	3 mm (0.12 in) toe-in to 3 mm (0.12 in) toe-out (nominally parallel)
Steering gear lubricant	Lithium based grease

Roadwheels
Wheel size	4¹/2 J x 13 or 5J x 13 steel or aluminium alloy

Tyres
Tyre size	6.15-13-4PR, 155 SR 13 or 175/70 SR 13

Tyre pressures – cold (all models):
Front and rear	1.8 bar (26 lbf/in²)

Torque wrench settings
Front suspension

	Nm	lbf ft
Swivel hub to suspension strut	80 to 119	59 to 88
Lower arm balljoint pinch-bolt	44 to 55	33 to 40
Balljoint to lower suspension arm	95 to 119	70 to 88
Brake disc to hub flange	44 to 55	33 to 40
Brake caliper mounting bracket to swivel hub	56 to 66	41 to 49
Driveshaft retaining nut	160 to 240	116 to 174
Suspension strut upper mounting to body	23 to 30	17 to 22
Suspension strut spindle to upper mounting	76 to 95	56 to 70
Lower suspension arm rear mounting bracket to body	60 to 75	44 to 55
Lower suspension arm front mounting bracket to body	95 to 119	70 to 88
Lower suspension arm to mounting bracket nuts	76 to 95	56 to 70
Anti-roll bar connecting link lock nut	12 to 18	9 to 13

Rear suspension

	Nm	lbf ft
Suspension strut upper mounting to body	22 to 27	16 to 20
Suspension strut spindle to upper mounting	56 to 82	41 to 60
Trailing arm to suspension strut	55 to 69	40 to 51
Trailing arm to body	60 to 75	44 to 55
Lateral links to stub axle	95 to 119	70 to 88
Lateral links to crossmember	95 to 119	70 to 88
Stub axle to suspension strut	95 to 119	70 to 88
Brake backplate to stub axle	46 to 68	34 to 50
Anti-roll bar to trailing arm	32 to 47	23 to 35

Steering

	Nm	lbf ft
Steering wheel retaining nut	40 to 50	29 to 37
Steering column retaining bolts	16 to 23	12 to 17
Universal joint clamp bolts	18 to 27	13 to 20
Steering gear mounting brackets to bulkhead	32 to 47	23 to 35
Steering gear tie-rod to rack	85 to 95	63 to 70
Tie-rod outer balljoint retaining nut	30 to 45	22 to 33
Tie-rod outer balljoint locknut	35 to 40	26 to 29

Roadwheels

	Nm	lbf ft
Wheel nuts (all models)	90 to 110	65 to 80

1 General description

The independent front suspension is of the MacPherson strut type, incorporating coil springs and integral telescopic shock absorbers. Lateral and longitudinal location of each strut assembly is by pressed steel lower suspension arms utilizing rubber inner mounting bushes and incorporating a balljoint at their outer ends. On 1500 GT models both lower suspension arms are interconnected by an anti-roll bar. The front swivel hubs, which carry the wheel bearings, brake calipers and the hub/disc assemblies, are bolted to the MacPherson struts and connected to the lower arms via the balljoints.

The fully independent rear suspension also utilizes MacPherson struts located by lateral and trailing links and interconnected by a rear anti-roll bar.

The steering gear is of the conventional rack and pinion type located behind the front wheels. Movement of the steering wheel is transmitted to the steering gear by an intermediate shaft and two universal joints. The front wheels are connected to the steering gear by tie-rods, each having an inner and outer balljoint.

2 Maintenance and inspection

1 At the intervals given in Routine Maintenance at the beginning of this manual a thorough inspection of all suspension and steering components should be carried out using the following procedure as a guide.

Front suspension and steering
2 Apply the handbrake, jack up the front of the car and support it securely on axle stands.

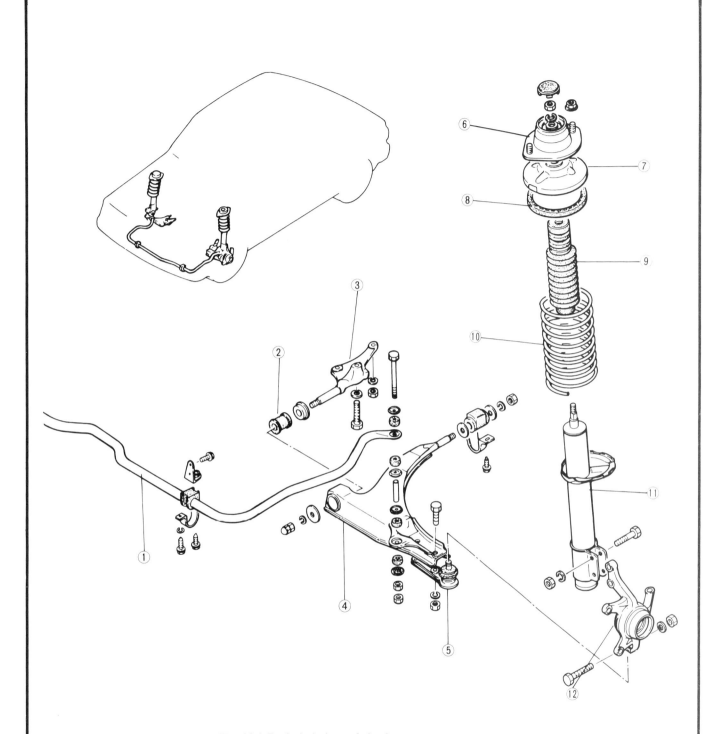

Fig. 10.1 Exploded view of the front suspension (Sec 1)

1 Anti-roll bar
2 Mounting block
3 Lower suspension arm front mounting bracket
4 Lower suspension arm
5 Lower suspension arm balljoint
6 Suspension strut upper mounting
7 Spring seat
8 Rubber ring
9 Strut spindle dust cover
10 Coil spring
11 Front suspension strut
12 Swivel hub

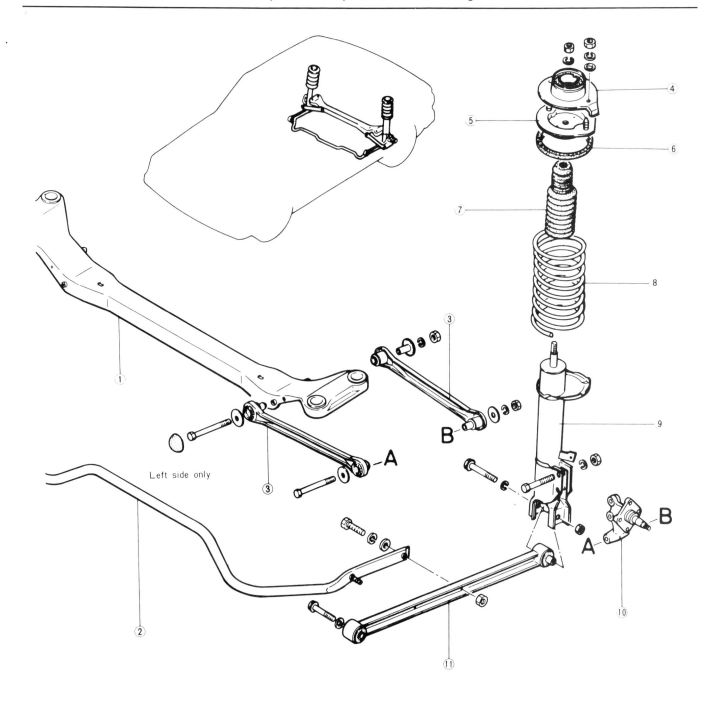

Fig. 10.2 Exploded view of the rear suspension (Sec 1)

1   Crossmember
2   Anti-roll bar
3   Lateral link
4   Suspension strut upper
    mounting
5   Spring seat
6   Rubber ring
7   Strut spindle dust cover
8   Coil spring
9   Rear suspension strut
10 Rear stub axle
11 Trailing arm

3   Visually inspect the lower balljoint dust covers and the steering gear rubber boots (photo) for splits, chafing, or deterioration. Renew the rubber boots or the balljoint assembly, as described in Sections 22 and 8 respectively, if any damage is apparent.
4   Grasp the roadwheel at the 12 o'clock and 6 o'clock positions and try to rock it. Very slight free play may be felt, but if the movement is appreciable further investigation is necessary to determine the source. Continue rocking the wheel while an assistant depresses the footbrake. If the movement is now eliminated or significantly reduced, it is likely that the hub bearings are at fault. If the free play is still evident with the footbrake depressed, then there is wear in the suspension joints or mountings. Pay close attention to the lower balljoint and lower arm

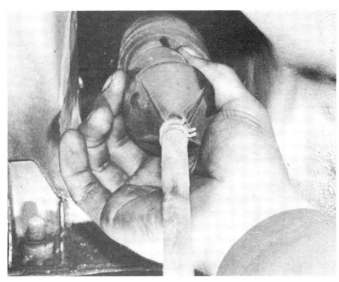

2.3 Check the steering gear rubber boot for splits, chafing or deterioration

mounting bushes. Renew any worn components, as described in the appropriate Sections of this Chapter.

5   Now grasp the wheel at the 9 o'clock and 3 o'clock positions and try to rock it as before. Any movement felt now may again be caused by wear in the hub bearings or the steering tie-rod inner or outer balljoints. If the outer balljoint is worn the visual movement will be obvious. If the inner joint is suspect, it can be felt by placing a hand over the rack and pinion rubber boot and gripping the tie-rod. If the wheel is now rocked, movement will be felt at the inner joint if wear has taken place. Repair procedures are described in Sections 4 and 25.

6   Using a large screwdriver or flat bar check for wear in the anti-roll bar mountings (where fitted) and lower arm mountings by carefully levering against these components. Some movement is to be expected, as the mountings are made of rubber, but excessive wear should be obvious. Renew any bushes that are worn.

7   With the car standing on its wheels, have an assistant turn the steering wheel back and forth about one eight of a turn each way. There should be no lost movement whatever between the steering wheel and roadwheels. If this is not the case, closely observe the joints and mountings previously described, but in addition check the intermediate shaft universal joints for wear and also the rack and pinion steering gear itself. Any wear should be visually apparent and must be rectified, as described in the appropriate Sections of this Chapter.

Rear suspension

8   Chock the front wheels, jack up the rear of the car and support it securely on axle stands.

9   Visually inspect the rear suspension components, attachments and linkages for any visible signs of wear or damage.

10 Grasp the roadwheel at the 12 o'clock and 6 o'clock positions and try to rock it. Any excess movement here indicates wear or maladjusted hub bearings which may also be accompanied by a rumbling sound when the wheel is spun. Repair procedures are described in Section 11.

Wheels and tyres

11 Carefully inspect each tyre, including the spare, for signs of uneven wear, lumps, bulges or damage to the sidewalls or tread face. Refer to Section 27 for further details.

12 Check the condition of the wheel rims for distortion, damage and excessive run-out. Also make sure that the balance weights are secure with no obvious signs that any are missing. Check the torque of the wheel nuts and check the tyre pressures.

Shock absorbers

13 Check for any signs of fluid leakage around the shock absorber body or from the rubber boot around the spindle. Should any fluid be noticed the shock absorber is defective internally and renewal is necessary.

14 The efficiency of the shock absorber may be checked by bouncing the car at each corner. Generally speaking the body will return to its normal position and stop after being depressed. If it rises and returns on a rebound, the shock absorber is probably suspect. Examine also the shock absorber upper and lower mountings for any sign of wear. Renewal procedures are contained in Sections 6 and 13.

3   Front swivel hub assembly – removal and refitting

1   Chock the rear wheels, firmly apply the handbrake then jack up the front of the car and support it on axle stands. Remove the appropriate front roadwheel.

2   Using a hammer and suitable chisel nosed tool, tap up the staking securing the driveshaft retaining nut to the groove in the constant velocity joint. Note that a new driveshaft retaining nut must be obtained for reassembly.

3   Have an assistant firmly depress the footbrake then using a socket and long bar, undo and remove the driveshaft retaining nut and washer.

4   If an anti-roll bar is fitted, undo the two locknuts and remove the connecting link bolt securing the anti-roll bar to the lower suspension arm. Recover the washers and rubber bushes noting their fitted positions.

5   Using a screwdriver, release the clip securing the flexible brake hose to the bracket on the suspension strut.

Fig. 10.3 Releasing the driveshaft retaining nut staking (Sec 3)

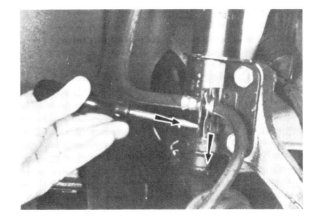

Fig. 10.4 Flexible brake hose retaining clip removal (Sec 3)

3.6 Brake caliper mounting bracket to swivel hub retaining bolts (arrowed)

Fig. 10.5 Front swivel hub assembly removal (Sec 3)

6   Undo the two bolts securing the brake caliper mounting bracket to the swivel hub (photo). Slide the caliper assembly, complete with disc pads, off the swivel hub and suspend it from one of the spring coils using string or wire.

7   Extract the split pin then unscrew the nut securing the tie-rod outer balljoint to the steering arm. Release the balljoint from the steering arm using a suitable extractor (see Section 21).

8   Undo the nut and remove the pinch-bolt securing the lower arm balljoint to the swivel hub.

9   Undo the nuts and remove the two bolts securing the swivel hub to the suspension strut.

10   Release the swivel hub from the strut and then lift the swivel hub while levering down on the lower arm to disengage the balljoint. Withdraw the swivel hub assembly from the driveshaft and remove it from the car.

11   Refitting the swivel hub is the reverse sequence of removal bearing in mind the following points:

    (a) Tighten all nuts and bolts to the specified torque

    (b) When fitting the new driveshaft retaining nut, tighten it to the specified torque then stake it into the groove in the constant velocity joint using a round nosed tool (Fig. 10.6)

    (c) Use a new split pin to secure the tie-rod balljoint retaining nut

Fig. 10.6 Driveshaft retaining nut staking (Sec 3)

more than
4 mm
0.16 in

---

4   Front hub bearings – removal and refitting

1   Remove the swivel hub assembly from the car as described in the previous Section.

2   Securely support the swivel hub in a vice and separate the hub and disc assembly by driving the hub out of the bearings using a hammer and tube of suitable diameter. Alternatively, if Mazda special tool 49 B001 726 can be obtained, this should be used to release the hub and disc assembly (Fig. 10.8).

3   The oil seal and outer bearing inner race will remain on the hub as it is removed. The bearing should now be withdrawn using a suitable puller. With the bearing removed, slide off the oil seal.

4   If the disc or hub require attention, undo the four bolts and separate the disc from the hub (photo).

5   Recover the spacer from the inner face of the bearing remaining in the swivel hub.

6   From the rear of the swivel hub extract the oil seal by prising it out with a screwdriver then lift out the inner bearing inner race.

7   Using a hammer and suitable drift, drive out one of the bearing outer races from the centre of the hub (Fig. 10.9). Remove the race gradually and carefully by tapping it a little bit at a time on one side,

then the other, taking care to keep it level in the hub bore. After removal of the first race, turn the hub over and remove the other race in the same way.

8   If necessary the disc dust cover can be removed by prising it off the hub using a screwdriver. Do not remove the dust cover unles it is damaged and requires renewal or is being transferred to a new swivel hub.

9   Wipe away any surplus grease from the bearings and swivel hub, then clean all the components thoroughly using paraffin or a suitable solvent. Dry the parts with a lint free rag.

10   Carefully examine the bearing inner and outer races, bearing rollers and roller cages for pitting, scoring or cracks and if at all suspect renew the bearings as a pair. It will also be necessary to renew the oil seals as they will have been damaged during removal. Check for any signs of damage to the swivel hub bore and hub flange and renew these components if necessary. Remove any burrs or score marks from the hub bore with a fine file or scraper.

11   Refit the disc dust cover to the swivel hub using a hammer and large bore tube to drive it into place. Make sure that the dust cover is positioned so that the distance from the flat edge to the brake caliper mounting bolt holes in the swivel hub is the same at the top and bottom (Fig 10.10).

12   Support the swivel hub in a vice with the disc dust cover uppermost.

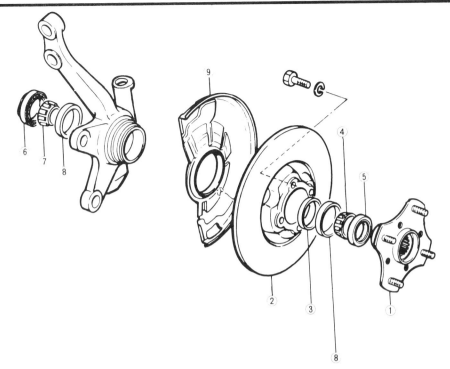

Fig. 10.7 Exploded view of
the front swivel hub
assembly (Sec 4)

1　Hub flange
2　Brake disc
3　Bearing spacer
4　Outer bearing inner race
5　Outer oil seal
6　Inner oil seal
7　Inner bearing inner race
8　Inner bearing outer race
9　Brake disc dust cover

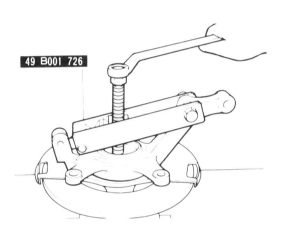

Fig. 10.8 Using a hub remover tool to separate the
hub and disc assembly from the swivel hub (Sec 4)

4.4 Removing the brake disc to hub retaining bolts

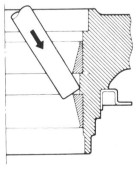

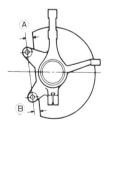

Fig. 10.9 Front hub bearing outer race removal (Sec 4)

Fig. 10.10 Refitting the brake disc dust cover (Sec 4)

Dimensions A and B must be equal

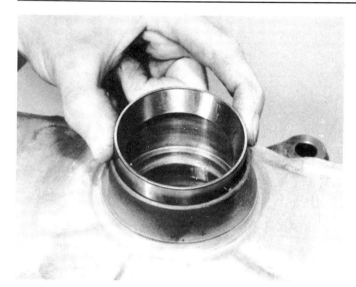

4.13 Fit the outer bearing outer race to the swivel hub

4.16B ... followed by the spacer ...

13 Place the outer bearing outer race in position in the swivel hub (photo) and carefully tap it into place with a hammer and drift, using the same procedure as for removal. Tap the race down until it contacts the shoulder in the centre of the swivel hub.
14 Turn the swivel hub over in the vice and repeat the procedure in paragraph 13 for the inner bearing outer race.
15 Before proceeding further it is necessary to adjust the bearing preload and to do this, Mazda special tool 49 B001 727 will be required together with a spring balance and torque wrench.
16 Pack both the bearing inner races with lithium based grease and place them in the swivel hub with the spacer in between (photos).
17 Refer to Fig. 10.11, and assemble tool 49 B001 727 through the bearings as shown.
18 Hook the end of the spring balance into one of the brake caliper mounting bolt holes in the swivel hub.
19 Tighten the nut on the special tool to 200 Nm (145 lbf ft) and check that the load required to start the swivel hub turning from rest, as shown on the spring balance scale is 230 to 900 g (0.5 to 1.9 lbs). Do this in 50 Nm (36 lbf ft) stages and turn the hub through one revolution by hand first, each time, to settle the bearings before checking the load with the spring balance.

4.16C ... then the inner bearing inner race

4.16A Fit the outer bearing inner race ...

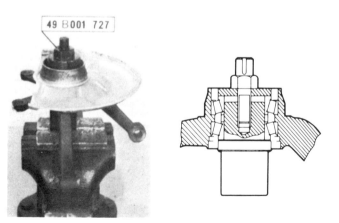

Fig. 10.11 Using the preload adjuster tool to check front hub bearing preload (Sec 4)

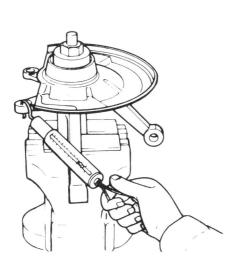

Fig. 10.12 Using a spring balance to check the load required to start the swivel hub turning (Sec 4)

4.21B ... and outer oil seals to the swivel hub

20 If the load required to turn the swivel hub is excessive a thicker spacer is required between the bearings. If the load is insufficient, a smaller spacer is required. Spacers are available in 21 different thicknesses increasing in increments of 0.04 mm (0.0015 in). Each spacer is stamped with a number (1 to 21) stamped on one face. If the bearing preload is to be altered, try the next size up or down as necessary by removing the special tool and bearing race, changing the spacer then repeating the checking procedure.
21 When the bearing preload is correct, remove the tool and pack the space between the hub bearings with grease then fit the new inner and outer oil seals (photos). Use a hammer and tube of suitable diameter to tap the seals into the hub until their edges are flush with the edges of the swivel hub.
22 If removed, refit the disc to the hub flange and secure with the four retaining bolts tightened to the specified torque.
23 Fit the assembled swivel hub assembly to the hub and disc (photo) then using a tube in contact with the inner bearing inner race, drive the swivel hub fully home. Alternatively use a press for this operation.
24 The swivel hub assembly can now be refitted to the car as described in Section 3.

4.23 Fit the swivel hub assembly to the hub flange and disc

4.21A Fit new inner ...

5 Front suspension strut – removal and refitting

1 Chock the rear wheels, firmly apply the handbrake, then jack up the front of the car and support it on axle stands. Remove the appropriate front roadwheel.
2 Using a screwdriver release the clip securing the flexible brake hose to the bracket on the suspension strut (photo). Lift the hose out of the bracket.
3 Undo the nuts and remove the two bolts securing the strut to the swivel hub.
4 Working in the engine compartment prise off the plastic cap in the centre of the strut upper mounting. Check that there is a triangular arrow marked on the mounting rubber and pointing towards the outside of the vehicle. If no mark can be seen, use a dab of white paint to mark the outer facing side of the mounting as a guide to reassembly.
5 Undo the two nuts each side (not the one in the centre) that secure the strut upper mounting to the body. Separate the strut from the swivel hub and remove the unit from under the wheel arch.

5.2 Flexible brake hose retaining clip (A) and strut to swivel hub retaining bolts (B)

the strut upper mounting and slacken **but do not remove** the strut spindle retaining nut.

3   Position the spring compressors on either side of the spring and compress the spring evenly until there is no tension on the spring seat or upper mounting.

4   Remove the strut spindle retaining nut then lift off the upper mounting followed by the spring seat, rubber ring, strut spindle dust cover and coil spring.

5   With the strut completely dismantled, the components can be examined as follows.

6   Examine the strut for signs of fluid leakage. Check the strut spindle for signs of wear or pitting along its entire length and check the strut body for signs of damage or elongation of the mounting bolt holes. Test the operation of the strut, while holding it in an upright position, by moving the spindle through a full stroke and then through short strokes of 50 to 100 mm (2 to 4 in). In both cases the resistance felt should be smooth and continuous. If the resistance is jerky or uneven, or if there is any visible sign of wear or damage to the strut, renewal is necessary.

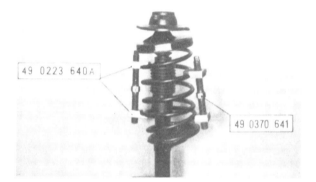

Fig. 10.14 Spring compressors in place on the front strut coil spring (Sec 6)

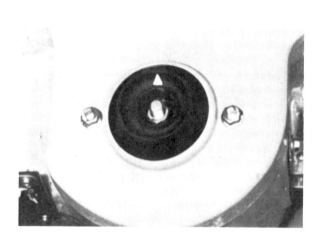

Fig. 10.13 Front suspension strut upper mounting reference arrow pointing towards the outside of the vehicle (Sec 5)

6   Refitting is the reverse sequence of removal bearing in mind the following points:

(a)   *Ensure that the triangular arrow on the strut upper mounting or the mark made during removal is positioned towards the outside of the car*

(b)   *Tighten all nuts and bolts to the specified torque*

---

6   Front suspension strut – dismantling and reassembly

Note: *Before attempting to dismantle the front suspension strut, a suitable tool to hold the coil spring in compression must be obtained. Adjustable coil spring compressors are readily available and are recommended for this operation. Any attempt to dismantle the strut without such a tool is likely to result in damage or personal injury.*

1   Remove the front suspension from the car as described in the previous Section.

2   Support the strut in a vice, remove the plastic cap in the centre of

7   If any doubt exists about the condition of the coil spring, remove the spring compressors and check the spring for distortion. Also measure the free length of the spring and compare the measurement with the figure given in the Specifications. Renew the spring if it is distorted or outside the specified length.

8   Begin reassembly by placing the compressed coil spring in place on the strut ensuring that the coil end seats properly in the lower mounting.

9   Pull the spindle our as far as it will go and locate the dust cover over the spindle and strut.

10 Place the rubber ring, spring seat and upper mounting on the strut and secure with the retaining nut. Tighten the nut to the specified torque after removing the spring compressors.

11 The strut assembly can now be refitted to the car as described in Section 5.

---

7   Front lower suspension arm – removal and refitting

1   Chock the rear wheels, firmly apply the handbrake then jack up the front of the car and support it on axle stands. Remove the appropriate front roadwheel.

2   If an anti-roll bar is fitted, undo the two locknuts and remove the connecting link bolt securing the anti-roll bar to the lower suspension arm. Recover the washers and rubber bush noting their fitted positions.

3   Undo the nut and remove the pinch-bolt securing the lower arm balljoint to the swivel hub (photo).

4   Using a long stout bar, lever the lower suspension arm down to release the balljoint shank from the swivel hub.

7.3 Lower arm balljoint to swivel hub pinch-bolt (arrowed)

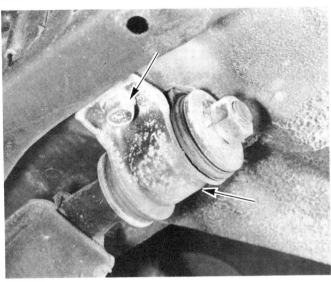

7.5B Lower arm rear mounting retaining bolts (arrowed)

5   Undo the bolts and nuts securing the lower arm mounting brackets to the underbody (photos), then remove the arm from under the car.
6   With the arm removed from the car, carefully examine the rubber mounting bushes for swelling or deterioration, the balljoint for slackness, and check for damage to the rubber boot. Renewal of the balljoint is described in Section 8. Renewal of the suspension arm mounting bushes may be carried out as follows.
7   Undo the retaining nut and withdraw the rear mounting and washers from the lower arm spindle. Renew the rear mounting as an assembly if the bushes are worn or damaged.
8   Undo the front mounting bracket retaining nut and remove the bracket and washers from the lower arm.
9   To renew the front mounting bushes, cut off the forward facing ear of the mounting bush using a hacksaw then press out the bush using suitable mandrels.
10 Press in a new bush from the front of the arm.
11 Refit the front and rear mounting brackets, but do not tighten the retaining nuts fully at this stage.

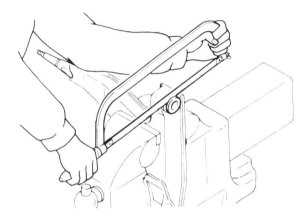

Fig. 10.15 Front lower suspension arm mounting bush renewal (Sec 7)

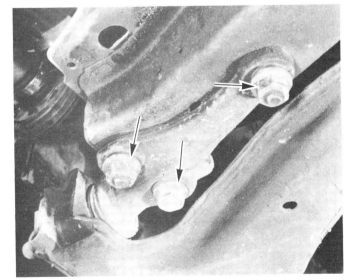

7.5A Lower arm front mounting bracket to body attachments (arrowed)

12 Refitting the suspension arm is the reverse sequence of removal bearing in mind the following points.

   (a) Tighten all retaining nuts and bolts to the specified torque
   (b) Do not fully tighten the lower arm to mounting bracket nuts until the weight of the car is standing on its wheels
   (c) After refitting check the front wheel toe setting as described in Section 26

8   Front lower suspension arm balljoint – removal and refitting

1   Chock the rear wheels, firmly apply the handbrake then jack up the front of the car and support it on axle stands. Remove the appropriate front roadwheel.
2   If an anti-roll bar is fitted, undo the two locknuts and remove the connecting link bolt securing the anti-roll bar to the lower suspension arm. Recover the washers and rubber bushes noting their fitted positions.
3   Undo the nut and remove the pinch-bolt securing the lower arm balljoint to the swivel hub.

4   Using a long stout bar, lever the lower suspension arm down to release the balljoint shank from the swivel hub.
5   Undo the two nuts and remove the bolts and washers securing the balljoint to the lower suspension arm (photo). Withdraw the balljoint from the end of the arm.
6   If the balljoint is excessively slack or in any way damaged it must be renewed as an assembly. If, however, only the rubber boot is damaged a new boot may be obtained separately.
7   Refitting the balljoint is the reverse sequence of removal.

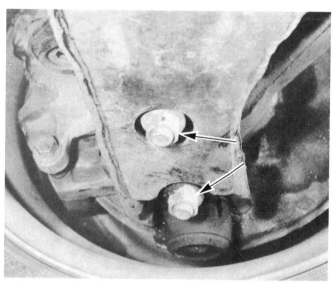

8.5 Lower arm balljoint retaining nuts (arrowed)

9   Front anti-roll bar – removal and refitting

1   Chock the rear wheels, firmly apply the handbrake then jack up the front of the car and support it on axle stands. Remove both front roadwheels.
2   Remove the engine undertray to gain access to the anti-roll bar mountings.
3   Undo the two locknuts and remove the connecting link bolt securing each end of the anti-roll bar to the lower suspension arms. Recover the washers and rubber bushes noting their fitted positions.
4   Undo the bolts securing the anti-roll bar front mounting clamps to the chassis member, then remove the bar from under the car.
5   Carefully examine the mountings, connecting links and anti-roll bar for signs of cracks, damage or deformation and renew any parts as necessary.

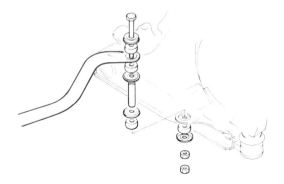

Fig. 10.16 Front anti-roll bar connecting link arrangement (Sec 9)

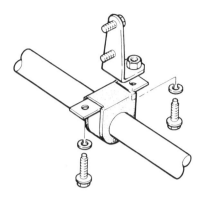

Fig. 10.17 Anti-roll bar front mounting details (Sec 9)

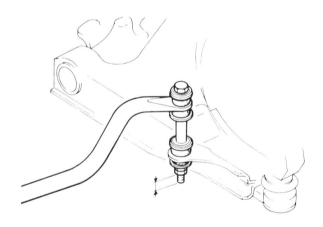

Fig. 10.18 Correct fitting of front anti-roll bar connecting link (Sec 9)

Thread protrusion below locknut = 6.2 mm (0.24 in)

6   To refit the anti-roll bar, position it under the car and fit the front mounting clamp bolts finger tight only at this stage.
7   Refer to Fig. 10.8 and refit the connecting links. Tighten the locknuts so that approximately 6.2 mm (0.24 in) of bolt thread protrudes below the locknuts.
8   Now securely tighten the front mounting clamp retaining bolts.
9   Refit the undertray and roadwheels then lower the car to the ground.

10   Rear hub assembly – removal and refitting

1   Chock the front wheels, jack up the rear of the car and securely support it on axle stands. Remove the appropriate rear roadwheel then make sure that the handbrake is fully released. Remove the hub cap.
2   Using a pointed tool, tap up the staking securing the rear hub retaining nut to the groove in the stub axle. Undo and remove the hub nut.
3   Pull the brake drum and hub assembly squarely off the stub axle while at the same time holding the outer bearing and thrustwasher in place with your thumbs to prevent them dropping out. If it is not possible to remove the assembly due to the brake shoes binding on the drum, remove the handbrake lever stop at the rear of the backplate using a screwdriver. If the brake shoes are still binding, extract the handbrake cable clevis pin and push the lever up against the backplate.

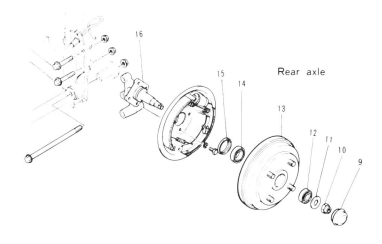
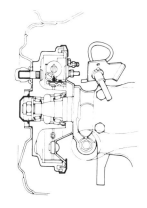

Fig. 10.19 Exploded view of the rear hub and stub axle assembly (Secs 10 and 11)

9 Hub cap
10 Hub retaining nut

11 Thrust washer
12 Outer bearing

13 Drum and hub assembly
14 Inner bearing

15 Oil seal
16 Stub axle

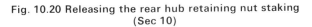

Fig. 10.20 Releasing the rear hub retaining nut staking (Sec 10)

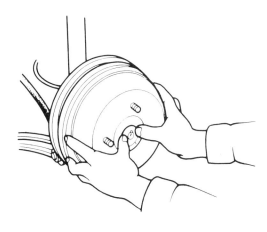

Fig. 10.21 Removing the drum and hub assembly (Sec 10)

Fig. 10.22 Rear hub bearing adjustment (Sec 10)

Fig. 10.23 Using a spring balance to check the load required to start the rear hub turning (Sec 10)

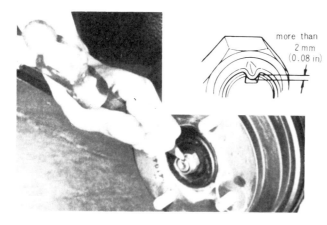

Fig. 10.24 Rear hub retaining nut staking (Sec 10)

This will increase the clearance between the brake shoes and drum and allow the drum and hub assembly to be removed.

4   To refit the drum and hub assembly place it in position on the stub axle while holding the outer bearing and thrustwasher in place as was done during removal.

5   Fit a new hub retaining nut to the stub axle and tighten it to a torque of 25 to 30 Nm (18 to 22 lbf ft) while at the same time turning the drum to settle the bearings. Now slacken the hub nut by one complete turn.

6   Using a spring balance connected to one of the wheel studs on the brake drum, measure the load required to start the hub turning from rest. This should be 0.4 to 1.0 kg (0.9 to 2.2 lbs). Tighten the hub retaining nut as necessary until the correct starting load is obtained.

7   With the hub bearings correctly adjusted, stake the retaining nut into the stub axle groove using a round nosed tool.

8   Refit the handbrake lever stop or handbrake cable clevis pin if these were removed to facilitate drum removal.

9   Refit the roadwheel and hub cap then lower the car to the ground.

11 Rear hub bearings – removal and refitting

1   Remove the appropriate rear hub assembly from the car as described in the previous Section.

2   Lift out the thrustwasher and outer bearing inner race.

3   Turn the hub over and extract the oil seal using a screwdriver to prise it out.

4   Lift out the inner bearing inner race.

5   Wipe away the surplus grease from the centre of the hub then using a hammer and suitable drift drive out one of the bearing outer races (Fig. 10.25). Remove the race gradually and carefully by tapping it a little bit at a time on one side, then the other, taking care to keep it level in the hub bore. After removal of the first race, turn the hub over and remove the other race in the same way.

6   Clean all the components thoroughly using paraffin or a suitable solvent. Dry the parts with a lint free rag.

7   Carefully examine the bearing inner and outer races, bearing rollers and roller cages for pitting, scoring or cracks and if at all suspect renew the bearings as a pair. It will also be necessary to renew the oil seal as it will have been damaged during removal. Remove any burrs or score marks from the hub bore using a fine file or scraper.

8   Place the outer bearing outer race in position in the hub and carefully tap it into place with a hammer and drift using the same procedure as for removal. Tap the race down until it contacts the shoulder in the centre of the hub.

9   Turn the hub over and repeat the procedure in paragraph 8 for the inner bearing outer race.

10 Pack the inner bearing inner race with lithium based grease and place it in position in the hub.

11 Lubricate the lip of the new oil seal with grease then tap it into place until its face is flush with the edge of the hub.

12 Pack the outer bearing inner race with grease and also the area between the bearings in the hub bore.

13 Place the outer bearing inner race and the thrustwasher in position and refit the hub as described in Section 10.

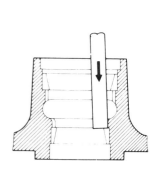

Fig. 10.25 Rear hub bearing inner race removal (Sec 11)

12 Rear suspension strut – removal and refitting

1   Chock the front wheels, jack up the rear of the car and securely support it on axle stands. Remove the appropriate rear roadwheel.

2   At the rear of the brake backplate, disconnect the handbrake cable return spring, extract the split pin and remove the clevis pin securing the handbrake cable end to the lever.

3   Using a brake hose clamp or similar tool, clamp the rear flexible brake hose to minimise brake fluid loss during subsequent operations.

4   Using a screwdriver, release the clip securing the flexible brake hose to the bracket on the suspension strut.

5   Wipe clean the area around the brake pipe union at the rear of the wheel cylinder.

6   Unscrew the brake pipe union nut, withdraw the pipe end from the wheel cylinder and move the pipe and hose clear of the suspension strut. Plug the pipe end and wheel cylinder orifice to prevent dirt entry.

7   Undo the nut and remove the bolt and washer securing the trailing arm to the base of the suspension strut.

8   Undo the nut and remove the bolt and washers securing the lateral links to the stub axle assembly.

9   From inside the luggage compartment, remove the side trim to gain access to the suspension strut upper mounting.

10 Undo the two nuts and remove the washers securing the strut upper mounting to the body. Ease the strut down, release the trailing arm and lateral links then remove the strut complete with brake and stub axle assemblies from under the wheel arch.

11 If further work is to be carried out on the suspension strut, undo the two nuts, remove the bolts and washers then separate the strut from the stub axle and brake assembly.

12 Refitting the suspension strut is the reverse sequence of removal bearing in mind the following points.

   (a) *If removed, first refit the stub axle and brake assembly and tighten the retaining bolts to the specified torque*

   (b) *Do not tighten the trailing arm and lateral link retaining bolts fully until the weight of the car is standing on its wheels; then tighten them to the specified torque*

   (c) *Use a new split pin to secure the handbrake cable clevis pin*

   (d) *Bleed the brake hydraulic system as described in Chapter 9 after refitting*

Fig. 10.26 Rear suspension strut upper mounting nuts (arrowed) (Sec 12)

13 Rear suspension strut – dismantling and reassembly

Note: *Before attempting to dismantle the rear suspension strut, a suitable tool to hold the coil spring in compression must be obtained. Adjustable coil spring compressors are readily available and are recommended for this operation. Any attempt to dismantle the strut without such a tool is likely to result in damage or personal injury.*

1   Remove the rear suspension strut from the car as described in the previous Section.
2   Support the strut in a vice and slacken, **but do not remove** the strut spindle retaining nut in the centre of the upper mounting.
3   Position the spring compressors on either side of the spring and compress the spring evenly until there is no tension on the spring seat or upper mounting (Fig. 10.14).
4   Remove the strut spindle retaining nut then lift off the upper mounting followed by the spring seat, rubber ring, strut spindle dust cover and coil spring.
5   With the strut completely dismantled, the components can be examined as follows.
6   Examine the strut body for signs of damage or corrosion, and for any trace of fluid leakage. Check the strut spindle for distortion, wear, pitting, or corrosion along its entire length. Test the operation of the strut, while holding it in an upright position, by moving the spindle through a full stroke and then through short strokes of 50 to 100 mm (2 to 4 in). In both cases the resistance felt should be smooth and continuous. If the resistance is jerky or uneven, or if there is any sign of wear or damage to the strut, renewal is necessary.
7   If any doubt exists about the condition of the coil spring, remove the spring compressors and check the spring for distortion. Also measure the free length of the spring and compare the measurement with the figure given in the Specifications. Renew the spring if it is distorted or not of the specified length.
8   Begin reassembly by placing the compressed coil spring in place on the strut ensuring that the coil end seats properly in the lower mounting.
9   Pull the spindle out as far as it will go and locate the dust cover over the spindle and strut.
10 Place the rubber ring, spring seat and upper mounting on the strut and secure with the retaining nut. Tighten the nut to the specified torque after removing the spring compressors.
11 The strut assembly can now be refitted to the car as described in Section 12.

14 Rear stub axle – removal and refitting

1   Refer to Section 10 and remove the rear hub assembly.
2   Using a brake hose clamp or similar tool, clamp the rear flexible brake hose to minimise fluid loss during subsequent operations.
3   Wipe clean the area around the brake pipe union at the rear of the wheel cylinder. Undo the union nut and withdraw the brake pipe from

the wheel cylinder. Plug the pipe end and wheel cylinder orifice to prevent dirt entry.
4   Disconnect the handbrake cable return spring then extract the split pin, remove the clevis pin and separate the cable end from the lever.
5   Undo the four bolts securing the brake backplate to the stub axle. Remove the backplate complete with brake shoes, as an assembly.
6   Undo the nut and remove the through-bolt and washers securing the lateral links to the stub axle.
7   Undo the two nuts and remove the bolts securing the stub axle to the rear suspension strut then withdraw the stub axle from its location.
8   Examine the stub axle for any signs of cracks or damage or for wear ridges on the oil seal flange. Surface corrosion or light scoring can be removed using fine emery cloth.
9   To refit the stub axle place it in position and refit the stub axle to suspension strut bolts, washers and nuts. Tighten the nuts to the specified torque while applying an upward load to the stub axle spindle.
10 Refit the through-bolt, washers and nut securing the lateral links to the stub axle. Do not fully tighten the nut at this stage.
11 Refit the backplate and brake assembly and tighten the four retaining bolts to the specified torque.
12 Refit the handbrake cable and clevis pin and secure the clevis pin using a new split pin. Connect the handbrake cable return spring.
13 Refit the brake pipe to the wheel cylinder and tighten the union nut securely. Remove the brake hose clamp.
14 Refer to Section 10 and refit the rear hub assembly.
15 Bleed the hydraulic system as described in Chapter 9 then refit the roadwheel and lower the car to the ground. With the weight of the car standing on its wheels, tighten the lateral links to stub axle retaining nut to the specified torque.

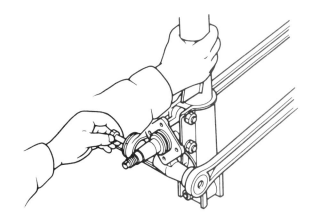

Fig. 10.27 Removing the lateral link through-bolt from the stub axle (Sec 14)

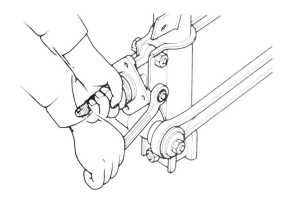

Fig. 10.28 Apply an upward load to the stub axle while tightening the stub axle to strut mounting bolts (Sec 14)

174 | Chapter 10 Suspension and steering

15 Rear lateral links – removal and refitting

1   Chock the front wheels, jack up the rear of the car and securely support it on axle stands. Remove the appropriate rear roadwheel.
2   Undo the nut and remove the through-bolt and washers securing the lateral links to the stub axle (photo).
3   Wipe clean the face of the notched eccentric washer located behind the lateral link to crossmember retaining nut (photo). On the face of the washer will be found a positioning mark and a corresponding lug on the link which will be engaged with one of the washer notches. Make a note of the number of notches clockwise or anti-clockwise. The positioning mark is situated in relation to the lug. The position of the washer determines the rear suspension toe setting and it is important to refit it in the same place otherwise the setting will be lost.
4   Having noted the position of the eccentric washer, undo the retaining nut, remove the bolt and washers and withdraw the lateral links from under the car. If the forward facing link on the left-hand side is being removed, it will be necessary to slacken the rear crossmember

mounting nuts, and lower the crossmember to provide sufficient clearance for removal of the bolt.
5   Examine the lateral links for signs of damage or distortion or for signs of deterioration of the mounting bushes. Renew the links if any of these conditions are found.
6   Refitting is the reverse sequence of removal bearing in mind the following points:

   (a) Refit the eccentric washer on the inner mounting in the position noted during removal
   (b) Do not fully tighten the retaining nuts until the weight of the car is standing on its wheels; then tighten them to the specified torque
   (c) If new lateral links have been fitted the rear toe setting should be checked as described in Section 26

16 Rear trailing arm – removal and refitting

1   Chock the front wheels, jack up the rear of the car and securely support it on axle stands. Remove the appropriate rear roadwheel.
2   Undo the two nuts and remove the bolts and washers securing the rear anti-roll bar to the trailing arm.
3   Undo the nut and remove the bolt and washers securing the trailing arm to the base of the rear suspension strut (photo). Separate the trailing arm from the strut.
4   Undo and remove the bolt securing the trailing arm to the underbody (photo) then withdraw the arm and remove it from under the car.
5   Examine the trailing arm for signs of damage or distortion or for signs of deterioration of the mounting bushes. Renew the trailing arm if any of these conditions are found.
6   Refitting is the reverse sequence of removal, but do not fully tighten the front and rear mountings until the weight of the car is standing on its wheels; then tighten them to the specified torque.

17 Rear anti-roll bar – removal and refitting

1   Chock the front wheels, jack up the rear of the car and securely support it on axle stands. Remove both rear roadwheels.
2   Undo the two nuts and remove the bolts securing the anti-roll bar to each rear trailing arm (photo).
3   Withdraw the anti-roll bar from the trailing arms, manipulate it over the exhaust system and remove it from under the car.
4   Check the anti-roll bar carefully for twists, cracks or other damage and renew the bar if evident.

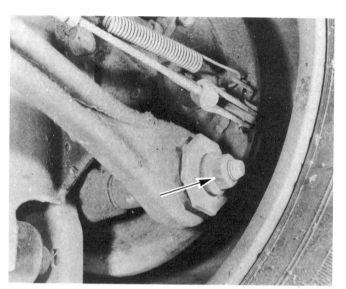

15.2 Lateral link to stub axle through-bolt and retaining nut (arrowed)

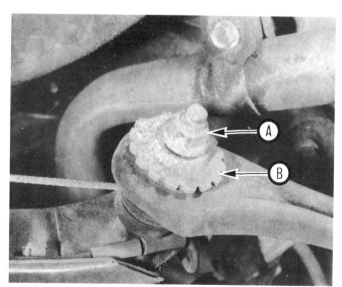

15.3 Lateral link to crossmember retaining nut (A) and eccentric washer (B) for toe setting adjustment

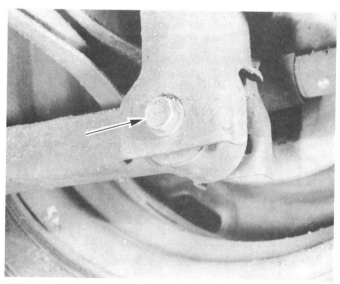

16.3 Trailing arm to suspension strut retaining bolt (arrowed)

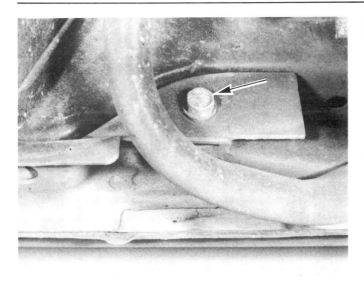

16.4 Trailing arm to underbody retaining bolt (arrowed)

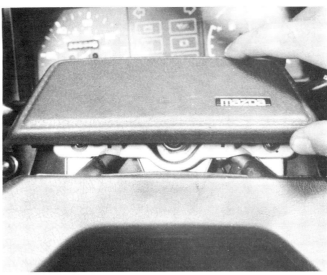

18.2 Prise up the horn push trim cover ...

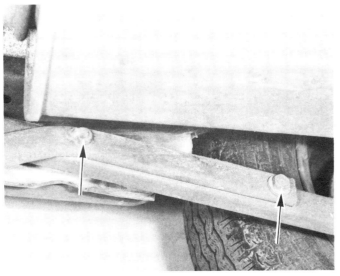

17.2 Anti-roll bar to trailing arm retaining bolts (arrowed)

18.3 ... then undo the steering wheel retaining nut (arrowed)

5   Refitting is the reverse sequence of removal, ensuring that the mountings are tightened to the specified torque.

18 Steering wheel – removal and refitting

1   Set the front wheels to the straight-ahead position.
2   Carefully prise up the horn push trim cover to gain access to the steering wheel retaining nut (photo).
3   Using a 21 mm socket, unscrew the nut securing the steering wheel to the column shaft (photo).
4   Using a dab of paint, mark the position of the steering wheel in relation to the shaft as an aid to refitting.
5   Using a suitable puller secured through the two threaded holes on either side of the shaft, draw the steering wheel off the shaft (Fig. 10.29).
6   Refitting is the reverse sequence of removal. Align the marks made during removal and tighten the retaining nut to the specified torque.

Fig. 10.29 Using a puller to remove the steering wheel (Sec 18)

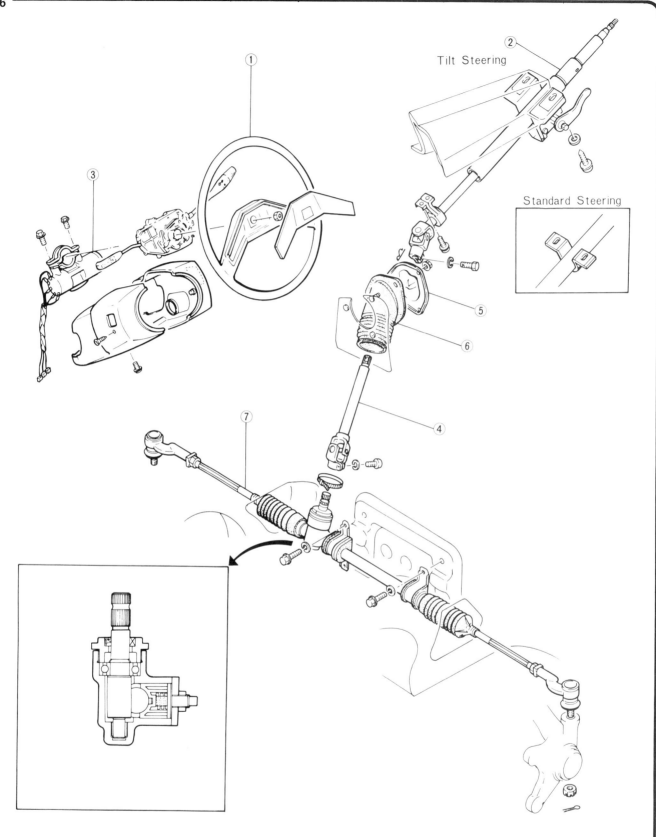

Tilt Steering

Standard Steering

Fig. 10.30 Exploded view of the steering wheel and column assembly (Secs 18 and 19)

1 Steering wheel
2 Steering column and shaft assembly
3 Steering lock/ignition switch
4 Intermediate shaft
5 Rubber boot retaining plate
6 Rubber boot
7 Steering gear and linkage

19 Steering column – removal, overhaul and refitting

1 Disconnect the battery negative terminal.

2 Refer to Section 18 and remove the steering wheel.

3 Remove the cover under the facia to gain access to the column and mountings.

4 Undo the nut and three screws securing the two halves of the steering column shroud to the column. Lift off the left-hand shroud, remove the bulbholder in the right-hand shroud by turning it anti-clockwise, then lift off the right-hand shroud.

5 Disconnect the wiring multi-plugs at the rear of the steering column combination switch. Undo the switch clamp bolt and slide the switch off the column.

6 Disconnect the ignition switch wiring at the harness connectors.

7 Undo the clamp bolt securing the steering column shaft universal joint to the intermediate shaft (photo).

8 Undo the upper and lower column mounting bracket retaining bolts, withdraw the universal joint from the intermediate shaft and remove the column assembly from the car.

9 If the intermediate shaft is also to be removed, open the bonnet and from within the engine compartment release the clip securing the rubber boot to the pinion housing on the steering gear.

10 Fold the boot back and undo the clamp bolt securing the intermediate shaft universal joint to the steering gear pinion.

11 Separate the intermediate shaft from the pinion by moving it upwards, then withdraw the shaft from the engine compartment.

12 Support the steering column in a vice with protected jaws.

13 Insert the key into the ignition switch and turn the switch so that the steering lock is released.

14 Remove the steering column shaft with a twisting action from the base of the column.

15 Check the steering column shaft for straightness and for signs of impact or damage to the collapsible portion. Similarly check for damage or distortion to the column. Check for wear or roughness in the column bearings and in the intermediate shaft universal joint. If any damage or wear is found the column and column shaft must be renewed as an assembly. It is however possible to obtain the column upper bearing separately, but all the other bearings are supplied only as part of the complete column assembly. Similarly if the intermediate shaft universal joint is worn, obtain a new shaft.

16 To renew the column upper bearing prise it out of the column tube using a screwdriver and carefully tap a new bearing into place.

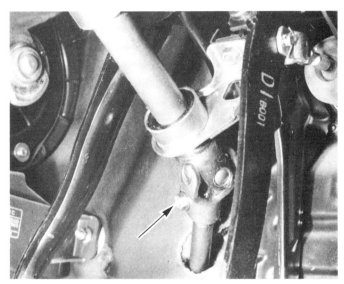

19.7 Steering column universal joint clamp bolt (arrowed)

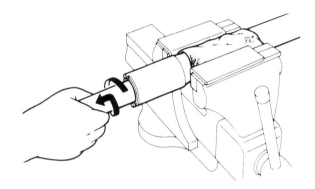

Fig. 10.32 Removing the steering column shaft from the column (Sec 19)

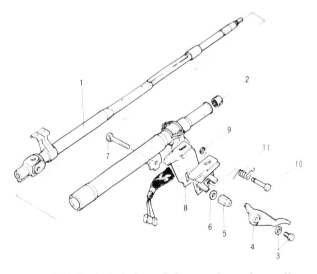

Fig. 10.33 Exploded view of the steering column tilt mechanism (Sec 19)

1	Steering column shaft	7	Bolt
2	Column upper bearing	8	Column upper mounting
3	Bolt and washer		bracket
4	Adjusting lever	9	Clip
5	Adjusting nut	10	Pin
6	Washer	11	Spring

(Items 9, 10 and 11 are fitted to early models only)

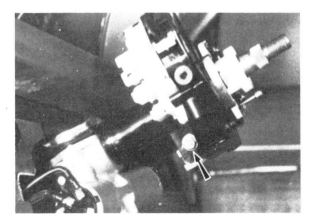

Fig. 10.31 Steering column combination switch clamp bolt (arrowed) (Sec 19)

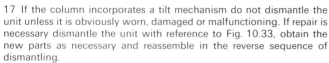

Fig. 10.34 Refit the column so that a small gap exists between the column shrouds and steering wheel (Sec 19)

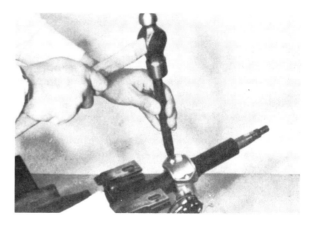

Fig. 10.35 Steering column lock shear bolt removal (Sec 20)

17 If the column incorporates a tilt mechanism do not dismantle the unit unless it is obviously worn, damaged or malfunctioning. If repair is necessary dismantle the unit with reference to Fig. 10.33, obtain the new parts as necessary and reassemble in the reverse sequence of dismantling.
18 To reassemble the steering column, lubricate the column bearings with a lithium based grease then refit the shaft through the base of the column.
19 Refit the intermediate shaft universal joint to the steering gear pinion then refit the clamp bolt and tighten it to the specified torque.
20 Fold back the rubber boot and secure it to the pinion housing with a new clip.
21 Align the hole in the steering column shaft universal joint with the flat on the intermediate shaft. Slide the universal joint onto the shaft, refit the clamp bolt and tighten it to the specified torque.
22 Refit the column upper and lower mountings bolts, but only tighten them finger tight at this stage.
23 Reconnect the ignition switch and combination switch wiring.
24 Refit the two steering column shroud halves then refit the steering wheel, referring to Section 18, if necessary.
25 Move the column up or down as necessary until a small gap exists between the steering wheel and column shrouds (Fig. 10.34). Hold the column in this position and tighten the upper and lower mounting bolts to the specified torque.
26 Refit the cover under the facia and reconnect the battery negative terminal.
27 Road test the car and check the position of the steering wheel. If necessary, refer to Section 18 and reposition the wheel so that the spokes are level when the car is driven in a straight line.

20 Steering column lock/ignition switch – removal and refitting

1   Remove the steering column as described in Section 19.
2   With the column assembly on the bench, use a hammer and chisel to cut a slot in the round heads of the clamp plate retaining shear bolts (Fig. 10.35).
3   Unscrew the shear bolts, lift off the clamp plate and remove the lock assembly.
4   To refit the lock, place it in position on the column, fit the clamp plate and screw in two new shear bolts. Tighten the bolts finger tight only at this stage.
5   Using the ignition key check the operation of the lock mechanism then tighten the bolts until the heads break off.
6   Refit the column to the car as described in Section 19.

21 Tie-rod outer balljoint – removal and refitting

1   Chock the rear wheels, firmly apply the handbrake then jack up the front of the car and support it on axle stands. Remove the appropriate front roadwheel.
2   Using a suitable spanner, slacken the balljoint locknut on the tie-rod by a quarter of a turn (photo).
3   Extract the split pin then undo the nut securing the balljoint to the steering arm (photo).
4   Release the tapered shank of the balljoint from the steering arm using a universal balljoint separator tool (photo).
5   Hold the square portion of the tie-rod with a spanner and unscrew the balljoint.
6   To refit the balljoint screw it onto the tie-rod until it contacts the locknut then engage the shank with the steering arm.
7   Refit the retaining nut, tighten it to the specified torque then align the next split pin hole with one of the retaining nut slots. Secure the nut with a new split pin.
8   Tighten the locknut on the tie-rod against the shoulder of the balljoint.
9   Refit the roadwheel and lower the car to the ground.
10 Check the front wheel toe setting as described in Section 26.

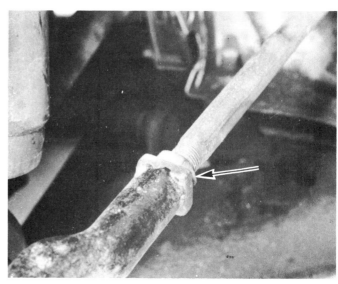

21.2 Tie-rod outer balljoint locknut (arrowed)

21.3 Tie-rod outer balljoint retaining nut and split pin (arrowed)

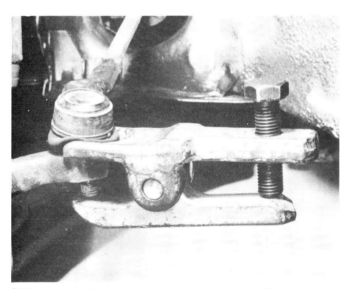

21.4 Using a balljoint separator tool to release the balljoint shank from the steering arm

22 Steering gear rubber boot – removal and refitting

1   Remove the tie-rod outer balljoint as described in the previous Section.
2   Mark the position of the outer balljoint locknut on the tie-rod using a dab of paint then unscrew the nut.
3   Using pliers release the rubber boot outer retaining clip and slide it off the tie-rod.
4   Remove the inner retaining clip by cutting it, then withdraw the rubber boot from the steering gear and tie-rod.
5   Fit the new rubber boot ensuring that it seats in the grooves in the steering gear and tie-rod.
6   Secure the inner end of the boot using a new retaining clip and secure the outer end by sliding the original clip up the tie-rod and into position on the boot.
7   Refit the balljoint locknut to the position marked during removal.
8   Refit the tie-rod outer balljoint as described in Section 21.

23 Steering gear – removal and refitting

1   Chock the rear wheels, apply the handbrake then jack up the front of the car and support it on axle stands. Remove both front roadwheels.
2   Extract the split pins, unscrew the retaining nuts and release the tie-rod outer balljoints from the steering arms using a universal balljoint separator tool (see Section 21).
3   Working in the engine compartment release the clip securing the large rubber boot to the pinion housing on the steering gear.
4   Fold the boot back and undo the clamp bolt securing the intermediate shaft universal joint to the steering gear pinion.
5   Undo the two bolts each side securing the steering gear mounting brackets to the engine compartment bulkhead.
6   Lift off the mounting brackets, release the pinion from the intermediate shaft universal joint and withdraw the steering gear sideways and out from under the wheel arch.
7   Refitting is the reverse sequence of removal, bearing in mind the following points.

(a)   Tighten all retaining nuts and bolts to the specified torque
(b)   Use new split pins to secure the tie-rod outer balljoint retaining nuts
(c)   After fitting the steering gear, centralize the steering wheel spokes (see Section 18) so that they are level with the roadwheels in the straight-ahead position
(d)   Check the front wheel toe setting as described in Section 26

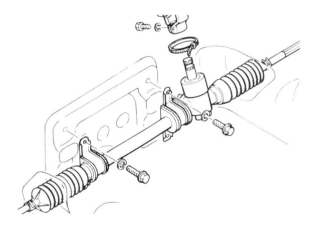

Fig. 10.36 Steering gear removal details (Sec 23)

24 Steering gear overhaul – general

Complete overhaul of the steering gear is considered to be beyond the scope of the average home mechanic owing to the complexity of the unit and the need for special tools and expertise to complete the task satisfactorily. If the steering gear is worn to such an extent that overhaul is being considered, it is usually preferable to obtain an exchange reconditioned unit.
Renewal of the steering gear rubber boots and tie-rods can, however, be carried out reasonably easily and these operations are described in Section 22 and the following Section respectively.

25 Steering gear tie-rod – removal and refitting

1   Remove the steering gear from the car as described in Section 23.
2   Hold the square portion of the tie-rod with a spanner and slacken the outer balljoint locknut.
3   Unscrew the outer balljoint and remove it from the tie-rod followed by the locknut.
4   Using pliers, release the rubber boot outer retaining clip then cut off the inner clip. Slide the rubber boot off the steering gear and tie-rod.

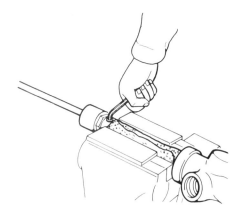

Fig. 10.37 Removing the tie-rod inner balljoint lock bolt
(Sec 25)

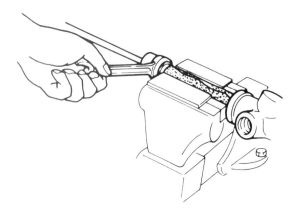

Fig. 10.38 Removing the tie-rod and inner balljoint assembly
from the rack (Sec 25)

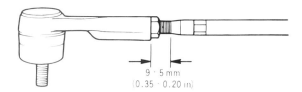

9 · 5 mm
(0.35 · 0.20 in)

Fig. 10.39 Tie-rod outer balljoint fitting position (Sec 25)

5   Turn the steering gear pinion so that the rack is protruding as far as possible on the side in which the tie-rod is to be removed.
6   Wrap a cloth around the exposed rack and lightly clamp it in a vice with the steering gear in an inverted position.
7   Using a suitable Allen key, unscrew the lock bolt securing the tie-rod inner balljoint to the rack.
8   Using a spanner, unscrew the balljoint and remove the tie-rod assembly from the rack.
9   Before fitting the new tie-rod assembly liberally lubricate the balljoint with lithium based grease, working it well into the ball and ball seat.
10 Screw the balljoint onto the rack and tighten it to the specified torque ensuring that the lock bolt holes in the rack and balljoint are aligned.

11 Apply a thread locking agent to the lock bolt threads, fit the lock bolt and tighten it securely.
12 Refit the rubber boot and secure it with the outer, and new inner retaining clips.
13 Refit the outer balljoint locknut and balljoint. Position the balljoint so that the distance from its shoulder to the end of the tie-rod threads is 4 to 14 mm (0.15 to 0.55 in). Hold the balljoint and tie-rod and tighten the locknut (Fig. 10.39).
14 The steering gear can now be refitted to the car as described in Section 23.

26 Wheel alignment and steering angles

1   Accurate wheel alignment is essential to provide positive steering and prevent excessive tyre wear. Before considering the steering/ suspension geometry, check that the tyres are correctly inflated, the front wheels are not buckled and the steering linkage and suspension joints are in good order without slackness or wear.
2   Wheel alignment consists of four factors:
Camber is the angle at which the front wheels are set from the vertical when viewed from the front of the car. 'Positive camber' is the amount (in degrees) that the wheels are tilted outward at the top from the vertical.
Castor is the angle between the steering axis and a vertical line when viewed from each side of the car. 'Positive castor' is when the steering axis is inclined rearward.
Steering axis inclination is the angle (when viewed from the front of the car) between the vertical and an imaginary line drawn between the suspension strut upper mounting and the lower suspension arm balljoint.
Toe setting is the amount by which the distance between the front inside edges of the roadwheels (measured at hub height) differs from the diametrically opposite distance measured between the rear inside edges of the roadwheels.
3   With the exception of the front and rear toe setting and front camber angle, all other steering angles on Mazda 323 models are set during manufacture and no adjustment is possible. It can be assumed, therefore, that unless the car has suffered accident damage all the preset steering angles will be correct. Should there be some doubt about their accuracy it will be necessary to seek the help of a Mazda dealer, as special gauges are needed to check the steering angles. Where adjustment is possible proceed as follows:

Front toe setting
4   Two methods are available to the home mechanic for checking the toe setting. One method is to use a gauge to measure the distance between the front and rear inside edges of the roadwheels. The other method is to use a scuff plate in which each front wheel is rolled across a movable plate which records any deviation, or scuff, of the tyre from the straight-ahead position as it moves across the plate. Relatively inexpensive equipment of both types is available from accessory outlets to enable these checks, and subsequent adjustments, to be carried out at home.
5   If, after checking the toe setting using whichever method is preferable, it is found that adjustment is necessary, proceed as follows.
6   Turn the steering wheel onto full left lock and record the number of exposed threads on the right-hand steering tie-rods. Now turn the steering onto full right lock and record the number of threads on the left-hand tie-rod. If there are the same number of threads visible on both tie-rods then subsequent adjustments can be made equally on both sides. If there are more threads visible on one side than the other it will be necessary to compensate for this during adjustment. *After adjustment there must be the same number of threads visible on each tie-rod. This is most important.*
7   To alter the toe setting slacken the locknut on the tie-rod and turn the rod using a spanner to achieve the desired setting. When viewed from the side of the car, turning the tie-rod clockwise will increase the toe-in, turning it anti-clockwise will increase the toe-out. Only turn the tie-rods by a quarter of a turn each time and then recheck the setting using the gauges, or scuff plate.
8   After adjustment tighten the locknuts and reposition the steering gear rubber boots if necessary, to remove any twist caused by turning the tie-rods.

Fig. 10.40 Adjusting the front wheel toe setting (Sec 26)

Rear toe setting

9   The procedure for checking the rear toe setting is the same as described in paragraph 4 except that the equipment is applied to the rear wheels.

10 Adjustment of the toe setting of each rear wheel is achieved using an eccentric washer located behind the rear lateral link to crossmember retaining nut. The washer has a number of notches around its periphery which engage with a lug on the lateral link.

11 If adjustment is necessary, slacken the retaining nut and turn the washer one notch at a time in whichever direction is necessary to obtain the correct setting. Note that one notch of the washer is equal to 2.5 mm (0.1 in) of toe setting adjustment. After repositioning the washer, tighten the retaining nut and recheck the setting. Repeat the procedure until the setting is as specified. Tighten the lateral link retaining nut to the specified torque after the final check.

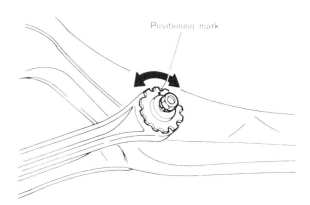

Fig. 10.41 Rear wheel toe setting adjustment point at lateral link eccentric washer (Sec 26)

Front camber angle

12 The front camber angle can be set to one of two positions by turning the front suspension strut upper mounting through 180°.

13 If, after checking the front wheel camber using suitable gauges, it is found to be incorrect, adjustment may be carried out as follows.

14 Jack up the front of the car and support it on axle stands.

15 From within the engine compartment undo the two strut upper mounting retaining nuts. Lower the strut slightly, turn the mounting through 180°, push the strut back up, and refit the two nuts. Tighten the nuts to the specified torque. If the mounting is turned so that the triangular arrow reference mark on the upper face of the mounting

rubber (Fig. 10.42) is turned from facing out to facing in, the camber alters in the positive direction. If the mark is turned from facing in to facing out, the change is to the negative.

16 Lower the car, bounce the suspension to settle the components and recheck the settings.

Fig. 10.42 Triangular reference mark on front strut upper mounting for camber adjustment (Sec 26)

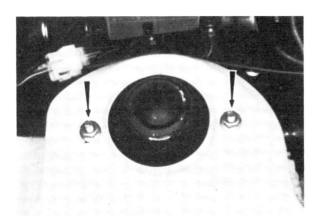

Fig. 10.43 Front strut upper mounting retaining nuts (arrowed) (Sec 26)

27 Wheels and tyres – general care and maintenance

Wheels and tyres should give no real problems in use provided that a close eye is kept on them with regard to excessive wear or damage. To this end, the following points should be noted.

Ensure that tyre pressures are checked regularly and maintained correctly. Checking should be carried out with the tyres cold and not immediately after the vehicle has been in use. If the pressures are checked with the tyres hot, an apparently high reading will be obtained owing to heat expansion. Under no circumstances should an attempt be made to reduce the pressures to the quoted cold reading in this instance, or effective underinflation will result.

Underinflation will cause overheating of the tyre owing to excessive flexing of the casing, and the tread will not sit correctly on the road surface. This will cause a consequent loss of adhesion and excessive wear, not to mention the danger of sudden tyre failure due to heat build-up.

Overinflation will cause rapid wear of the centre part of the tyre tread coupled with reduced adhesion, harsher ride, and the danger of shock damage occurring in the tyre casing.

Regularly check the tyres for damage in the form of cuts or bulges, especially in the sidewalls. Remove any nails or stones embedded in the tread before they penetrate the tyre to cause deflation. If removal of a nail *does* reveal that the tyre has been punctured, refit the nail so that its point of penetration is marked. Then immediately change the wheel and have the tyre repaired by a tyre dealer. Do *not* drive on a tyre in such a condition. In many cases a puncture can be simply repaired by the use of an inner tube of the correct size and type. If in any doubt as to the possible consequences of any damage found, consult you local tyre dealer for advice.

Periodically remove the wheels and clean any dirt or mud from the inside and outside surfaces. Examine the wheel rims for signs of rusting, corrosion or other damage. Light allow wheels are easily damaged by 'kerbing' whilst parking, and similarly steel wheels may become dented or buckled. Renewal of the wheel is very often the only course of remedial action possible.

The balance of each wheel and tyre assembly should be maintained to avoid excessive wear, not only to the tyres but also to the steering and suspension components. Wheel imbalance is normally signified by vibration through the vehicle's bodyshell, although in many cases it is particularly noticeable through the steering wheel. Conversely, it should be noted that wear or damage in suspension or steering components may cause excessive tyre wear. Out-of-round or out-of-true tyres, damaged wheels and wheel bearing wear/maladjustment also fall into this category. Balancing will not usually cure vibration caused by such wear.

Wheel balancing may be carried out with the wheel either on or off the vehicle. If balanced on the vehicle, ensure that the wheel-to-hub relationship is marked in some way prior to subsequent wheel removal so that it may be refitted in its original position.

General tyre wear is influenced to a large degree by driving style – harsh braking and acceleration or fast cornering will all produce more rapid tyre wear. Interchanging of tyres may result in more even wear, but this should only be carried out where there is no mix of tyre types on the vehicle. However, it is worth bearing in mind that if this is completely effective, the added expense of replacing a complete set of tyres simultaneously is incurred, which may prove financially restrictive for many owners.

Front tyres may wear unevenly as a result of wheel misalignment. The front wheels should always be correctly aligned according to the settings specified by the vehicle manufacturer.

Legal restrictions apply to the mixing of tyre types on a vehicle. Basically this means that a vehicle must not have tyres of differing construction on the same axle. Although it is not recommended to mix tyre types between front axle and rear axle, the only legal permissible combination is crossply at the front and radial at the rear. When mixing radial ply tyres, textile braced radials must always go on to the front axle, with steel braced radials at the rear. An obvious disadvantage of such mixing is the necessity to carry two spare tyres to avoid contravening the law in the event of a puncture.

In the UK, the Motor Vehicles Construction and Use Regulations apply to many aspects of tyre fitting and usage. It is suggested that a copy of these regulations is obtained from your local police if in doubt as to the current legal requirements with regard to tyre condition, minimum tread depth, etc.

28 Fault diagnosis – suspension and steering

Note: *Before diagnosing suspension or steering faults, be sure that the trouble is not due to incorrect tyre pressures, mixture of tyre types or binding brakes.*

Symptom	Reason(s)
Vehicle pulls to one side	Incorrrect front hub bearing adjustment Incorrect wheel alignment Wear in suspension or steering components Accident damage to steering or suspension components Faulty tyre
Steering stiff or heavy	Seized balljoint or suspension mounting Steering rack or column bent or damaged Lack of steering gear lubricant Incorrect wheel alignment
Excessive play in steering	Incorrect front hub bearing adjustment Worn steering or suspension joints or mountings Wear in steering column shaft universal joints Worn steering gear rack and pinion
Wheel wobble and vibration	Tyres out of balance Roadwheels buckled or damaged Incorrect front hub bearing adjustment Worn steering or suspension joints or mountings Faulty or damaged tyre Wheel nuts loose Faulty front suspension strut Steering column bearings or shaft universal joints worn
Tyre wear uneven	Incorrect front hub bearing adjustment Incorrect wheel alignment Worn steering or suspension components Tyres out of balance Faulty tyre Accident damage

Chapter 11 Bodywork and fittings

For modifications, and information applicable to later models, see Supplement at end of manual

Contents

1 General description

The bodyshell and underframe is of all steel welded construction incorporating progressive crumple zones at the front and rear and a rigid centre safety cell. To facilitate accident damage repair many of the main body panels are supplied as part panel replacements and are bolted rather than welded in place, particularly at the front of the vehicle.

Mazda 323 models covered by this manual are available in three-door or five-door hatchback or four-door notchback body styles.

2 Maintenance – bodywork and underframe

The general condition of a vehicle's bodywork is the one thing that significantly affects its value. Maintenance is easy but needs to be regular. Neglect, particularly after minor damage, can lead quickly to further deterioration and costly repair bills. It is important also to keep watch on those parts of the vehicle not immediately visible, for instance the underside, inside all the wheel arches and the lower part of the engine compartment.

The basic maintenance routine for the bodywork is washing – preferably with a lot of water, from a hose. This will remove all the loose solids which may have stuck to the vehicle. It is important to flush these off in such a way as to prevent grit from scratching the finish. The wheel arches and underframe need washing in the same way to remove any accumulated mud which will retain moisture and tend to encourage rust. Paradoxically enough, the best time to clean the underframe and wheel arches is in wet weather when the mud is thoroughly wet and soft. In very wet weather the underframe is usually cleaned of large accumulations automatically and this is a good time for inspection.

Periodically, except on vehicles with a wax-based underbody protective coating, it is a good idea to have the whole of the underframe of the vehicle steam cleaned, engine compartment included, so that a thorough inspection can be carried out to see what minor repairs and renovations are necessary. Steam cleaning is available at many garages and is necessary for removal of the accumulation of oily grime which sometimes is allowed to become thick in certain areas. If steam cleaning facilities are not available, there are one or two excellent grease solvents available which can be brush applied. The dirt can then be simply hosed off. Note that these methods should not be used on vehicles with wax-based underbody protective coating or the coating will be removed. Such vehicles should be inspected annually, preferably just prior to winter, when the underbody should be washed down and any damage to the wax coating repaired. Ideally, a completely fresh coat should be applied. It would also be worth considering the use of such wax-based protection for injection into door panels, sills, box sections, etc, as an additional safeguard against rust damage where such protection is not provided by the vehicle manufacturer.

After washing paintwork, wipe off with a chamois leather to give an unspotted clear finish. A coat of clear protective wax polish will give added protection against chemical pollutants in the air. If the paintwork sheen has dulled or oxidised, use a cleaner/polisher combination to restore the brilliance of the shine. This requires a little effort, but such dulling is usually caused because regular washing has been neglected. Care needs to be taken with metallic paintwork, as special non-abrasive cleaner/polisher is required to avoid damage to the finish. Always check that the door and ventilator opening drain holes and pipes are completely clear so that water can be drained out. Bright work should be treated in the same way as paint work. Windscreens and windows can be kept clear of the smeary film which often appears by the use of a proprietary glass cleaner. Never use any form of wax or other body or chromium polish on glass.

3 Maintenance – upholstery and carpets

Mats and carpets should be brushed or vacuum cleaned regularly to keep them free of grit. If they are badly stained remove them from the vehicle for scrubbing or sponging and make quite sure they are dry before refitting. Seats and interior trim panels can be kept clean by wiping with a damp cloth. If they do become stained (which can be more apparent on light coloured upholstery) use a little liquid detergent and a soft nail brush to scour the grime out of the grain of the material. Do not forget to keep the headlining clean in the same way as the upholstery. When using liquid cleaners inside the vehicle do not over-wet the surfaces being cleaned. Excessive damp could get into the seams and padded interior causing stains, offensive odours or even rot. If the inside of the vehicle gets wet accidentally it is worthwhile taking some trouble to dry it out properly, particularly where carpets are involved. *Do not leave oil or electric heaters inside the vehicle for this purpose.*

4 Minor body damage – repair

The photographic sequences on pages 190 and 191 illustrate the operations detailed in the following sub-sections.
Note: *For more detailed information about bodywork repair, the Haynes Publishing Group publish a book by Lindsay Porter called The Car Bodywork Repair Manual. This incorporates information on such aspects as rust treatment, painting and glass fibre repairs, as well as details on more ambitious repairs involving welding and panel beating.*

Repair of minor scratches in bodywork

If the scratch is very superficial, and does not penetrate to the metal of the bodywork, repair is very simple. Lightly rub the area of the scratch with a paintwork renovator, or a very fine cutting paste, to remove loose paint from the scratch and to clear the surrounding bodywork of wax polish. Rinse the area with clean water.
Apply touch-up paint to the scratch using a fine paint brush; continue to apply fine layers of paint until the surface of the paint in the

scratch is level with the surrounding paintwork. Allow the new paint at least two weeks to harden: then blend it into the surrounding paintwork by rubbing the scratch area with a paintwork renovator or a very fine cutting paste. Finally, apply wax polish.
Where the scratch has penetrated right through to the metal of the bodywork, causing the metal to rust, a different repair technique is required. Remove any loose rust from the bottom of the scratch with a penknife, then apply rust inhibiting paint to prevent the formation of rust in the future. Using a rubber or nylon applicator fill the scratch with bodystopper paste. If required, this paste can be mixed with cellulose thinners to provide a very thin paste which is ideal for filling narrow scratches. Before the stopper-paste in the scratch hardens, wrap a piece of smooth cotton rag around the top of a finger. Dip the finger in cellulose thinners and then quickly sweep it across the surface of the stopper-paste in the scratch; this will ensure that the surface of the stopper-paste is slightly hollowed. The scratch can now be painted over as described earlier in this Section.

Repair of dents in bodywork

When deep denting of the vehicle's bodywork has taken place, the first task is to pull the dent out, until the affected bodywork almost attains its original shape. There is little point in trying to restore the original shape completely, as the metal in the damaged area will have stretched on impact and cannot be reshaped fully to its original contour. It is better to bring the level of the dent up to a point which is about ⅛ in (3 mm) below the level of the surrounding bodywork. In cases where the dent is very shallow anyway, it is not worth trying to pull it out at all. If the underside of the dent is accessible, it can be hammered out gently from behind, using a mallet with a wooden or plastic head. Whilst doing this, hold a suitable block of wood firmly against the outside of the panel to absorb the impact from the hammer blows and thus prevent a large area of the bodywork from being 'belled-out'.
Should the dent be in a section of the bodywork which has a double skin or some other factor making it inaccessible from behind, a different technique is called for. Drill several small holes through the metal inside the area – particularly in the deeper section. Then screw long self-tapping screws into the holes just sufficiently for them to gain a good purchase in the metal. Now the dent can be pulled out by pulling on the protruding heads of the screws with a pair of pliers.
The next stage of the repair is the removal of the paint from the damaged area, and from an inch or so of the surrounding 'sound' bodywork. This is accomplished most easily by using a wire brush or abrasive pad on a power drill, although it can be done just as effectively by hand using sheets of abrasive paper. To complete the preparation for filling, score the surface of the bare metal with a screwdriver or the tang of a file, or alternatively, drill small holes in the affected area. This will provide a really good 'key' for the filler paste.
To complete the repair see the Section on filling and re-spraying.

Repair of rust holes or gashes in bodywork

Remove all paint from the affected area and from an inch or so of the surrounding 'sound' bodywork, using an abrasive pad or a wire brush on a power drill. If these are not available a few sheets of abrasive paper will do the job just as effectively. With the paint removed you will be able to gauge the severity of the corrosion and therefore decide whether to renew the whole panel (if this is possible) or to repair the affected area. New body panels are not as expensive as most people think and it is often quicker and more satisfactory to fit a new panel than to attempt to repair large areas of corrosion.
Remove all fittings from the affected area except those which will act as a guide to the original shape of the damaged bodywork (eg headlamp shells etc). Then, using tin snips or a hacksaw blade, remove all loose metal and any other metal badly affected by corrosion. Hammer the edges of the hole inwards in order to create a slight depression for the filler paste.
Wire brush the affected area to remove the powdery rust from the surface of the remaining metal. Paint the affected area with rust inhibiting paint; if the back of the rusted area is accessible treat this also.
Before filling can take place it will be necessary to block the hole in some way. This can be achieved by the use of aluminium or plastic mesh, or aluminium tape.
Aluminium or plastic mesh is probably the best material to use for a large hole. Cut a piece to the approximate size and shape of the hole to be filled, then position it in the hole so that its edges are below the level

of the surrounding bodywork. It can be retained in position by several blobs of filler paste around its periphery.

Aluminium tape should be used for small or very narrow holes. Pull a piece off the roll and trim it to the approximate size and shape required, then pull off the backing paper (if used) and stick the tape over the hole; it can be overlapped if the thickness of one piece is insufficient. Burnish down the edges of the tape with the handle of a screwdriver or similar, to ensure that the tape is securely attached to the metal underneath.

Bodywork repairs – filling and re-spraying

Before using this Section, see the Sections on dent, deep scratch, rust holes and gash repairs.

Many types of bodyfiller are available, but generally speaking those proprietary kits which contain a tin of filler paste and a tube of resin hardener are best for this type of repair. A wide, flexible plastic or nylon applicator will be found invaluable for imparting a smooth and well contoured finish to the surface of the filler.

Mix up a little filler on a clean piece of card or board – measure the hardener carefully (follow the maker's instructions on the pack) otherwise the filler will set too rapidly or too slowly. Using the applicator apply the filler paste to the prepared area; draw the applicator across the surface of the filler to achieve the correct contour and to level the filler surface. As soon as a contour that approximates to the correct one is achieved, stop working the paste – if you carry on too long the paste will become sticky and begin to 'pick up' on the applicator. Continue to add thin layers of filler paste at twenty-minute intervals until the level of the filler is just proud of the surrounding bodywork.

Once the filler has hardened, excess can be removed using a metal plane or file. From then on, progressively finer grades of abrasive paper should be used, starting with a 40 grade production paper and finishing with 400 grade wet-and-dry paper. Always wrap the abrasive paper around a flat rubber, cork, or wooden block – otherwise the surface of the filler will not be completely flat. During the smoothing of the filler surface the wet-and-dry paper should be periodically rinsed in water. This will ensure that a very smooth finish is imparted to the filler at the final stage.

At this stage the 'dent' should be surrounded by a ring of bare metal, which in turn should be encircled by the finely 'feathered' edge of the good paintwork. Rinse the repair area with clean water, until all of the dust produced by the rubbing-down operation has gone.

Spray the whole repair area with a light coat of primer – this will show up any imperfections in the surface of the filler. Repair these imperfections with fresh filler paste or bodystopper, and once more smooth the surface with abrasive paper. If bodystopper is used, it can be mixed with cellulose thinners to form a really thin paste which is ideal for filling small holes. Repeat this spray and repair procedure until you are satisfied that the surface of the filler, and the feathered edge of the paintwork are perfect. Clean the repair area with clean water and allow to dry fully.

The repair area is now ready for final spraying. Paint spraying must be carried out in a warm, dry, windless and dust free atmosphere. This condition can be created artificially if you have access to a large indoor working area, but if you are forced to work in the open, you will have to pick your day very carefully. If you are working indoors, dousing the floor in the work area with water will help to settle the dust which would otherwise be in the atmosphere. If the repair area is confined to one body panel, mask off the surrounding panels; this will help to minimise the effects of a slight mis-match in paint colours. Bodywork fittings (eg chrome strips, door handles etc) will also need to be masked off. Use genuine masking tape and several thicknesses of newspaper for the masking operations.

Before commencing to spray, agitate the aerosol can thoroughly, then spray a test area (an old tin, or similar) until the technique is mastered. Cover the repair area with a thick coat of primer; the thickness should be built up using several thin layers of paint rather than one thick one. Using 400 grade wet-and-dry paper, rub down the surface of the primer until it is really smooth. While doing this, the work area should be thoroughly doused with water, and the wet-and-dry paper periodically rinsed in water. Allow to dry before spraying on more paint.

Spray on the top coat, again building up the thickness by using several thin layers of paint. Start spraying in the centre of the repair area and then, using a circular motion, work outwards until the whole repair area and about 2 inches of the surrounding original paintwork is covered. Remove all masking material 10 to 15 minutes after spraying on the final coat of paint.

Allow the new paint at least two weeks to harden, then, using a paintwork renovator or a very fine cutting paste, blend the edges of the paint into the existing paintwork. Finally, apply wax polish.

5 Major body damage – repair

Where serious damage has occurred or large areas need renewal due to neglect, it means that completely new sections or panels will need welding in, and this is best left to professionals. If the damage is due to impact, it will also be necessary to completely check the alignment of the bodyshell structure. Due to the principle of construction, the strength and shape of the whole car can be affected by damage to one part. In such instances the services of a Mazda dealer with specialist checking jigs are essential. If a body is left misaligned, it is first of all dangerous, as the car will not handle properly, and secondly uneven stresses will be imposed on the steering, engine and transmission, causing abnormal wear or complete failure. Tyre wear may also be excessive.

6 Maintenance – hinges and locks

1 Lubricate the hinges of the bonnet, boot lid or tailgate and doors with a drop or two of light oil at regular intervals.
2 At the same time lightly oil the bonnet release mechanism and all the door locks.
3 Do not attempt to lubricate the steering lock.

7 Door rattles – tracing and rectification

1 Check first that the door is not loose at the hinges, and that the lock is holding the door firmly in position. Check also that the door lines up with the aperture in the body and adjust the door hinges or striker if necessary.
2 If the lock is holding the door in the correct position but still rattles, the lock mechanism is worn and should be renewed.
3 Other rattles from the door could be caused by wear in the window regulator or glass channels. Loose or disconnected lock control rods can also be a source of rattles.

8 Bonnet – removal and refitting

1 With the bonnet open, undo the two bolts securing the stay to the bonnet inner panel (photo).

8.1 Remove the bonnet stay retaining bolts

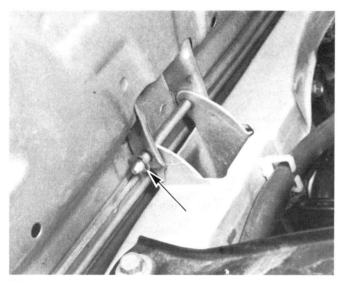

8.2 Extract the hinge retaining circlips (arrowed)

8.3 Remove the hinge pins and lift off the bonnet

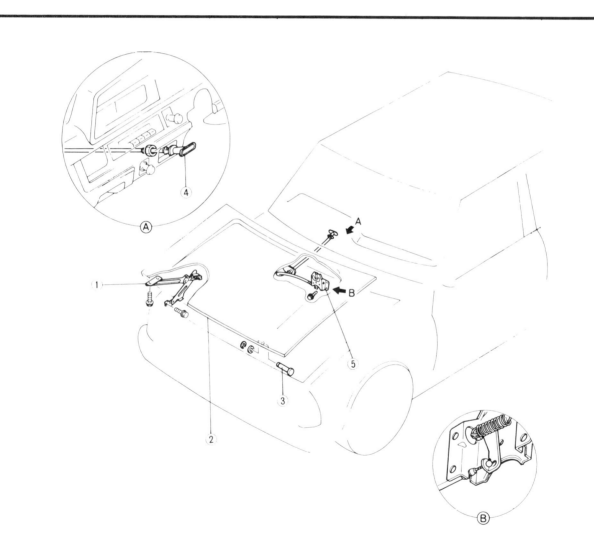

Fig. 11.1 Layout of the bonnet, bonnet lock and release cable (Secs 8, 9 and 10)

1 Bonnet stay
2 Bonnet
3 Hinge pin
4 Release cable knob
5 Bonnet lock
Inset A and B show release cable attachments

2   With an assistant supporting the bonnet, extract the two hinge retaining circlips and remove the washers (photo).
3   Withdraw the two hinge pins and remove the bonnet from the car (photo).
4   Refitting is the reverse sequence of removal.

9   Bonnet lock – adjustment

1   If the bonnet does not close satisfactorily, slacken the retaining bolts, move the lock up or down as required and tighten the bolts.
2   Check for proper operation and repeat the procedure until a satisfactory closing action is achieved.

10   Bonnet lock release cable – removal and refitting

1   Disconnect the battery negative terminal.
2   Working in the engine compartment disconnect the cable from the lock mechanism lever and release the cable sheath from the bracket.
3   From inside the car remove the steering column shrouds to gain access to the cable.
4   Undo the cable retaining nut from the rear of the facia and pull the cable through from the engine compartment.
5   Refitting is the reverse sequence of removal.

11   Radiator grille – removal and refitting

1   Insert a screwdriver into the centre of one of the grille retaining clips and carefully spread the clip ears as you pull outward on the grille

11.1 Radiator grille retaining clip (arrowed)

(photo). Repeat this procedure on all the remaining clips until the grille comes free and can be lifted away.
2   To refit the grille, locate it in its aperture and push it inwards until the clips engage and it snaps into place.

12   Boot lid – removal and refitting

1   Remove the boot lid lock as described in Section 13 then release the cable from its retaining clips on the boot lid.
2   Using a soft pencil mark the outline of the hinges on the boot lid.
3   Have an assistant support the boot lid then undo the hinge retaining bolts and lift the boot lid away.

4   Refitting is the reverse sequence of removal. Align the hinges with the outline marks made during removal. Adjust the hinge position slightly if necessary so that the lid closes easily and is in correct alignment. Further adjustment is possible by repositioning the striker plate.

13   Boot lid lock – removal and refitting

1   Disconnect the private lock operating rod from the boot lid lock.
2   Disconnect the lock release cable from its retaining clips and from the lock assembly.
3   Undo the retaining bolts and remove the lock from the boot lid.
4   Refitting is the reverse sequence of removal.

14   Boot lid private lock – removal and refitting

1   Disconnect the operating rod from the private lock lever.
2   Extract the large horseshoe shaped clip securing the private lock to the boot lid.
3   Withdraw the private lock from the boot lid and recover the washer.
4   Refitting is the reverse sequence of removal.

15   Tailgate – removal and refitting

1   Disconnect the battery negative terminal.
2   Refer to Chapter 12 and remove the courtesy light from the tailgate.
3   Remove the tailgate interior trim retaining buttons by unscrewing their centre part then prising out the button body with a screwdriver (photo). Withdraw the trim panel.

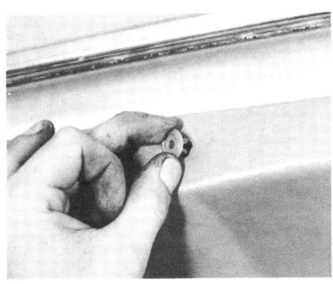

15.3 Removing the trim retaining button body

4   Disconnect the water hose from the tailgate washer and withdraw the hose from the tailgate.
5   Disconnect the tailgate wiper motor and rear window demister wiring and release the loom from its clips. Withdraw the complete loom from the tailgate.
6   Have an assistant support the tailgate then undo the two bolts each side securing the support strut brackets to the body (photo).
7   Undo the hinge retaining nuts and carefully lift off the tailgate.
8   Refitting is the reverse sequence of removal. Adjust the hinge positions as necessary so that the tailgate locates centrally in the body aperture. Further adjustment is possible by repositioning the striker plate to obtain satisfactory closure (photo).

15.6 Tailgate strut bracket retaining bolts

15.8 Tailgate striker plate retaining bolts (arrowed)

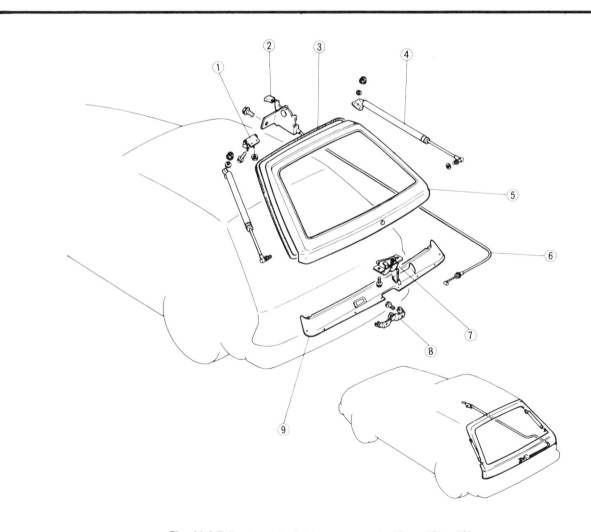

Fig. 11.2 Tailgate and related components (Secs 15 to 18)

1 Hinge	4 Support strut	7 Lock assembly
2 Tailgate release lever	5 Tailgate	8 Striker plate
3 Weatherstrip	6 Release cable	9 Interior trim

16 Tailgate support strut – removal and refitting

1   Support the tailgate in the open position using a stout length of wood or an assistant.
2   Undo the nut securing the support strut end fitting to the tailgate and the two bolts securing the bracket to the body. Withdraw the strut.
3   Refitting is the reverse sequence of removal.

17 Tailgate lock – removal and refitting

1   Refer to Chapter 12 and remove the courtesy light from the tailgate.
2   Remove the tailgate interior trim retaining buttons by unscrewing their centre part then prising out the button body using a screwdriver. Withdraw the trim panel.
3   Disconnect the private lock operating rod from the tailgate lock lever.
4   Undo the two retaining bolts and remove the lock from the tailgate.
5   Refitting is the reverse sequence of removal.

18 Tailgate private lock – removal and refitting

1   Refer to Chapter 12 and remove the courtesy light from the tailgate.
2   Remove the tailgate interior trim retaining buttons by unscrewing their centre part then prising out the button body with a screwdriver. Withdraw the trim panel.
3   Disconnect the operating rod from the private lock lever.
4   Extract the horseshoe shaped retaining clip and withdraw the private lock from the tailgate.
5   Refitting is the reverse sequence of removal.

19 Windscreen, tailgate window and stationary quarter window glass – removal and refitting

1   The windscreen, tailgate window and stationary quarter window glass are all sealed in place with a special adhesive and sealant compound. Removal of the trim mouldings and the adhesive compound entails the use of special tools and equipment making glass renewal a complex operation.
2   In view of this it is not recommended that stationary glass renewal be attempted by the home mechanic. If renewal is necessary due to breakage or leakage, the work should be entrusted to a Mazda dealer or glass replacement specialist.

20 Door inner trim panel – removal and refitting

1   Undo the door inner handle retaining screw, disengage the operating rod (photo) and remove the handle from the door.
2   Remove the window regulator handle horseshoe clip by hooking it out with a screwdriver or bent piece of wire, then pull the handle off the spindle.
3   Extract the trim caps (where applicable) over the armrest retaining screws then remove the screws and the armrest (photos).
4   Release the trim panel retaining studs by carefully levering between the panel and door with a screwdriver or suitable flat bar (photo). When all the studs are released lift the panel upwards and off the door.
5   To gain access to the door components, carefully peel back the polythene water shield as necessary (photo).
6   Refitting the trim panel is the reverse sequence of removal. When refitting the window regulator handle, fit the clip to the handle first then push the handle onto the regulator spindle (photo).

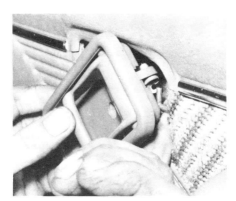

20.1 Disengage the operating rod from the door inner handle

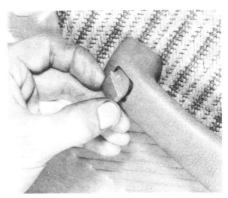

20.3A Extract the trim caps ...

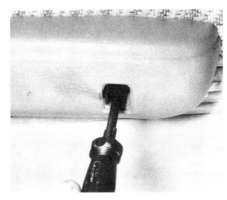

20.3B ... then undo the armrest retaining screws

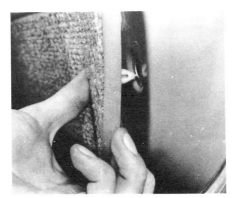

20.4 Release the trim panel retaining studs

20.5 Peel back the water shield for access to the door components

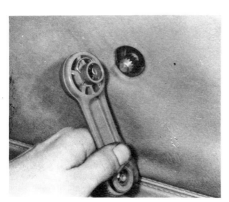

20.6 Refit the clip to the regulator handle before fitting the handle to the spindle

This sequence of photographs deals with the repair of the dent and paintwork damage shown in this photo. The procedure will be similar for the repair of a hole. It should be noted that the procedures given here are simplified – more explicit instructions will be found in the text

In the case of a dent the first job – after removing surrounding trim – is to hammer out the dent where access is possible. This will minimise filling. Here, the large dent having been hammered out, the damaged area is being made slightly concave

Now all paint must be removed from the damaged area, by rubbing with coarse abrasive paper. Alternatively, a wire brush or abrasive pad can be used in a power drill. Where the repair area meets good paintwork, the edge of the paintwork should be 'feathered', using a finer grade of abrasive paper

In the case of a hole caused by rusting, all damaged sheet-metal should be cut away before proceeding to this stage. Here, the damaged area is being treated with rust remover and inhibitor before being filled

Mix the body filler according to its manufacturer's instructions. In the case of corrosion damage, it will be necessary to block off any large holes before filling – this can be done with aluminium or plastic mesh, or aluminium tape. Make sure the area is absolutely clean before ...

... applying the filler. Filler should be applied with a flexible applicator, as shown, for best results; the wooden spatula being used for confined areas. Apply thin layers of filler at 20-minute intervals, until the surface of the filler is slightly proud of the surrounding bodywork

Initial shaping can be done with a Surform plane or Dreadnought file. Then, using progressively finer grades of wet-and-dry paper, wrapped around a sanding block, and copious amounts of clean water, rub down the filler until really smooth and flat. Again, feather the edges of adjoining paintwork

Again, using plenty of water, rub down the primer with a fine grade wet-and-dry paper (400 grade is probably best) until it is really smooth and well blended into the surrounding paintwork. Any remaining imperfections can now be filled by carefully applied knifing stopper paste

The top coat can now be applied. When working out of doors, pick a dry, warm and wind-free day. Ensure surrounding areas are protected from over-spray. Agitate the aerosol thoroughly, then spray the centre of the repair area, working outwards with a circular motion. Apply the paint as several thin coats

The whole repair area can now be sprayed or brush-painted with primer. If spraying, ensure adjoining areas are protected from over-spray. Note that at least one inch of the surrounding sound paintwork should be coated with primer. Primer has a 'thick' consistency, so will find small imperfections

When the stopper has hardened, rub down the repair area again before applying the final coat of primer. Before rubbing down this last coat of primer, ensure the repair area is blemish-free — use more stopper if necessary. To ensure that the surface of the primer is really smooth use some finishing compound

After a period of about two weeks, which the paint needs to harden fully, the surface of the repaired area can be 'cut' with a mild cutting compound prior to wax polishing. When carrying out bodywork repairs, remember that the quality of the finished job is proportional to the time and effort expended

21 Front door lock assembly – removal and refitting

1   Remove the door inner trim panel as described in Section 20.
2   Working through the door aperture disconnect the private lock, inner handle and inner lock button control rods by releasing their plastic clips (photo).
3   Disconnect the exterior handle control rod at the handle.
4   Undo the three screws securing the lock assembly to the door and remove the lock through the door aperture (photo).
5   Refitting is the reverse sequence of removal.

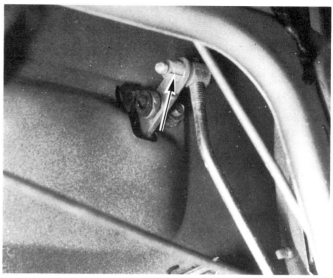

22.2 Disconnect the control rod (arrowed) at the exterior handle

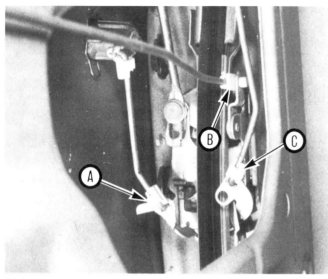

21.2 Private lock (A), inner handle (B), and inner lock button (C) control rod retaining clips

23 Front door private lock – removal and refitting

1   Remove the door inner trim panel as described in Section 20.
2   Disconnect the door lock control rod at the private lock by releasing the plastic clip (photo).
3   Extract the wire retaining clip and withdraw the private lock from the door.
4   Refitting is the reverse sequence of removal.

21.4 Undo the door lock retaining screws

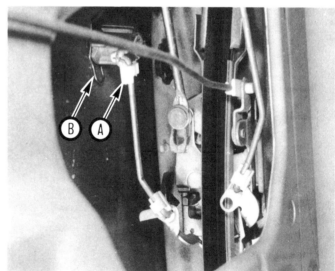

23.2 Control rod clip (A) and private lock wire retaining clip (B)

24 Front door glass and regulator – removal and refitting

1   Remove the door inner trim panel as described in Section 20.
2   Remove the two sealing strips from the top edge of the door panel by carefully releasing the retaining clips.
3   Working through the door aperture, undo the two screws securing the glass to the regulator frame.
4   Lift the glass upwards and remove it from the door.

22 Front door exterior handle – removal and refitting

1   Remove the door inner trim panel as described in Section 20.
2   Disconnect the door lock control rod, undo the two retaining nuts and withdraw the lock from the door (photo).
3   Refitting is the reverse sequence of removal.

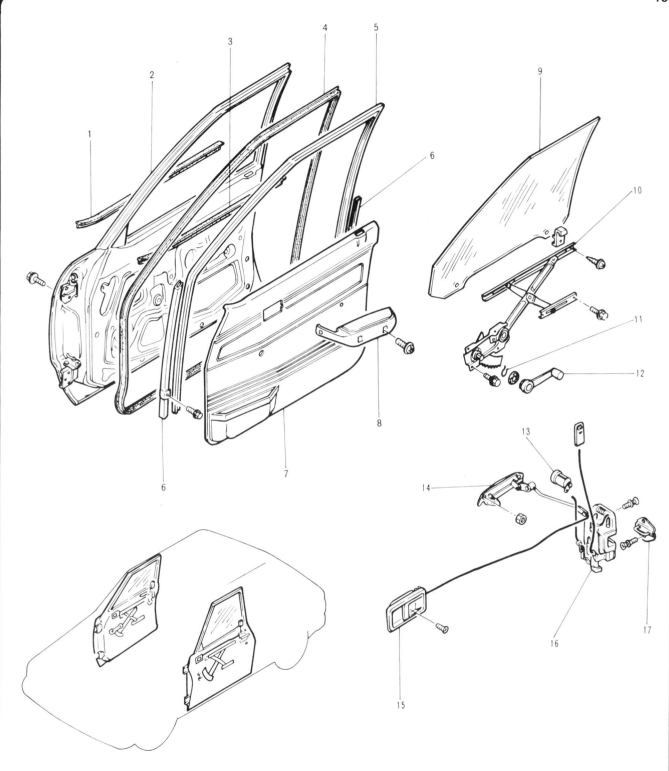

Fig. 11.3 Exploded view of the front door (Secs 20 to 24)

1 Outer sealing strip
2 Door frame
3 Inner sealing strip
4 Weatherstrip
5 Glass channel
6 Glass guide

7 Inner trim panel
8 Armrest
9 Window glass
10 Window regulator
11 Regulator handle horseshoe clip
12 Regulator handle

13 Private lock
14 Outer handle
15 Inner handle
16 Door lock
17 Striker

Fig. 11.4 Door glass to regulator frame retaining screws (4) (Sec 24)

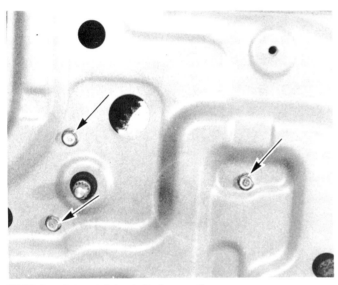

24.5A Regulator retaining bolts (arrowed) ...

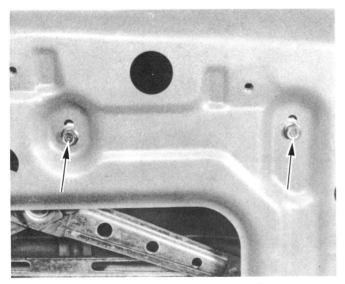

24.5B ... and regulator guide retaining bolts (arrowed)

5   Undo the bolts securing the regulator and regulator guide to the door panel and manipulate the assembly out through the door aperture (photos).
6   Refitting is the reverse sequence of removal, but before refitting the trim panel, adjust the regulator as follows.
7   Raise the glass to its highest position using the regulator. Adjust the position of the regulator guide so that the glass closes fully and moves smoothly in its guide channels.

25 Rear door lock assembly – removal and refitting

1   Remove the door inner trim panel as described in Section 20.
2   Working through the door aperture disconnect the inner handle and inner lock button control rods by releasing their plastic clips.
3   Undo the three screws securing the lock assembly to the door and remove the lock through the door aperture.
4   Refitting is the reverse sequence of removal.

26 Rear door exterior handle – removal and refitting

1   Remove the door inner trim panel as described in Section 20.
2   Undo the two retaining nuts and withdraw the lock from the door.
3   Refitting is the reverse sequence of removal.

27 Rear door quarter window glass – removal and refitting

1   Remove the door inner trim panel as described in Section 20.
2   Move the weatherstrip aside along the top of the door frame to gain access to the centre guide channel upper retaining screw. Undo this screw and the lower retaining screw then withdraw the channel from the door.
3   Ease the quarter window glass away from the door frame and remove it from the door.
4   Refitting is the reverse sequence of removal.

28 Rear door glass and regulator – removal and refitting

1   Remove the quarter window glass as described in Section 27.
2   Remove the two sealing strips from the top edge of the door panel by carefully releasing the retaining clips.
3   Lower the rear portion of the glass and disengage the roller on the regulator arm from the glass holder.
4   Lift the glass upwards and remove it from the door.
5   Undo the bolts securing the regulator to the door panel and manipulate the assembly out through the door aperture.
6   Refitting is the reverse sequence of removal. Adjust the centre guide channel at the lower retaining screw so that the glass is well supported but slides freely.

29 Door striker – adjustment

1   The door striker should be adjusted so that the door closes without slamming, is flush with the adjacent body panels when closed, and does not rattle when closed. The striker can be moved up and down or in and out to achieve this condition.
2   If adjustment is necessary, slacken the two striker retaining screws very slightly and move the striker as required. Hold the outer handle so that the door will not lock and slowly close the door. Check that the striker bar is parallel with the slot in the lock and check that the lock does not hit the striker as the door is closed. Tighten the striker retaining screws and close the door in the normal way. If necessary repeat the adjustment until satisfactory closing is achieved.

30 Rear quarter window – removal and refitting

1   Using a screwdriver carefully prise off the hinge covers.
2   Slacken the screws securing the hinges to the body.

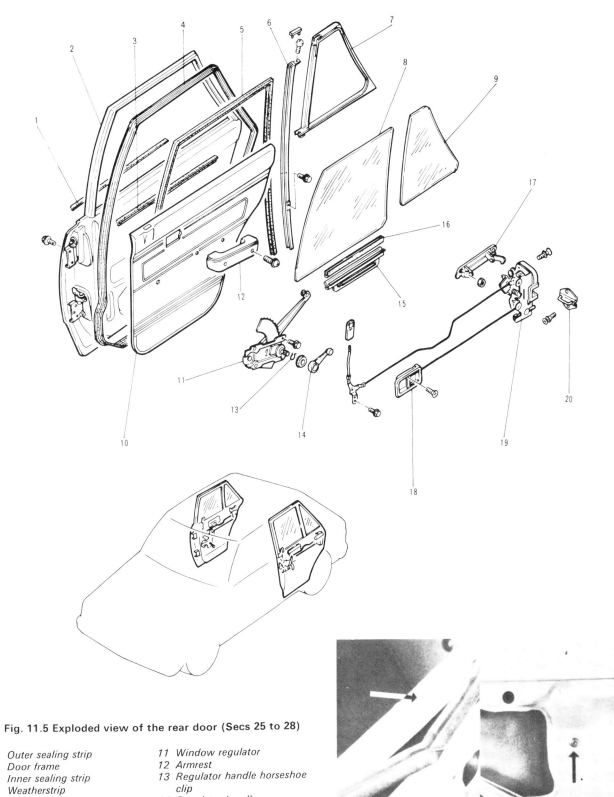

Fig. 11.5 Exploded view of the rear door (Secs 25 to 28)

1 Outer sealing strip
2 Door frame
3 Inner sealing strip
4 Weatherstrip
5 Glass channel
6 Centre guide channel
7 Quarter window glass
   channel
8 Door glass
9 Quarter window glass
10 Inner trim panel

11 Window regulator
12 Armrest
13 Regulator handle horseshoe
   clip
14 Regulator handle
15 Glass holder
16 Rubber strip
17 Outer handle
18 Inner handle
19 Door lock
20 Striker

Fig. 11.6 Quarter window centre guide channel retaining
screws (arrowed) (Sec 27)

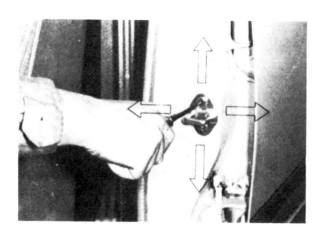

Fig. 11.7 Door striker adjustment (Sec 29)

3 Open the window and undo the screw securing the retaining catch to the body.
4 Have an assistant support the weight of the glass then undo the hinge retaining screws. Remove the window from its location.
5 Refitting is the reverse sequence of removal.

31 Front and rear bumpers – removal and refitting

1 If removing the front bumper on later models, undo the direction indicator lens retaining screws, withdraw the lens and light body and disconnect the wiring. Remove the direction indicators.
2 If removing a rear bumper prise up the number plate light body, disconnect the wiring and remove the light.
3 Refer to Fig. 11.8 and undo the nuts securing the bumper mounting bracket to the body.
4 Release the bumper wrap around section from the plastic slides and remove the bumper from the car.
5 Refitting is the reverse sequence of removal.

32 Door mirror – removal and refitting

1 Carefully prise off the mirror adjustment lever trim cap (photo).
2 Undo the retaining screw and remove the adjustment lever from the arm.
3 Undo the trim capping front screw and remove the capping (photo).
4 Undo the two remaining screws, lift off the stiffener plate and remove the mirror from the door (photos).
5 Refitting is the reverse sequence of removal.

33 Front and rear seats – removal and refitting

Front seat
1 Move the seat forwards as necessary to gain access to the rear seat rail retaining bolts. Undo the two bolts then move the seat rearwards.
2 Undo the two front seat rail retaining bolts and remove the seat from the car.
3 Refitting is the reverse sequence of removal.

Rear seat
4 Detach the seat back from the striker catch and push the seat rearward.
5 Remove the seat back fasteners and remove the mat.
6 Undo the seat back retaining bolts and remove the seat back from the car.

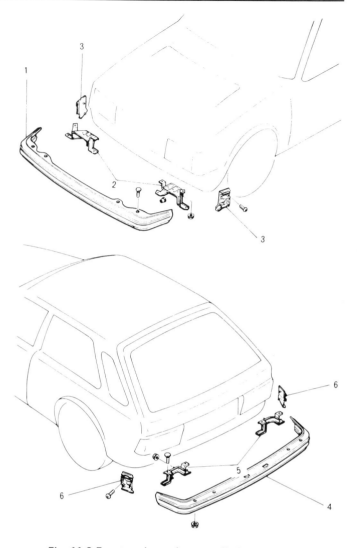

Fig. 11.8 Front and rear bumper fittings (Sec 31)

1	Front bumper	4	Rear bumper
2	Mounting bracket	5	Mounting bracket
3	Slide	6	Slide

32.1 Prise off the lever trim cap

32.3 Remove the trim capping front screw

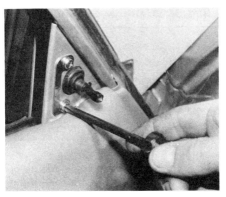
32.4A Undo the two remaining screws ...

32.4B ... and remove the mirror

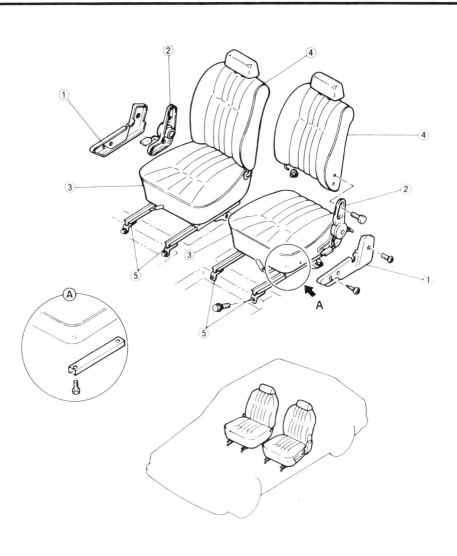

Fig. 11.9 Exploded view of the front seats (Sec 33)

1   Cover
2   Reclining assembly
3   Seat cushion
4   Seat back
5   Seat rails

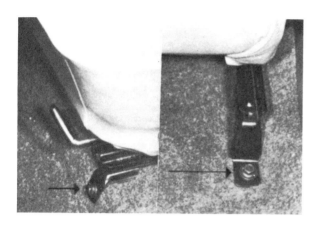

Fig. 11.10 Front seat rail attachments (arrowed) (Sec 33)

7   Where fitted undo the bolts securing the rear of the seat cushion to the floor.
8   Push the front of the cushion downwards and rearwards to release the front catch then remove it from the car.
9   Refitting is the reverse sequence of removal.

34 Centre console – removal and refitting

1   Carefully prise the upper panel out of its locating catches (photo), lift it up over the gear lever or selector lever and remove it.
2   Undo the two screws in the centre (photo) and the two screws at the rear sides securing the console in position. Lift the console up and remove it from the car.
3   Refitting is the reverse sequence of removal.

35 Facia panel – removal and refitting

1   Refer to Chapter 12 and remove the instrument panel.
2   Undo the retaining screws and remove the oddments tray from under the centre of the facia (photo).

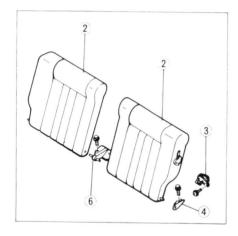

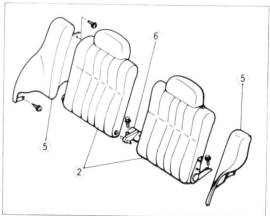

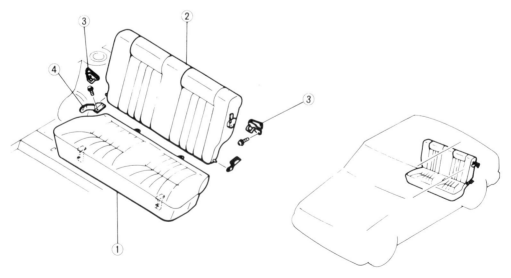

Fig. 11.11 Rear seat attachment details (Sec 33)

1   Seat cushion
2   Seat back
3   Striker catch
4   Side mounting bracket
5   Side trim
6   Centre mounting bracket

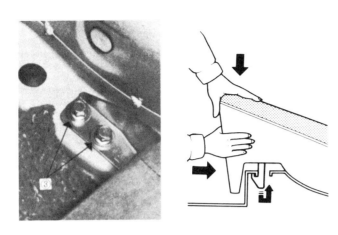

Fig. 11.12 Rear seat removal (Sec 33)

Seat back mounting bracket (left), removing rear seat cushion (right)

35.2 Oddments tray retaining screws (arrowed)

34.1 Console upper panel locating catches (arrowed)

3   Remove the radio control knobs and retaining nuts.
4   Undo the choke knob retaining grub screw and pull off the knob.
5   Undo the knurled retaining nut (photo) securing the choke cable to the switch panel.
6   Undo the screws along the upper edge securing the left and right-hand halves of the switch panel (photos).
7   Pull the upper part of the switch panel outwards then disengage the lower catches. Remove the left-hand panel, disconnect the switch wiring and remove the right-hand panel.
8   Undo the two screws securing the radio to the facia (photo). Withdraw the radio, disconnect the wiring and aerial connections and remove the radio.
9   Undo the two clock retaining screws (photo). Disconnect the wiring and remove the clock.
10 Undo the screws securing the glovebox lid striker and remove the striker.
11 Undo the screws securing the glovebox lid and glovebox to the facia (photo). Lift off the lid and remove the glovebox (photo).
12 Undo the nuts securing the heater controls to the facia frame and separate the controls and frame (photo).
13 Undo the fusebox retaining screws and separate the fusebox from the facia.

34.2 Console centre retaining screws (arrowed)

35.5 Choke cable knurled retaining nut (arrowed)

35.6A Undo the screws securing the left-hand ...

35.6B ... and right-hand halves of the switch panel

35.8 Radio retaining screws (arrowed)

35.9 Clock retaining screws (arrowed)

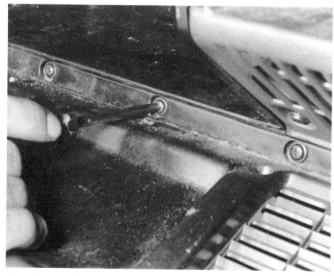

35.11A Undo the glovebox retaining screws ...

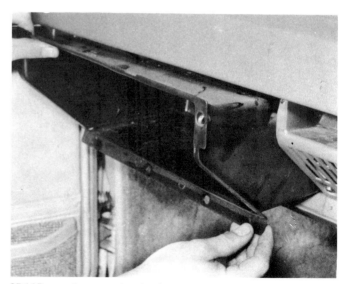

35.11B ... and remove the glovebox

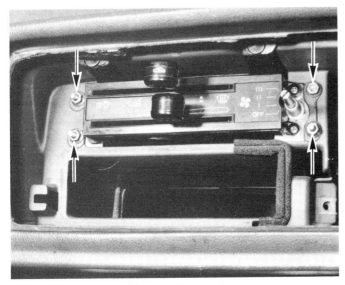

35.12 Heater control retaining nuts (arrowed)

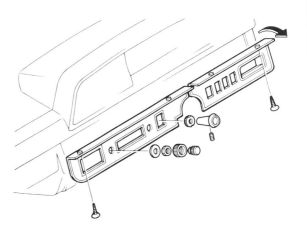

Fig. 11.13 Facia switch panel removal (Sec 35)

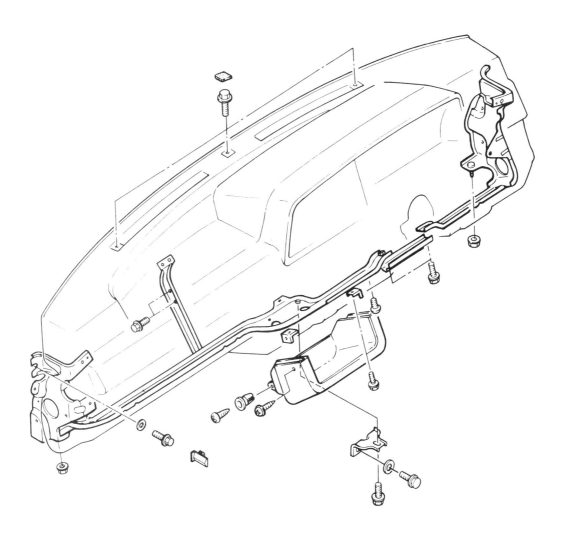

Fig. 11.14 Facia and facia frame attachments (Sec 35)

14 Referring to Chapter 10 if necessary, undo the steering column mounting bolts and lower the column clear of the facia.
15 Refer to Fig. 11.14 and undo the bolts securing the facia and frame to the bulkhead (photos). Ease the facia away from its location and, as access improves, disconnect the heater ducts and any remaining wiring. Remove the facia from the car.
16 Refitting is a reverse of the removal sequence.

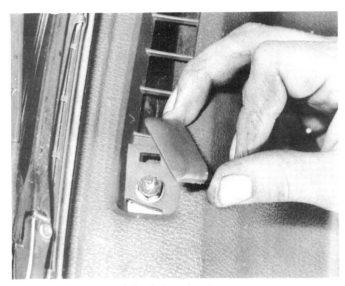

35.15A Facia upper retaining bolt under trim cap ...

35.15B ... and side retaining bolt (arrowed)

36 Heater controls – adjustment

1 Before carrying out any adjustments disconnect the battery negative terminal.

Air control adjustment
2 Move the air control lever fully to the left.
3 Release the control cable retaining clip at the air flap on the lower left-hand side of the heater (accessible from the passenger's footwell).
4 Move the flap fully clockwise, hold it in this position and refit the control cable retaining clip.

5 A second control cable from the air control lever operates a flap valve on the air intake to open or close the intake to outside air.
6 To adjust the air intake flap valve pull the control lever knob out and release the retaining clip at the air intake flap valve.
7 Move the flap valve fully anti-clockwise, hold it in this position and refit the control cable retaining clip.

Air temperature control adjustment
8 Move the air temperature control lever fully to the right.
9 Release the control cable retaining clip at the air flap on the lower right-hand side of the heater (accessible from the driver's footwell).
10 Move the flap fully clockwise, hold it in this position and refit the control cable retaining clip.
11 Now move the air temperature control lever fully to the left.

36.12 Control cable retaining clip (arrowed)

12 From within the engine compartment release the control cable retaining clip at the water valve (photo). Move the valve lever fully anti-clockwise, hold it in this position and refit the control cable retaining clip.

37 Heater controls – removal and refitting

1 Disconnect the battery negative terminal.
2 Pull the knob off the heater blower control.
3 Undo the four screws securing the upper part of the instrument panel shroud to the facia. Pull the bottom part of the shroud out of its retaining clips and remove it.
4 Undo the grub screws securing the knobs to the heater control levers and remove the knobs (photo).
5 Undo the screws securing the heater control faceplate and remove the faceplate.
6 Undo the heater control retaining nuts and withdraw the control assembly from the facia. Release the control cable retaining clips, disconnect the cables and remove the heater control assembly.
7 Refitting is the reverse sequence of removal, but adjust the controls as described in Section 36 after refitting.

38 Heater blower motor – removal and refitting

1 Disconnect the battery negative terminal.
2 Remove the cover undo the facia on the driver's side.
3 Disconnect the motor wiring connector, undo the three retaining

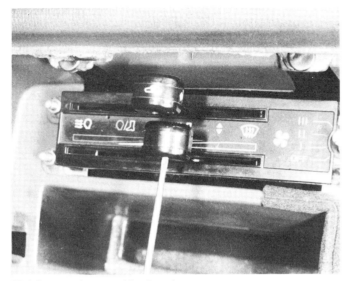

37.4 Remove the control knob grub screws

Fig. 11.15 Exploded view of the heater
(Secs 36 to 39)

1 Water valve
2 Heater controls
3 Demister nozzle
4 Side demister hose
5 Ventilator duct
6 Side ventilator grille
7 Centre ventilator grille
8 Heater unit
9 Demister hose
10 Duct
11 Air intake
12 Boost ventilator duct
13 Retaining button
14 Elbow joint
15 Rear compartment duct

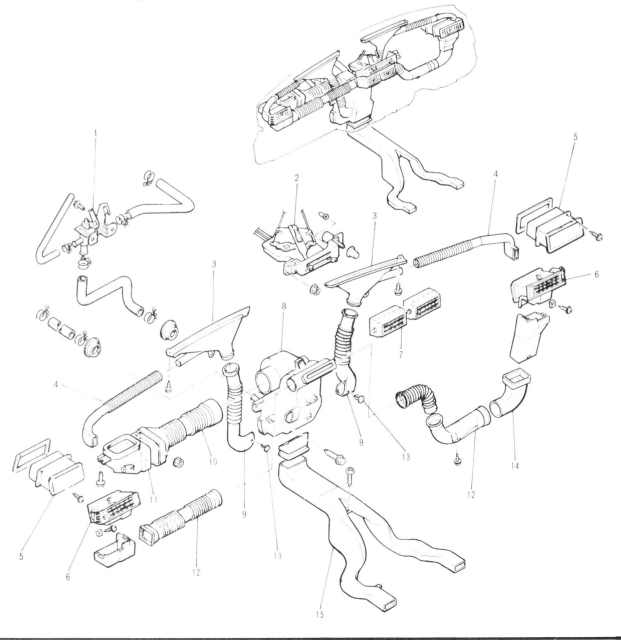

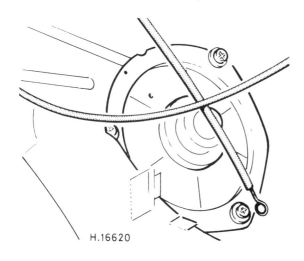

H.16620

Fig. 11.16 Heater blower motor removal (Sec 38)

screws and withdraw the motor from the heater unit. For greater access remove the air ducts under the facia as necessary.

4   Refitting is the reverse sequence of removal.

39 Heater unit – removal and refitting

1   Disconnect the battery negative terminal.
2   Refer to Chapter 2 and drain the cooling system.
3   Remove the facia as described in Section 35 of this Chapter.
4   From within the engine compartment disconnect the heater hoses at the matrix outlets.
5   Release the retaining clips and disconnect the control cables at the heater unit.
6   Disconnect the blower motor wiring at the connector.
7   Disconnect the air ducts and demister ducts at the heater unit.
8   Undo the bolts securing the heater in position and ease it away from the engine compartment bulkhead. Tip the unit back so that the matrix outlets are uppermost to prevent water spillage then remove the unit from the car.
9   Refitting is the reverse sequence of removal bearing in mind the following points:

(a) Refill the cooling system as described in Chapter 2
(b) Adjust the heater control cables as described in Section 36

Chapter 12 Electrical system

For modifications, and information applicable to later models, see Supplement at end of manual

Contents

Specifications

System type .... 12 volt, negative earth

Battery
Type .... 12 volt, low maintenance
Capacity .... 33 Amp hour, or 50 Amp hour

Alternator
Type .... Mitsubishi
Maximum output .... 50 Amps
Brush length:
    Standard .... 18 mm (0.7 in)
    Wear limit .... 8 mm (0.3 in)

Starter motor
Type .... Mitsubishi pre-engaged
Brush length:
    Standard .... 17 mm (0.6 in)
    Wear limit .... 11.5 mm (0.45 in)
Drive pinion gap .... 0.5 to 2.0 mm (0.02 to 0.08 in)

Bulbs
	Wattage
Headlight	60/55
Front direction indicator	21
Side repeater	5
Front sidelight	5

	Wattage
Rear direction indicator	21
Rear tail light	5
Rear stop-light	21
Reversing light	21
Number plate light	5
Rear foglight	21
Interior courtesy light	10
Map light	6
Luggage compartment light	5
Instrument warning and panel illumination lights	1.4 or 3.4

Torque wrench settings

	Nm	lbf ft
Alternator pivot mounting bolt	38 to 64	28 to 47
Starter motor retaining bolts	38 to 64	28 to 47

1 General description

The electrical system is of the 12 volt negative earth type, and consists of a 12 volt battery, alternator, starter motor and related electrical accessories, components and wiring. The battery is of the low maintenance type and is charged by an alternator which is belt-driven from the crankshaft pulley. The starter motor is of the pre-engaged type incorporating an integral solenoid. On starting, the solenoid moves the drive pinion into engagement with the flywheel ring gear before the starter motor is energised. Once the engine has started, a one-way clutch prevents the motor armature being driven by the engine until the pinion disengages from the flywheel.

Further details of the major electrical systems are given in the relevant Sections of this Chapter.

Caution: *Before carrying out any work on the vehicle electrical system, read through the precautions given in Safety First! at the beginning of this manual and in Section 2 of this Chapter.*

Fig. 12.1 Electrolyte level markings on battery case (Sec 3)

2 Electrical system – precautions

It is necessary to take extra care when working on the electrical system to avoid damage to semi-conductor devices (diodes and transistors), and to avoid the risk of personal injury. In addition to the precautions given in Safety First! at the beginning of this manual, observe the following items when working on the system.

1 *Always remove rings, watches, etc before working on the electrical system.* Even with the battery disconnected, capacitive discharge could occur if a component live terminal is earthed through a metal object. This could cause a shock or nasty burn.

2 *Do not reverse the battery connections.* Components such as the alternator or any other having semi-conductor circuitry could be irreparably damaged.

3 If the engine is being started using jump leads and a slave battery, connect the batteries *positive to positive* and *negative to negative*. This also applies when connecting a battery charger.

4 Never disconnect the battery terminals, or alternator multiplug connector, when the engine is running.

5 The battery leads and alternator wiring must be disconnected before carrying out any electric welding on the car.

6 Never use an ohmmeter of the type incorporating a hand cranked generator for circuit or continuity testing.

3 Maintenance and inspection

1 At the service intervals given in Routine Maintenance at the beginning of this Manual carry out the following maintenance and inspection operations on the electrical system components.

2 Check that the level of electrolyte in the battery is maintained between the upper and lower level markings on the side of the battery case. If topping up is necessary, unscrew the cell filler caps and add distilled water to each cell until the level is correct. Refit the filler caps and wipe off any spilled water.

3 Check the operation of all the electrical equipment, ie wipers, washers, lights, direction indicators etc. Refer to the appropriate Sections of this Chapter if any components are found to be inoperative.

4 Visually check all accessible wiring connectors, harnesses and retaining clips for security, or any signs of chafing or damage. Rectify any problems encountered.

5 Check the alternator drivebelt for cracks, fraying or damage. Renew the belt if worn or, if satisfactory, check and adjust the belt tension. These procedures are covered in Chapter 2.

6 Check the condition of the wiper blades and if they are cracked or show signs of deterioration, renew them, as described in Section 27. Check the operation of the windscreen washers. Adjust the nozzles if necessary.

7 Check the battery terminals and, if there is any sign of corrosion, disconnect and clean them thoroughly. Smear the terminals and battery posts with petroleum jelly before refitting the plastic covers. If there is any corrosion on the battery tray, remove the battery, clean the deposits away and treat the affected metal with an anti-rust preparation. Repaint the tray in the original colour after treatment.

8 Top up the windscreen washer reservoir and check the security of the pump wires and water pipes.

9 It is advisable to have the headlight aim adjusted using optical beam setting equipment.

10 While carrying out a road test check the operation of all the instruments and warning lights, and the operation of the direction indicator self-cancelling mechanism.

4 Battery – removal and refitting

1 Slacken the negative (-) terminal clamp bolt and lift the terminal off the battery post (photo).

2 Lift the plastic cover from the positive (+) terminal, slacken the clamp bolt and lift the terminal off the battery post.

3 Undo the retaining nuts and lift off the battery clamp.

4 Withdraw the battery from the carrier tray.

5 Refitting is the reverse sequence of removal.

4.1 Battery negative terminal disconnected

5 Battery – charging

1   It is possible that in winter, when the load on the battery cannot be recuperated during normal driving time, external charging may be necessary. This can be confirmed by checking the state of charge of the battery by means of a hydrometer. To do this unscrew the cell filler caps on the battery and measure the specific gravity of the electrolyte in each cell. Compare the readings obtained with the following chart to determine the state of charge of the battery.

	Climate below 26.7°C (80°F)	Climate above 26.7°C (80°F)
Fully charged	1.270 to 1.290	1.210 to 1.230
Half charged	1.190 to 1.210	1.120 to 1.150
Discharged completely	1.110 to 1.130	1.050 to 1.070

Note: If the electrolyte temperature is significantly different from 15.6°C (60°F) then the specific gravity will be affected. For every 2.8°C (5°F) it will increase or decrease with the temperature by 0.002.

When the vehicle is being used in cold climates, it is essential to maintain the battery fully charged because the charge affects the freezing point of the electrolyte. The densities below have been corrected to suit measurement at 26.7°C (80°F):

Specific gravity 1.200 freezes   -37.5°C (-35°F)
Specific gravity 1.160 freezes   -18°C (0°F)

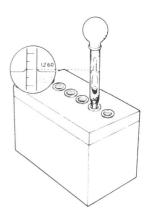

Fig. 12.2 Checking battery condition with a hydrometer (Sec 5)

2   If charging is necessary this should be done at a trickle rate of about 1 to 1.5 Amps overnight. Alternatively, if a more sophisticated charger is available then this should be set to charge at 10% of the battery's capacity over a 10 hour period i.e. for a 33 Amp hour battery, charge at 3.3 Amps for 10 hours from a fully discharged state.

3   Before connecting the battery charger ensure that the electrolyte level is correct and top up with distilled water if necessary to bring the level between the upper and lower level markings on the battery case. Disconnect the battery negative terminal and make sure that the charging takes place in a well ventilated area. Do not smoke or allow naked flame anywhere near the battery while charging takes place.

6 Alternator – removal and refitting

1   Disconnect the battery negative terminal.
2   For greater access, apply the handbrake, chock the rear wheels and jack up the front of the car. Support the car on axle stands then remove the undertrays as necessary.
3   Disconnect the wiring at the rear of the alternator (photo).
4   Slacken the alternator pivot mounting bolt and the adjusting arm

6.3 Disconnect the wiring (arrowed) at the alternator

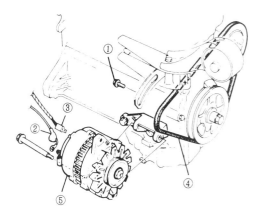

Fig. 12.3 Alternator mounting details (Sec 6)

1   Adjusting arm bolt
2   Alternator lead to battery
3   Alternator lead to ignition switch
4   Drivebelt
5   Alternator

bolt then move the alternator towards the engine. Slip the drivebelt off the alternator pulley.

5   Remove the adjusting arm bolt and pivot mounting bolt then withdraw the alternator from the engine.

6   Refitting is the reverse sequence of removal, but before tightening the mounting and adjusting arm bolt, tension the drivebelt as described in Chapter 2.

7   Alternator – fault tracing and rectification

1   Owing to the specialist knowledge and equipment required to test or repair an alternator, it is recommended that, if performance is suspect, the car be taken to an automobile electrician who will have the facilities for such work.

2   The most obvious sign of a fault is the alternator warning lamp on the instrument panel light, particularly at low speeds. This indicates that the alternator is not charging. Other symptoms are a low battery charge, evidenced by dim headlights and the starter motor turning the engine over slowly.

3   The first check should always be of the drivebelt tensioner (Chapter 2) followed by making sure that all electrical connections are secure and free of dirt and corrosion.

4   If the drivebelt tension, electrical connections and battery condition are good, an internal fault in the alternator or internal voltage regulator is indicated.

5   An exploded view of the alternator is given in Fig. 12.4 for reference purposes but as stated above, repair should be left to a specialist. If the alternator has seen considerable service a practical alternative may be to replace it with an exchange reconditioned unit.

8   Starter motor – testing in the car

1   If the starter motor fails to operate, first check the condition of the battery by switching on the headlights. If they glow brightly then gradually dim after a few seconds, the battery is in an uncharged condition.

2   If the battery is satisfactory, check the starter motor main terminal and the engine earth cable for security. Check the terminal connections on the starter solenoid – located on top of the starter motor.

3   If the starter still fails to turn use a voltmeter, or 12 volt test lamp and leads, to ensure that there is battery voltage at the solenoid main terminal (containing the cable from the battery positive terminal).

4   With the ignition switched on and the ignition key in position III, check that voltage is reaching the solenoid terminal with the spade connector, and also the starter main terminal.

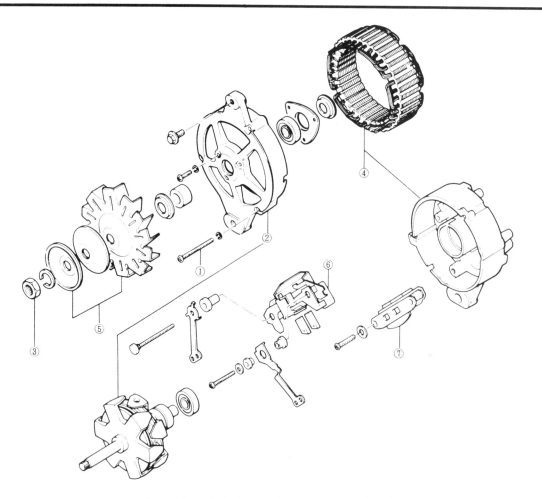

Fig. 12.4 Exploded view of the alternator (Sec 7)

1 Through-bolt	4 Commutator end bracket and stator	6 Brush holder assembly
2 Drive-end bracket and rotor	5 Pulley and fan	7 Rectifier diode
3 Pulley retaining nut		

5   If there is no voltage reaching the spade connector there is a wiring or ignition switch fault. If voltage is available, but the starter does not operate, then the starter or solenoid is likely to be at fault.

9   Starter motor – removal and refitting

1   Disconnect the battery negative terminal.
2   Disconnect the starter motor wiring at the rear of the solenoid.
3   Undo the three retaining bolts and remove the starter from the engine (photo).
4   Refitting is the reverse sequence of removal.

10   Starter motor – overhaul

1   Remove the starter from the car as described in the previous Section.
2   At the rear of the solenoid, unscrew the nut and disconnect the lead from the field windings.
3   Undo and remove the two screws securing the solenoid to the drive-end housing. Disengage the solenoid plunger from the engaging lever and withdraw the solenoid.
4   Undo and remove the two through-bolts and withdraw the rear cover.
5   Slip the field brushes out of the brush holder and remove the holder assembly. Recover the remaining brush and the brush springs.
6   Withdraw the yoke followed by the armature from the drive-end housing.
7   Using a tube of suitable diameter, tap the thrust collar on the end of the armature shaft toward the drive pinion to expose the retaining circlip. Extract the circlip then slide the thrust collar and drive pinion off the armature shaft.
8   With the starter motor now completely dismantled, clean all the components in paraffin or a suitable solvent and wipe dry.
9   Check the brush length and renew the brushes if they are worn to below the minimum length given in the Specifications. Also check the condition of the springs and renew any that are distorted or broken.
10 Check that the brushes move freely in their holders and clean the brushes and holders with a petrol moistened rag if they show any tendency to stick. If necessary use a fine file on the brushes if they still stick after cleaning.

9.3 Removing the starter motor

11 Check the armature shaft for distortion and examine the commutator for excessive scoring, wear or burns. If necessary the commutator may be skimmed in a lathe and then polished with fine glass paper. After skimming check that the commutator segments are still proud of the mica insulation (Fig. 12.7) and if necessary increase the depth of the mica grooves.
12 Check the taping of the field coils, check all joints for security and check the coils and commutator for signs of burning.
13 Check the drive pinion assembly, drive-end housing, engaging lever and solenoid for wear or damage. Make sure that the drive pinion one-way clutch permits movement of the pinion in one direction only and renew the complete assembly if necessary.
14 Check the condition of the bushes in the drive-end housing and

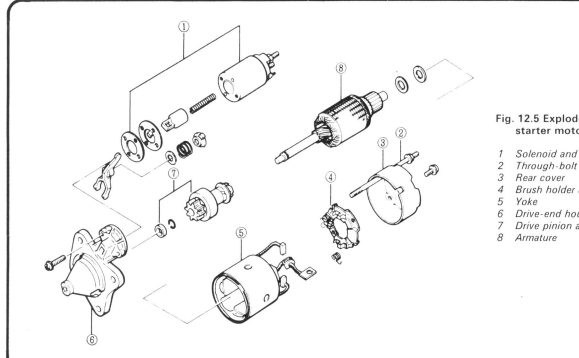

Fig. 12.5 Exploded view of the starter motor (Sec 10)

1   Solenoid and spacers
2   Through-bolt
3   Rear cover
4   Brush holder assembly
5   Yoke
6   Drive-end housing
7   Drive pinion and thrust collar
8   Armature

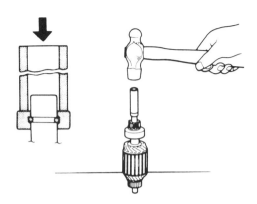

Fig. 12.6 Using a hammer and tube to release the thrust collar (Sec 10)

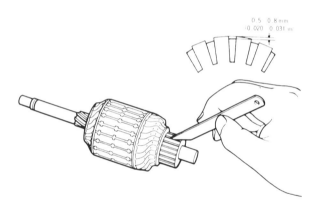

0.5 0.8 mm
(0.020 0.031 in)

Fig. 12.7 Increasing the depth of commutator mica insulation (Sec 10)

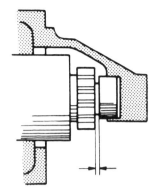

Fig. 12.8 Drive pinion gap measuring point (Sec 10)

11 Fuses and fusible links – general

1   The fusebox is situated on the front of the facia just to the right of the steering column. Lift off the fusebox lid to gain access to the fuses (photo).
2   To remove a fuse from its location hook it out using the small plastic removal tool provided (photo). This is located in the fusebox lid. Hook the tool over the fuse and pull upwards to remove. Refit the fuse by pressing it firmly into its location.
3   Always renew a fuse with one of an identical rating. Never renew a fuse more than once without finding the source of the trouble. Each fuse is colour coded and has its rating stamped on it. The circuits protected by each fuse are shown on the fusebox.
4   Additionally the headlights are further protected by two fusible links located in the engine compartment just behind the battery (photo).
5   If the headlights fail to operate and the relevant fuses are not blown, check the fusible links. If either of the links has melted it must be replaced. Note however that if this happens there may be a fault in the circuit and a thorough check should be carried out.

12 Ignition switch/steering column lock – removal and refitting

The ignition switch is an integral part of the steering column lock; removal and refitting procedures are given in Chapter 10.

rear cover and renew them if worn. Soak the new bushes in engine oil for 24 hours before fitting.
15 Accurate checking of the armature, commutator and field coil windings and insulation requires the use of special test equipment. If the starter motor was inoperative when removed from the car and the previous checks have not highlighted the problem, then it can be assumed that there is a continuity or insulation fault and the unit should be renewed.
16 If the starter is in a satisfactory condition, or if a fault has been traced and rectified, the unit can be reassembled using the reverse of the dismantling procedure.
17 With the starter motor reassembled the drive pinion gap should be checked as follows.
18 Disconnect the lead from the field windings to the solenoid terminal.
19 Attach a lead from the negative terminal of a 12 volt battery to the starter motor body and hold a positive lead from the battery against the spade terminal on the solenoid. As this is done the drive pinion will move out. Measure the gap between the extended pinion and the thrust collar on the armature shaft using feeler gauges (Fig. 12.8). This is the drive pinion gap and should be as given in the Specifications. During this check do not allow the pinion to remain in the extended position for more than 20 seconds at a time otherwise the solenoid will be damaged. If the gap is not as specified, adjust by increasing or decreasing the number of spacers between the solenoid and the drive-end housing. Increasing the number of spacers decreases the gap and vice versa.
20 On completion of the adjustment refit the starter motor as described in Section 9.

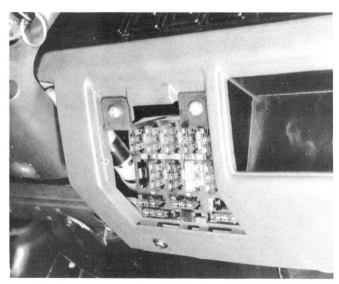

11.1 Lift off the fusebox lid to gain access to the fuses

11.2 Using the tool provided to remove a fuse

13.3A Undo the retaining screws (arrowed) and lift off the steering column shrouds

11.4 Fusible links location in engine compartment

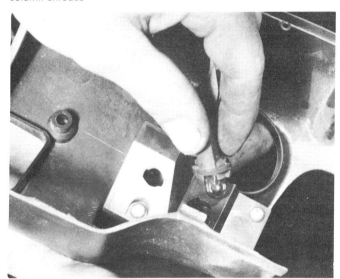

13.3B Removing the bulbholder from the right-hand shroud

13 Steering column combination switch – removal and refitting

1   Disconnect the battery negative terminal.
2   Refer to Chapter 10 and remove the steering wheel.
3   Undo the screws securing the two halves of the steering column shroud to the column (photo). Lift off the left-hand shroud, remove the bulbholder in the right-hand shroud by turning it anti-clockwise (photo), then lift off the right-hand shroud.
4   Undo the clamp retaining screw and remove the clamp (photo).
5   Disconnect the wiring multi-plugs and remove the combination switch assembly. If necessary the switches can be removed from the main body after undoing the retaining screws at the rear.
6   Refitting is the reverse sequence of removal.

14 Instrument panel – removal and refitting

1   Remove the steering column combination switch as described in the previous Section.

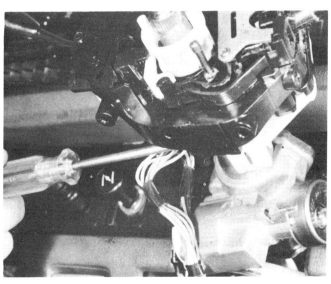

13.4 Undo the combination switch clamp retaining screw

2   Pull the knob off the heater blower motor switch then undo the four upper retaining screws securing the instrument panel shroud to the facia (photo).

3   Push down on the flat surface of the shroud below the instrument panel and pull the left-hand side of the shroud outwards. Now withdraw the shroud from the facia (photo).

14.2 Undo the instrument panel shroud retaining screws ...

14.3 ... and remove the shroud

4   Undo the four screws securing the instrument panel to the facia frame (photo).

5   Pull the instrument panel out slightly then reach behind and disconnect the panel wiring connectors and multi-plugs (photo), and the speedometer cable. Make a note of the location of the wiring connectors as they are disconnected then remove the instrument panel.

6   Refitting is the reverse sequence of removal.

---

15 Instrument panel and instruments – dismantling and reassembly

---

1   Remove the instrument panel from the car, as described in the previous Section.

14.4 Undo the four instrument panel retaining screws ...

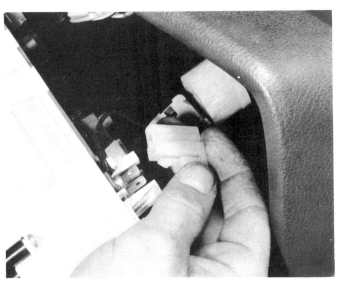

14.5 ... and disconnect the wiring and cables at the rear of the panel

Panel illumination and warning light bulbs

2   The bulbholders are secured to the rear of the instrument panel by a bayonet fitting and are removed by turning the holders anti-clockwise (photo). The bulbs can be removed from their holders in the same way, but note that some of the bulbs are not removable separately and are supplied with the holder as a unit.

3   Refit the bulbs and holders by turning them clockwise until they lock.

Instruments

4   Undo the retaining screws (photo), release the lower tags and separate the meter cover from the meter case.

5   Undo the retaining screws or nuts as applicable and remove the relevant instrument from the case.

6   Refitting is the reverse sequence of removal.

Voltage regulator

7   Disconnect the regulator lead at the spade terminal.

8   Undo the retaining screw and remove the regulator from the rear of the instrument panel.

9   Refitting is the reverse sequence of removal.

15.2 Instrument panel bulb removal

15.4 Meter cover to meter case retaining screws (arrowed)

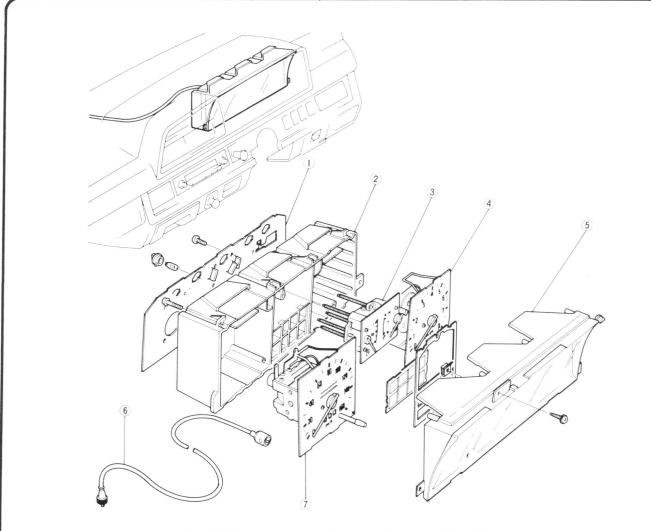

Fig. 12.9 Exploded view of the instrument panel (Sec 15)

1 Printed circuit	3 Fuel and temperature gauges	5 Meter cover
2 Meter case	4 Tachometer	6 Speeedometer cable
		7 Speedometer

15.10 Component locations on the rear of the instrument panel

16.3 Disconnect the wiring from the panel switches

Printed circuit

10 Remove the bulbholders, retaining nuts and screws at the rear of the instrument panel and lift off the printed circuit (photo).
11 Refitting is the reverse sequence of removal.

16 Facia switches – removal and refitting

1 Disconnect the battery negative terminal.
2 Undo the screws along the upper edge securing the right-hand half of the switch panel to the facia.
3 Pull the upper part of the switch panel outwards then disengage the lower catches. Disconnect the switch wiring and remove the panel (photo).
4 Depress the switch retaining tags (photo) and withdraw the switches from the panel.
5 To remove the switches on the auxiliary panel adjacent to the fusebox, remove the cover under the facia then disconnect the wiring and release the relevant switch by reaching up behind the facia.
6 Refitting is the reverse sequence of removal.

16.4 Remove the switches by depressing the retaining tags

17 Clock – removal and refitting

1 Disconnect the battery negative terminal.
2 Remove the radio control knobs and retaining nuts.
3 Undo the choke knob retaining grub screw and pull off the knob.
4 Undo the knurled retaining nut securing the choke cable to the switch panel.
5 Undo the screws along the upper edge securing the left-hand half of the switch panel to the facia.
6 Pull the upper part of the switch panel outwards then disengage the lower catches. Remove the panel.
7 Undo the two clock retaining screws and withdraw it from the facia (photo).
8 Disconnect the clock wiring and remove the unit.
9 Refitting is the reverse sequence of removal.

18 Radio – removal and refitting

1 Refer to the previous Section and carry out the operations described in paragraphs 1 to 7 inclusive.
2 Undo the two screws securing the radio to the facia.
3 Withdraw the radio and disconnect the wiring and aerial lead at the rear of the unit then remove it from the facia.
4 Refitting is the reverse sequence of removal.

17.7 Clock retaining screws (arrowed)

19 Headlight bulb – renewal

1   From within the engine compartment pull off the wiring connector at the rear of the headlight bulb (photo).
2   Slip off the rubber cover, remove the bulb retaining ring and withdraw the bulb (photos). Take care not to touch the bulb glass with your fingers; if touched, clean the bulb with methylated spirit.
3   Refit the bulb using the reverse of the removal procedure.

20 Sidelight bulb – renewal

1   Undo the screws and remove the sidelight lens.

2   Remove the bulb from the holder by turning anti-clockwise (photo).
3   Refit the bulb using the reverse of the removal procedure.

21 Front direction indicator bulb – renewal

1   Undo the screws and remove the direction indicator lens which is integral with the sidelight on early models or located in the front bumper on later models (photo).
2   Remove the bulb from the holder by turning anti-clockwise (photo).
3   To renew the side repeater bulb, undo the two screws and remove the lens (photo).
4   Withdraw the push fit bulb from the holder (photo).
5   Refitting is the reverse sequence of removal.

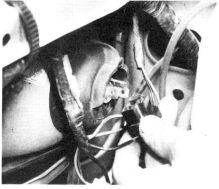

19.1 Disconnect the headlight wiring plug

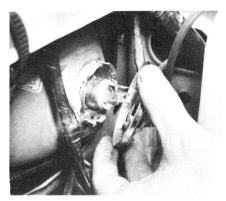

19.2A Remove the bulb retaining ring ...

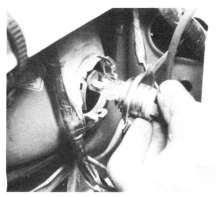

19.2B ... and withdraw the bulb

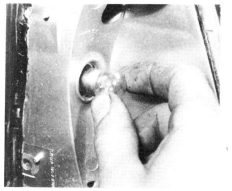

20.2 Sidelight bulb renewal

21.1 Undo the direction indicator lens retaining screws ...

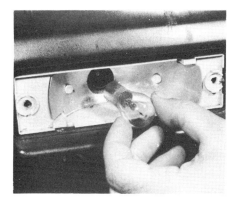

21.2 ... and remove the lens followed by the bulb

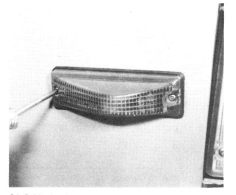

21.3 Undo the side repeater lens retaining screws then remove the lens ...

21.4 ... and withdraw the push fit bulb

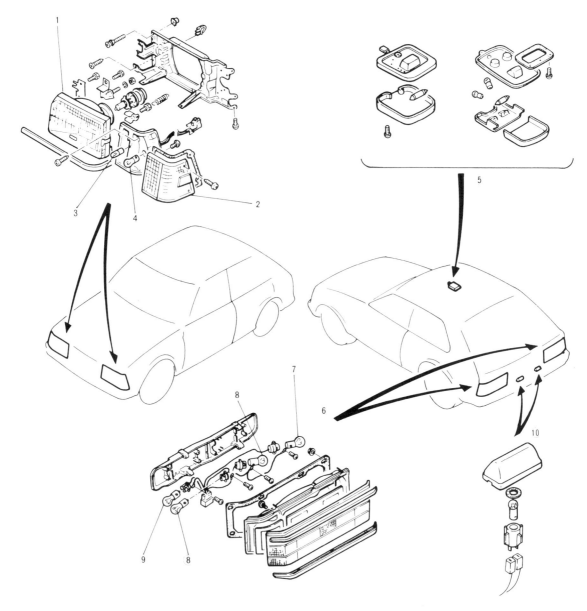

Fig 12.10 Exploded view of the vehicle lighting assemblies – early models (Secs 19 to 25)

1 *Headlight lens unit*	4 *Direction indicator bulb*	8 *Stop/tail light bulb*
2 *Direction indicator/*	5 *Interior courtesy light*	9 *Direction indicator bulb*
sidelight lens	6 *Rear light clusters*	10 *Number plate light*
3 *Sidelight bulb*	7 *Reversing light bulb*	

22 Rear light cluster bulbs – renewal

1   Working in the luggage compartment depress the catches and withdraw the bulb panel from the lens unit (photos).
2   The relevant bulb can now be removed from the panel as required. All the bulbs are removed by turning them anti-clockwise (photo).
3   Refitting is the reverse sequence of removal.

23 Number plate light bulb – renewal

1   Carefully prise the light unit out of the bumper then turn the bulbholder anti-clockwise to remove it from the unit (photos).
2   Remove the bulb by turning it anti-clockwise (photo).
3   Refitting is the reverse sequence of removal.

24 Interior courtesy light bulb – renewal

1   Ease the lens off the light unit then remove the festoon bulb from its edge contacts (photos).
2   For greater access slip the light unit out of its location by lifting out one end then disengaging the tags at the other end (photo). The bulb can now be removed.
3   Refitting is the reverse sequence of removal.

25 Headlight lens unit – removal and refitting

1   Remove the radiator grille as described in Chapter 11.
2   From within the engine compartment disconnect the wiring at the

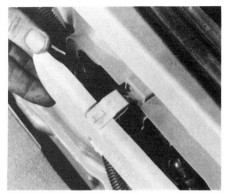

22.1A Depress the catches and withdraw the rear bulb panel ...

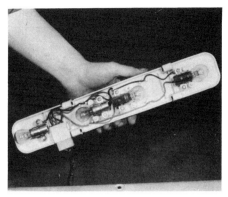

22.1B ... containing the rear light cluster bulbs

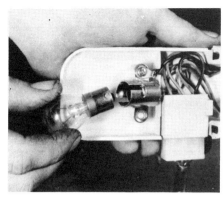

22.2 Rear light bulb renewal

23.1A Remove the number plate light unit from the bumper ...

23.1B ... and release the bulbholder from the unit

23.2 Remove the number plate light bulb from the holder

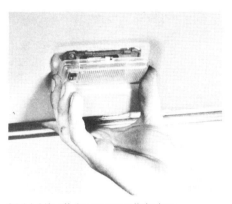

24.1A Lift off the courtesy light lens ...

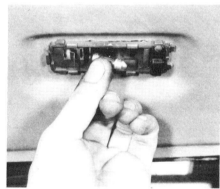

24.1B ... and withdraw the festoon bulb

24.2 Courtesy light unit removal

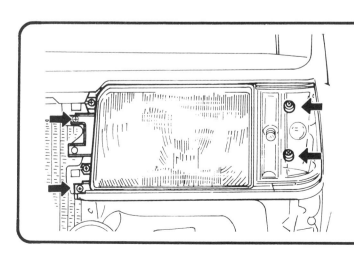

Fig. 12.11 Headlight lens unit attachments (arrowed) (Sec 25)

rear of the headlight bulb. Disconnect the side and direction indicator light wiring at the connectors.
3   Undo the screws and remove the direction indicator lens.
4   Undo the screws securing the headlight body and direction indicator assembly (Fig. 12.11) and remove the unit from the car.
5   Refitting is the reverse sequence of removal.

26 Headlight aim – adjustment

1   At regular intervals headlight aim should be checked and if necessary adjusted.
2   Owing to the light pattern of the lenses fitted to current vehicles, optical beam setting equipment must be used to achieve satisfactory aim of the headlights. It is recommended therefore that this work be entrusted to a Mazda dealer.

27 Wiper blades and arms – removal and refitting

Wiper blades
1   The wiper blades should be renewed when they no longer clean the windscreen or tailgate window effectively.
2   Lift the wiper arm away from the glass.
3   Release the spring retaining catch and separate the blade from the wiper arm (photo).
4   Insert the new blade into the arm, making sure that the spring retaining catch is engaged properly.

Wiper arms
5   Lift up the hinged cover and unscrew the wiper arm retaining nut (photo).
6   Carefully prise the arm off the spindle.
7   Before refitting the arm, switch the wipers on and off allowing the mechanism to return to the 'park' position.
8   Refit the arm to the spindle with the blade positioned at the bottom of the screen.
9   Refit the retaining nut and the hinged cover.

28 Windscreen wiper motor – removal and refitting

1   Disconnect the battery negative terminal.
2   Remove the wiper arms as described in the previous Section.
3   Undo the screw securing the windscreen washer nozzle to the motor access cover on the engine compartment bulkhead (photo).
4   Undo the access cover retaining screws and withdraw the cover (photo).

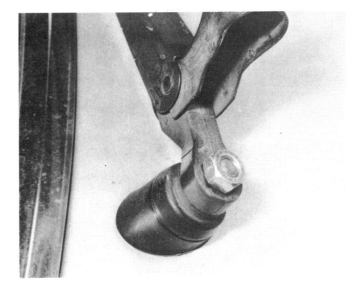

27.5 Lift up the cover to gain access to the arm retaining nut

28.3 Washer nozzle retaining screw (arrowed)

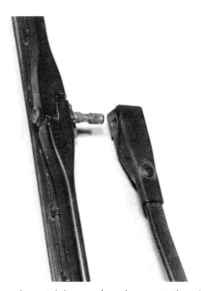

27.3 Release the spring retaining catch and separate the wiper blade from the arm

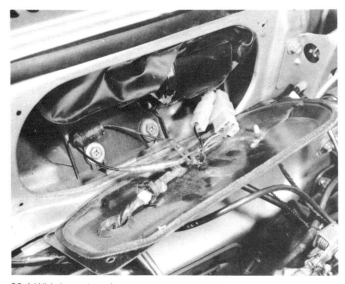

28.4 Withdraw the wiper motor access cover

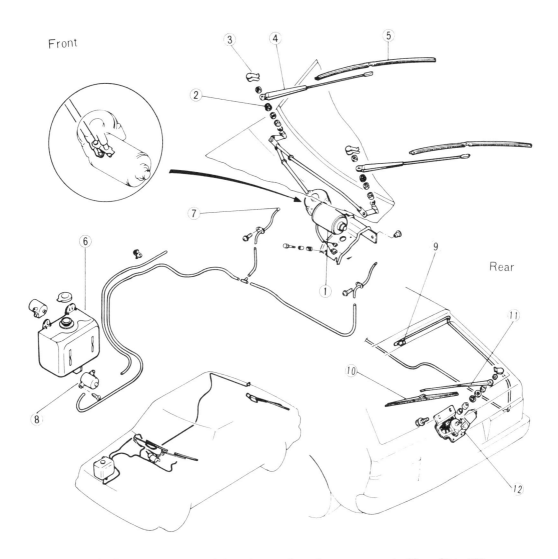

Fig. 12.12 Exploded view of the wiper and washer components (Secs 27 to 29)

1 Windscreen wiper motor	5 Wiper blade	9 Tailgate washer nozzle
2 Seal cover	6 Washer reservoir	10 Tailgate wiper blade
3 Hinged cover	7 Washer nozzle	11 Tailgate wiper arm
4 Wiper arm	8 Washer pump	12 Tailgate wiper motor

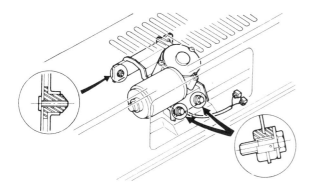

Fig. 12.13 Windscreen wiper motor attachments (arrowed) (Sec 28)

5 Lift off the covers and undo the nuts securing the wiper spindles to the scuttle. Lift off the rubber grommets and push the spindles throught the scuttle.

6 Disconnect the wiper motor wiring at the harness connectors.

7 Undo the screws securing the motor mounting plate to the body and withdraw the wiper motor through the opening.

8 Manipulate the linkage arms out of the opening and remove the assembly from the car.

9 If necessary the motor can be removed from the mounting plate after undoing the retaining screws and removing the primary crank arm. Before disturbing the crank arm mark its position on the motor spindle and in relation to the motor body and ensure that it is refitted in the same place.

10 Refitting the motor assembly is the reverse sequence of removal.

29 Tailgate wiper motor – removal and refitting

1 Disconnect the battery negative terminal.

2 Remove the interior courtesy light as described in Section 24.

3   Remove the tailgate interior trim retaining buttons by unscrewing their centre part then prising out the button body with a screwdriver. Withdraw the trim panel.
4   Remove the wiper arm as described in Section 27.
5   Lift off the cover and undo the nut securing the wiper spindle to the tailgate.
6   Disconnect the motor wiring at the connector then undo the four motor retaining bolts (photo).
7   Withdraw the wiper motor from the tailgate.
8   Refitting is the reverse sequence of removal.

30 Speedometer cable – removal and refitting

1   Refer to Section 14 paragraphs 1 to 4 inclusive and disconnect the speedometer cable from the speedometer.
2   Release the grommet from the bulkhead and pull the cable through into the engine compartment.
3   Undo the bolt securing the cable and gear assembly to the transmission and withdraw the gear.
4   Release the clips and ties and remove the cable from the car.
5   Refitting is the reverse sequence of removal.

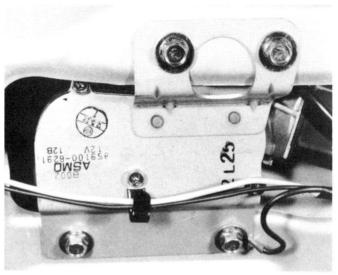

29.6 Tailgate wiper motor retaining bolts

31 Fault diagnosis – electrical system

Symptom	Reason(s)
Starter fails to turn engine	Battery discharged or defective Battery terminal and/or earth leads loose Starter motor connections loose Starter solenoid faulty Starter brushes worn or sticking Starter commutator dirty or worn Starter field coils earthed Starter inhibitor switch faulty (automatic transmission only)
Starter turns engine very slowly	Battery discharged Starter motor connections loose Starter brushes worn or sticking
Starter spins but does not turn engine	Pinion or flywheel ring gear teeth broken or badly worn Starter pinion sticking
Starter noisy	Pinion or flywheel ring gear teeth badly worn Mounting bolts loose
Battery will not hold charge for more than a few days	Battery defective internally Battery terminals loose Alternator drivebelt slipping Alternator or regulator faulty Short circuit
Ignition light stays on	Alternator faulty Alternator drivebelt broken
Ignition light fails to come on	Warning bulb blown Indicator light open circuit Alternator faulty
Instrument readings increase with engine speed	Faulty instrument voltage regulator
Fuel or temperature gauge gives no reading	Wiring open circuit Sender unit faulty Faulty instrument voltage regulator
Fuel or temperature gauge gives continuous maximum reading	Wiring short circuit Sender unit faulty Faulty instrument voltage regulator Faulty gauge

Symptom	Reason(s)
Lights inoperative	Bulb blown Fuse blown Fusible link blown Battery discharged Switch faulty Wiring open circuit Bad connection due to corrosion
Failure of component motor	Commutator dirty or burnt Armature faulty Brushes sticking or worn Armature bearings dry or misaligned Field coils faulty Fuse blown Relay faulty Poor or broken wiring connections
Failure of an individual component	Fuse blown Relay faulty Poor or broken wiring connections Switch faulty Component faulty

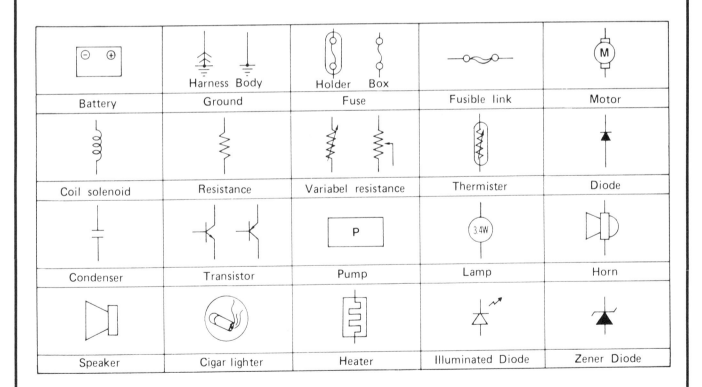

Fig. 12.14 Symbols used in the wiring diagrams

DESCRIPTION OF HARNESS	SYMBOL	DESCRIPTION OF HARNESS	SYMBOL
Front harness	[F]	No. 1 Door harness	[Dr1]
Engine harness	[E]	No. 2 Door harness	[Dr2]
Instrument panel harness	[I]	No. 3 Door harness	[Dr3]
Rear harness	[R]	No. 4 Door harness	[Dr4]
Interior light harness	[In]	Air-Cond harness	[A]
Floor harness	[Fr]	Others	

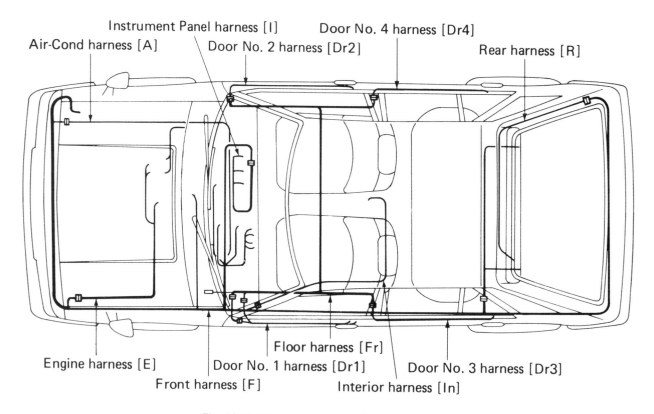

Fig. 12.15 Wiring harness locations and symbols

Abbr.	Term	Abbr.	Term
St	Start	A	Ampere
IG	Ignition	W	Watt
ACC	Accessory	R	Resistance
AS	Auto stop	Tr	Transistor
INT	Intermittent	M	Motor
Lo	Low	SW	Switch
Mi	Middle	Sq	Square per millimeter
Hi	High		
R.H.	Right hand	A/T	Automatic transmission
L.H.	Left hand		
F.R	Front righ	M/T	Manual transmission
F.L	Front left		
R.R	Rear right	NO	Normal opened
R.L	Rear left	NC	Normal closed
V	Volt		

CODE	COLOR	CODE	COLOR
B	Black	Lg	Light green
Br	Brown	O	Orange
G	Green	R	Red
Gy	Gray	W	White
L	Blue	Y	Yellow
Lb	Light blue		

Abbreviations and colour codes

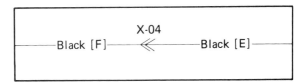

Fig. 12.16 Wiring diagram explanation

In the illustration shown Black indicates the wire colour (which may appear in the diagrams as a letter indicating the colour or two letters where a tracer colour is used). The letter in brackets indicates the wiring harness where this is shown. In this case (F) is the front harness and (E) is the engine harness. The arrow symbol indicates a harness connector and X-04 is the connector number

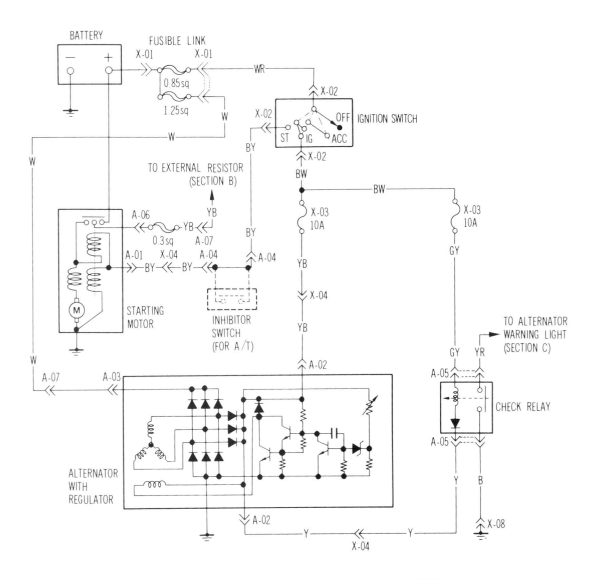

Fig. 12.17 Charging and starting system wiring diagram (1981 models)

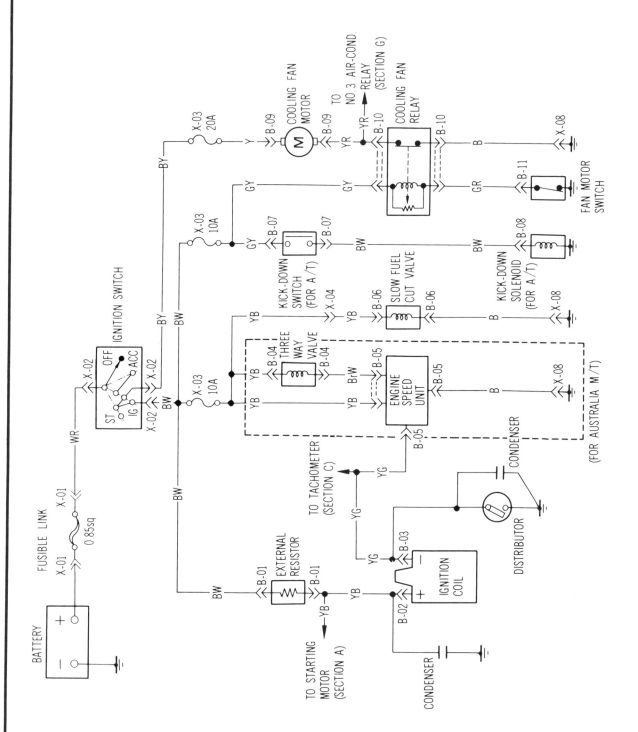

Fig. 12.18 Fuel, ignition, cooling fan and automatic transmission kickdown system wiring diagram (1981 models)

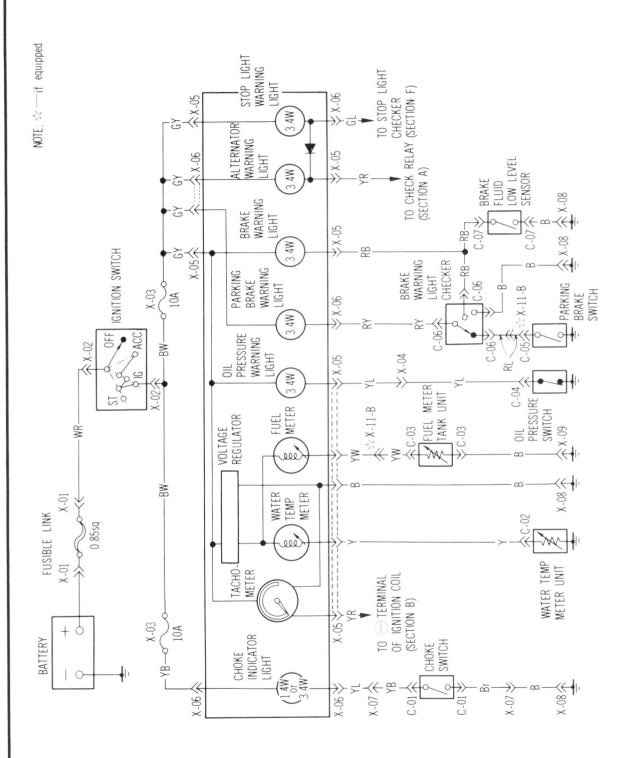

Fig. 12.19 Instrument and warning light wiring diagram (1981 models)

226

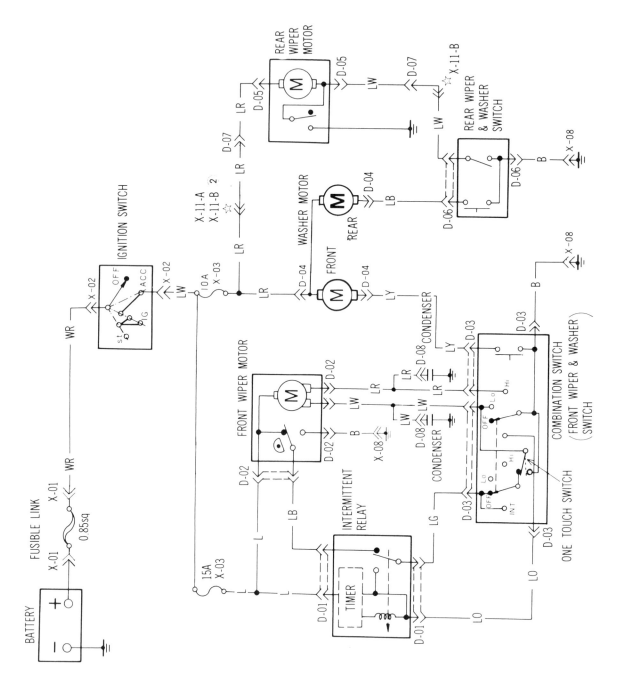

Fig. 12.20 Front and rear wiper and washer wiring diagram (1981 models)

227

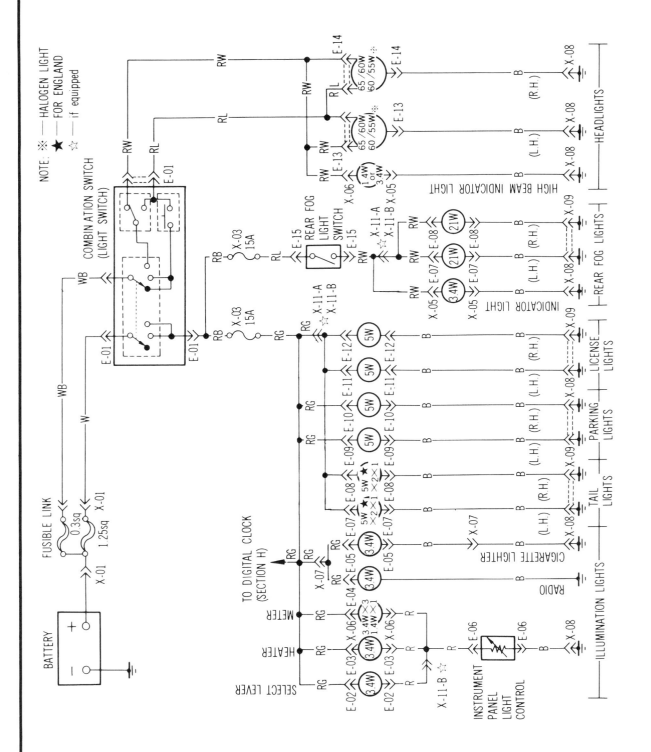

Fig. 12.21 Headlight, sidelight, stop/tail light, number plate light, and interior light wiring diagram (1981 models)

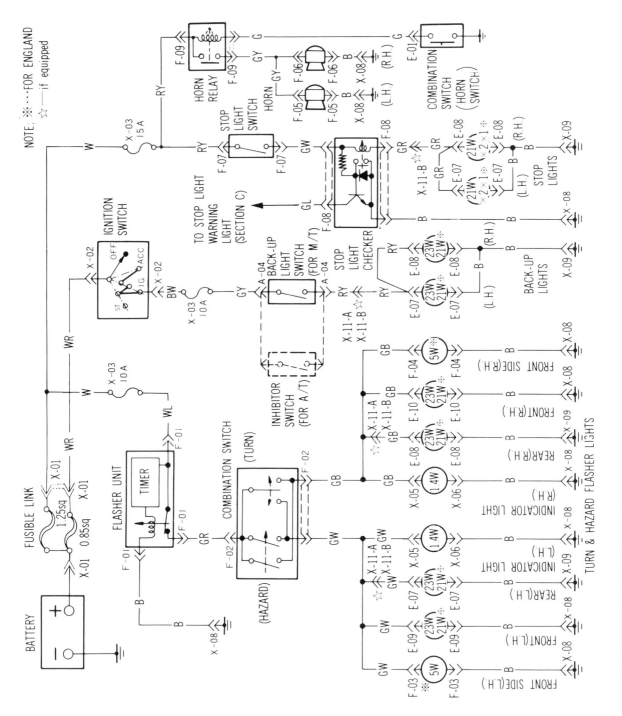

Fig. 12.22 Direction indicator, hazard warning, horn, reversing light and stop-light wiring diagram (1981 models)

229

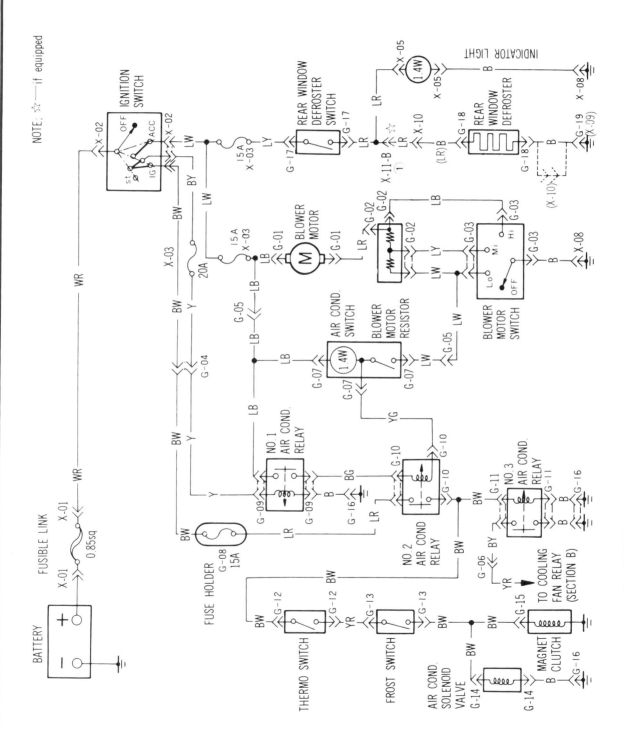

Fig. 12.23 Heater, air conditioner and rear screen demister wiring diagram (1981 models)

230

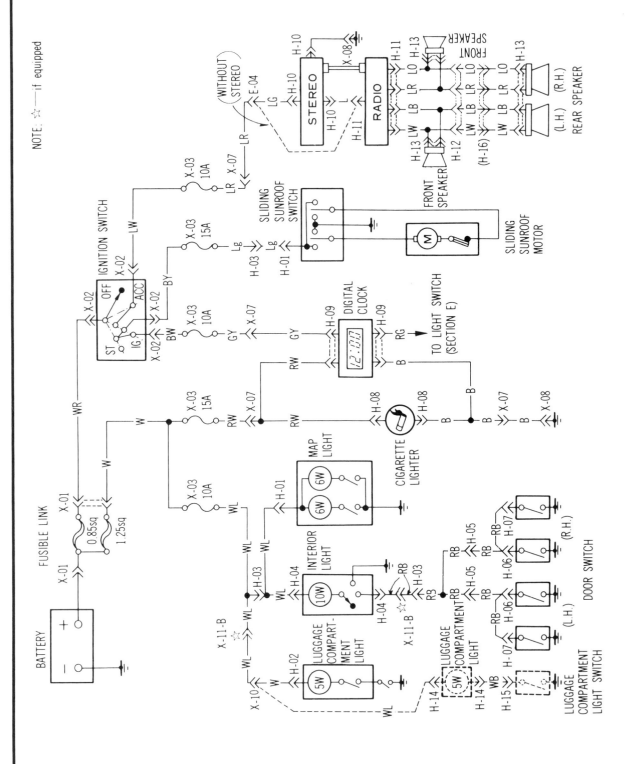

Fig. 12.24 Radio, stereo, luggage compartment light, interior light, cigarette lighter, clock and sun roof wiring diagram (1981 models)

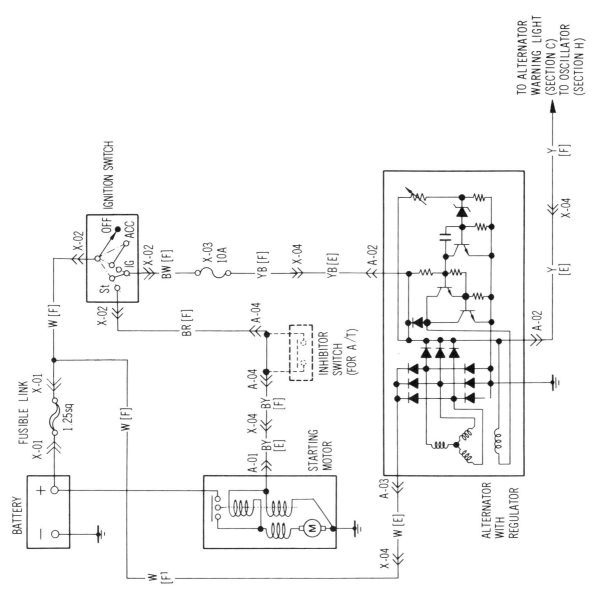

Fig. 12.25 Charging and starting system wiring diagram (1982 models onwards)

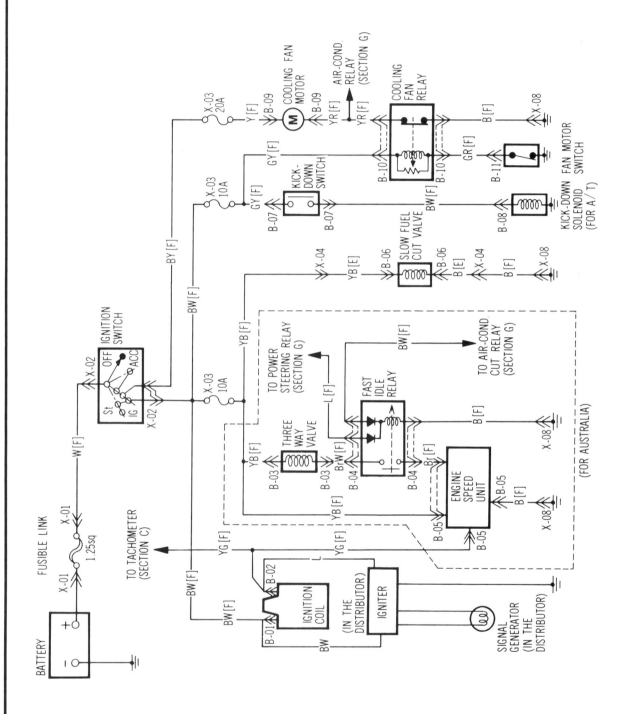

Fig. 12.26 Fuel, ignition, cooling fan and automatic transmission kickdown system wiring diagram (1982 models onwards)

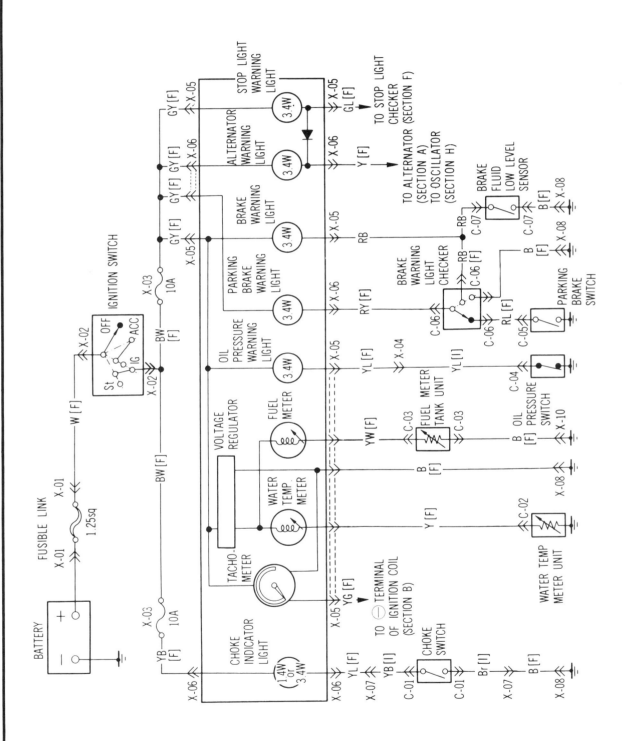

Fig. 12.27 Instrument and warning light wiring diagram (1982 models onwards)

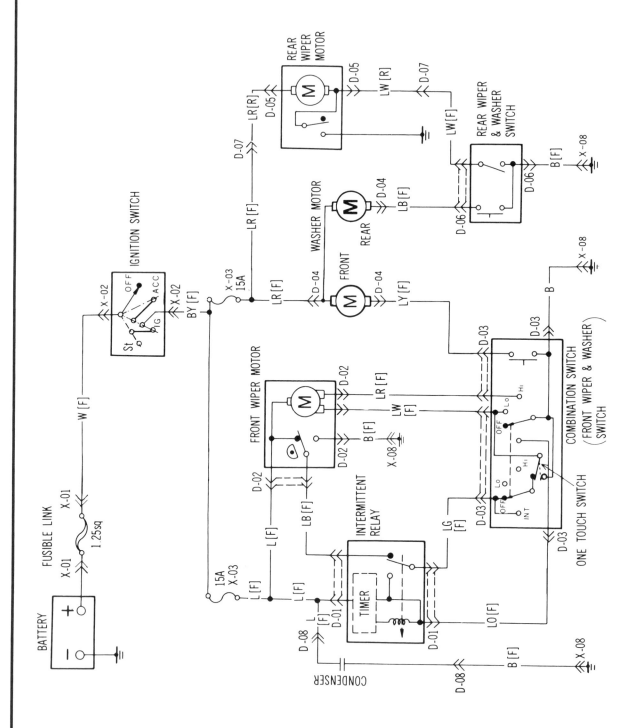

Fig. 12.28 Front and rear wiper and washer wiring diagram (1982 models onwards)

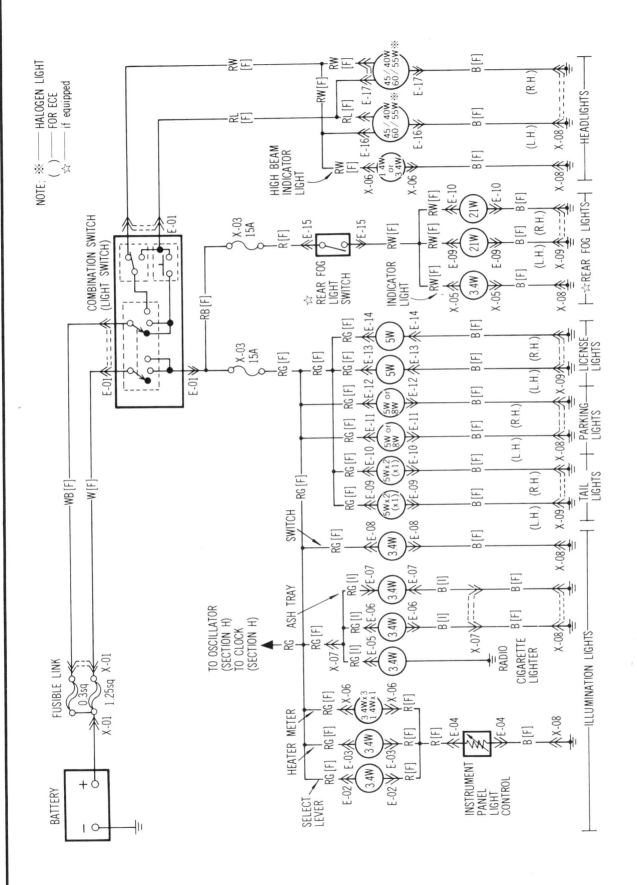

Fig. 12.29 Headlight, sidelight, stop/tail light, number plate light and interior light wiring diagram (1982 models onwards)

236

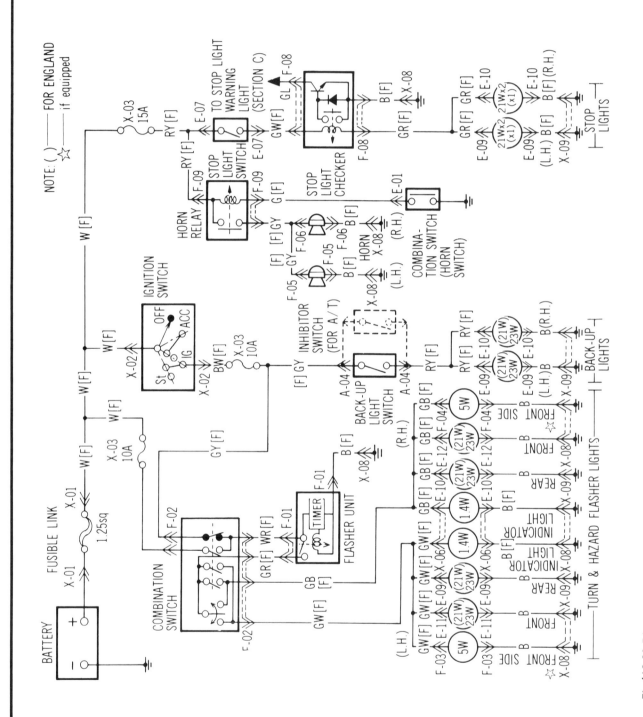

Fig. 12.30 Direction indicator, hazard warning, horn, reversing light and stop-light wiring diagram (1982 models onwards)

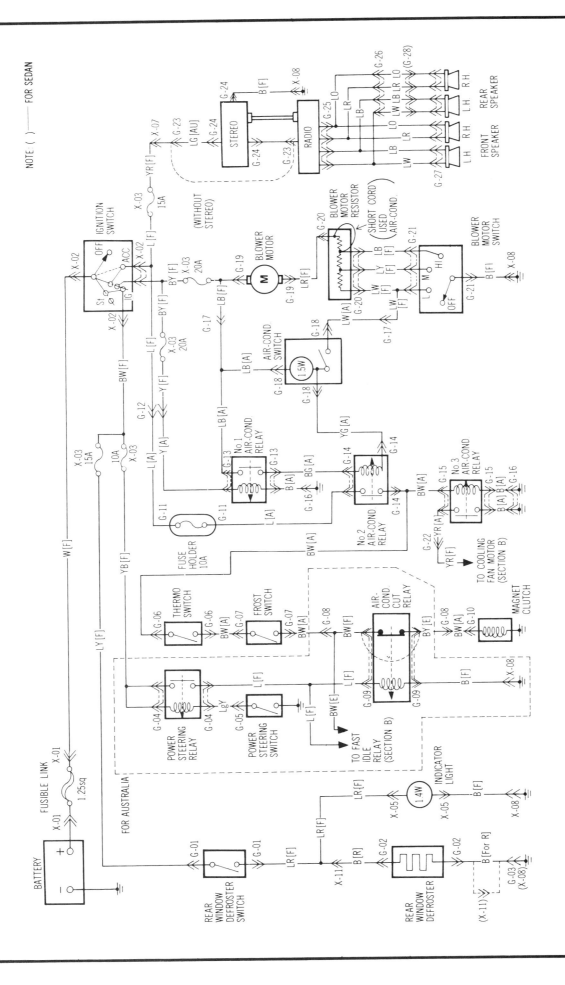

Fig. 12.31 Radio, stereo, air conditioner and rear screen demister wiring diagram (1982 models onwards)

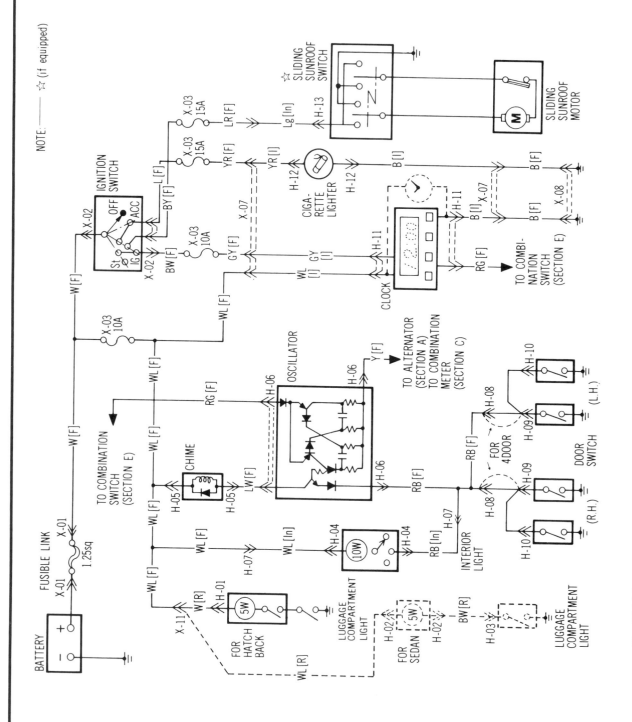

Fig. 12.32 Luggage compartment light, interior light, cigarette lighter and sliding sun roof wiring diagram (1982 models onwards)

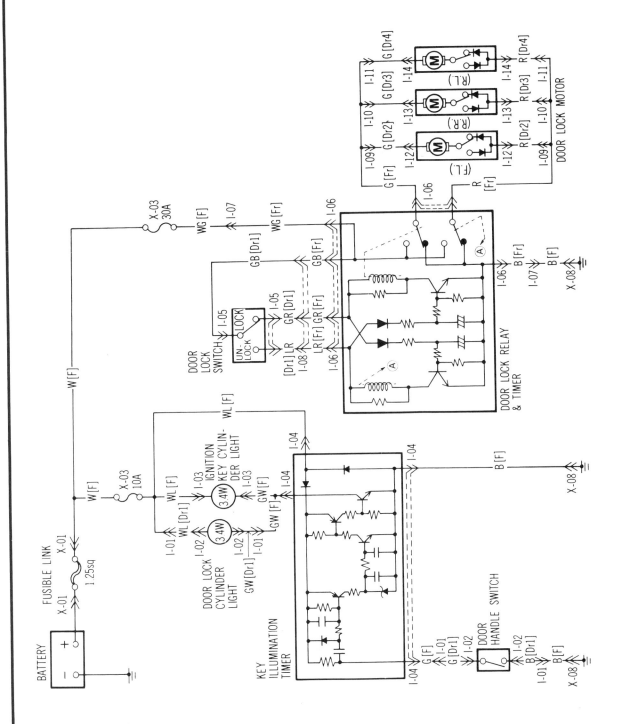

Fig. 12.33 Ignition key light, door lock light and central locking wiring diagram (1982 models onwards)

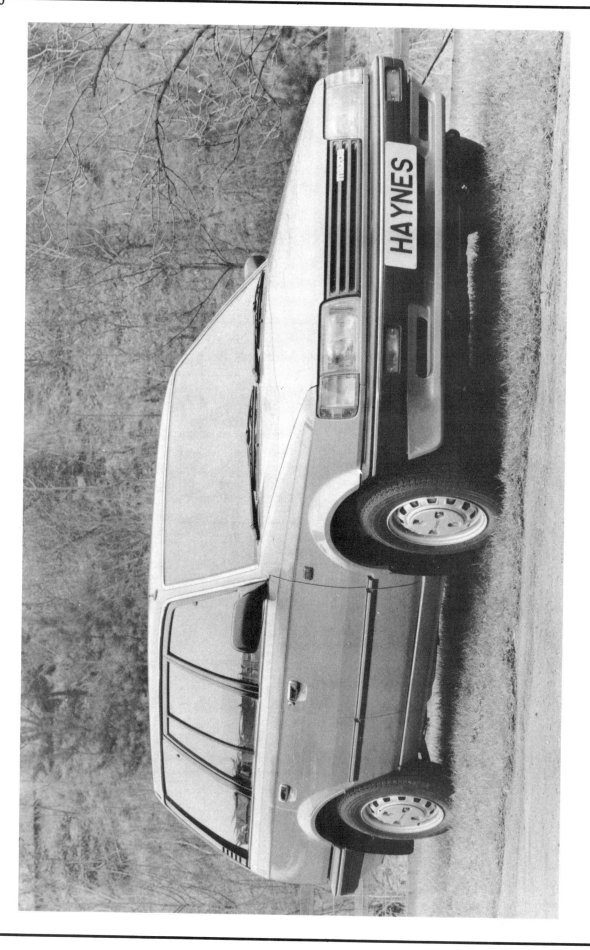

Mazda 323 Estate 1500 GLX

Chapter 13 Supplement:
Revisions and information on later models

Contents

1 Introduction

Since the introduction in the spring of 1981, the Mazda 323 front-wheel-drive models have had a number of modifications and improvements made to them. This Chapter deals mainly with modifications made from September 1985 onwards, but in some instances, information applicable to earlier models, which was not available when this manual was originally produced, is also included.

In order to use this Supplement to the best advantage, particularly with later models, it is suggested that it is referred to before the main Chapter(s) of the manual. This will ensure that any relevant information can be incorporated into the procedures given in Chapters 1 to 12, thus ensuring that a particular job is completed correctly, and hence saving time and money.

Although, as stated previously, most of the information in this Supplement relates to the new models, in the case of modification and rationalisation, some of the design changes are incorporated into older models by the fitting of modified parts. It is therefore necessary when replacing parts to pay close attention to interchangeability, and to note any Specification changes which may occur from fitting modified parts. Where any doubt exists about interchangeability, then the advice of your local Mazda dealer should be sought.

Project vehicle

The vehicle used in the preparation of this Supplement and appearing in many of the photographic sequences was a Mazda 323 Estate 1500 GLX.

2 Specifications

The specifications listed here are revised or supplementary to the main specifications given at the start of each Chapter.

Engine
Engine oil capacity (from September 1985)
Total (dry engine)	3.4 litres (6.0 Imp pints)
Sump (engine oil change)	3.0 litres (5.3 Imp pints)
Oil filter	0.30 litre (0.53 Imp pint)

Torque wrench setting
	Nm	lbf ft
Cylinder head bolts – from September 1985	85 to 91	63 to 67

Cooling system
Cooling system capacity
Automatic transmission models	6.0 litres (10.6 Imp pints)

Thermostat – from September 1985
Starts to open	82°C (180°F)
Fully open	95°C (203°F)
Lift height	8.5 mm (0.335 in)

Radiator cooling fan
Motor current consumption:	
300 mm (11.81 in) diameter fan	6.1 to 7.3 amps

Fuel and exhaust systems
Fuel tank capacity
From September 1985	45 litres (9.9 Imp gals)

Carburettor – from September 1985
Type .... Aisan, dual throat downdraught

Calibration and adjustment data – 1100 cc models:

	Primary	Secondary
Throat diameter	28 mm	32 mm
Venturi diameter	20 mm x 11 mm	25 mm x 11 mm
Main nozzle	2.40 mm	2.40 mm
Main jet	0.79 mm	1.13 mm
Main air bleed	0.60 mm	0.70 mm
Slow jet	0.50 mm	0.80 mm
Slow air bleed	1.60 mm (No 1)	0.50 mm
Power jet	0.40 mm	0.40 mm

Float settings:	
Float-to-air horn clearance ('L')	45 to 49 mm (1.771 to 1.929 in)
Float-to-air horn clearance ('H')	4 to 5 mm (0.1574 to 0.1968 in)
Fast idle cam adjustment	0.23 to 0.53 mm (0.0090 to 0.0208 in)
Choke vacuum diaphragm operating vacuum	120 to 126 mm Hg
Accelerator linkage free play (at carburettor)	1.0 to 3.0 mm (0.040 to 0.118 in)
Idle compensator valve opening temperature	63° to 71°C (145 to 159°F)
Idle speed:	
Manual transmission model	800 to 900 rpm
Automatic transmission model (Selector in 'N' position)	900 to 1000 rpm
Idle-up system operating engine speed:	
Manual or automatic transmission models (selector in 'N' position) with power steering	1100 to 1300 rpm
Manual or automatic transmission models (selector in 'N' position) with air conditioning	1350 to 1450 rpm
CO concentration (%)	1.5 to 2.0

Calibration and adjustment data – 1300 and 1500 cc models:

	Primary	Secondary
Throat diameter	28 mm	32 mm
Venturi diameter	22 mm x 11 mm	27 mm x 11 mm
Main nozzle	2.40 mm	2.40 mm
Main jet	0.93 mm	1.29 mm
Main air bleed	0.55 mm	0.70 mm
Slow jet	0.50 mm	0.90 mm
Slow air bleed	1.60 mm (No 1)	0.50 mm
Power jet	0.45 mm	0.45 mm
Float level settings	As per 1100 cc models with Aisan carburettor	
Fast idle cam adjustment	0.35 to 0.65 mm (0.0137 to 0.0255 in)	
Choke vacuum diaphragm operating vacuum	120 to 260 mm Hg	
Unloader clearance	1.55 to 2.05 mm (0.061 to 0.081 in)	
Accelerator linkage free play (at carburettor)	1.0 to 3.0 mm (0.04 to 0.118 in)	
Idle speed:		
Manual transmission model	800 to 900 rpm	
Automatic transmission model (selector in 'N' position)	900 to 1000 rpm	
CO concentration (%)	1.5 to 2.0	
Idle-up system:		
Single diaphragm types	As per 1100 cc models	
Dual diaphragm types (models with power steering and air conditioning):		
Stage 1 (Vacuum at port 'A')	1350 to 1450 rpm	
Stage 2 (Vacuum at port 'B')	1100 to 1300 rpm	

Ignition system
Spark plugs

Suitable alternatives to those listed in Chapter 4	Champion RN9Y or RN9YC
Electrode gap for Champion plugs	0.80 mm (0.031 in)

Clutch
Clutch cover – from September 1985

Grinding limit	0.5 mm (0.020 in)
Release fork and pin clearance	1.5 to 2.5 mm (0.06 to 0.10 in)

Clutch adjustment – from September 1985

Pedal height	214.5 to 219.5 mm (8.44 to 8.64 in)
Pedal free play	9.0 to 15.0 mm (0.35 to 0.59 in)
Pedal minimum distance to floor (pedal depressed)	85 mm (3.3 in)

Flywheel

Run-out limit	0.2 mm (0.008 in)
Regrind limit	0.5 mm (0.020 in)

Torque wrench setting

	Nm	lbf ft
Clutch pedal pivot bolt nut	20 to 35	14.5 to 25

Automatic transmission
Torque wrench settings

	Nm	lbf ft
Selector cable:		
Adjuster locknuts (shift lever end)	8 to 11	6 to 8
Shift lever knob locknut	15 to 20	11 to 14

Driveshafts
Joint types

Manual transmission	Double offset inner joint, ball outer joint
Automatic transmission	Tripod inner joint, ball outer joint

Driveshaft diameter

	22 mm (0.87 in)

Driveshaft length

	Manual transmission	Automatic transmission
1100 cc engine:		
Left-hand	384.1 mm (15.12 in)	–
Right-hand	660.6 mm (26.00 in)	–
1300 cc engine:		
Left-hand	384.1 mm (15.12 in)	373.7 mm (14.71 in)
Right-hand	660.6 mm (26.00 in)	652.7 mm (25.70 in)
1500 cc engine:		
Left-hand	380.5 mm (14.98 in)	373.7 mm (14.71 in)
Right-hand	657.0 mm (25.87 in)	652.7 mm (25.70 in)

Torque wrench setting

	Nm	lbf ft
Driveshaft retaining nut	157 to 235	116 to 174

1 Engine oil dipstick
2 Washer reservoir
3 Engine oil filler cap
4 Alternator
5 Brake master cylinder
6 Vehicle identification plate
7 Carburettor
8 Fuel pump
9 Windscreen wiper motor
10 Fuses
11 Battery
12 Ignition coil
13 Ignition distributor
14 Clutch adjuster
15 Cooling fan
16 Radiator filler cap

Engine and underbonnet component locations on later models (air cleaner removed for clarity)

1 Radiator coolant drain plug
2 Gearbox
3 Gearbox drain plug
4 Tie-rod
5 Brake lines
6 Gearchange rod
7 Exhaust system
8 Steering gear gaiter
9 Front lower suspension arm
10 Driveshaft
11 Engine sump drain plug
12 Anti-roll bar
13 Bottom coolant hose
14 Exhaust downpipes

Front underbody view on later models (undertrays removed)

246

1 Fuel tank
2 Brake lines
3 Trailing arm
4 Anti-roll bar
5 Spare wheel and carrier
6 Rear lateral link (adjustable)
7 Rear suspension strut
8 Lateral link (non adjustable)
7 Exhaust system
10 Exhaust mounting rubber
11 Handbrake cable

Rear underbody view – Estate model

Braking system
Ventilated type front disc brake
Disc diameter .... 238 mm (9.37 in)
Disc thickness:
    New .... 18 mm (0.71 in)
    Minimum .... 15 mm (0.63 in)
Maximum disc run-out .... 0.10 mm (0.004 in)
Disc pad thickness:
    New .... 10 mm (0.39 in)
    Minimum .... 1.0 mm (0.04 in)

Rear brakes
Drum diameter (internal):
    New .... 200 mm (7.87 in)
    Maximum .... 201 mm (7.91 in)
Brake lining thickness:
    New .... 5.0 mm (0.20 in)
    Minimum .... 1.0 mm (0.04 in)

General (from September 1985)
Handbrake:
    Adjustment (forward pull cable type) – at lever pull of 196 N
    (44 lb) force .... 7 to 11 notches
Brake pedal height (right-hand drive models) .... 219 to 224 mm (8.6 to 8.8 in)
Brake pedal free play .... 4.0 to 7.00 mm (0.16 to 0.28 in)

Torque wrench setting (from September 1985)

	Nm	lbf ft
Rear wheel cylinder to backplate	10 to 13	8 to 10

Suspension and steering
Front suspension (from September 1985)
Coil spring free length:
    Standard .... 365.5 mm (14.39 in)
    Heavy duty .... 380.5 mm (13.98 in)
Number of spring coils:
    Standard 4.90
    Heavy duty 5.50

Rear suspension (from September 1985)

	Saloon and Hatchback	Estate
Coil spring free length:		
Standard	345.0 mm (13.58 in)	363.0 mm (14.29 in)
Heavy duty	361.5 mm (14.23 in)	–
Number of coils:		
Standard	4.60	7.25
Heavy duty	5.20	–

Rear wheel toe setting:
    Saloon and Hatchback variants .... −3 to +3 mm (−0.12 to +0.12 in)
    Estate:
        Early models .... −3 to +3 mm (−0.12 to +0.12 in)
        Later models (adjustable lateral links) .... +5.08 to +10.16 mm (+0.2 to +0.4 in)

Steering – general
Geometry – from September 1985:
    Camber angle .... 0° 48′ ± 45′
    Caster angle .... 1° 35′ ± 45′
    Steering axis inclination .... 12° 22′
    Toe-in .... 1 to 5 mm (0.04 to 0.20 in)

Power steering
Type .... Rack and pinion with hydraulic assistance
Turns lock-to-lock 3.2
Operating force .... 40 N (9 lbf)
Lubricant (fluid) type .... ATF (M2C33-F)
Fluid capacity .... 0.6 litre (0.53 Imp pint)
Pump drivebelt deflection at force of 98 N (22 lbf):
    New belt .... 8 to 10 mm (0.31 to 0.39 in)
    Used belt .... 10 to 12 mm (0.39 to 0.47 in)

Electrical system
Alternator – from September 1985
Maximum output .... 55 Amps
Brush length:
    Standard .... 16.5 mm (0.65 in)
    Wear limit .... 10.0 mm (0.39 in)

Vehicle dimensions
Estate model
Overall length .... 4225 mm (166.3 in)
Overall width .... 1645 mm (64.7 in)
Overall height .... 1430 mm (56.3 in)
Track:
    Front .... 1390 mm (54.7 in)
    Rear .... 1415 mm (55.7 in)

---

3   Routine maintenance

The routine maintenance operations and intervals given at the start of this manual remain unchanged, with the following exceptions.

Every 6000 miles (10 000 km) or 6 months – whichever comes first

---

Power steering system (Chapter 13, Section 11):
    Check the fluid level in the pump reservoir and top up if required
    Check tension and condition of pump drivebelt
    Check system lines and hoses for condition and any sign of leaks

---

Every 12 000 miles (20 000 km) or 12 months – whichever comes first

---

Fuel system:
    Check the throttle positioner system (Chapter 13, Section 6)

---

4   Engine

1   The following modifications have been made to the engine on later models to improve its performance and efficiency. These differences should be noted when ordering replacement parts which may be affected.

Cylinder block
2   The cylinder block has had its shape modified to reduce vibrations and noise.
3   The right-hand engine mounting is now secured to the block at three points (two previously) on manual and automatic transmission models. On automatic transmission models the mounting position on the body has been moved 50 mm (1.97 in) further forward, enabling the mounting to be in line with the engine – see Fig. 13.1 (photo).
4   The front engine mounting has also been modified and is now as shown (photos).

Valves, rocker arms and camshaft
5   To reduce the operating noise of the valves and wear on the rocker arm shaft, the rocker arms have been modified and are now straight in

shape, and the camshaft lobes have been relocated to suit. At the same time, the inlet and exhaust valve stems were increased in length by 2.9 mm (0.11 in) to suit, and the inlet valve rear face was reprofiled to improve air flow – see Fig. 13.2 (photos).
6   The rocker arm shaft springs have been increased in length to 17 mm (0.67 in) on the inlet side and 30.5 mm (1.20 in) on the exhaust side.

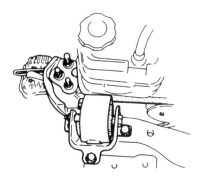

Fig. 13.1 Right-hand engine mounting location on later automatic transmission models (Sec 4)

Fig. 13.2 Sectional view showing reprofiled valve seat on later models (Sec 4)

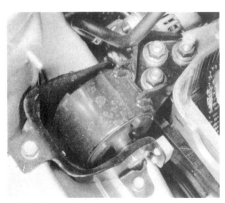

4.3 Right-hand engine mounting on later models

4.4A Front mounting viewed from above

4.4B Front mounting viewed from underneath

4.5A 'Straight' type rocker arms are fitted to later models

4.5B General view of rocker assemblies on later models

5.3 Radiator top mounting bracket and filler cap on later models

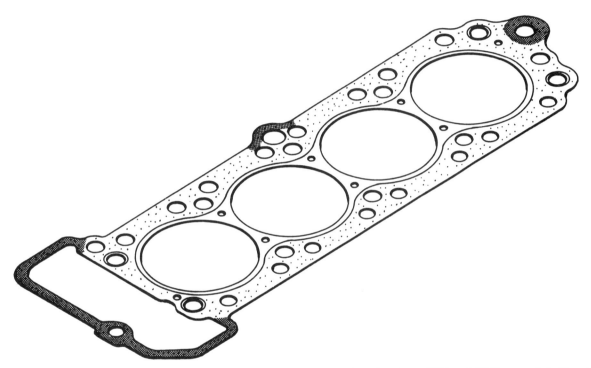

Fig. 13.3 Cylinder head gasket showing silicon areas (shaded), as fitted to later 1300 and 1500 cc models (Sec 4)

Note: Fit silicon-coated face towards cylinder head

Cylinder head gasket (1300 and 1500 cc engines)
7   A new head gasket has been introduced for use with these engines in order to prevent oil leakage. The gasket has silicone applied to areas on its lower face as shown in Fig. 13.3.
8   When fitting this type of gasket, ensure that the side with the silicone areas faces the cylinder block.

5   Cooling system

1   The following cooling system items have been modified on later models.

Radiator
2   The radiator fitted to late models differs from earlier types in that the filler neck is located on the right-hand side, and a small diameter hose is connected between the filler neck and the cooling system expansion tank, which is mounted on the left-hand side of the engine compartment. The procedures for checking and topping-up the cooling system are as described for earlier models in Chapter 2.
3   The radiator is now secured at its top by brackets bolted to the front crossmember. This later type of radiator is **not** interchangeable with the earlier types (photo).

Cooling fan
4   On later models, the cooling fan has a revised blade shape and size in order to reduce noise when in operation. The cooling fan motor is lighter in construction, and whilst its operating speed remains the same, it requires less current to drive it than on earlier models. The later type cooling fan and motor are **not** interchangeable with the earlier type.

Water pump
5   Later models are fitted with an improved type of water pump which has a larger bearing and a more efficient seal than the earlier type pump. Whilst the later type water pump can be fitted to earlier models, the reverse is not the case.

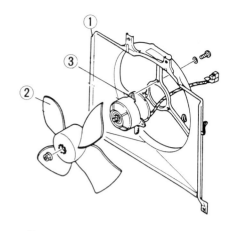

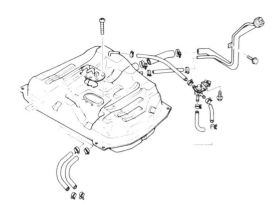

Fig. 13.5 Fuel tank and associated components on later models (Sec 6)

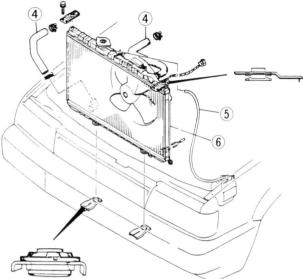

Fig. 13.4 Radiator, cooling fan and associated components on later models (Sec 5)

1	Radiator cowling	4	Radiator hoses
2	Fan	5	Expansion tank hose
3	Fan motor	6	Radiator

6 Fuel and exhaust systems

Maintenance and inspection – later models
1 The procedures for later models are similar to those specified for earlier models in Chapter 3. When checking the idle speed, mixture setting and choke system on later models fitted with an Aisan carburettor, refer to the appropriate paragraphs of this Section.

Fuel tank
2 The main feed and return hose connections at the fuel tank on later models are as shown in Fig. 13.5. The removal and refitting details are otherwise the same as those described for earlier models in Chapter 3 (photo).

Aisan carburettor – description
3 Later models are fitted with an Aisan carburettor of twin choke downdraught design. A schematic diagram showing the main components is given in Fig. 13.6.
4 When the engine is idling, fuel flows from the float chamber through the primary main jet and slow jet, mixes with air drawn through the primary slow air bleed and passes through the idle part.
5 To prevent the engine from running on when switched off, a solenoid valve cuts off the fuel supply to the idle system.

6.2 Fuel tank sender unit and line connections are accessible with cover removed

6 On acceleration, the primary throttle valve is opened, fuel is drawn from the float chamber through the emulsion tube, into the main jet where it mixes with air supplied through the primary main air bleed. The resultant fuel/air mixture is discharged to the primary main nozzle and then into the inlet manifold.
7 When the primary throttle valve is opened 50° or more, it opens the secondary throttle valve a small amount by means of a cam. The resultant increase in engine speed correspondingly increases the vacuum, to the air jet, activating the vacuum diaphragm, and causing the secondary throttle valve to slowly open, thus maintaining the correct fuel/air mixture.
8 The secondary main system only comes into operation when the throttle is opened wider for high speed operation.
9 An accelerator pump is fitted, and this is mechanically operated by a cam on the carburettor throttle shaft. When the accelerator pedal is depressed, fuel is injected into the main venturi. The pump is of a diaphragm type which ensures an efficient discharge of fuel as required.
10 A power valve is fitted, and its function is to supply the extra fuel needed under heavy load conditions. Low manifold vacuum causes a vacuum piston to open the power valve, and additional fuel is then allowed through the emulsion tube for discharge into the main nozzle (with fuel from the main system).
11 A fully automatic choke is fitted, the main parts of which are the choke valve, a bi-metal heater, the fast idle cam, a choke breaker diaphragm and a fast idle cam breaker (FICB) diaphragm (Fig. 13.7 and 13.8).
12 The fast idle cam opens the throttle valve relative to the choke valve

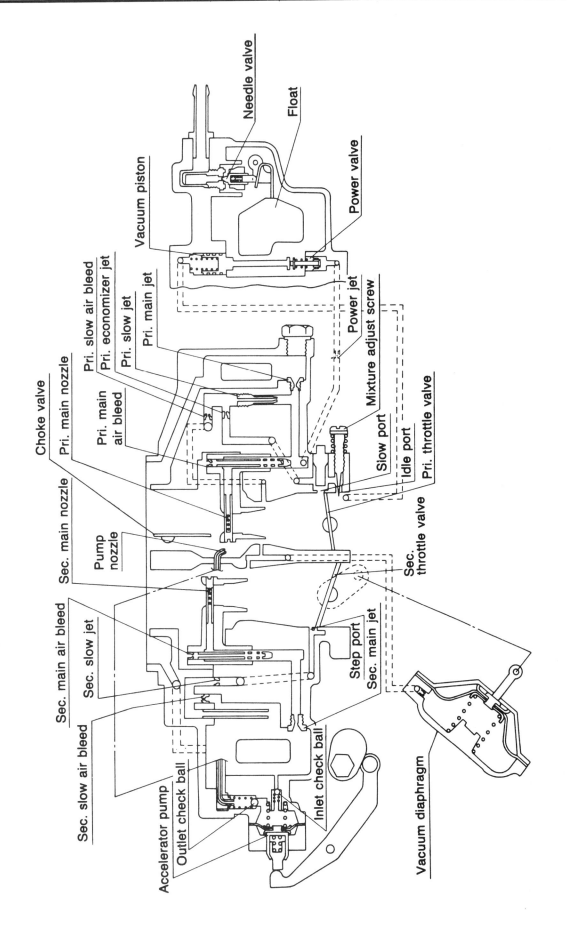

Fig 13.6 Sectional view of the Aisan carburettor and its main components (Sec 6)

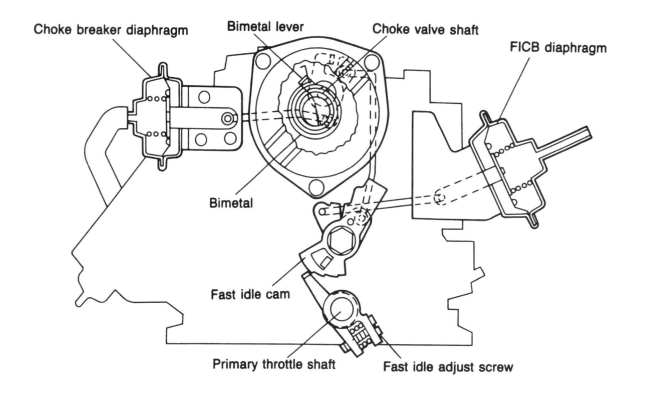

Choke breaker diaphragm

Bimetal lever

Choke valve shaft

FICB diaphragm

Bimetal

Fast idle cam

Primary throttle shaft

Fast idle adjust screw

Bimetal and heater

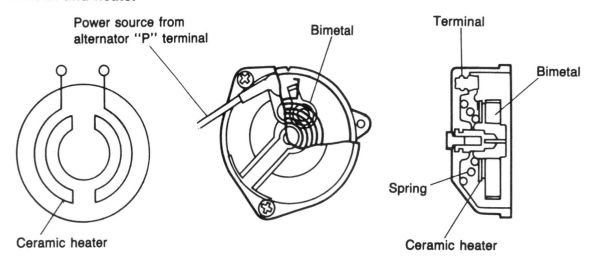

Power source from alternator "P" terminal

Bimetal

Terminal

Bimetal

Spring

Ceramic heater

Ceramic heater

Fig. 13.7 Choke system components – Aisan carburettor (Sec 6)

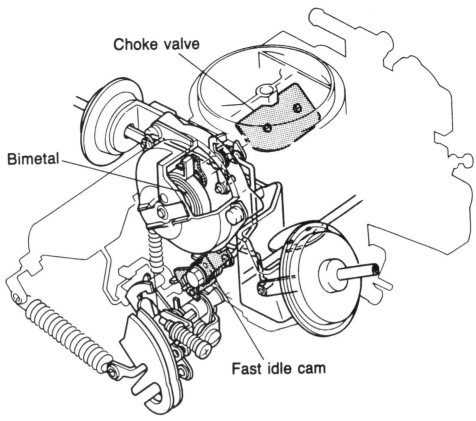

Choke valve

Bimetal

Fast idle cam

Before depressing the accelerator pedal, choke valve is open.

After depresseing the accelerator pedal, choke valve is closed.

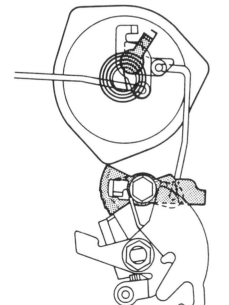

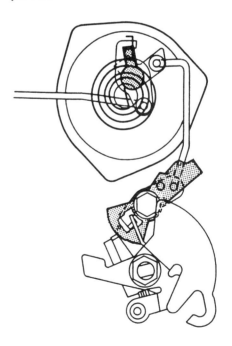

Fig. 13.8 Choke system and fast idle cams – Aisan carburettor (Sec 6)

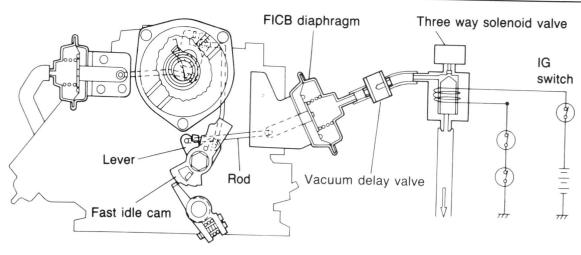

Fig. 13.9 Fast idle cam breaker (FICB) system – Aisan carburettor (Sec 6)

opening and provides the correct mixture. The choke valve is operated in accordance with the bi-metal heater strip.

13 When the engine is started the choke breaker diaphragm opens the choke valve a sufficient amount to provide the correct mixture ratio. In the event of the engine flooding with fuel when cold, a choke unloader opens the choke partially to weaken the mixture.

14 As the engine temperature rises and reaches 40°C (104°F), the coolant temperature sensor switch causes the three-way solenoid valve to open, allowing vacuum from the inlet manifold to be directed to the FICB diaphragm. This then shuts down the fast idle cam to reduce the engine speed (Fig. 13.9).

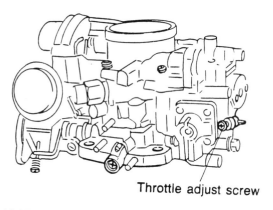

Fig. 13.10 Throttle (idle) speed adjustment screw location (Sec 6)

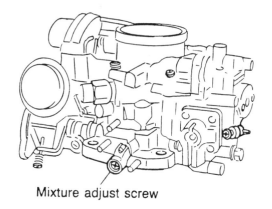

Fig. 13.11 Idle mixture adjustment screw location (Sec 6)

15 The vacuum delay valve fitted to 1100 cc and 1300 cc engine models delays the operation of the FICB diaphragm by 10 to 20 seconds.

Aisan carburettor – adjustments
16 Prior to checking or making adjustments to the idle speed or idle mixture, first observe the preliminary requirements given in paragraphs 1 to 4 inclusive in Section 9 of Chapter 3. On automatic transmission models Select 'N'.

17 **Idle speed:** Ensure that the choke valve is fully opened in the venturi, then check the idle speed. If adjustment is necessary, turn the adjuster screw in the required direction to set the idle speed at that specified (Fig. 13.10).

18 **Idle mixture:** Connect up an exhaust gas analyser in accordance with the manufacturer's instructions. Disconnect the secondary air hoses from the reed valves and plug them (where applicable). Compare the exhaust CO reading with that specified.

19 If idle mixture adjustment is necessary, remove the blind cap from the mixture adjuster screw recess (Fig. 13.11). The cap will probably break as it is removed, in which case do not refit it.

20 Turn the mixture adjustment screw as required to meet the specified CO requirement. If the idle speed is affected, readjust it as described previously.

21 On completion a new blind cap should be fitted to the mixture screw recess, the air cleaner refitted and the tachometer and CO meter disconnected.

Aisan carburettor – removal and refitting
22 The removal and refitting details for this carburettor are similar to those described for the carburettor fitted to earlier models in Chapter 3.

23 When removing the carburettor, first disconnect the battery earth lead, then referring to Fig. 13.12, disconnect the items in the numerical order shown. Make a note of the vacuum hose connections to avoid the possibility of confusion when refitting (photos).

24 When the carburettor is refitted, restart the engine and check the idle speed and mixture setting adjustments as described elsewhere in this Section. Check for fuel leaks and also, with the engine held at idle speed, check that the fuel level in the float chamber is maintained at the centre mark in the window (photo).

Aisan carburettor – dismantling and reassembly
25 The carburettor can be dismantled as required by referring to Fig. 13.13, disconnect the various components in the numerical sequence given. During dismantling, care must be taken not to damage the components, particularly the jets. Do not remove the throttle valve assemblies unless absolutely necessary.

26 As the components are removed, lay them out on a cleaned area for inspection, and where required, label them for identification and orientation to avoid possible confusion during reassembly.

27 Examine the various components as described for earlier carburettors, referring to paragraphs 18 to 24 inclusive in Section 14 of Chapter 3.

6.23A Aisan carburettor showing accelerator cable connection

28 Reassemble the carburettor in the reverse order of dismantling. Ensure that all parts are clean as they are fitted, and do not overtighten the jets and fastenings. The following items should be checked for adjustment as they are fitted.

29 **Choke bi-metal heater:** When assembling the bi-metal heater unit ensure that the lever is hooked onto the angled tang of the bi-metal (Fig. 13.14). The matching marks of the bimetal heater and case must align (photo).

30 **Float height adjustment:** To check the float height, the air horn (top cover) must be removed and held in its normal position as shown in Fig. 13.15. The clearance (L) between the base of the float and the bottom flange face of the air horn (without its gasket) must be as given in the Specifications at the start of this Chapter. If required, adjust the float level by bending the float stopper (A) to suit using a pair of needle-nosed pliers.

31 Invert the air horn and let the float pivot down towards it under its own weight. Now measure the clearance (H) between the air horn flange face and the float at the points shown in Fig. 13.16. If adjustment is necessary, bend the arm to suit and set the clearance to that specified (see Specifications at the start of this Chapter).

32 **Choke breaker diaphragm:** This check requires the use of a vacuum pump and gauge. Entrust this check to your Mazda dealer if they are not available.

33 The air cleaner must be removed and the vacuum pump connected to the diaphragm as shown in Fig. 13.17. Check that the choke valve is shut, then apply a vacuum of 400 mm Hg (15.7 Hg) to the diaphragm. Insert a gauge rod (a drill will do) with a diameter to suit the specified

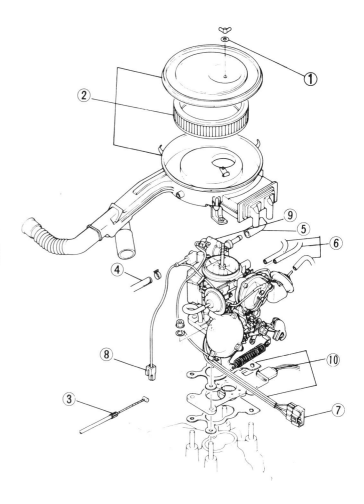

Fig. 13.12 Aisan carburettor and air cleaner components – remove in numerical sequence shown (Sec 6)

1 Air cleaner cover wing nut
2 Air cleaner assembly
3 Accelerator cable
4 Fuel feed hose
5 Evaporation hose (where applicable)
6 Vacuum hoses
7 Wiring connector
8 Bi-metal heater wire (where applicable)
9 Carburettor
10 Gasket and PTC heater

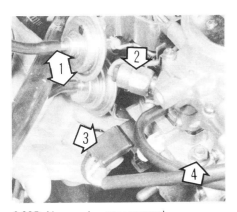

6.23B Aisan carburettor removal
1 Vacuum diaphragm hoses
2 Fuel cut-off solenoid
3 PTC heater
4 Carburettor retaining nut

6.24 Fuel level viewing window (arrowed)

6.29 Align index marks of bi-metal heater and case

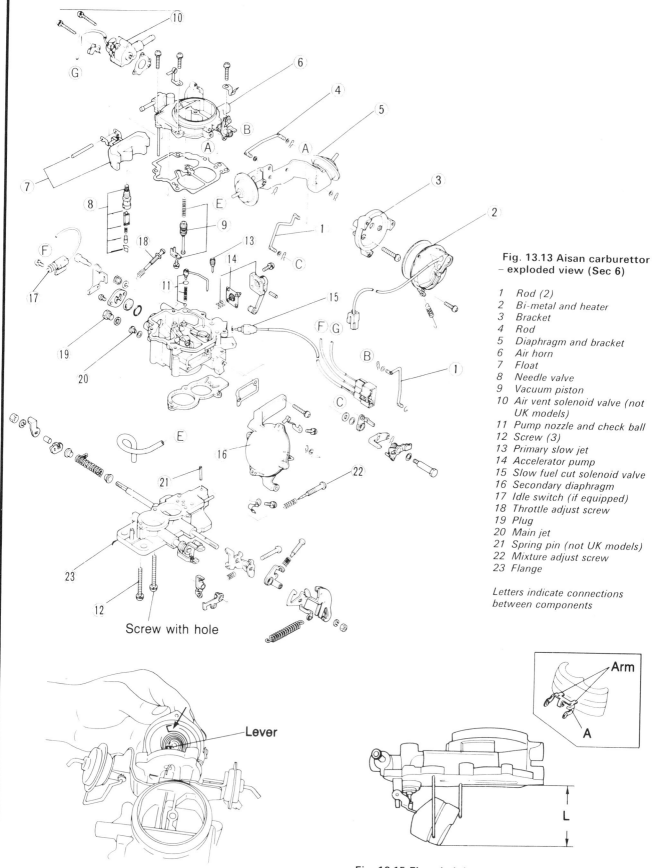

Fig. 13.13 Aisan carburettor
– exploded view (Sec 6)

1 Rod (2)
2 Bi-metal and heater
3 Bracket
4 Rod
5 Diaphragm and bracket
6 Air horn
7 Float
8 Needle valve
9 Vacuum piston
10 Air vent solenoid valve (not
    UK models)
11 Pump nozzle and check ball
12 Screw (3)
13 Primary slow jet
14 Accelerator pump
15 Slow fuel cut solenoid valve
16 Secondary diaphragm
17 Idle switch (if equipped)
18 Throttle adjust screw
19 Plug
20 Main jet
21 Spring pin (not UK models)
22 Mixture adjust screw
23 Flange

Letters indicate connections
between components

Screw with hole

Fig. 13.14 Engage tang (arrowed) on bi-metal with lever
(Sec 6)

Fig. 13.15 Float height adjustment check. For clearance
'L', see Specifications. Bend float stopper 'A' to adjust
(Sec 6)

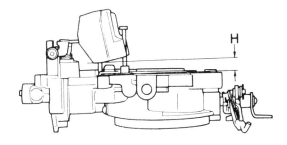

Fig. 13.16 Float height adjustment check. 'H' must equal specified clearance (Sec 6)

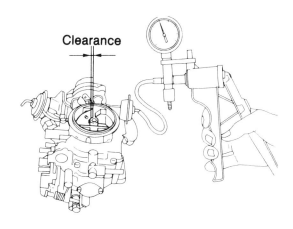

Fig. 13.17 Choke breaker diaphragm check method. Clearance must be as specified according to type (Sec 6)

1100 cc engine – 0.85 to 1.35 mm (0.033 to 0.053 in)
1300 and 1500 cc engines – 1.30 to 1.80 mm (0.051 to 0.071 in)

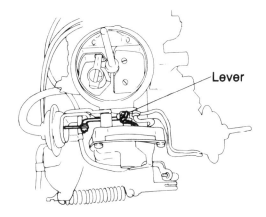

Fig. 13.18 Choke breaker clearance adjustment-bend lever (Sec 6)

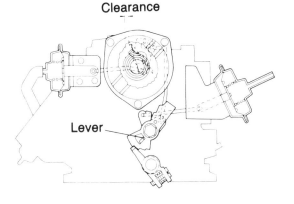

Fig. 13.20 Fast idle cam on second step to check the choke valve clearance (Sec 6)

Clearance – 0.67 to 1.17 mm (0.026 to 0.046 in)

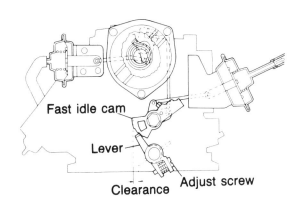

Fig. 13.19 Fast idle cam on third step to check clearance which must be as specified (Sec 6)

1100 cc engine – 0.23 to 0.53 mm (0.009 to 0.021 in)
1300 and 1500 cc engines – 0.35 to 0.65 mm (0.014 to 0.026 in)

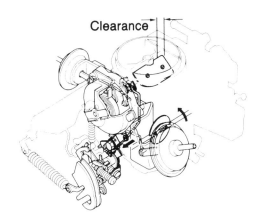

Fig. 13.21 Checking the unloader system (Sec 6)

Clearance – 1.55 to 2.05 mm (0.061 to 0.081 in)

clearance, between the air horn and choke valve. If the clearance is not as specified, bend the lever to suit using a pair of needle-nosed pliers (Fig. 13.18).

34 **Fast idle cam:** Set the fast idle cam onto the third step position, then check the primary throttle valve-to-carburettor wall clearance using a gauge rod (or drill) with a diameter of the specified clearance. If adjustment is necessary, turn the adjuster screw as required (Fig. 13.19).

35 **Choke valve clearance:** Move the fast idle cam onto the second step position and measure the choke valve clearance (Fig. 13.20). If adjustment is necessary, bend the operating lever to suit.

36 **Unloader system:** Fully open the primary throttle valve and measure the choke valve clearance (Fig. 13.21). The clearance should be as specified.

37 **Secondary throttle valve:** When the primary throttle valve is opened 47° to 53°, the secondary throttle valve should just start to open. The clearance between the primary throttle valve and the throttle bore should be as specified (see Fig. 13.22) when the secondary throttle valve starts to open (contacting the lever and tab). Use a gauge rod or drill with the same diameter as the specified clearance to check the clearance requirement.
38 If adjustment is necessary, bend the tab to suit using a pair of needle-nosed pliers.

Idle-up system (including throttle positioner system)
39 This system is fitted to models with power steering, or air conditioning (single servo diaphragm type system) or both (dual servo diaphragm system). The accompanying diagrams show the layout and components of the system types used. If required they can be checked and adjusted as follows according to type.

Single servo diaphragm type
40 When this system is in operation, the engine speeds should be as given in the Specifications. If adjustment is necessary, detach the hose between the servo diaphragm and the three-way solenoid valve.
41 Connect up a tachometer and run the engine. With intake manifold vacuum applied to the servo diaphragm, set the engine speed to that specified according to model – see Fig. 13.26.
42 On completion, reconnect the hose to the servo unit and three-way valve. Detach the tachometer.

Dual servo diaphragm type
43 Stage I: Proceed as described above for the single servo diaphragm type (paragraphs 40 and 41), but refer to Fig. 13.27 and detach the hose from diaphragm port 'A' to make the check/adjustment. If required, set the engine speed to that specified for Stage I.
44 Stage II: Reconnect the hose to the vacuum port 'A' and detach the vacuum hose from the servo diaphragm. Repeat the procedures in paragraphs 40 and 41. If required set the engine speed to that given for the Stage II adjustment in the Specifications, at the step 2 adjuster shown in Fig. 13.27.
45 On completion, detach the tachometer and reconnect the vacuum hose to the servo diaphragm valve.

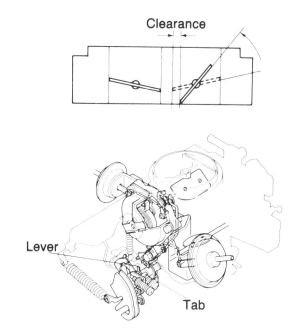

Fig. 13.22 Secondary throttle valve opening check (Sec 6)

Clearance at primary valve – 5.4 to 6.4 mm (0.213 to 0.252 in) when secondary valve starts to open

Economy drive indicator system
46 This system is fitted to later five-speed models, and its object is to improve the fuel consumption by warning the driver when he is using excessive throttle and when the vehicle is being driven in as inappropriate gear.

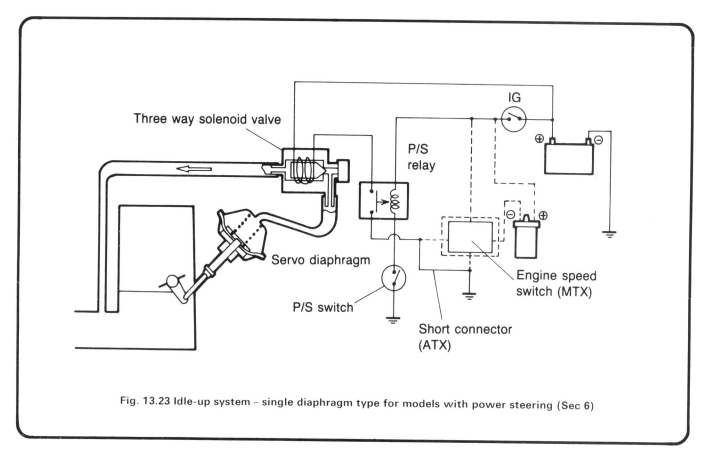

Fig. 13.23 Idle-up system – single diaphragm type for models with power steering (Sec 6)

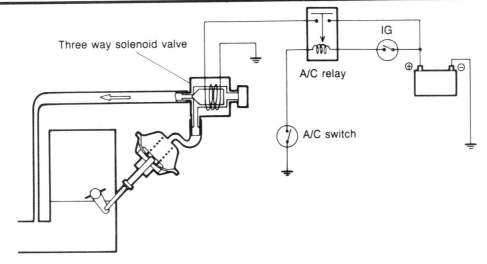

Fig. 13.24 Idle-up system – single diaphragm type for automatic transmission models with air conditioning (Sec 6)

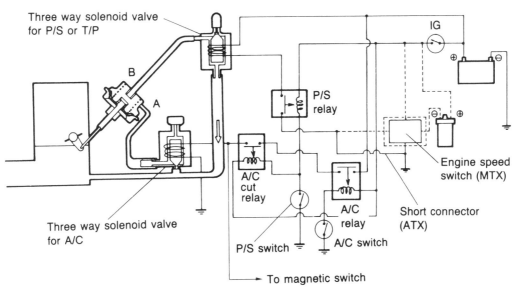

Fig. 13.25 Idle-up system – dual servo type for models with power steering and air conditioning (Sec 6)

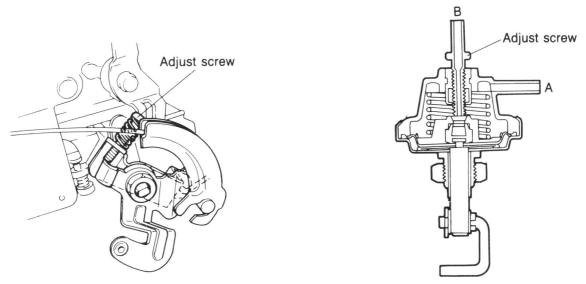

Fig. 13.26 Adjust engine speed if required by turning screw indicated (Sec 6)

Fig. 13.27 Dual diaphragm port connections and Stage II adjuster screw (Sec 6)

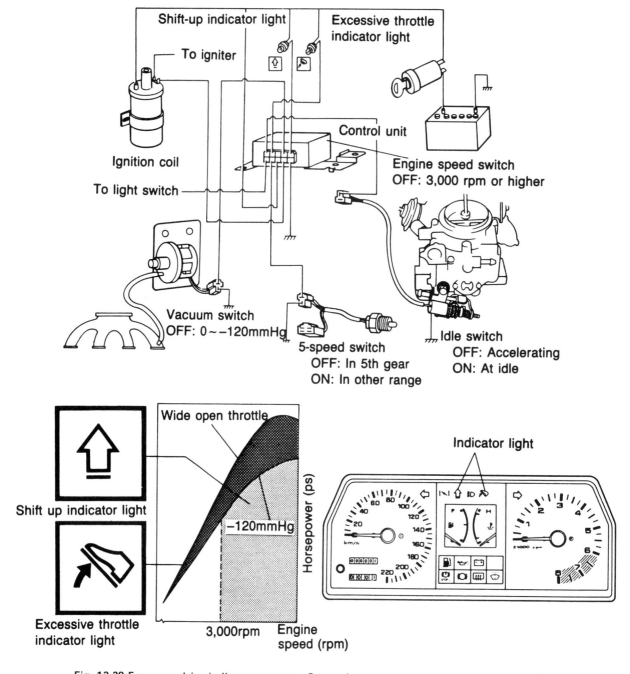

Fig. 13.28 Economy drive indicator system – 5-speed manual transmission models (Sec 6)

47 It does this by means of a warning indicator light which operates in any gear except fifth. Fig. 13.28 shows the system components and layout.

48 As the throttle pedal is depressed, the vacuum in the inlet manifold is reduced and when it drops to 4.72 in Hg (120 mm Hg), the warning light comes on.

49 A 'shift-up' indicator light is also fitted and this illuminates when the engine speed exceeds 3000 rpm in each gear (except fifth). When the engine is decelerating the idle switch is activated and the 'shift-up' light does not illuminate.

Emission control system (later models) – description

50 To assist in reducing the harmful CO emissions from the exhaust, later models are fitted with certain emission control components. The type and number of emission control devices fitted is dependent on the model and operating territory. The items dealt with below are those fitted to UK models only.

51 **Deceleration control system:** On manual transmission models this system is operated by the throttle positioner, whilst automatic transmission models have an anti-afterburn valve (AAV) which supplies air to the inlet manifold when decelerating.

52 **PTC heater system:** This system comprises the PTC heater, a relay, and a water temperature switch. With this system the air/fuel mixture is heated when the engine temperature is low (below 60°C/40°F) to improve fuel atomization.

53 **Fast idle cam breaker control system:** This system comprises the fast idle cam breaker, a three-way solenoid valve, a delay valve and a water temperature switch. The system is designed to operate when the engine coolant temperature is above 40°C (104°F) or the radiator coolant temperature is above 17°C (62°F). Once these temperatures are reached, the fast idle cam disengages and the engine speed is reduced (see Fig. 13.9).

54 **Idle compensator:** The function of this devise is to maintain a constant idle speed in accordance with the changes in operating

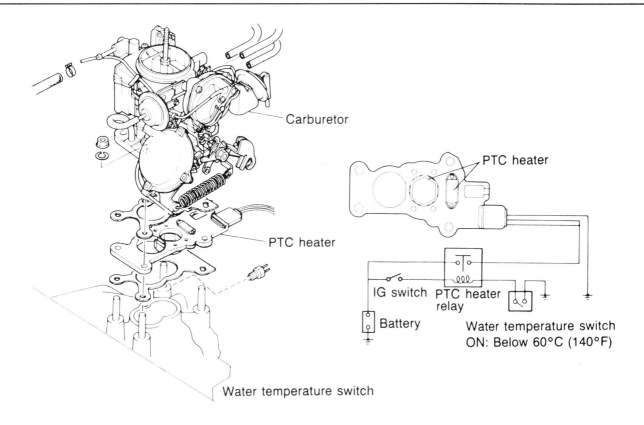

Fig. 13.29 PTC heater system (Sec 6)

temperature. A valve located in the base of the air cleaner body is connected by a hose to the inlet manifold and allows additional air into the manifold in accordance with the temperature.

55 **Positive crankcase ventilation (PCV) system:** The function of this system is to draw blow-by gases from the crankcase and rocker chamber and direct them into the inlet manifold. From here the gases are drawn into the combustion chambers with the fuel/air mixture and burnt in the combustion process.

56 **Evaporative emission control system:** The function of this system is to reduce the amount of fuel vapour released into the atmosphere. The system is activated by a two-way check valve near the fuel tank.

57 Maintenance of the emission control system components is basic and comprises mainly of periodical checks of the system hoses and connections for condition and security.

58 When removing and refitting any of the fuel system components, note the positions of the emission control hoses and wiring connections to avoid confusion during reassembly.

59 When removing any of the system water temperature switches, disconnect the wiring to the switch and partially drain the cooling system as described in Chapter 2 before unscrewing the switch.

60 If any of the system components are suspected of malfunction, have them checked by a Mazda dealer.

Fault diagnosis – fuel and exhaust systems

The fault diagnosis for later models fitted with an Aisan carburettor and emission control components is similar to that given for earlier models in Chapter 3, but the following additional items should be considered and checked, according to model and symptom.

Symptom	Reason(s)
Engine difficult to start	PCV valve faulty
Engine will not idle or idles erratically	PCV valve faulty Evaporative emission control system fault Blocked jets in carburettor Idle compensator faulty Vacuum hose(s) faulty
Idle speed too high	Idle compensator faulty Idle-up system faulty
Poor performance	Power valve faulty Dirty air cleaner

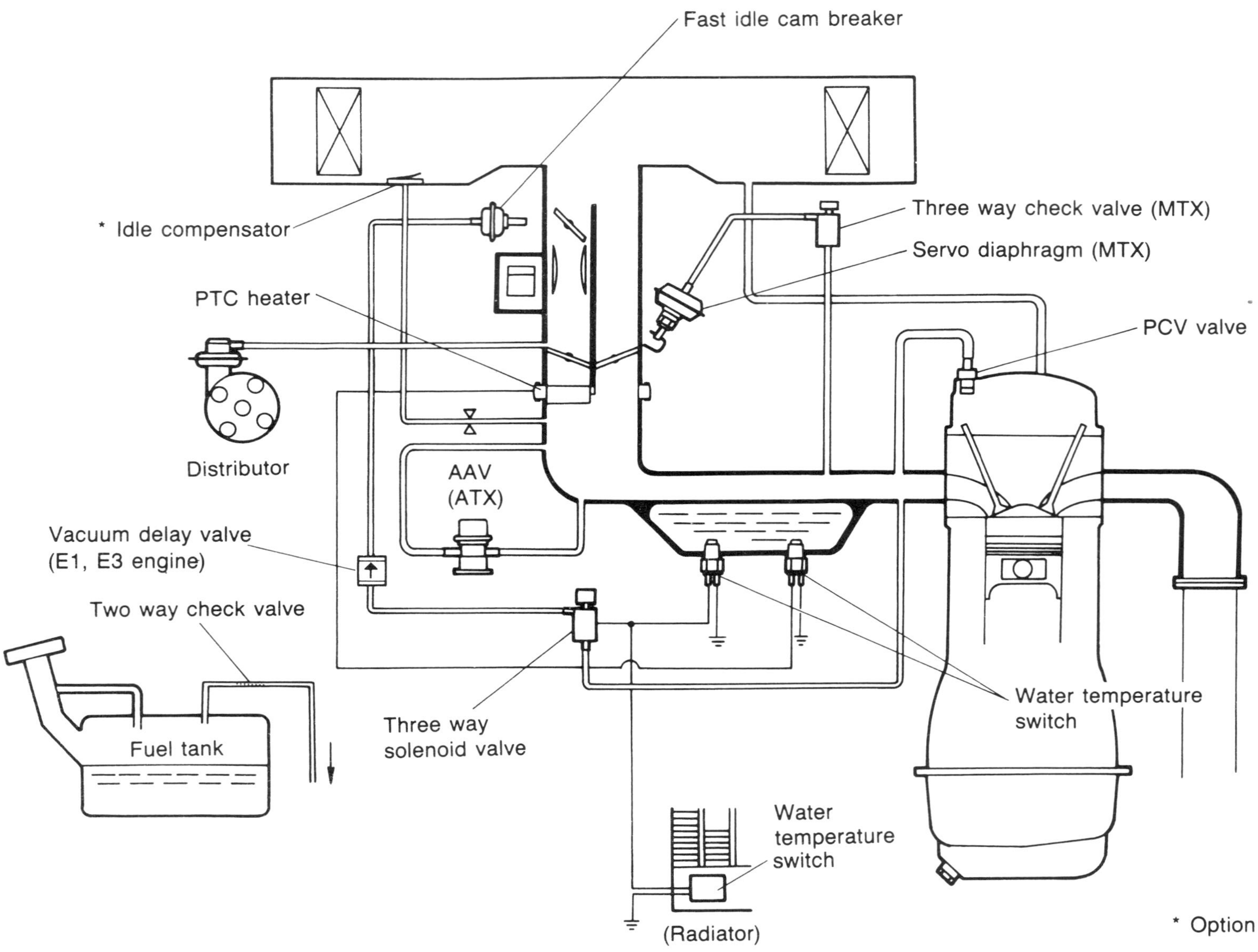

262

Fast idle cam breaker

Three way check valve (MTX)

Servo diaphragm (MTX)

PCV valve

Water temperature switch

Water temperature switch

(Radiator)

* Option

* Idle compensator

PTC heater

Distributor

AAV (ATX)

Three way solenoid valve

Vacuum delay valve (E1, E3 engine)

Two way check valve

Fuel tank

Fig. 13.30 Emission control system layout (Sec 6)

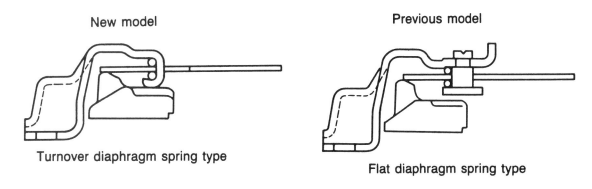

New model

Turnover diaphragm spring type

Previous model

Flat diaphragm spring type

Fig. 13.31 Sectioned views showing the later and earlier type clutch cover assemblies (Sec 7)

7 Clutch

Clutch unit – later models
1   A modified clutch cover and driven plate (disc) are fitted to later models. The cover is lighter in weight and is of a different shape to the earlier type (Fig. 13.31). The driven plate lining is harder wearing for longer life. The fitting direction for early and late type driven plates is critical and must be as shown in Fig. 13.32.
2   The later type cover and disc can be fitted to earlier models, and renewal procedures for the later type are the same as given in Chapter 5 for earlier models.

Clutch pedal – later models
3   A clutch pedal assist spring is fitted to later 1500 cc engine models. The object of the spring is to reduce the pedal pressure required to

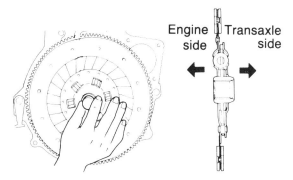

Engine side   Transaxle side

Fig. 13.32 Clutch driven plate (disc) must be fitted as shown (Sec 7)

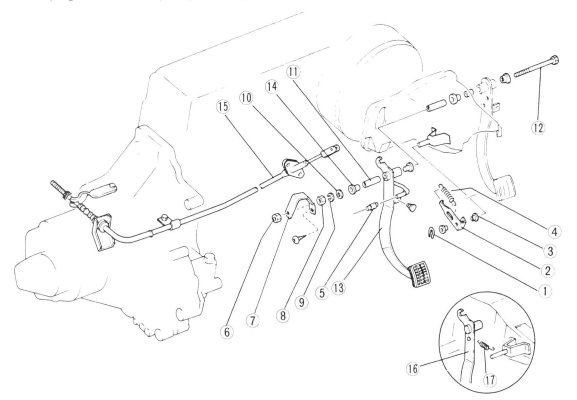

Fig. 13.33 Clutch pedal and cable components – later models (Sec 7)

1 Retaining ring	6 Nut	10 Plain washer	14 Bush
2 Lever	7 Cover	11 Spacer	15 Clutch cable
3 Bush	8 Nut	12 Through-bolt	16 Clutch pedal
4 Return spring	9 Spring washer	13 Clutch pedal	17 Return spring
5 Bush			

operate the clutch. The clutch pedal return spring on the later smaller engine variants also differs to that shown for earlier models in Chapter 5.

4   When checking the clutch pedal height and free play on later models, refer to the Specifications at the start of this Chapter.

Clutch pedal (later models) – removal and refitting

5   Disconnect the battery earth lead, then remove the cover under the facia on the driver's side.

6   Prise free the retaining clip, then remove the lever bushes and return spring (Fig. 13.33).

7   Undo the retaining nut from the pivot bolt, remove the cover, the second nut, washers and spacer, and withdraw the pivot bolt. Remove the clutch pedal, disengaging the cable and return spring.

8   Renew the pedal bushes if they are excessively worn. Renew any other parts which are damaged or worn.

9   Refitting is a reversal of the removal procedure. Smear the pedal bushes, cable and hook connection points with a lithium-based grease. On 1500 cc models with an assist spring, fit the spring as shown in Fig. 13.34.

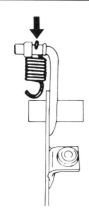

Fig. 13.34 Return spring installation position – 1500 cc models (Sec 7)

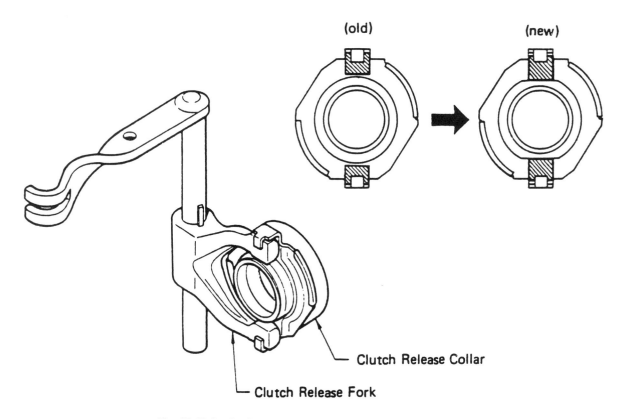

Fig. 13.35 Revised type clutch release bearing and fork (Sec 7)

10 Tighten the pivot bolt retaining nut to the specified torque setting.

11 On completion, check the pedal height and free play and adjust if required as described in Section 2 of Chapter 5, but refer to the setting requirements in the Specifications at the start of this Chapter.

Clutch release bearing and fork

12 A later improved type of release bearing and fork has been introduced on later models, the release bearing material now being resin (Fig. 13.35).

13 The new bearing and fork can be fitted to earlier models, but only as a complete assembly.

8   Automatic transmission

Kickdown switch – checking and adjustment

1   The kickdown switch is located on the accelerator pedal bracket. To check the switch for satisfactory operation, connect up a circuit tester as shown in Fig. 13.36. Fully depress the accelerator pedal. A continuity reading should be indicated when the pedal is depressed by approximately $7/8$ of its total movement.

2   If necessary, adjust the switch by detaching its wiring connector, loosening its locknut and turning the switch as required. Retighten the locknut and reconnect the wires to the switch, then recheck the adjustment. If satisfactory, disconnect the circuit tester.

3   If the kickdown switch is found to be defective it must be renewed. When fitting the switch, adjust it as described previously prior to fully tightening the locknut.

Modifications

4   The automatic transmission has had some design improvements made to quieten its operation and to make the gear changes smoother. The procedures described in Chapter 7 remain the same, with the following exceptions.

5   **Driveshaft removal**: When removing a driveshaft from models with the later automatic transmission, it should be noted that the side

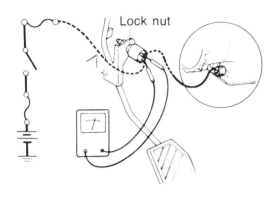

Fig. 13.36 Kickdown switch testing (Sec 8)

Shift cable adjustment:

8   Loosen the locknut, and unscrew and remove the selector lever knob. Undo the retaining screws and lift the centre console clear of the shift unit.
9   Check that the handbrake is fully applied and place chocks against the roadwheels. The engine should be warmed up to its normal operating temperature with the idle speed as specified, but switch the engine off during the adjustment procedures.
10 At the shift lever end of the cable, loosen off the locknuts and then move the selector lever to 'N', (detent roller must be fully engaged in the 'N' position – see Fig. 13.39).
11 Move the selector lever at the transmission to 'N' (see Fig. 13.40), then reverting to the cable at the shift lever end, screw the lower locknut up the cable thread so that it contacts the 'T' joint, then screw the upper locknut against the 'T' joint from the top end, tightening it to the specified torque.

New model

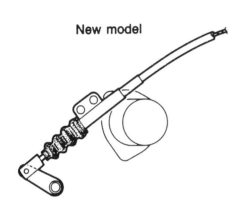

New model

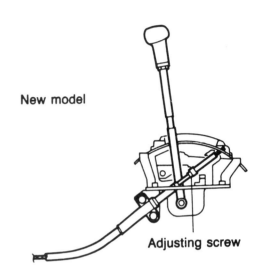

Adjusting screw

Previous model

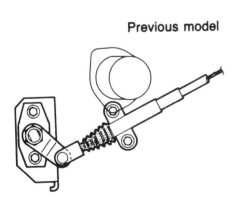

Previous model

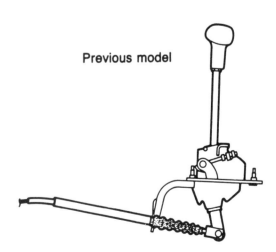

Fig. 13.37 Automatic transmission shift control types used (Sec 8)

bearing housings now have a notch in them, in which a lever can be inserted to assist when withdrawing the driveshaft from the transmission.
6   **Shift control:** The shift control on later models is a cable type rather then the lever rod type used on earlier models. Two cable types have been used, the main difference between them being the routing – see Fig. 13.37.
7   An exploded view of the later type shift cable assembly and associated components is shown in Fig. 13.38. If required the shift cable can be adjusted as follows.

12 Press the button on the shift lever knob and move the lever towards the 'R' position, to the point where the select lever on the transmission starts to operate. Measure the amount of selector lever movement ('a' in Fig. 13.41).
13 Now pull the shift lever back to the 'D' position and measure the amount of movement at 'b'. The movements measured for 'a' and 'b' should be equal. If they are not, loosen off the upper cable locknuts at the shift lever end and adjust them to suit. When the movements 'a' and 'b' are equal, tighten the locknuts, then check the manual linkage for satisfactory movement and engagement throughout the range.

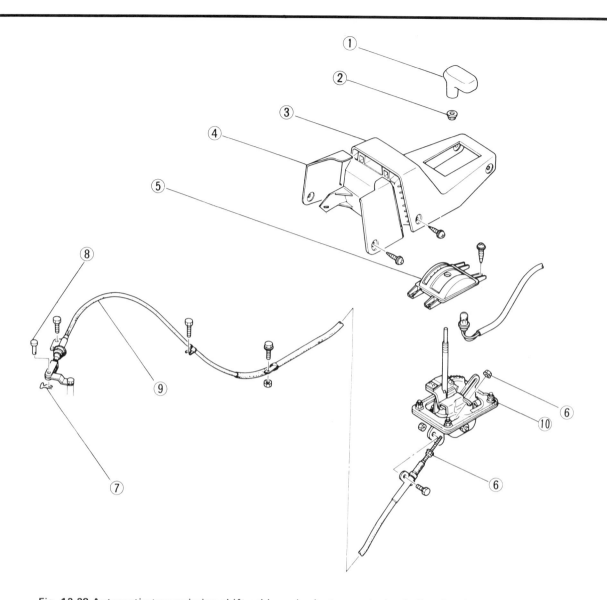

Fig. 13.38 Automatic transmission shift cable and selector control unit fitted to later models (Sec 8)

1	Selector lever knob	4	Side trim	7	Snap pin	9	Selector cable
2	Knob locknut	5	Selector indicator panel	8	Joint pin	10	Locknut
3	Centre console	6	Cable locknut				

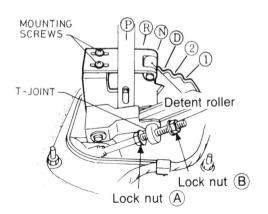

Fig. 13.39 Shift control cable adjustment showing locknuts and detent roller engaged in the 'N' position (Sec 8)

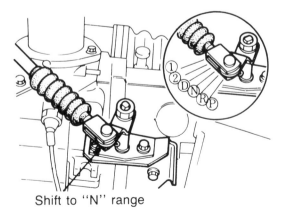

Fig. 13.40 Move selector lever at transmission to 'N' position (Sec 8)

14 If the shift lever operation is not satisfactory, set it in the 'P' position, loosen off the detent roller mounting screws and move the detent roller to suit. Retighten the detent roller mounting screw, then recheck the cable shift adjustments as described above (Fig. 13.39).

15 **Shift lever knob adjustment:** Screw the adjuster locknut fully down the shift lever, then screw the knob fully down the shaft. From this position unscrew the knob no more than one full turn to position it correctly, and tighten the locknut against it to secure. Check that the lever movement and engagement is satisfactory through its range.

16 Remove the wheel chocks and roadtest the vehicle.

9 Driveshafts

Driveshafts – automatic transmission models

1 Later models with an automatic transmission are fitted with driveshafts which have a tripod type inner CV joint. This type of joint improves smoothness in operation (Fig. 13.42).

2 The removal and overhaul procedures for this type of driveshaft are the same as those described in Section 5 of Chapter 8, but before separating the joint from the shaft, mark the relative positions of the outer ring, the tripod joint and the driveshaft. Dismantle the inner joint as shown in Fig. 13.45, but do not knock the roller bearings when dismantling the joint from the shaft.

3 Reassemble in reverse, following the procedures described in Section 5 of Chapter 8, but align the marks made during removal when reassembling the tripod joint driveshaft and outer ring.

10 Braking system

Modifications – general

1 To improve the efficiency of the braking system on later models the following items have been modified.

(a) *Front brake discs:* Ventilated type front brake discs are now fitted to aid cooling of the front brake units. The front brake calipers and pads are also modified

(b) *Rear drum brakes:* The brake drums at the rear are now larger in diameter but reduced in width and the brake shoes are modified to suit

(c) *Handbrake:* A 'forward' pull action handbrake system is now fitted instead of the 'cross' pull system used on earlier models. Although the adjustment procedures are the same as for earlier models, refer to the Specifications at the start of this Chapter for the applicable handbrake adjustment data

(d) *Dual proportioning valve:* This unit is enlarged on later models to increase the brake efficiency. As with earlier models it is mounted on the bulkhead in the engine compartment (photo)

(e) *Rear wheel cylinder:* On later models the wheel cylinder has had its inner diameter reduced from 54.0 to 50.8 mm

(f) *Master cylinder:* On later models the master cylinder inner diameter is enlarged from 20.64 mm to 22.22 mm (photo)

2 With the exception of the following items, the removal and refitting details of the later components listed previously are the same as those

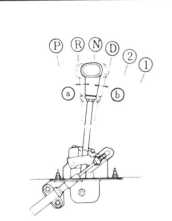

Fig. 13.41 Selector lever movements between 'a' and 'b' must be equal (Sec 8)

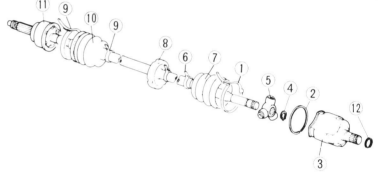

Fig. 13.42 Exploded view of the driveshaft fitted to later automatic transmission models showing tripod inner joint (Sec 9)

1 Boot band	8	Damper (right-hand side only)
2 Clip	9	Boot band
3 Outer ring	10	Boot
4 Snap ring	11	Shaft/balljoint unit
5 Tripod joint	12	Clip
6 Boot band		
7 Boot		

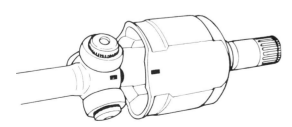

Fig. 13.43 Mark the tripod joint and outer ring (do not use a punch) for alignment before dismantling (Sec 9)

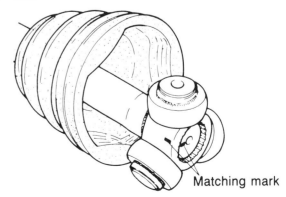

Matching mark

Fig. 13.44 Mark the tripod joint and shaft for alignment before dismantling (Sec 9)

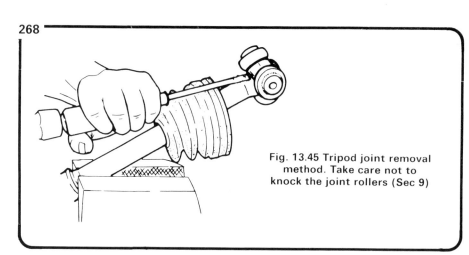

Fig. 13.45 Tripod joint removal method. Take care not to knock the joint rollers (Sec 9)

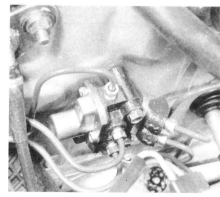

10.1A Dual proportioning valve fitted to later models

10.1B The master cylinder and servo unit fitted to later models

10.5A Release the retaining clip ...

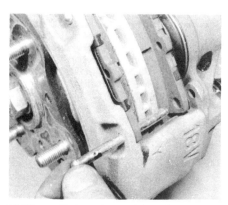

10.5B ... withdraw the retaining pins ...

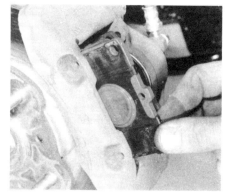

10.5C ... remove the outer pad and shims ...

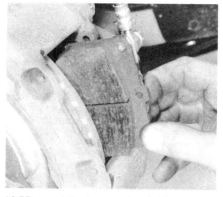

10.5D ... and the inner pad and shims

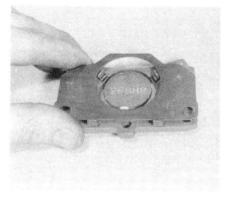

10.7A Locate the inner pad first shim ...

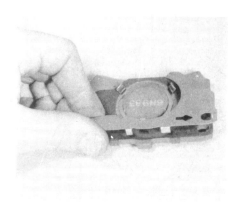

10.7B ... then fit the second as shown (arrow points in direction of disc rotation)

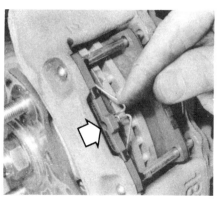

10.8A Engage retaining clip into pad hole (arrowed) ...

10.8B ... and clip ends into pins (arrowed)

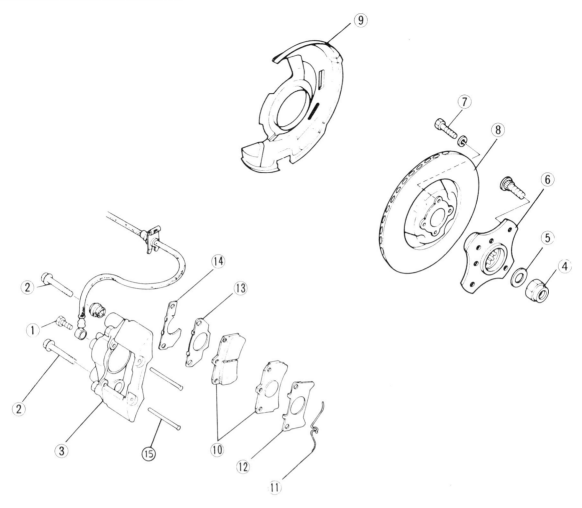

Fig. 13.46 Later type ventilated front disc, caliper and associated components (Sec 10)

1	Bolt	5	Washer
2	Sleeve bolts	6	Hub
3	Caliper	7	Bolt
4	Nut	8	Disc plate

9	Dust cover	13	Shim
10	Disc pad	14	Shim
11	Clip	15	Pad pin
12	Shim		

described for earlier models in Chapter 9, but care must be taken to order the correct replacement when renewing an item.

Brake pedal height and free play – checking and adjustment
3   The procedures for checking and adjusting the brake pedal height and free play remain the same for later models as for earlier models described in Chapter 9, but note that the free play and pedal height requirements differ on later models (see Specifications at the start of this Chapter).

Front disc pads (ventilated disc type) – inspection and renewal
4   To inspect the pads for excessive wear, proceed as described in paragraphs 1 and 2 of Section 4, Chapter 9.
5   To remove the pads, extract the spring retainer from the pads and retainer pins using suitable pliers, withdraw the retainer pins, then remove the pads and shims. Note the orientation of the shims as they are removed (photos).
6   Clean and inspect the components as described in paragaphs 7 and 8 of Section 4, Chapter 9.
7   To refit the pads, assemble the shims to them as noted during removal and shown in the photographs. Fit the inner and outer pads and shims into position.
8   Locate the pins and wire spring retainer as shown (photos).
9   Depress the footbrake two or three times to bring the piston into

contact with the pads, then refit the roadwheel and lower the car to the ground. Tighten the roadwheel nuts to the specified torque when the car is on its wheels, then check the fluid level in the master cylinder reservoir.
10 Roadtest the car to complete.

Front brake caliper (later models) – removal, overhaul and refitting
11 Apply the handbrake and slacken the front wheel retaining nuts. Jack up the front of the vehicle and support it on axle stands. Remove the applicable front roadwheel.
12 Remove the brake pads as described previously in this Section.
13 Now refer to Section 5 of Chapter 9 and proceed as described in paragraphs 4 to 6 inclusive.
14 To remove the caliper completely (and this is preferable, so that it can be thoroughly cleaned, inspected and reassembled on the workbench), undo the two sleeve bolts and withdraw the caliper unit.
15 With the caliper on the bench, wipe away all traces of dust and dirt, but **take care to avoid inhaling the dust as it is injurious to health.**
16 Fully withdraw the partially ejected piston from the caliper body and remove the dust seal.
17 Extract the caliper/piston hydraulic seal ring using a small screwdriver (or similar tool) as a lever but take care not to damage the caliper/piston surfaces.
18 Examination and reassembly of the caliper is similar to that

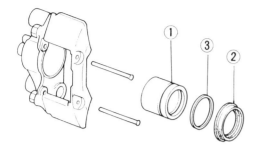

Fig. 13.47 Exploded view showing the caliper, piston (1) dust seal (2) and piston seal (3) (Sec 10)

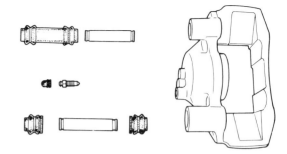

Fig. 13.48 Check the condition of the caliper guide pins and bushes (Sec 10)

Fig. 13.49 Piston seal fitting method (Sec 10)

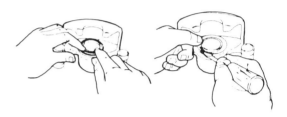

Fig. 13.50 Dust seal fitting method (Sec 10)

described for earlier models in paragraphs 11 to 17 inclusive of Section 5, Chapter 9.

19 Refit the caliper and pads in the reverse order of removal. Bleed the brakes to complete, as described in Section 14 of Chapter 9.

Rear brake shoes (later models) – inspection and renewal

20 The modified type rear brake assembly fitted to later models is shown in Fig. 13.51 and photos.

21 The procedures for removing the brake drum and shoes is similar

to that described for earlier models in Section 7 of Chapter 9, but the following differences apply.

(a) The right-hand hub nut has a left-hand thread on later models and must therefore be turned clockwise to loosen it. This nut is galvanized for identification

(b) The self-adjust mechanism differs to suit the later type handbrake cable, but it also has a manual adjuster quadrant to loosen off the shoe adjustment when removing or refitting the brake drum (Fig. 13.52)

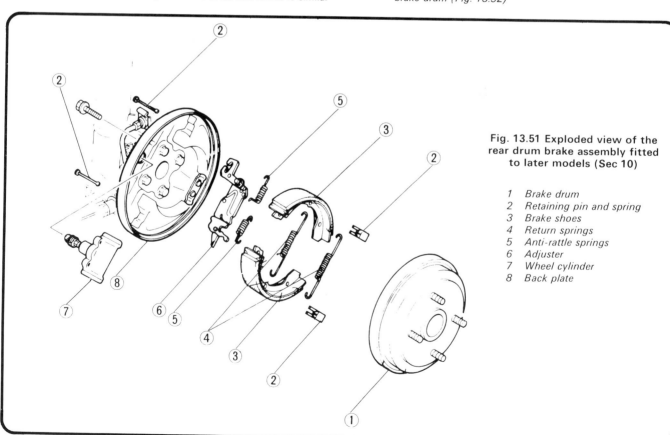

Fig. 13.51 Exploded view of the rear drum brake assembly fitted to later models (Sec 10)

1 Brake drum
2 Retaining pin and spring
3 Brake shoes
4 Return springs
5 Anti-rattle springs
6 Adjuster
7 Wheel cylinder
8 Back plate

10.20A Rear drum upper return spring and adjuster locations on later models

    (c) Refer to later paragraphs in this Section for details on disconnecting and reconnecting the handbrake cable
    (d) When refitting the hub nut ensure that a new nut is used, adjust the bearing pre-load as described in Section 7 of Chapter 9, but when measuring the torque at which the drum starts to turn, the rotation starting torque must be set between 0.15 to 0.49 Nm (1.30 to 4.34 in lb). Stake the locknut as described to set the pre-load at this setting

Handbrake cable (forward pull type) – removal and refitting
22 The forward pull type handbrake cable layout is shown in Fig.

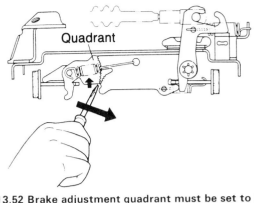

Fig. 13.52 Brake adjustment quadrant must be set to loosen adjustment of brake shoes (Sec 10)

13.53. From the cable equaliser a separate cable goes back to each rear brake unit and one or both cables can be removed for renewal as required. Renewal of both cables at the same time is recommended.
23 To remove a cable, chock the front roadwheels, jack up the rear of the car and support it on axle stands.
24 Undo the retaining screws and remove the centre console from the handbrake.
25 Unscrew the handbrake cable adjuster nut and remove the front cable from the handbrake lever. This cable can now be pulled through the floor pan from underneath the car and removed with the equaliser and spring as required (photos).
26 To remove the left and/or right-hand brake cable, detach the inner cable nipple from the equaliser at the front end. If the front cable has not been removed, the handbrake must be fully released and the adjuster on the handbrake lever loosened off.
27 Unbolt the outer cable-to-floor location bracket and also unbolt the cable from the backplate (photos).
28 Detach the cable clevis from the operating lever at the rear end (photo). Remove the cable.

10.20B Lower brake shoe and return spring locations on later models

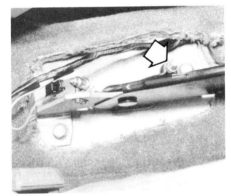

10.25A Handbrake lever and cable adjuster (arrowed)

10.25B Handbrake cable equalizer (arrowed) and return spring

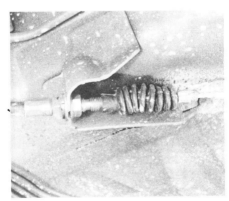

10.27A Handbrake outer cable-to-floor pan bracket showing locknuts

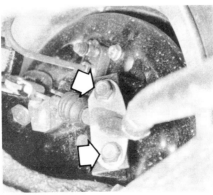

10.27B Handbrake cable-to-backplate bolts (arrowed)

10.28 Handbrake cable-to-brake unit clevis (arrowed)

Fig. 13.53 Handbrake cable and lever attachments on later
models (Sec 10)

1 Adjuster nut
2 Equalizer
3 Return spring
4 Front section cable
5 Rear section cable

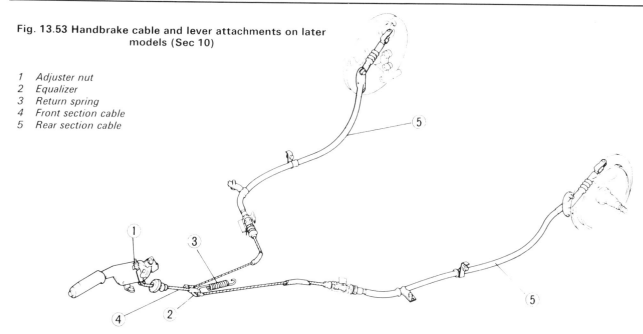

29 Refitting is a reversal of the removal procedure. Lubricate exposed
linkages and cable guides with a multi-purpose grease during
assembly. On completion, adjust the cable, referring to Section 15 of
Chapter 9, but note that the adjustment requirement differs (see
Specifications at the start of this Chapter).

11 Suspension and steering

Front and rear wheel hub modifications
1 **Front wheel hub**: Later models are fitted with a modified front
wheel hub which although similar in design to the earlier type, differs
as follows (Fig. 13.54).

(a) The brake caliper-to-knuckle angle is changed by 15°
     (upward)
(b) The brake disc dust cover shape is changed (Fig 13.55)
(c) The outer hub oil seal is changed in shape (Fig. 13.56)

2 If using a Mazda puller when removing the later type hub, use
special tool number 49 G030 725 as shown in Fig. 13.57.
3 The overhaul procedures for the front wheel hub are otherwise as
described for the earlier models in Chapter 10. When ordering spare
parts, be specific regarding the type you require.
4 **Rear wheel hub**: Later models are fitted with a modified rear
wheel hub which although similar in design to the earlier type differs as
follows.

(a) The rear wheel hub spindle diameter is increased in size and a
     larger bearing is fitted to suit

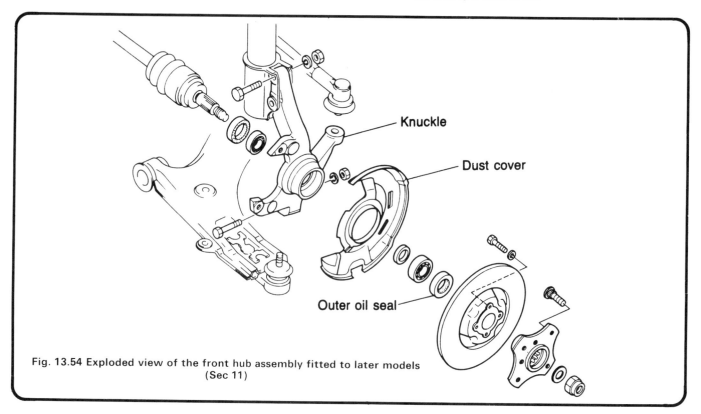

Knuckle

Dust cover

Outer oil seal

Fig. 13.54 Exploded view of the front hub assembly fitted to later models
(Sec 11)

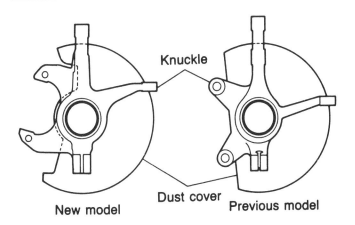

Fig. 13.55 Brake disc dust cover and knuckle identification features (Sec 11)

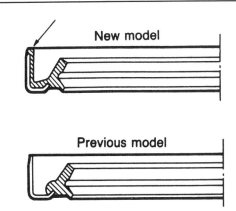

Fig. 13.56 Outer hub oil seal profiles (Sec 11)

(b) The right-hand hub nut now has a left-hand thread to prevent the nut self-tightening. This nut has a galvanised finish for identification and is tightened to the same torque setting as that specified for the earlier type with the right-hand thread. The left-hand hub nut remains the same
(c) The rear hub spindle lateral link fitting angle is changed from 90° to 83° on later models

5   The overhaul procedures for the rear wheel hub are otherwise as described for the earlier models in Chapter 10. When ordering spare parts, be specific regarding the type required.

Lower suspension arm
6   On later models the lower suspension arm front mounting bracket is replaced by a pivot bolt which locates in the lower arm and underbody and is secured by a captive nut. The bolt is fitted from the front. A later design of suspension arm is fitted to suit and the lower arm bush also differs, being a double bush type with a metal sleeve (Fig. 13.58).

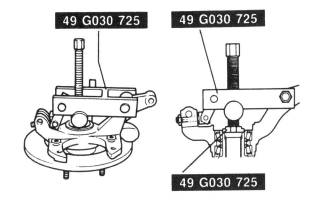

Fig. 13.57 Mazda wheel hub puller tools for later models (Sec 11)

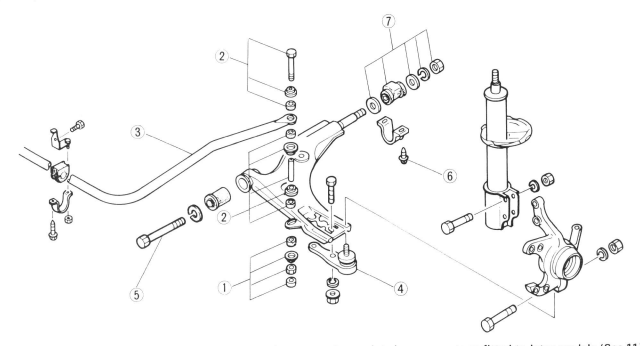

Fig. 13.58 Exploded view of the front lower suspension arm and associated components as fitted to later models (Sec 11)

1 Nut, bush and retainer assembly	2 Bolt, retainer and bush assembly	4 Lower arm balljoint	6 Bolt
	3 Stabilizer	5 Bolt	7 Nut and bush assembly

7   The removal and refitting details for the lower suspension arm and associated components are as described for the earlier type in Chapter 10, but note the following when renewing the bushes.

> (a) *Mount the suspension arm in a vice for support and then cut free the bush collar using a hacksaw, but take care not to damage the suspension arm (see Fig. 10.15)*
>
> (b) *To withdraw the bush from the eye in the suspension arm, use a piece of metal tubing of suitable diameter, or Mazda special tool number 49 BO92 625A as shown in Fig. 13.59*
>
> (c) *Refit in the reverse order, but smear the new bush with soapy water to ease fitting. **Do not** lubricate the bush with oil or grease*

Front stabilizer

8   The front stabilizer bar fitted to later models is hollow in its cross-section to save weight. It should be noted that it is not possible to fit a stabilizer bar to automatic transmission models. The removal and refitting of the later type bar is the same as that described for the earlier type in Chapter 10.

Rear suspension modifications

9   The following items have been modified on later models to effect improvements to the rear suspension system.

> (a) *A revised type of rubber spring seat is fitted to the top of the rear suspension strut to prevent the ingress of water into the luggage area. In addition, a plastic seat is inserted between the suspension tower unit and the upper mounting, its function being to reduce noise*
>
> (b) *The rear suspension stabilizer is changed in shape to allow for the larger fuel tank. Also, in order to reduce weight, the stabilizer is now hollow in cross-section*
>
> (c) *The trailing arm-to-shock absorber mounting is lowered by 10 mm (0.39 in)*
>
> (d) *The rear crossmember is modified in order to save weight*
>
> (e) *The length of the lateral link bolt is now increased to 275 mm (10.8 in) from 251 mm (9.8 in) for previous models*
>
> (f) *The rear suspension pivot bushes are of double type construction, in rubber with a metal sleeve, and are similar to the later type bushes, now fitted to the front suspension arm front inner pivots*
>
> (g) *The lateral links are modified in shape and are now secured by a locknut on the pivot bolts. Estate models differ again in that the rearmost lateral link on each side is completely different in design, and is adjustable for length to set the rear toe-in as specified (photo)*

10 The removal and refitting procedures for the modified items mentioned are as described for the earlier type fittings in Chapter 10, except for the following.

11 When renewing the suspension pivot bushes, the procedure is similar to that described for the front suspension arm bushes in paragraph 7 of this Section.

Rear lateral links (Estate models) – removal, refitting and adjustment

12 The removal and refitting procedures for the rear lateral link arms on Estate models is similar to that described for other models in Section 15 of Chapter 10, but the adjustment references differ.

13 Ignore the references to alignment marking made in paragraph 3 of Section 15 (Chapter 10), since an eccentric washer type adjustment is not used on Estate models. Provided that the length of the lateral link arm is not changed, the toe setting will remain the same.

14 Although not recommended, if a rear lateral link arm is to be dismantled, or its length changed for any reason, measure the lengths of exposed thread between the central adjuster and the locknut prior to loosening the locknut. Note that the length of the lateral arm each side should be equal. Having noted the length, this can be used as a setting guide when refitting the lateral link arm. On completion, an accurate alignment check will need to be made as described in Section 26 of Chapter 10.

15 If adjustment is required to correct the rear toe setting, loosen off the lateral arm adjuster locknut(s) and then turn the adjuster(s) in the required direction to adjust the setting, which must be as specified (see Specifications at the start of this Chapter).

16 The rear lateral link arm lengths must be kept the same each side.

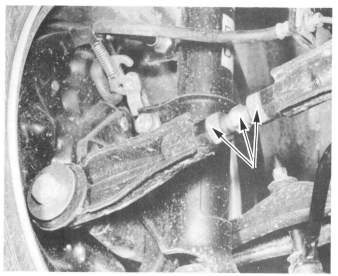

11.9 Rear lateral link on Estate models showing adjuster and locknuts (arrowed)

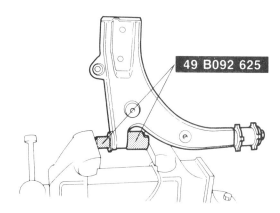

49 B092 625

Fig. 13.59 Lower arm bush removal method using Mazda special tools (late models) (Sec 11)

To increase the toe setting, turn the right-hand link adjuster clockwise and the left-hand link adjuster anti-clockwise, and *vice versa* to reduce the setting. Retighten the locknuts on completion.

Rear anti-roll bar – removal and refitting

17 Chock the front wheels, jack up the rear of the vehicle and securely support it on axle stands.

18 Undo the two nuts and detach the link bolts from the lateral arm on each side. Note the order and orientation of the washers and insulator bushes (photo).

19 Undo the stabilizer bar-to-crossmember saddle clamp bolt each side and remove the stabilizer (photo).

20 If the anti-roll bar is distorted, cracked or damaged it must be renewed. Renew the insulator mounting bushes if they are damaged or perished.

21 Refit in the reverse order of removal. **Do not** fully tighten the fastenings until after the vehicle is free standing.

Rear trailing arm – removal and refitting

22 Proceed as described in Section 16 of Chapter 10, but note the following differences.

> (a) *The anti-roll bar on later models is attached to the lateral link arm, not the trailing arm as on previous models*
>
> (b) *Disconnect the handbrake cable retainer strap from the trailing arm*

11.18 Rear stabilizer bar-to-lateral link connecting bolt on later models

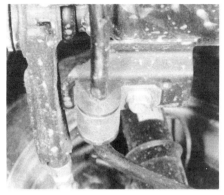

11.19 Rear stabilizer bar-to-crossmember mounting on later models

11.25 View showing the later type steering column tilt lock

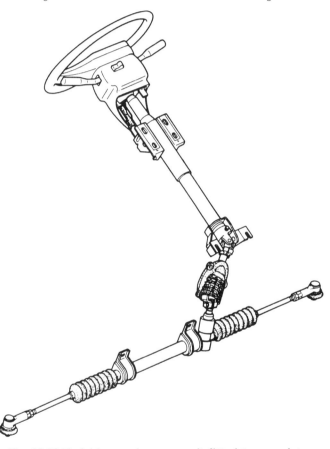

Fig. 13.60 Variable steering gear unit fitted to some later models – left-hand drive shown (Sec 11)

Steering gear – manual with variable gear ratio
23 Some later models are fitted with a manual rack and pinion steering gear unit which is of the variable ratio type. The advantage of a variable ratio type steering gear unit is that the gear ratio changes as the movement of the steering increases and this has the effect of reducing the amount of steering force required (Fig. 13.60).
24 The removal and refitting details for the variable ratio steering gear unit are the same as those for the constant ratio type described in Chapter 10. The specification differences for the variable ratio type are given in the Specifications at the start of this Chapter.

Steering column tilt lock – later models
25 On later models the tilt steering lock lever is located underneath the column, rather than on the side as with earlier models (photo).
26 On the later type, the column mounting bracket is attached by four mounting bolts to reduce the vibrations at the steering wheel.
27 The removal and refitting of the later column is otherwise the same as that described for the earlier type in Chapter 10.

Steering pinion gear
28 The steering pinion gear on later models differs in that it is now only partially notched in the coupling spline area for the intermediate shaft (Fig. 13.61).
29 When disconnecting this type of coupling it is advisable to make alignment marks on the pinion shaft and intermediate shaft universal joint as they are uncoupled.
30 These marks can then be used to correctly align the shaft and joint when refitting, so that the coupling bolt hole and notch are in exact alignment. If the alignment between the two is not exact when reassembling, then the pinion shaft, joint coupling and/or the retaining bolt could be damaged and will then require renewal.

Tie-rod outer balljoint
31 The tie-rod outer balljoints on later models differ in that they no longer have the square section on the inner end, and the left and right-hand balljoints are now the same.
32 The removal and refitting procedures are otherwise as described in Section 21 of Chapter 10.

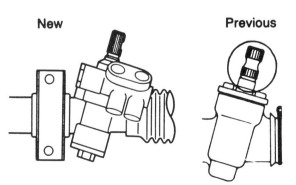

Fig. 13.61 Views illustrating the two types of steering pinion gear used (Sec 11)

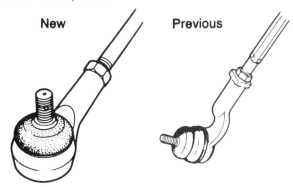

Fig. 13.62 Views illustrating the two types of steering tie-rod end used (Sec 11)

Power steering system – description and maintenance

33 A power-assisted steering system became available as an optional fitting on later models. The system layout is shown in Fig. 13.63, and the main components comprise a rack and pinion steering gear unit, a belt-driven hydraulic pump and fluid reservoir, and the hydraulic fluid feed and return lines between the steering gear and the pump unit.

34 Maintenance comprises of periodically making a visual inspection of the fluid level in the fluid reservoir, inspecting the hydraulic line connection points for any signs of leakage, and checking the condition and tension of the pump drivebelt cause a drop in the fluid level in the reservoir and/or a noticeable difference in the pressure required to turn the steering wheel when in motion.

35 Any defects in the power steering lines must be rectified at the earliest opportunity. When checking the hydraulic lines for leakage, run the engine and get an assistant to turn the steering wheel from lock to lock in each direction, but do not hold the steering wheel in the full lock position for a period exceeding 15 seconds. The most likely points at which leaks may occur are indicated in Fig. 13.63.

36 The fluid level in the reservoir is easily checked by removing the cap. The cap has a dipstick attached, with high (H) and low (L) level markings on it. The fluid level must be kept between the two marks. If required, top up the level using ATF type F fluid, but do not overfill. Ensure that the cap is fully tightened. Do not allow dirt to enter the hydraulic system.

37 Check the condition and tension of the power steering pump drivebelt as follows. Check the tension midway between the pulleys, applying a pressure of about 98 N (22 lb). The deflection should be as specified. To adjust the drivebelt tension, loosen off the pump mounting bolt and the adjuster locknut, then turn the adjuster in the required direction to set the tension as specified, and retighten the locknut and mounting bolt.

38 If the drivebelt is to be renewed, loosen off the tensioner so that the

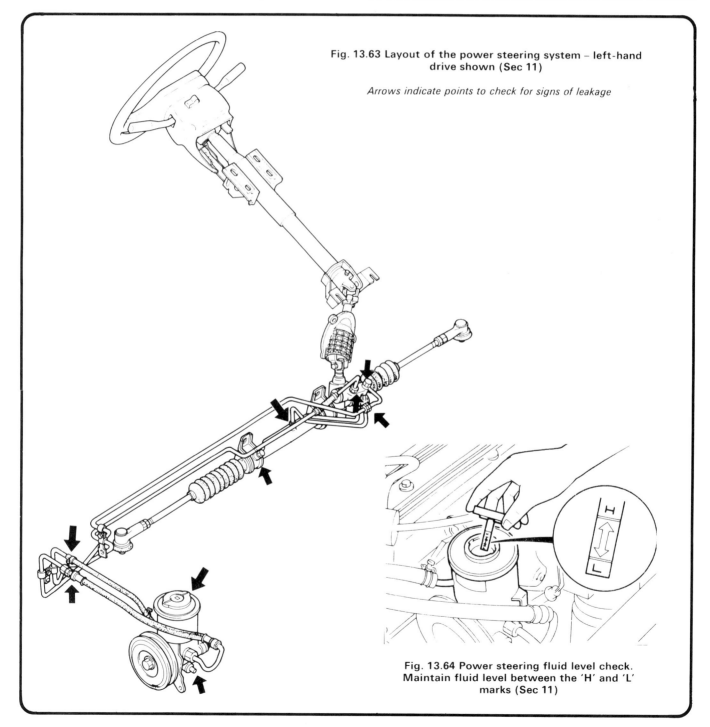

Fig. 13.63 Layout of the power steering system – left-hand drive shown (Sec 11)

Arrows indicate points to check for signs of leakage

Fig. 13.64 Power steering fluid level check. Maintain fluid level between the 'H' and 'L' marks (Sec 11)

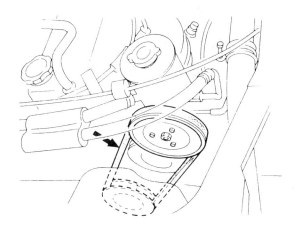

Fig. 13.65 Check the power steering drivebelt (arrowed) for condition and tension (Sec 11)

old belt can be disengaged from the two pulleys. Fit the new belt and tension it as described in the previous paragraph.

39 After fitting a new drivebelt, recheck its tension after an initial mileage has been covered (say 500 miles). It is normal for the belt to stretch a little, and for the tension to slacken off during this period. Further adjustment may then be necessary.

Power steering system – bleeding

40 Apply the handbrake and chock the rear wheels, then raise and support the front of the vehicle on axle stands so that the front wheels are clear of the ground.

41 Check the fluid level in the power steering pump reservoir. If necessary, top up the level whilst turning the steering from lock to lock. Add more fluid as necessary to maintain the level whilst continuing to

turn the steering. When the fluid level stabilizes, lower the vehicle so that it is free standing.

42 Start and run the engine at idle speed, then turn the steering from lock to lock a few times and check that the fluid level does not drop below the 'L' line on the level dipstick.

43 If when turning the steering an abnormal noise is heard from the fluid lines, it indicates that there is still air in the system. Further check this by moving the wheels to the straight ahead position and switching off the engine. If the fluid level in the reservoir rises, then air is present in the system and further bleeding is necessary – until it is removed. During the bleeding process, ensure that the level of the fluid does not drop below the 'L' line on the reservoir dipstick.

44 If the air in the system is difficult to remove, raise the temperature of the system fluid to between 50 and 80°C (122 to 176°F) by continuously turning the steering from lock to lock with the engine running. When this temperature is reached, switch off the engine for a few moments, then recheck the fluid level as described in paragraph 42, but make this check within five minutes of switching off the engine. If necessary repeat this operation to completely bleed the system.

Power steering gear – removal and refitting

45 The removal and refitting procedures for the power steering gear unit are similar to those described for the manual type in Section 23 of Chapter 10, but the following additional points should be noted.

(a) Allow for fluid spillage when disconnecting the hydraulic fluid feed and return lines from the steering gear unit and have a container ready to catch it in. This fluid must be disposed of and new fluid of the specified type used when refilling. **Do not** allow dirt to enter the hydraulic system. Plug the hose connections to prevent excessive fluid leakage and the possible ingress of dirt

(b) When refitting the steering gear unit, ensure that the plugs are removed from the hose connections and also ensure that the connections are clean

(c) On completion, top up and bleed the hydraulic system as described previously in this Section

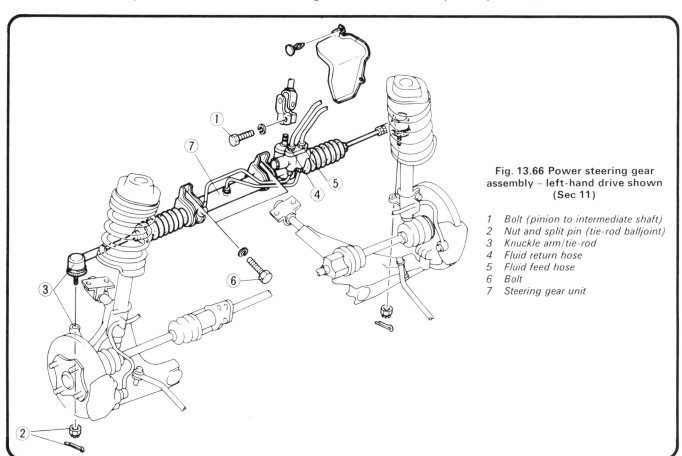

Fig. 13.66 Power steering gear assembly – left-hand drive shown (Sec 11)

1   *Bolt (pinion to intermediate shaft)*
2   *Nut and split pin (tie-rod balljoint)*
3   *Knuckle arm/tie-rod*
4   *Fluid return hose*
5   *Fluid feed hose*
6   *Bolt*
7   *Steering gear unit*

Power steering gear – overhaul
46 As with the manual steering gear, the complete overhaul of the power steering gear is not within the scope of the average home mechanic, and any repairs possible should therefore be entrusted to a Mazda dealer (see Section 24 of Chapter 10).

Power steering pump unit – removal and refitting
47 Raise the front of the vehicle and support it on axle stands.
48 Loosen off the drivebelt adjustment and disengage the drivebelt from the power steering pump pulley.
49 Disconnect the hydraulic lines (feed and return) from the pump unit by loosening the retaining clips and pulling the hoses free. Allow for fluid spillage, and if possible plug the connections to prevent excessive spillage and the possible ingress of dirt. Wipe any spilt fluid from surrounding components or body paintwork.
50 Unscrew and remove the pump mounting bolt and nut from the support bracket and lift the pump clear.
51 If required, undo the retaining bolts to remove the support bracket from the engine.
52 Overhaul of the power steering pump unit is not a task for the average home mechanic and any repairs necessary should therefore be entrusted to a Mazda dealer.
53 Refitting is a reversal of the removal procedure. When the pump unit is in position, the drivebelt will need to be fitted and adjusted for tension (see paragraphs 37 and 39).
54 Top up the fluid level in the pump reservoir and bleed the hydraulic system as described previously in this Section.

12 Bodywork and fittings

Estate models
1 An Estate model was added to the Mazda 323 front-wheel-drive range of vehicles in July of 1982. As with the Saloon and Hatchback variants, the Estate model is of all steel welded construction with the same built in safety features.

Bodywork repair – plastic components
2 With the use of more and more plastic body components by the vehicle manufacturers (eg bumpers, spoilers, and in some cases major body panels), rectification of damage to such items has become a matter of either entrusting repair work to a specialist in this field, or renewing complete components. Repair by the DIY owner is not really feasible owing to the cost of the equipment and materials required for effecting such repairs. The basic technique involves making a groove along the line of the crack in the plastic using a rotary burr in a power drill. The damaged part is then welded back together by using a hot air gun to heat up and fuse a plastic filler rod into the groove. Any excess plastic is then removed and the area rubbed down to a smooth finish. It is important that a filler rod of the correct plastic is used, as body components can be made of a variety of different types (eg polycarbonate, ABS, polypropylene).
3 If the owner is renewing a complete component himself, he will be left with the problem of finding a suitable paint for finishing which is compatible with the type of plastic used. At one time the use of a

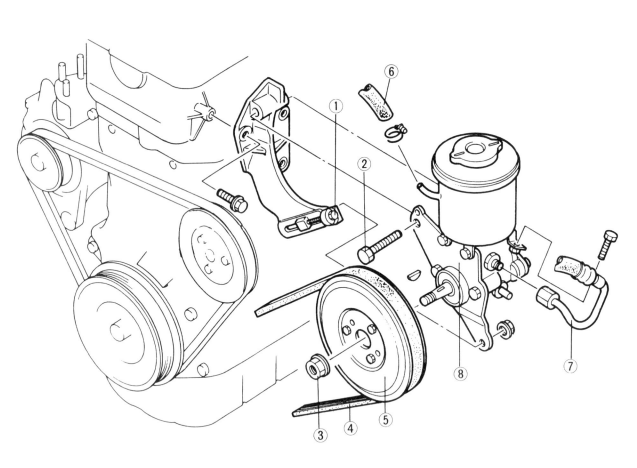

Fig. 13.67 Power steering pump unit and attachments (Sec 11)

| 1 | Adjuster bolt | 3 | Pulley nut | 5 | Pulley | 7 | Fluid feed hose |
| 2 | Pump bracket bolt | 4 | Drivebelt | 6 | Fluid return hose | 8 | Oil pump and reservoir unit |

universal paint was not possible owing to the complex range of plastics encountered in body component applications. Standard paints, generally speaking, will not bond to plastic or rubber satisfactorily. However, it is now possible to obtain a plastic body parts finishing kit which consists of a pre-primer treatment, a primer and coloured top coat. Full instructions are normally supplied with a kit, but basically the method of use is to first apply the pre-primer to the component concerned and allow it to dry for up to 30 minutes. Then

the primer is applied and left to dry for about an hour before finally applying the special coloured top coat. The result is a correctly coloured component where the paint will flex with the plastic or rubber, a property that standard paint does not normally possess.

Bonnet (later models) – removal and refitting

4   Raise the bonnet and get an assistant to support it, then using a pencil or felt tip pen, mark the outline position of each bonnet hinge relative to the bonnet. These outline markings will act as a guide when refitting the bonnet to ensure correct alignment.
5   Undo the retaining bolts and carefully lift the bonnet clear. Store it out of the way in a safe place.
6   Refitting is a reversal of the removal procedure. Loosely fit the hinge bolts each side, align the hinges and bonnet adjustment markings and then tighten the retaining bolts.
7   Check the bonnet for alignment with the adjacent panels when it is closed. If necessary, loosen off the hinge bolts and realign the bonnet to suit, then retighten the bolts.
8   Check that the bonnet fastens and releases in a satisfactory manner. If adjustment is necessary, loosen the bonnet lock screws and adjust the position of the lock to suit (Fig. 13.69).

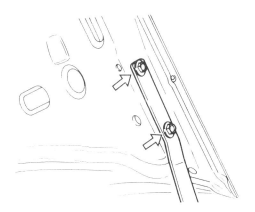

Fig. 13.68 Bonnet hinge retaining/adjustment bolts – later models (Sec 12)

Tailgate (Estate) – removal and refitting

9   Disconnect the battery earth lead.
10 Unclip and remove the tailgate trim panel and peel back the plastic insulation panel.
11 Disconnect the wiring to the rear wiper motor, the heated rear window and the central locking unit as applicable.
12 Get an assistant to support the weight of the tailgate and disconnect the strut on each side.
13 Use a pencil or felt tip pin and mark the position of each tailgate hinge on the tailgate by marking around the periphery of each hinge. Undo the hinge-to-tailgate bolts and remove the tailgate (photo).
14 Refit in the reverse order of removal. Check that the tailgate shuts correctly and is adjusted relative to the surrounding bodywork. If necessary loosen the hinge bolts and adjust the position of the tailgate to suit.
15 Ensure that the electrical and earth wire connections are secure before refitting the trim panel.
16 If required, the tailgate striker can be adjusted by loosening the retaining screws and moving it in the required direction. Retighten the screw when adjustment is correct.

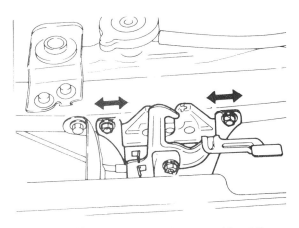

Fig. 13.69 Bonnet lock adjustment (Sec 12)

Tailgate lock (Estate models with central locking) – removal and refitting

17 The removal and refitting details are the same as those described for the manual lock type on other models in Chapter 11, but when removing the lock unit, also disconnect the lock button connecting rod and the catch unit rod (photo).

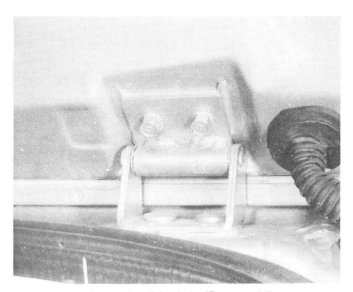

12.13 Tailgate hinge and retaining bolts (Estate model)

12.17 Tailgate lock and lock button connecting rod connections (Estate model)

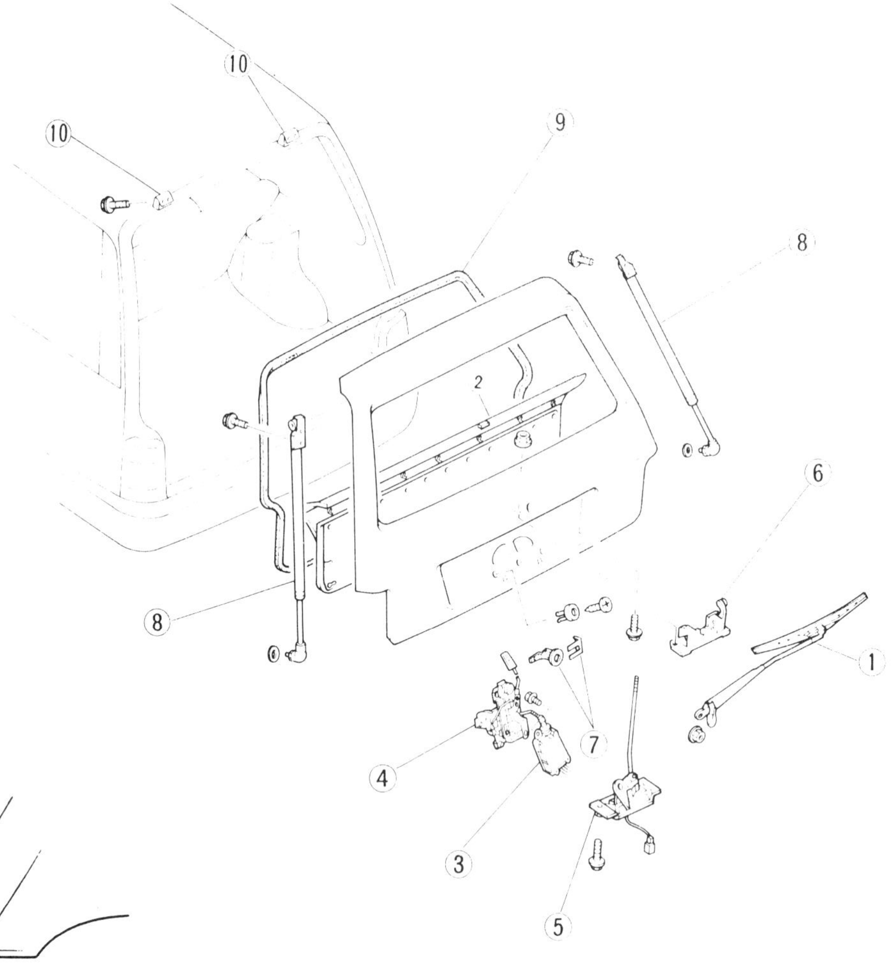
10
10
9
8
2
6
8
1
7
4
3
5

Fig. 13.70 Exploded view of the Estate model tailgate (Sec 12)

1 Rear wiper arm and blade
2 Tailgate trim
3 Lock controller
4 Lock unit
5 Remote release
6 Outer handle
7 Key lock and retainer
8 Damper (strut)
9 Weatherstrip
10 Hinge

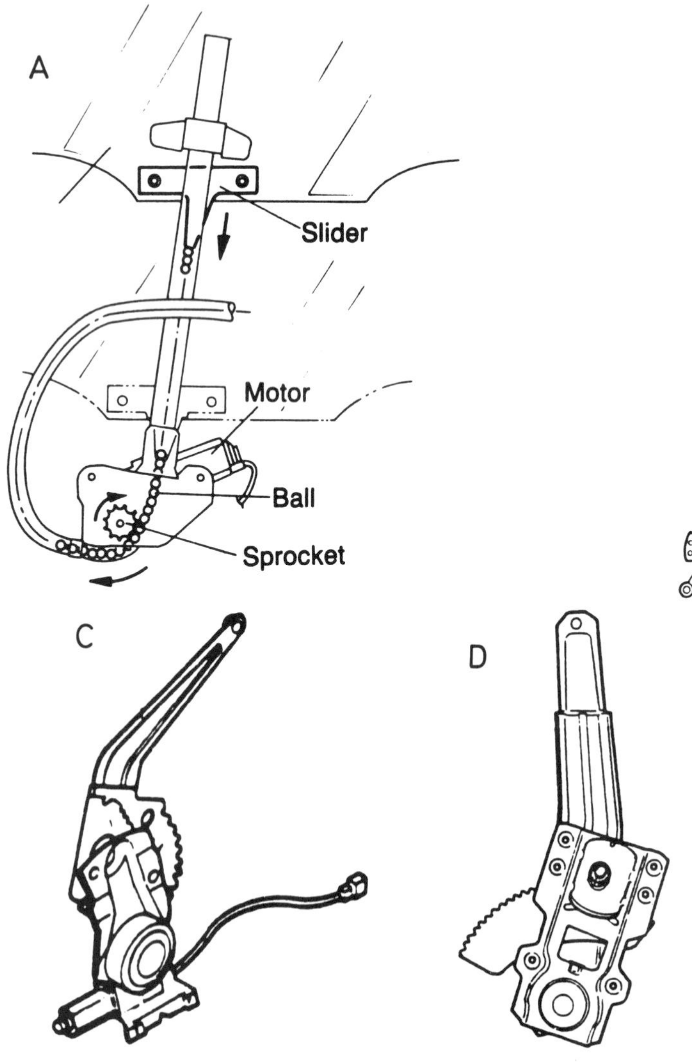
A
Slider
Motor
Ball
Sprocket
C
D

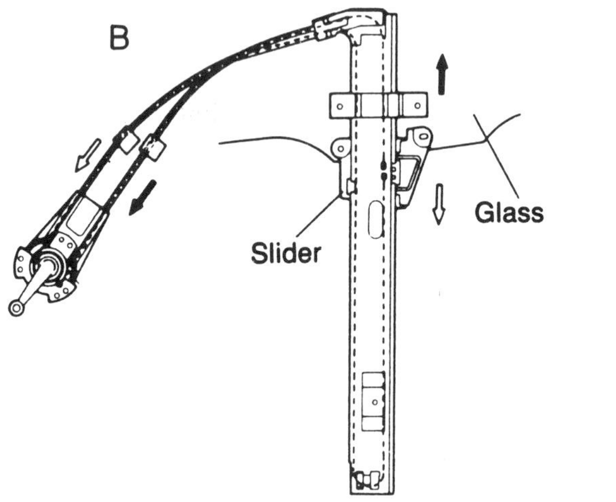
B
Glass
Slider

Fig. 13.71 Door window regulator types fitted (Sec 12)

A Ball type (power-operated window) – front door
B Cable type (manually-operated window) – front door
C Rear door power window regulator unit
D Rear door manual window regulator unit

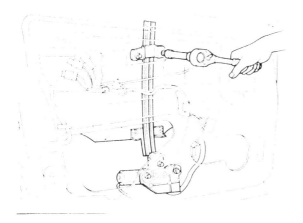

Fig. 13.72 Power window regulator refitting (Sec 12)

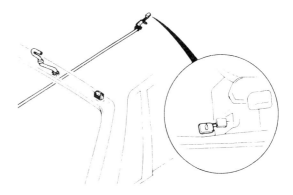

Fig. 13.73 Boot lid remote release cable-to-lever
connections (Sec 12)

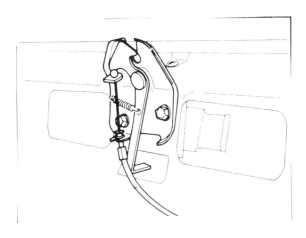

Fig. 13.74 Boot lid remote release cable-to-lock unit
connection (Sec 12)

12.27 Fuel filler cap and lid release mechanism (Estate)

Door locks (central locking) – removal and refitting
18 When removing the door locks on models with central locking, also
disconnect the connecting rod between the lock unit and the solenoid
switch.
19 The removal and refitting details are otherwise the same as those
described for the manual locking types in Chapter 11.

Door window regulator
20 The front door window regulator on later models will be either a
ball type (power operation) or a cable type (manual operation) – see
Fig. 13.71.
21 The rear door window regulator on later models will be a lever arm
and quadrant type for both power and manually-operated types.
22 Removal of the regulator unit is as described for early models in
Chapter 11, but on power-operated types, first disconnect the wiring
from the regulator motor.
23 When refitting the power type regulator, reconnect the wiring and
run the regulator down to the position shown (Fig. 13.72) before
fitting and tightening the retaining bolts.

Boot lid remote release cable – removal and refitting
24 Undo the retaining bolt and detach the boot lid release cable from
the lever in the car (Fig. 13.73).
25 Disconnect the release cable from the lock unit in the boot and
withdraw the cable (Fig. 13.74).
26 Refitting is a reversal of the removal procedure. Check for
satisfactory operation on completion.

Fuel filler remote release cable – removal and refitting
27 The procedure is similar to that described for the boot lid remote
cable renewal. At the fuel filler lid end, open the lid, detach the release
cable from the opener, then withdraw the cable (photo).

Facia panels (later models) – removal and refitting
28 An exploded diagram showing the main facia panel and its
associated fittings is shown in Fig. 13.75. If removing the complete
facia assembly, the components are best removed in the numerical
sequence shown. In most cases, the panels and their associated
fittings are secured by screws, bolts and/or clips. The screw and bolt
sizes vary, so note their locations as they are removed. Some screws
and bolts are only accessible after removing plastic covers (which can
usually be prised free) or an associated fitting. Items such as the
ashtray and coin holder simply lift out, in the latter case after prising
free from the outer side (photos).
29 When removing any of the switches or panels with switches,
always detach the battery earth lead first. The switches in the
right-hand vent/switch panel can be prised out, but care will be
needed not to damage the panel in the process.
30 The principle sub-panels can be removed as follows.
31 **Right-hand vent/switch panel:** Disconnect the battery earth
lead, undo the retaining screws and remove the instrument panel hood.
32 Remove the coin holder box by prising it free at its outside edge.
Pull free the right-hand vent control knob (photo).
33 Undo the two retaining screws through the coin holder box recess
and the single screw on the left-hand side (photo).
34 The vent/switch panel can now be withdrawn and the switch wires
disconnected (photo).

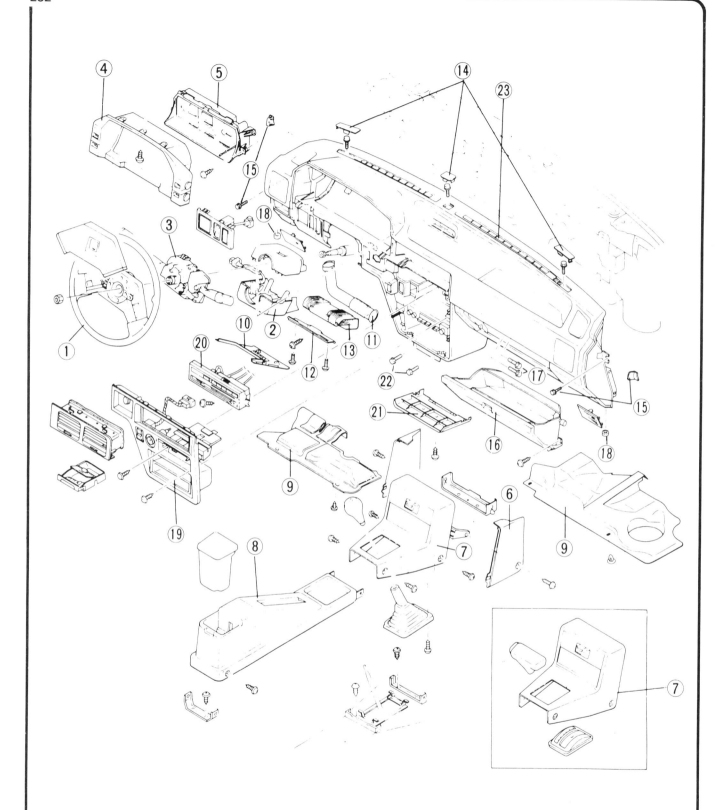

Fig. 13.75 Facia, instrument panel and associated fittings – later models (left-hand drive shown) (Sec 12)

1	Steering wheel	7	Front console	13	Lower louvre	19	Centre panel
2	Column shroud	8	Rear console	14	Bolts and covers	20	Heater console
3	Combination switch	9	Under cover	15	Bolts	21	Lower cover
4	Instrument panel hood	10	Lower panel	16	Glovebox	22	Bolts
5	Instrument panel	11	Duct	17	Bolts	23	Facia panel
6	Front console side wall	12	Reinforcement plate	18	Nuts		

12.28A Facia undercover retaining clip removal (driver's side cover)

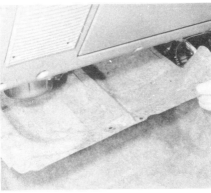
12.28B Facia undercover removal (passenger side)

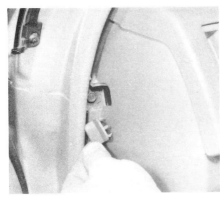
12.28C Facia side mounting bolt is accessible after prising free the plastic cover

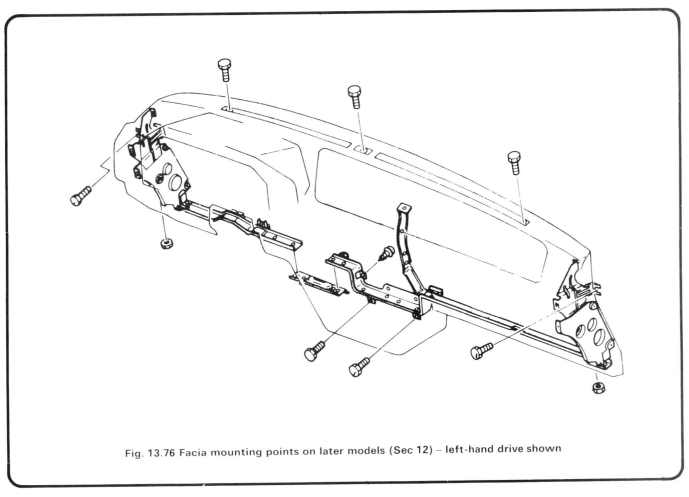
Fig. 13.76 Facia mounting points on later models (Sec 12) – left-hand drive shown

12.32 Coin box removal gives access ...

12.33 ... to the vent/switch panel retaining screws

12.34 Vent/switch panel removal

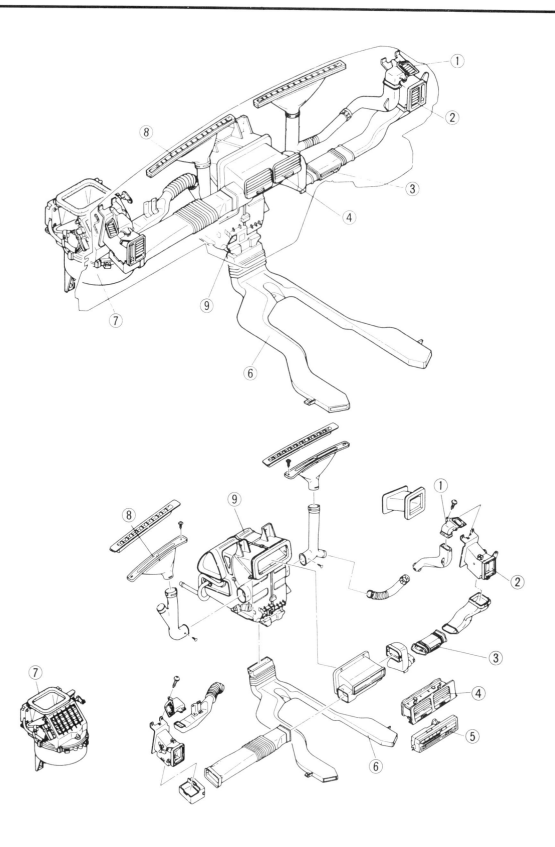

Fig. 13.77 The heater unit and associated components fitted to later models – left-hand drive shown (Sec 12)

1	Side defroster vent	4	Central vent	6	Rear heater duct	8	Front screen defroster air
2	Side louvre vent	5	Heater control panel	7	Blower motor unit		outlet
3	Lower vent					9	Heater unit

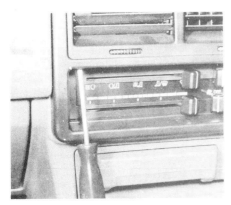

12.35A Undo the retaining screws ...

12.35B ... to remove the central vent panel

12.36A Undo screws in ashtray aperture ...

12.36B ... to remove the radio/ashtray panel (radio removed). Note side retainer clip position (arrowed)

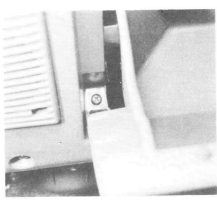

12.38A Glovebox retaining screw

12.38B Black cover removal from the glovebox aperture

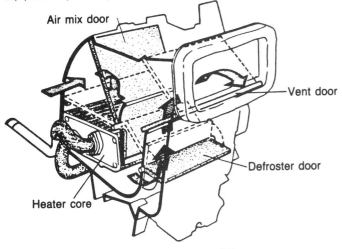

Air flow during MAX HOT

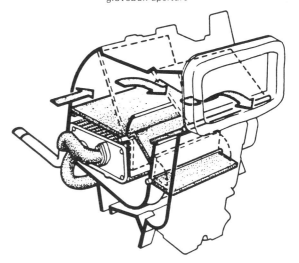

Air flow during MAX COLD

Fig. 13.78 Airflow diagram through heater unit on later models (Sec 12)

35 **Central vent panel:** Undo the two retaining screws and withdraw the panel as shown (photos).
36 **Central radio/ashtray panel:** Remove the ashtray for access to the two retaining screws. Compress the side clips using a screwdriver blade or similar implement and withdraw the panel. There are two clips on the right and one on the left of the panel (photos).
37 If the panel is being fully removed, disconnect the wiring connections from the radio/cassette unit and the cigar lighter.
38 **Glovebox:** Open the glovebox and then unscrew the two hinge screws (one each side at the bottom). Withdraw the glovebox. If required the black metal panel in the upper section of the glovebox aperture can be removed by undoing its retaining screws and withdrawing it (photos).

39 In all cases, refitting is a reversal of the removal procedure. Ensure that all electrical connections are securely made.

Heater – modifications
40 On later models the heater differs to the earlier type, the main differences being that the blower motor unit is now located on the left-hand side under the passenger facia, and is now separate from the heater unit casing; and the heater coolant valve is no longer used, the heater system now being a full flow type in which the air mix door shuts off completely when the controls are set to the cold position. This then allows only cool air to flow through the heater unit (Fig. 13.78).
41 In addition to the above modifications, a revised lever type control

unit is now fitted, whilst on some models, a 'Logic' control system is used.

42 The logic control system differs in that the air control lever functions are replaced by a push button electronic control system.

43 Reference to Fig. 13.79 shows the two control systems with the controls set in the 'Vent' position.

Heater controls (later lever type) – adjustments

44 Access to the heater and its control wires is gained after removing the front console and lower facia panels on each side (photos).

45 **Mode control wire:** Position the mode control knob at the 'DEF' position, then at the heater unit pivot the control lever fully downwards, as indicated (Fig. 13.80), to the stop position and engage the wire loop onto the lever peg.

46 Now pull the connecting rod down fully so that it is on its stop, slide the connecting rod into position in its fastener and fit a retaining clip (Fig. 13.81).

47 Check for satisfactory operation by moving the fan speed control to the number 4 setting. When the fan is switched on there should be full air circulation.

48 **Air mix door control wire:** Move the temperature control lever to the maximum cold setting, then at the heater unit, pivot the air mix control lever clockwise to the stop position and engage the control wire loop on the lever peg (Fig. 13.82).

49 Now pull the connecting rod lever up to its stop position and fit the connecting rod and retaining clip. Move the fan speed control to the number 4 position and check for satisfactory operation.

50 **Recirculating fresh air (REC/FRESH) control selector wire:** With the selector lever set at the fresh air inlet position, push the control lever on the blower unit to its extreme stop position and then place the wire loop over the lever peg (Fig. 13.83). Operate the blower motor to ensure that the recirculating fresh air operation is satisfactory.

Heater blower motor (later type) – removal and refitting

51 Disconnect the battery earth lead.

52 Remove the lower facia trim panel and the glove box and black metal cover (as described previously in this Section).

53 Disconnect the wiring connections to the heater (photo).

54 Detach the duct between the heater unit and the blower unit.

55 Disconnect the fresh air recirculation control wire, undo the three retaining bolts and remove the heater blower motor (photos). Note the following points when removing the blower motor if the vehicle is fitted with a 'Logic' type heater control and/or air conditioning:

(a) Removal of the instrument panel bracket will ease withdrawal of the unit

(b) Set the REC/FRESH air control selector at the REC position to ease removal of the upper retaining nuts

Lever control type

Logic   control type

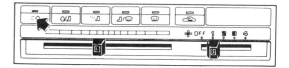

Fig. 13.79 The two heater/ventilation control systems used with the controls set in the 'Vent' position (Sec 12)

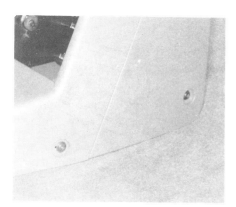

12.44A Undo the console retaining screws each side at the front ...

12.44B ... and rear ...

12.44C ... remove the console ...

12.44D ... the lower cover ...

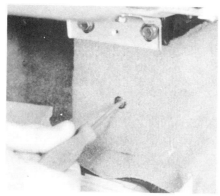

12.44E ... and carpet for access ...

12.44F ... to the lower facia and heater mountings and control cables

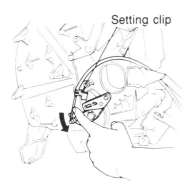

Fig. 13.80 Mode control wire adjustment. Pull lever down and engage wire (Sec 12)

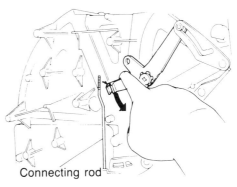

Fig. 13.81 Engage connecting rod into fastener (Sec 12)

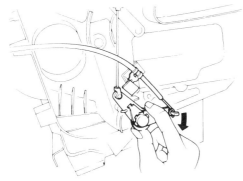

Fig. 13.82 Engage air mix wire on lever (Sec 12)

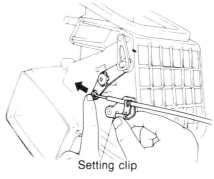

Fig. 13.83 Engage the air control wire on its lever (Sec 12)

12.53 Blower motor wiring connector

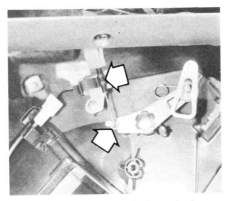

12.55A Detach the control wire at the lever and outer cable retainer clip (arrows) ...

12.55B ... undo the retaining bolts ...

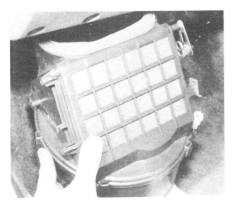

12.55C ... and carefully remove the blower motor

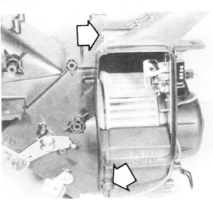

12.55D General view of the blower motor unit showing the air intake and fan. To separate the housings, remove screws and release clips (arrowed)

12.55E General view of the blower motor unit showing the blower motor unit retaining screws (arrowed)

56 Refitting is a reversal of the removal procedure. Adjust the REC/FRESH air control wire as described in paragraph 50 of this Section.

Heater unit (later type) – removal and refitting
57 Access to the heater unit for its removal is not good as it is surrounded by numerous facia and trim panels. However, it is unusual to require the removal of the complete heater unit, the normal items which may require attention being the control cables and lever connections, or the heater core. The heater core can be removed separately leaving the heater in position.
58 Access to the control cables on either side of the heater unit can be gained after removing the lower facia trim panel on the side concerned.
59 Access to the heater core can be gained by removing the lower facia trim on the passenger side, and the glovebox (see paragraph 38 of this Section).
60 When removing the heater core, either on its own or together with the heater unit, the cooling system must first be drained as described in Chapter 2.
Heater core removal
61 With the cooling system drained and the glovebox and lower trim removed, the core can be withdrawn from the heater unit as follows.
62 Disconnect the mode control cable and undo the screw securing the pivot control lever. Move the lever and cable out of the way, then undo the inlet and outlet coolant pipe connecting flange nuts. Detach

the pipes from the end face of the core, but allow for coolant spillage.
63 Undo the two retaining screws and withdraw the core from the heater body. Removal of the ducting will improve access to the bulkhead side retaining screw. The ducting is held in place by two plastic screws.
64 When removing the core, take care not to spill any remaining coolant over the carpets and upholstery.
65 Refit the core in the reverse order of removal. Ensure a good seal is made between the inlet and outlet pipes and the core. On completion top up the coolant level as described in Chapter 2 and adjust the mode control cable as described elsewhere in this Section.
Heater unit removal (complete)
66 Disconnect the battery earth lead and drain the cooling system (Chapter 2).
67 Remove the lower facia trim panels each side, the glovebox, the forward console unit, lower cover, and carpet trim (see photos 12.44A to 12.44E inclusive).
68 Disconnect the heater control cables from the heater connections.
69 Disconnect the coolant inlet and outlet pipes from the heater core. Allow for a certain amount of coolant spillage as they are detached.
70 Disconnect the airflow ducts from the heater unit and where necessary, remove the ducts completely to allow subsequent heater unit removal.
71 Undo the heater unit retaining nuts and bolts and withdraw the unit. Check that all items are disconnected from it as it is removed, and

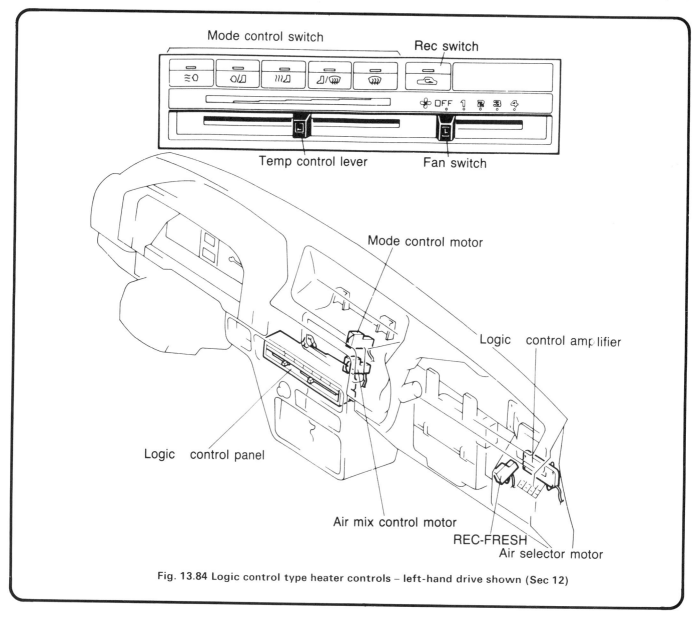

Fig. 13.84 Logic control type heater controls – left-hand drive shown (Sec 12)

allow for coolant spillage from the heater core as the unit is removed from the vehicle.

72 Refitting is a reversal of the removal procedure. Loosely assemble each fastener until the heater is fully in position and the various ductings are connected.

73 On completion, top up the cooling system as described in Chapter 2 and adjust the heater control cables as described elsewhere in this Section.

Heater controls (later type) – removal and refitting

74 Disconnect the battery earth lead.

75 Undo the two retaining screws and remove the central vent panel (see paragraph 35).

76 Remove the lower facia trim panels each side for access to the cable connections at the heater unit and blower motor.

77 Disconnect the cables, then undo the control unit retaining screws and withdraw the unit and cables (photo). Disconnect the wiring multi-plug from the unit as it is removed.

78 Refit in the reverse order of removal. Adjust the control cables as described previously in this Section.

Heater controls – 'Logic' type

79 The logic control panel and the associated components of the system are shown in Fig. 13.84. The functions of each are as follows:

   (a) *Logic control panel: This is a one touch push button control panel*

   (b) *Logic control amplifier: This controls the air mixer valve motor and protects it in the event of a malfunction*

   (c) *Mode control motor: This controls the air outlet during each mode, operating the ventilation valve and defrost valve*

   (d) *Air mixture control motor: This controls the outgoing air temperature by operating the air mixer valve in accordance with the signal from the logic control amplifier*

   (e) *REC-FRESH air selector motor: This motor operates the valve for the REC-FRESH shift by the selector lever*

80 If a malfunction occurs in the 'Logic' type heater system, the checking procedures are considerable and require the use of a special 'Logicon checker' unit. For this reason any faults in the system will have to be diagnosed and repaired by a Mazda dealer.

Fig. 13.85 The charging system circuit and alternator
connections on later models (Sec 13)

12.77 Heater/ventilation control unit and retaining screws (arrowed)

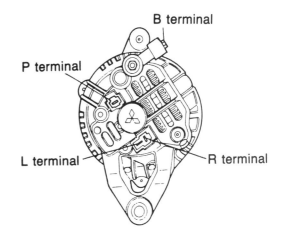

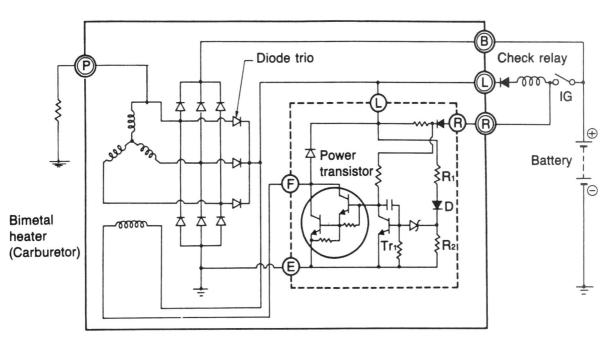

13.7 Fuse box location on later models. The cover shows the individual circuits protected and fuse rating requirements.

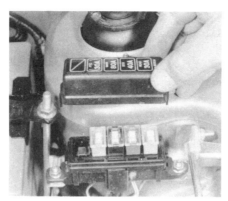

13.9A The main fuses in the engine compartment on later models

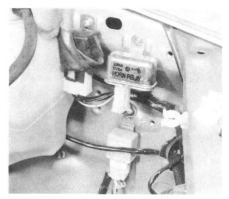

13.9B Engine compartment relays

13 Electrical system

Alternator – later type

1   The alternator fitted to later models is similar in construction to the earlier types, but it is now more compact, has an increased output (55 amps) and the 'B' terminal now faces upwards for improved access.

2   A 'P' terminal is also now fitted and this supplies power to the automatic choke heater on the carburettor (Fig. 13.85).

3   The removal and refitting details are otherwise the same as for earlier models.

Starter motor – later type

4   The starter motor fitted to later models is both shorter in length and lighter in weight than the type fitted to earlier models.

5   Apart from being reduced in size, the new type starter motor differs

from the earlier type in having a flush mounted rear bearing, and the magnetic switch solenoid now incorporates the lever return spring.

6   The removal and refitting details are otherwise the same as described for earlier models in Chapter 12.

Fuses – later models

7   The fusebox on later models is located on the right-hand corner of the lower facia within the car (beneath the bonnet release lever). Further main fuses are located in the engine compartment adjacent to the battery (photo).

8   Each fuse rating is marked and if renewal is necessary first check the cause of the old fuse failure, repair the fault, then replace the fuse with one of the correct rating.

9   Additional circuit switches and relays are located beneath the facia and in the engine compartment as shown in Figs. 13.86 and 13.87 and photos.

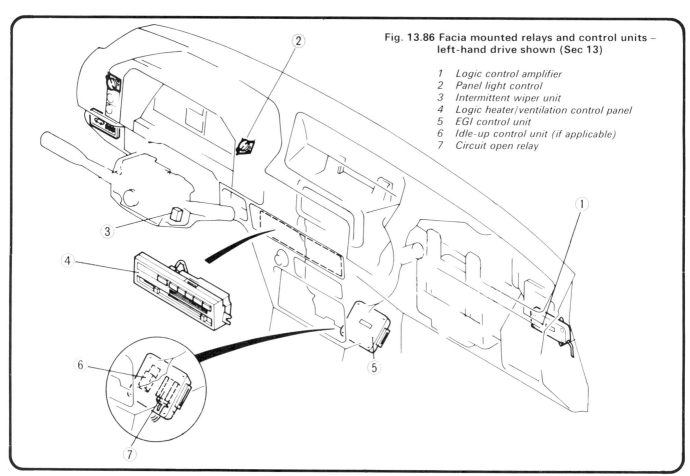

Fig. 13.86 Facia mounted relays and control units – left-hand drive shown (Sec 13)

1   Logic control amplifier
2   Panel light control
3   Intermittent wiper unit
4   Logic heater/ventilation control panel
5   EGI control unit
6   Idle-up control unit (if applicable)
7   Circuit open relay

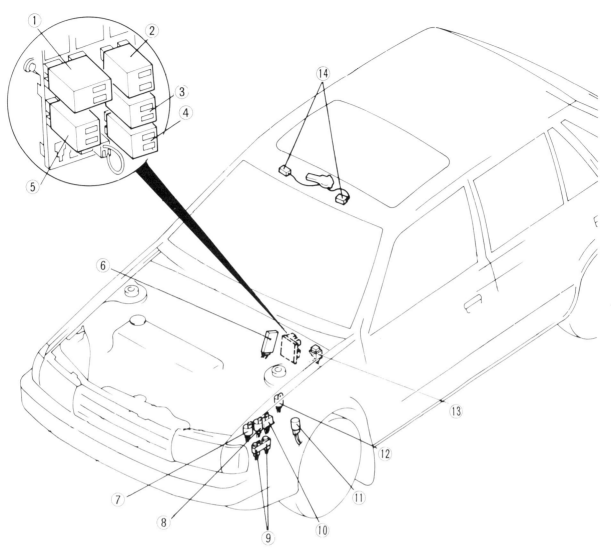

Fig. 13.87 Engine compartment relays and control units (Sec 13)

1	Door lock timer unit	5	Oscillator
2	Flasher unit	6	Cruise control unit (where
3	Entry timer unit		applicable)
4	Stop light checker	7	Electric fan relay

8 Idle-up relay (where applicable)
9 EGI main relay (fuel-injected model only)

10 Horn relay
11 PTC heater relay
12 NP relay (where applicable)
13 Cooling fan relay
14 Sliding roof relay

Instrument panel (later models) – removal and refitting

10 Disconnect the battery earth lead, then remove the steering column combination switches as described in Section 13 of Chapter 12.
11 Undo and remove the three screws securing the instrument panel shroud under its upper edge (photo).
12 Undo and remove the two retaining screws from the bottom of the panel shroud, one each side as shown (photo).
13 Withdraw the panel shroud and detach the switch wiring connectors (photo).
14 Undo the four retaining screws and withdraw the instrument panel cluster unit. As it is withdrawn, disconnect the wiring connectors and the speedometer cable. We found it necessary to detach the speedometer cable at the gearbox end to allow the panel cluster and cable to be withdrawn sufficiently to separate them at the rear of the cluster (photos).
15 Renewal of the instrument panel bulbs and dismantling of the instrument panel cluster is similar to that described for the earlier models in Chapter 12.
16 Refitting is a reversal of the removal procedure. Check the various switch and instrument functions on completion.

Facia switches (later models) – removal and refitting

17 Before removing any of the facia switches, always disconnect the battery earth lead.

Instrument panel shroud switches

18 Remove the instrument panel shroud as described previously in this Section (paragraphs 12 and 13).
19 Undo the switch retaining screws on the rear face of the panel and withdraw the switch unit from the panel (Fig. 13.88).

Rocker switches

20 These switches are secured to the underside of the panel by plastic clips at the top and bottom faces of the switch. As both clips need to be compressed to allow switch removal, the panel will need to be removed to allow access to the clips (see photo 13.25).
21 To remove the panel, pull free the vent control knob, then withdraw the coin box from the location in the panel.
22 Remove the instrument panel cluster shroud as described previously in this Section.
23 Undo the three panel retaining screws and withdraw the panel (photos 12.33 and 12.34).

13.11 Remove the instrument panel shroud
upper ...

13.12 ... and lower retaining screws

13.13A Withdraw the instrument panel
shroud ...

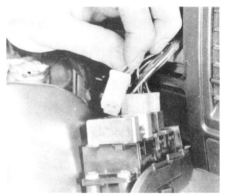

13.13B ... and detach the wiring connectors

13.14A Instrument panel retaining screws
(arrowed)

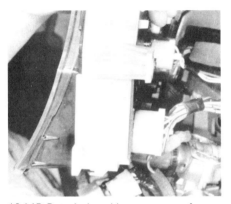

13.14B Detach the wiring connectors from
the rear of the instrument panel

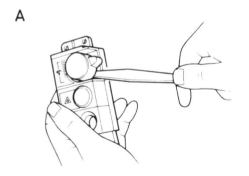

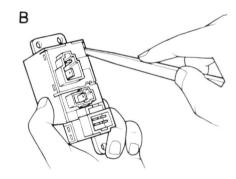

Fig. 13.88 Instrument panel shroud switch removal (Sec 13)

A   Prise free the knob (where applicable)
B   Carefully prise switch free from the rear face of the panel

24 Detach the wiring connector from the switch concerned and then
compress the retaining clips and withdraw the switch.
25 Refitting is a reversal of the removal procedure. If required the
panels can be refitted first, then the switch wire connector attached
and the switch pushed into position in its aperture (photo).

Cigarette lighter – removal and refitting
26 Disconnect the battery earth lead.
27 Access to the cigarette lighter unit wiring connections, and retainer
on the rear face is not good, and the facia panel in which it is mounted
is best removed. On later models this is the radio/ashtray holder panel
and this is secured by compression clips on each side (photo).
28 With the panel withdrawn, detach the wiring connector from the
rear of the cigarette lighter unit, also the bulb holder from its plastic
retainer (photos).
29 Undo the retaining screw and remove the plastic housing (photo).

30 To remove the cigarette lighter, compress the retaining clips and
withdraw it from the front face of the panel (photo).
31 Refitting is a reversal of the removal procedure.

Rear light cluster bulbs (Estate) – renewal
32 Open the tailgate, then undo the two lens/cluster unit retaining
screws (photo).
33 Withdraw the cluster unit, then untwist the bulbholder(s) from the
rear to inspect/renew the bulb as required (photo).
34 Refit in the reverse order of removal.

Number plate bulb (Estate) – renewal
35 Raise the tailgate, undo the two retaining screws and remove the
lens. Twist and remove the bulb from its holder (photo).
36 Refit in the reverse order of removal.

13.25 Refitting a rocker switch (with panel in position). Note retaining clips (arrowed)

13.27 Cigarette lighter location showing facia panel retaining clips (arrowed)

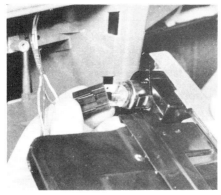

13.28A Detach the wiring connector from the cigarette lighter ...

13.28B ... and remove the bulbholder

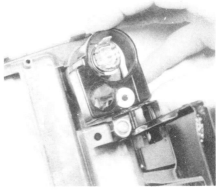

13.29 Remove the plastic housing

13.30 Cigarette lighter retaining clip (arrowed)

13.32 Remove the rear light unit retaining screws (Estate)

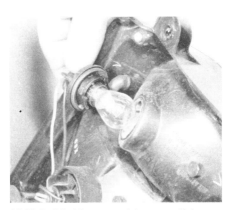

13.33 Bulbholder removal from rear light unit (Estate)

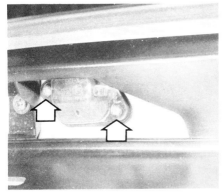

13.35 Number plate light unit on Estate showing lens retaining screws (arrowed)

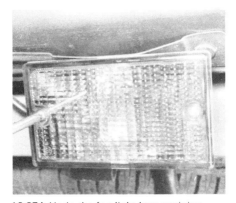

13.37A Undo the fog light lens retaining screws and remove lens ...

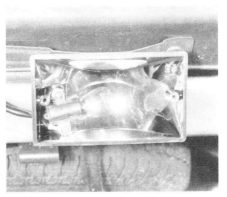

13.37B ... for access to the bulb (Estate)

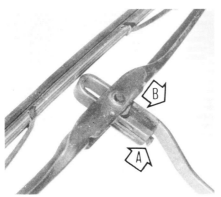

13.40 Windscreen wiper blade removal on later models: Press clip 'A' and withdraw blade from arm in direction of arrow 'B'

Rear foglight bulb (Estate) – renewal
37 Undo the two lens retaining screws, remove the lens, and then press and twist the bulb to remove it from its holder (photos).
38 Refit in the reverse order of removal.

Windscreen wiper blades and arms (later models) – renewal
39 The windscreen wiper arms and blades on later models are removed and refitted in a similar manner to that described for earlier models in Chapter 12.
40 When removing the wiper blade from the arm however, press the retaining clip in to release the blade and move the blade from the arm clevis as shown (photo).
41 The tailgate window wiper arm and blade on the Estate model is removed in the same manner.
42 Refitting is a reversal of the removal procedure. Check that the wiper arms are correctly positioned on the spindle and that they park correctly.

Windscreen wiper motor (later models) – removal and refitting
43 The layout of the windscreen wiper and washer components on later models is shown in Fig. 13.89.
44 To remove the windscreen wiper motor, disconnect the wiring connector from it, then working on the rear side of the bulkhead undo the wiper driveshaft-to-connecting link retaining nut, or release the connecting rod-to-link balljoint (photo).
45 Undo the four wiper motor retaining bolts and remove the motor from the bulkhead (photo).
46 Refit in the reverse order of removal, and on completion check the motor for satisfactory operation and also that the wiper arms park correctly.

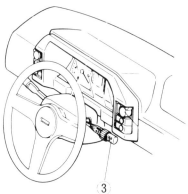
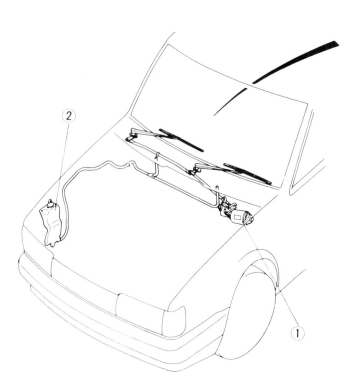

Fig. 13.89 Windscreen wiper and washer layout on later models (Sec 13)

1 Wiper motor unit   2 Washer reservoir   3 Wiper control switch

13.44 Wiper motor connecting rod and link (later models)

13.45 Windscreen wiper motor, retaining bolts and wiring connector (later models)

13.51 Tailgate wiper spindle and retaining nut

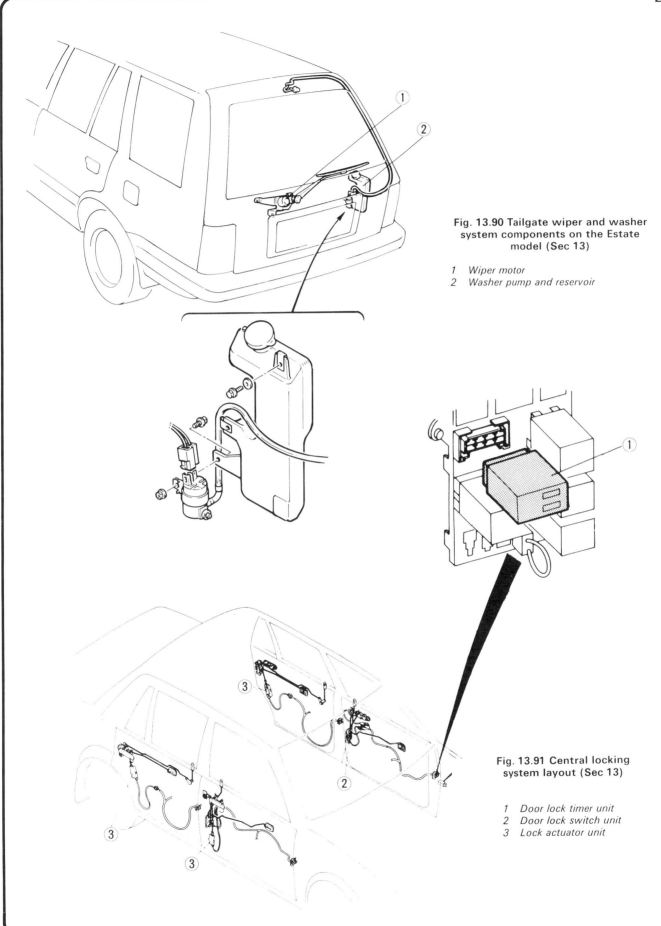

Fig. 13.90 Tailgate wiper and washer
system components on the Estate
model (Sec 13)

1   Wiper motor
2   Washer pump and reservoir

Fig. 13.91 Central locking
system layout (Sec 13)

1   Door lock timer unit
2   Door lock switch unit
3   Lock actuator unit

Tailgate wiper motor (Estate) – removal and refiting
47 Disconnect the battery earth lead.
48 Remove the rear wiper arm and blade.
49 Raise the tailgate and remove its inner trim panel.
50 Disconnect the wiring to the wiper motor.
51 Undo and remove the drive spindle nut (photo).
52 Undo the three retaining bolts, noting how the two earth leads are secured under two of them. Withdraw the wiper motor from the tailgate aperture.

53 Refitting is a reversal of the removal procedure. Check the operation of the wiper motor on completion and also that the wiper arm parks correctly.

Central locking system
54 The layout and principal components of the system are shown in Fig. 13.91.
55 The door lock timer unit is fitted to the main fuse/relay unit located under the driver's side facia panel (left-hand drive variant shown).

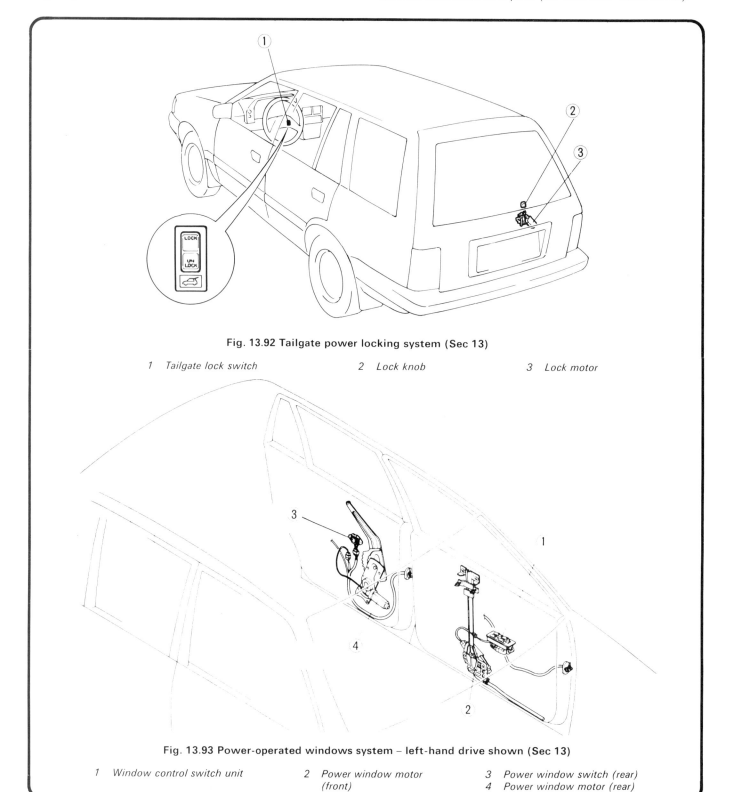

Fig. 13.92 Tailgate power locking system (Sec 13)

1 Tailgate lock switch	*2 Lock knob*	*3 Lock motor*

Fig. 13.93 Power-operated windows system – left-hand drive shown (Sec 13)

1 Window control switch unit	*2 Power window motor (front)*	*3 Power window switch (rear)*
		4 Power window motor (rear)

56 Access to the door switch and actuators is achieved by removing the appropriate door trim panel.
57 The tailgate lock is operated in a similar manner, but is on a separate circuit – see Fig. 13.92.
58 If a malfunction occurs, check the system wiring for poor connections or shorting. If removing any part of the system, always disconnect the battery earth lead first.
59 Any suspect components should be checked by a Mazda dealer and if defective, must be renewed.

Power-operated windows system
60 The layout and components of this system are shown in Fig. 13.93 (left-hand drive variant shown).
61 The testing and removal procedures are the same as those described for the central locking system in the previous sub-section.

Cruise control system
62 Fitted as an optional extra on some models, the main components and layout of the system are shown in Fig. 13.94.
63 If a malfunction in the system develops, have the system checked out by a Mazda dealer, as special test equipment is required.

Sunroof and motor – removal, refitting and adjustment
64 The sunroof motor and panel assemblies are shown in Fig. 13.95. Their removal procedures are as follows.
65 Disconnect the battery earth lead, then open the sunshade fully, but keep the sliding panel shut.
66 Carefully prise free the lower panel cover, working in the order shown in Fig. 13.96. Protect the glass from damage with cloth or tape when levering the panel free.
67 Undo the three sliding and lower panel retaining nuts each side, push the sliding panel upwards to remove it, and open the panel.
68 Hold down the deflector links and detach the links from the connectors. Remove the deflector (Fig. 13.97).
69 Undo the retaining screws and remove the set plate and the guide rail cover.
70 Undo the retaining screws and remove the bracket unit, the drip rail link and then the lower panel (upwards).
71 Detach and remove the interior rear view mirror, the overhead console and the seaming welt (Fig. 13.98). This then gives access to the sunroof motor.
72 Detach the sunroof motor wiring connectors, undo the three retaining screws and remove the motor unit. If required, the guide

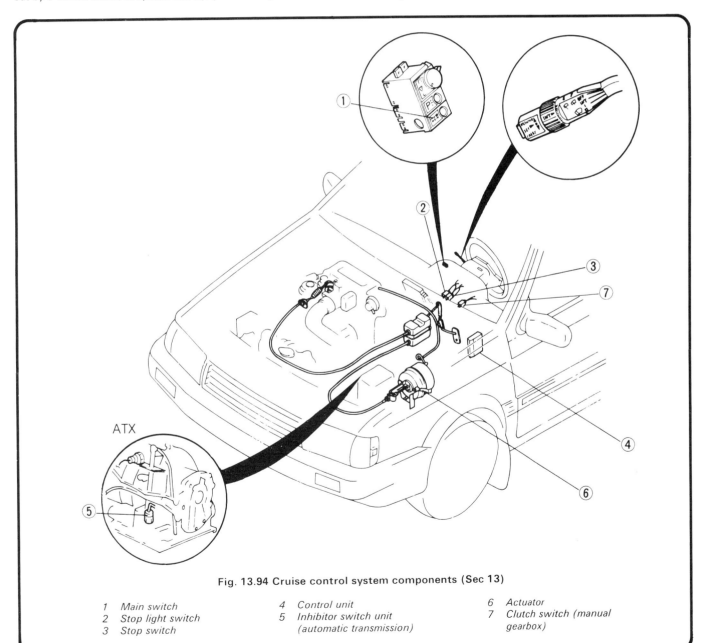

Fig. 13.94 Cruise control system components (Sec 13)

1 Main switch
2 Stop light switch
3 Stop switch
4 Control unit
5 Inhibitor switch unit (automatic transmission)
6 Actuator
7 Clutch switch (manual gearbox)

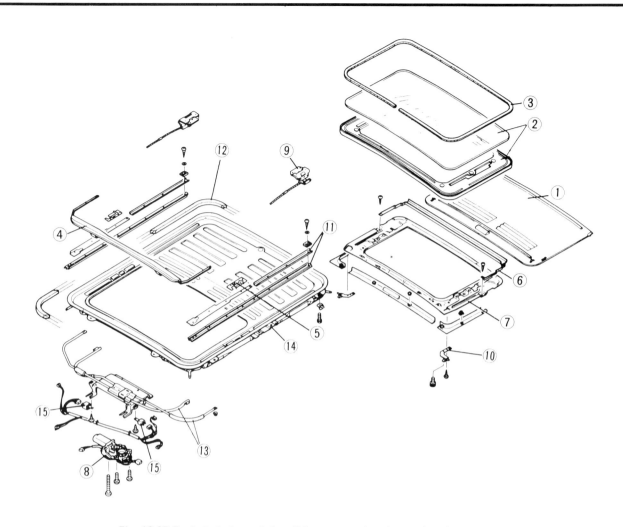

Fig. 13.95 Exploded view of the sliding sunroof and associated components

1 Sunshade	5 Stopper	9 Guide bracket (rear)	13 Tube assembly
2 Sliding panel/glass	6 Rail assembly	10 Guide bracket (front)	14 Frame assembly
3 Weatherstrip	7 Lower panel	11 Guide rail assembly	15 Sunroof relay
4 Deflector	8 Motor unit	12 Packing	

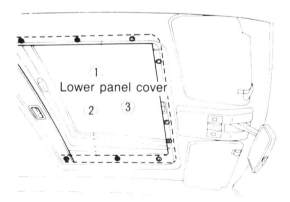

Fig. 13.96 Lower panel cover removal. Remove cover in order shown (Sec 13)

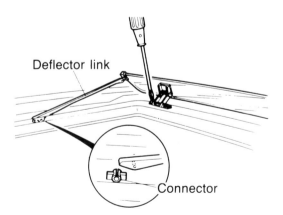

Fig. 13.97 Detach the deflector links whilst holding down the deflector as shown (Sec 13)

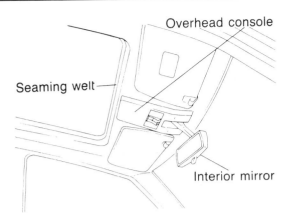

Fig. 13.98 Remove the items indicated for access to the sunroof motor (Sec 13)

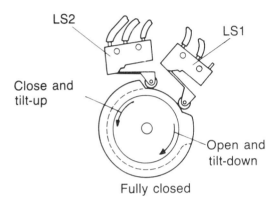

Fig. 13.100 Limit switches LS1 and LS2 at the off position (Sec 13)

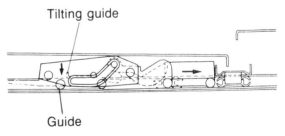

Fig. 13.101 Check that the guide roller is properly fitted to its rail (Sec 13)

B—B cross-section

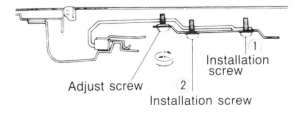

Fig. 13.103 Sliding roof panel adjustment at point B-B (Sec 13)

Loosen installation screws, turn adjuster screws in direction required, then retighten installation screws

Note: *For 2 mm (0.08 in) adjustment or less, do not loosen screw No 1*

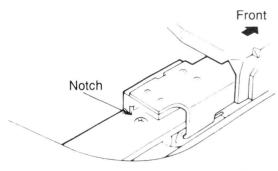

Fig. 13.99 Engage bracket rear end into the rail notch (Sec 13)

bracket unit can be removed from the rail and the drive cable pulled free.

73 If the drive motor unit is defective, it must be renewed. Inspect all parts for excessive wear and renew if necessary.

74 Before refitting the cable back into the tube, lubricate the cable and the sliding surfaces of the cam and guide shoe.

75 Adjust the guide cable each side. With the guide rail fitted into position in its bracket, engage the rear end of the bracket into the notch in the rear of the rail (Fig. 13.99).

76 Before refitting the drive motor, ensure that the limit switches LS1 and LS2 are in the off position as shown in Fig. 13.100. If necessary set the cam position manually.

77 Refit the drive motor and reconnect the wiring switch connectors.

78 Fit the lower panel to the guide bracket, then pull out the drip rail at the rear and tighten its link arm.

79 Manually open the slide panel fully by winding the motor by hand, but ensure that the guide roller is properly fitted to the guide rail to avoid the possibility of the slide panel and the sun shade coming into contact with each other. As the motor is turned, assist by pushing the cable (Fig. 13.101).

80 The remaining reassembly details are a reversal of the removal procedures. When the sliding panel is secured, check it for adjustment. The difference in height between the sliding roof panel and the outer panel surround must not exceed that specified – see Fig. 13.102. If adjustment is necessary at any of the points indicated, adjust as shown in Fig. 13.103 or 13.104 as applicable.

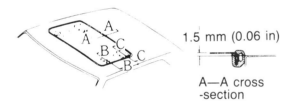

Fig. 13.102 Check the roof panel height adjustment between points indicated. Difference between panels must not exceed 1.5 mm (0.06 in) (Sec 13)

C—C cross-section

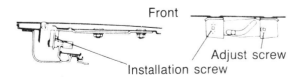

Fig. 13.104 Sliding roof panel adjustment at point C-C (Sec 13)

Loosen installation screw (a little) and adjuster screw, move panel as required to adjust, retighten adjuster screw, then retighten installation screw

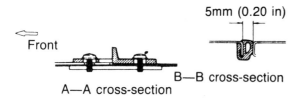

Fig. 13.105 Roof panel gap must not exceed amount shown
(Sec 13)

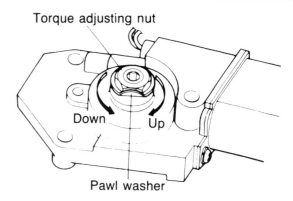

Fig. 13.106 Sliding roof motor torque adjuster (Sec 13)

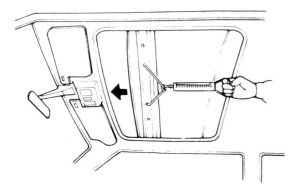

Fig. 13.107 Checking the sliding panel sliding (torque) load
(Sec 13)

81 Prior to refitting the header panel, check that the roof panel opens and shuts in a satisfactory manner. If the panel movement is sluggish, check that the battery is fully charged, check for dirt or foreign matter on the sliding parts, and also ensure that when opened, the roof panel does not contact the rear part of the roof surround. If it does, the stopper is in need of adjustment (Fig. 13.105).

82 The sunroof motor is adjustable for torque loading by peening back the 'lock ear' on the pawl washer, loosening the locknut and turning the torque adjuster as required (Fig. 13.106). The torque loading on the sliding panel should be checked using a spring gauge as shown in Fig. 13.107.

83 When the torque loading is set, retighten the lockwasher and bend up the pawl washer to secure.

84 Refit the header panel sun visors and rear view mirror to complete.

Wiring diagrams

85 The colour codes, symbols and harness details applicable to the Estate model wiring diagrams are the same as those given for earlier models in Chapter 12.

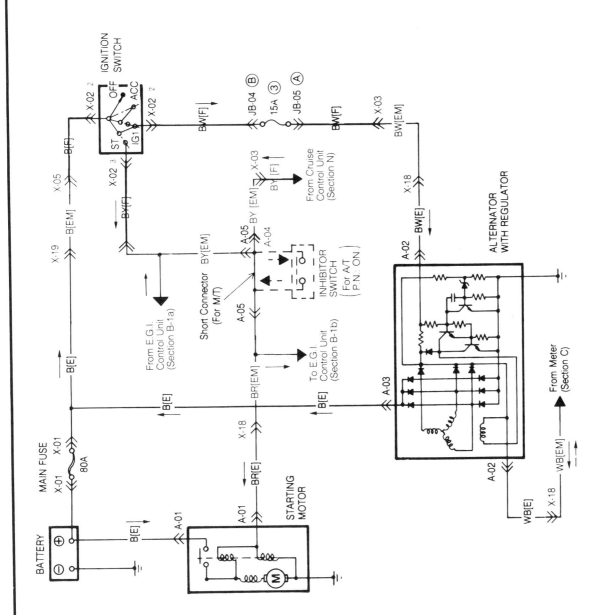

Fig. 13.108 Charging and starting wiring diagram (Estate model)

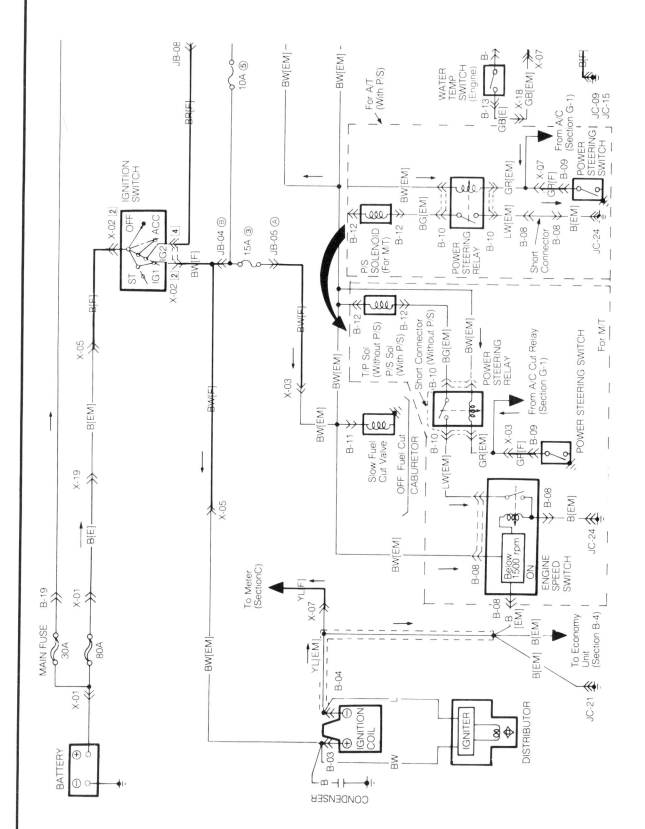

Fig. 13.109 Cooling fan, ignition system, engine control, kickdown system (automatic transmission) and PTC heater wiring diagram (Estate model)

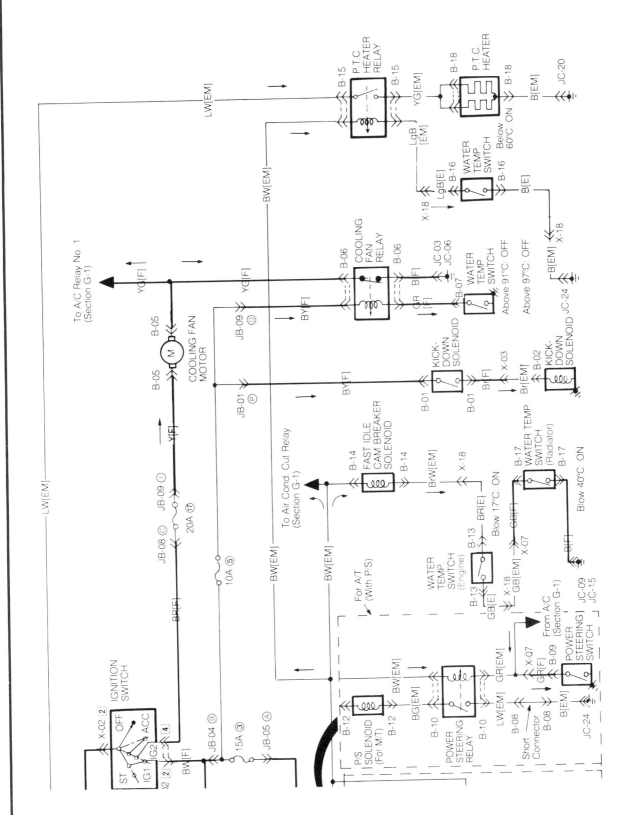

Fig. 13.109 Cooling fan, ignition system, engine control, kickdown system (automatic transmission) and PTC heater wiring diagram (Estate model) (continued)

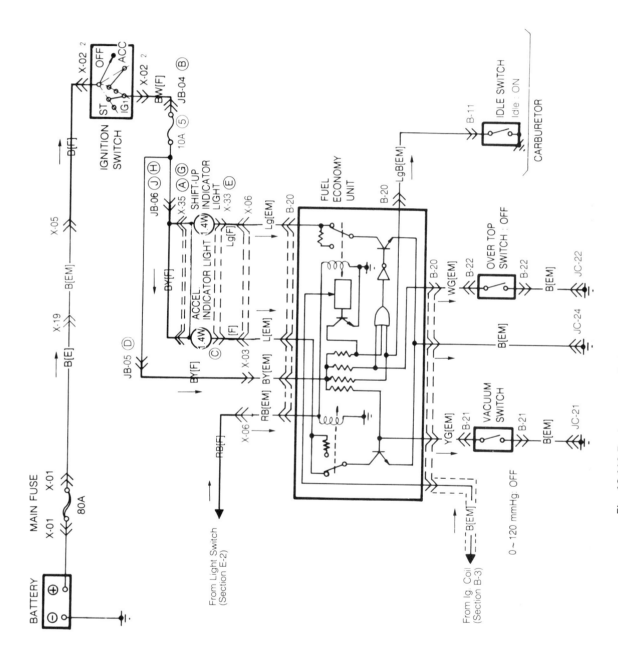

Fig. 13.110 Fuel economy indicator system wiring diagram (Estate model)

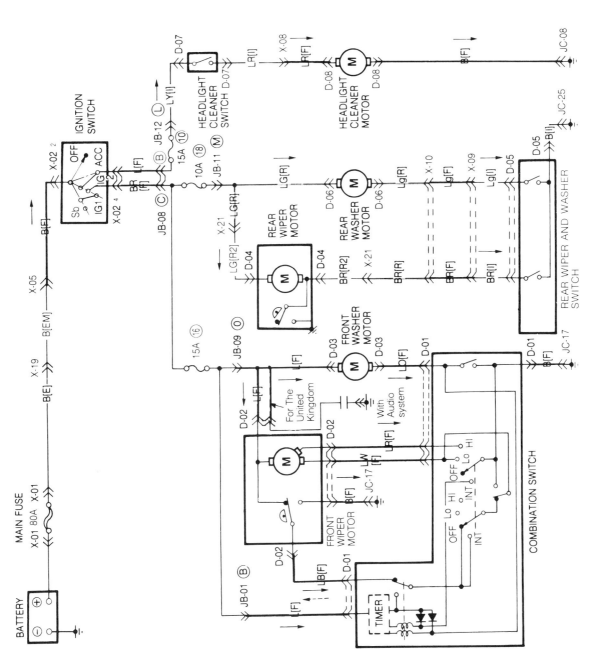

Fig. 13.111 Wipers, washers and headlamp cleaners wiring diagram (Estate model)

306

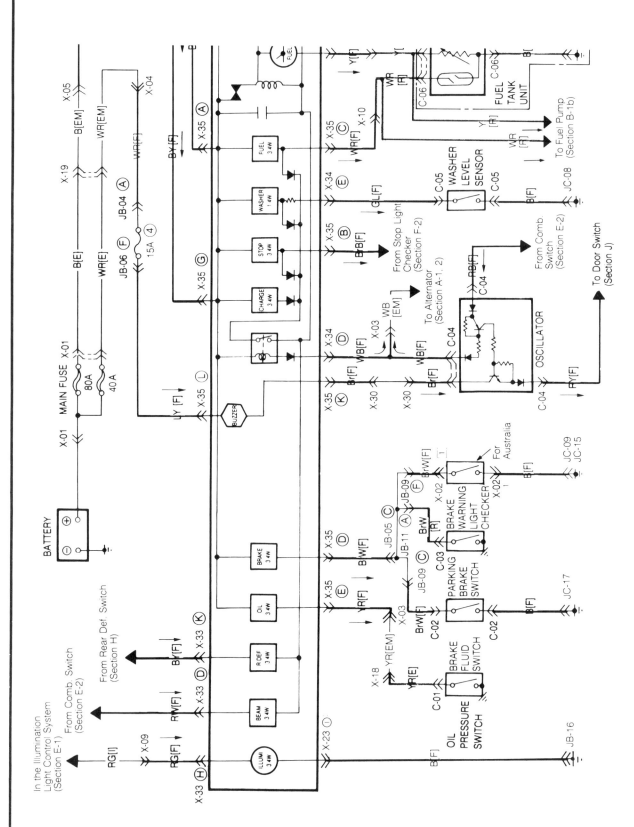

Fig. 13.112 Meters and warning lights wiring diagram (Estate model)

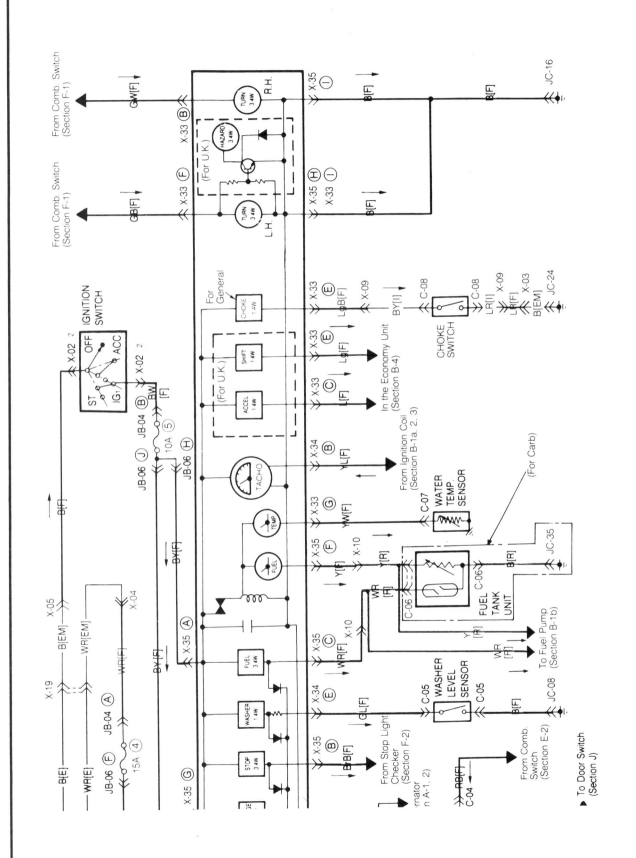

Fig. 13.112 Meters and warning lights wiring diagram (Estate model) (continued)

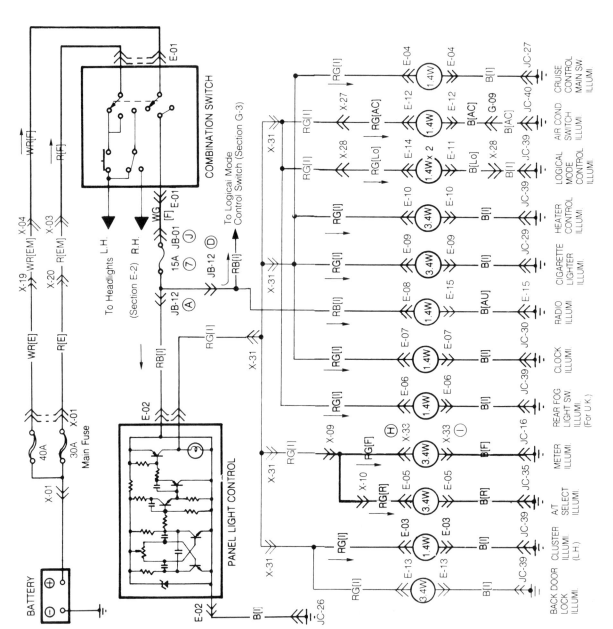

Fig. 13.113 Instrument illumination light control system wiring diagram (Estate model)

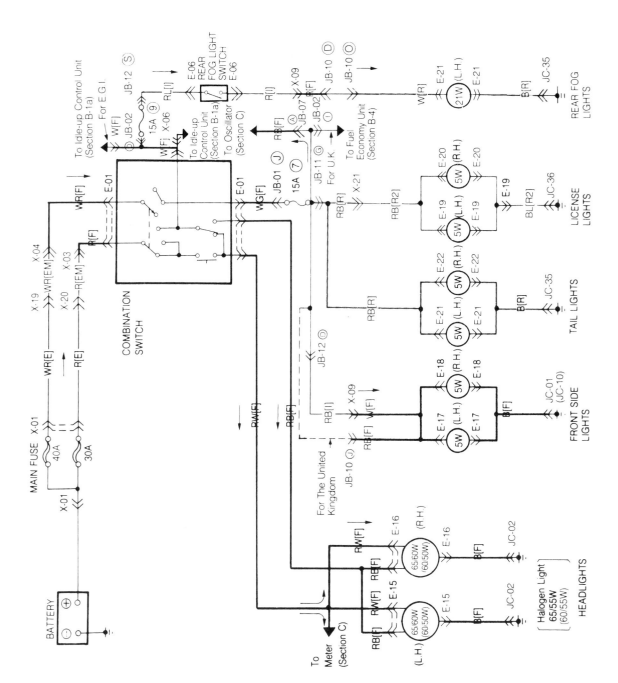

Fig. 13.114 Front side lights, headlights, tail lights, number plate and rear fog lights wiring diagram (Estate model)

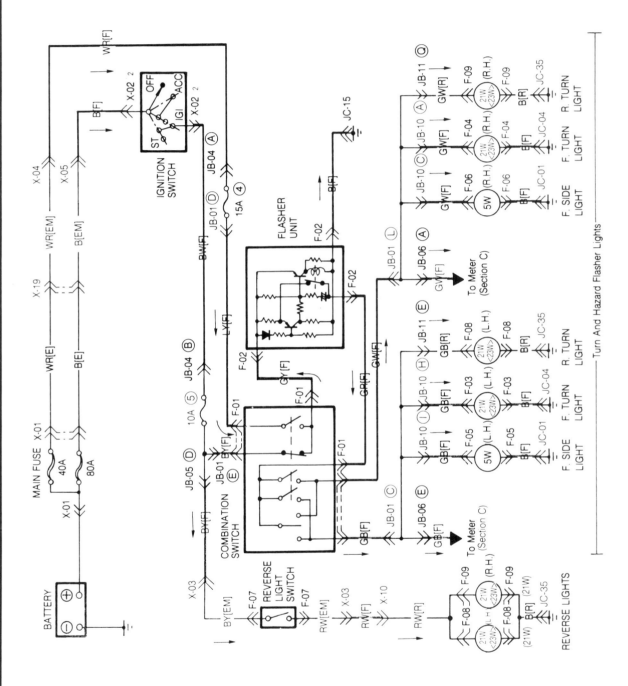

Fig. 13.115 Reversing lights and indicators wiring diagram (Estate model)

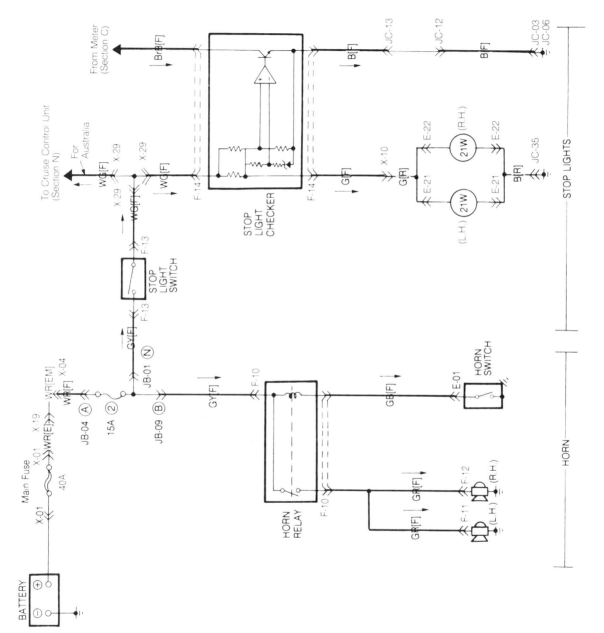

311

Fig. 13.116 Horn and stop lights wiring diagram (Estate model)

312

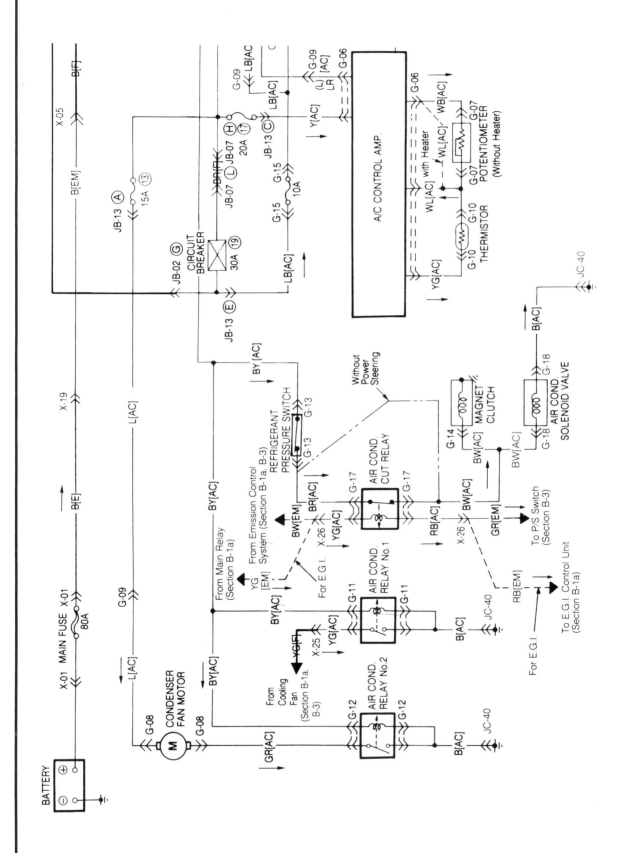

Fig. 13.117 Heater and air conditioning systems (as applicable) wiring diagram (Estate model)

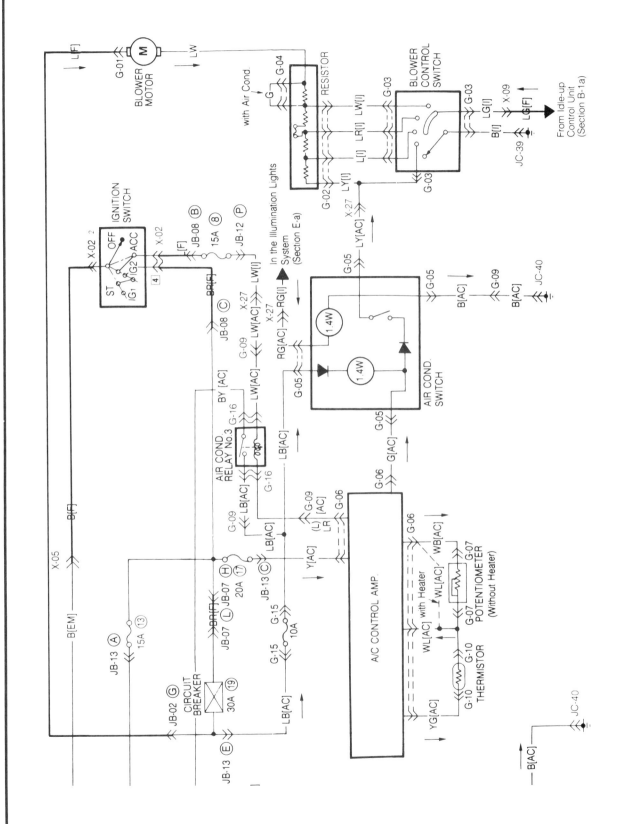

Fig. 13.117 Heater and air conditioning systems (as applicable) wiring diagram (Estate model) (continued)

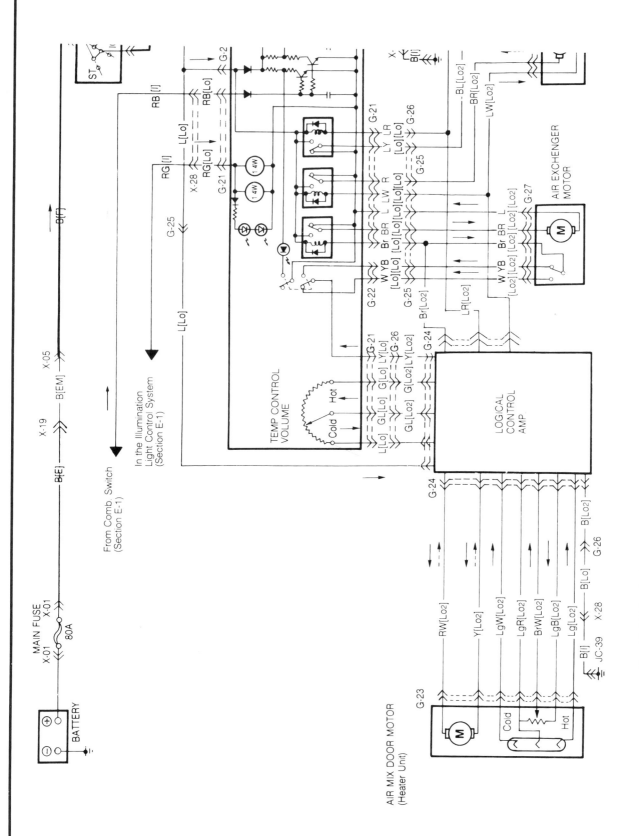

Fig. 13.118 Logic ('Logical') mode heater control system wiring diagram (Estate model)

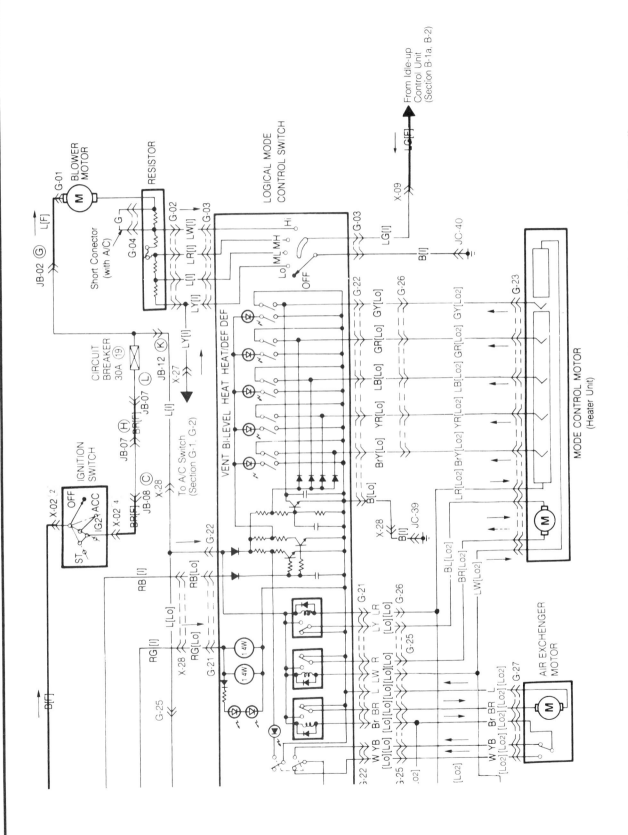

Fig. 13.118 Logic ('Logical') mode heater control system wiring diagram (Estate model) (continued)

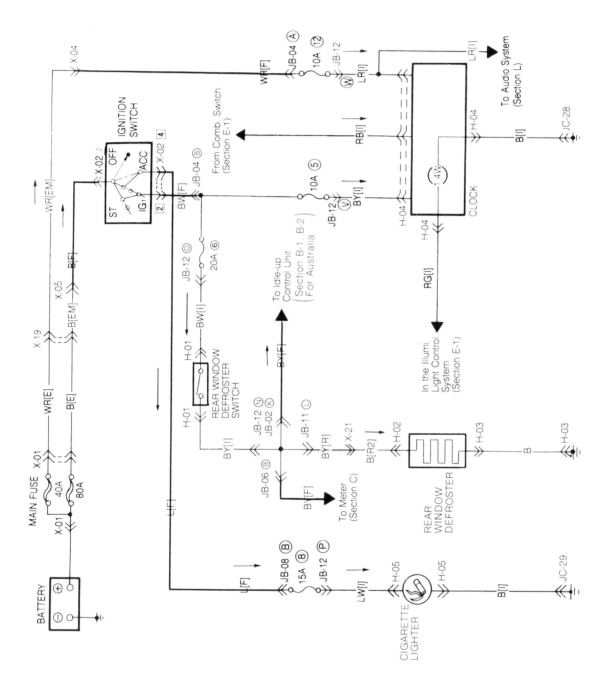

Fig. 13.119 Automatic clock and heated rear window wiring diagram (Estate model)

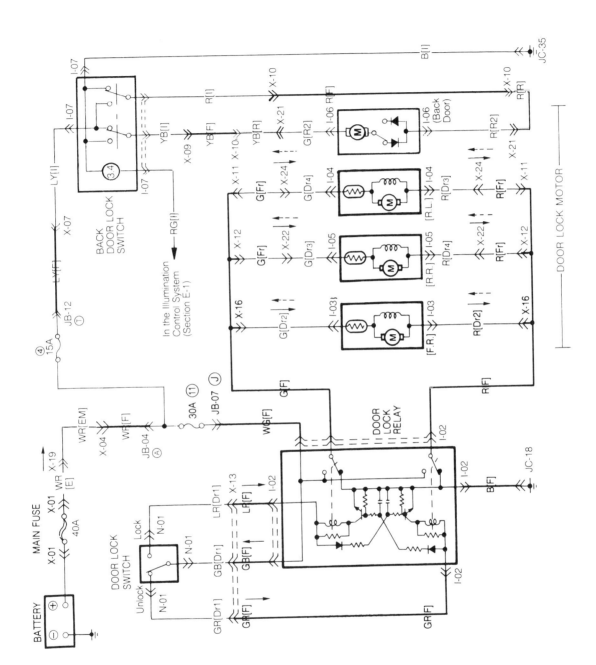

Fig. 13.120 Central locking (power door lock) system wiring diagram (Estate model)

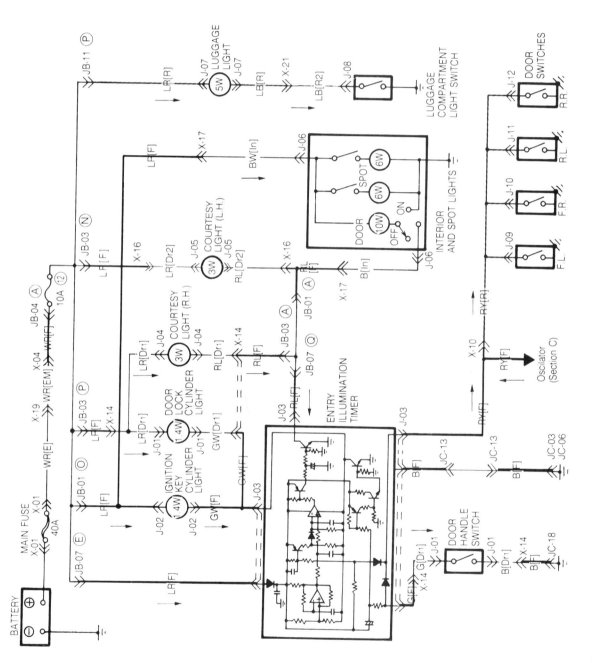

Fig 13.121 Courtesy lights, door lock cylinder lights, ignition key lock unit illumination light, interior and spot lights and luggage compartment light wiring diagram (Estate model)

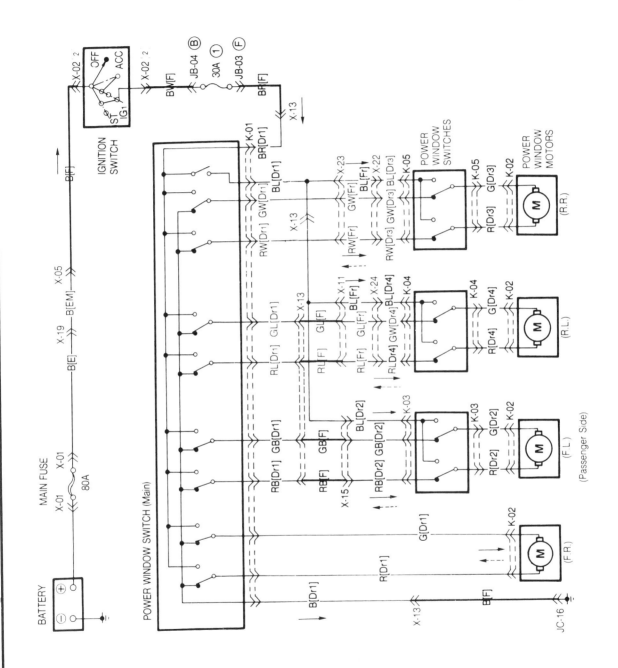

Fig. 13.122 Electric (power) window wiring diagram (Estate model)

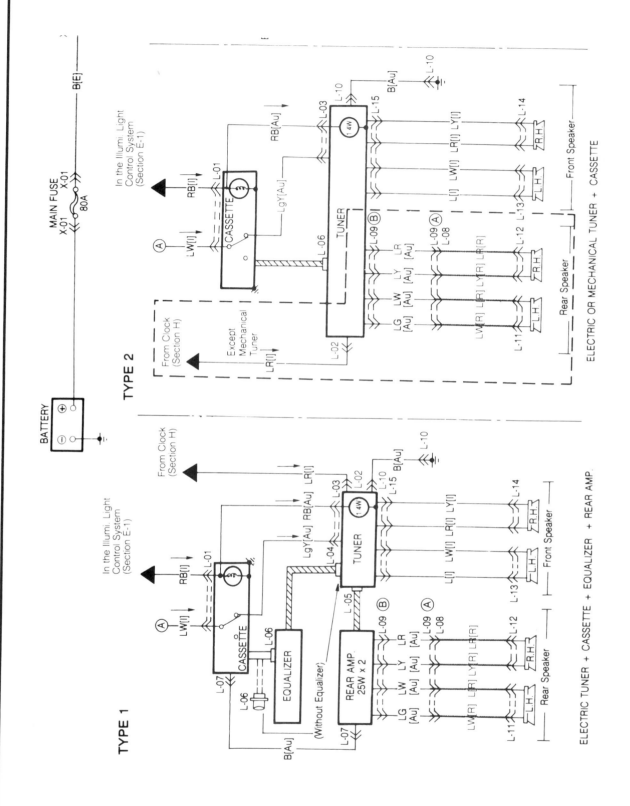

Fig. 13.123 Audio system wiring diagram (Estate model)

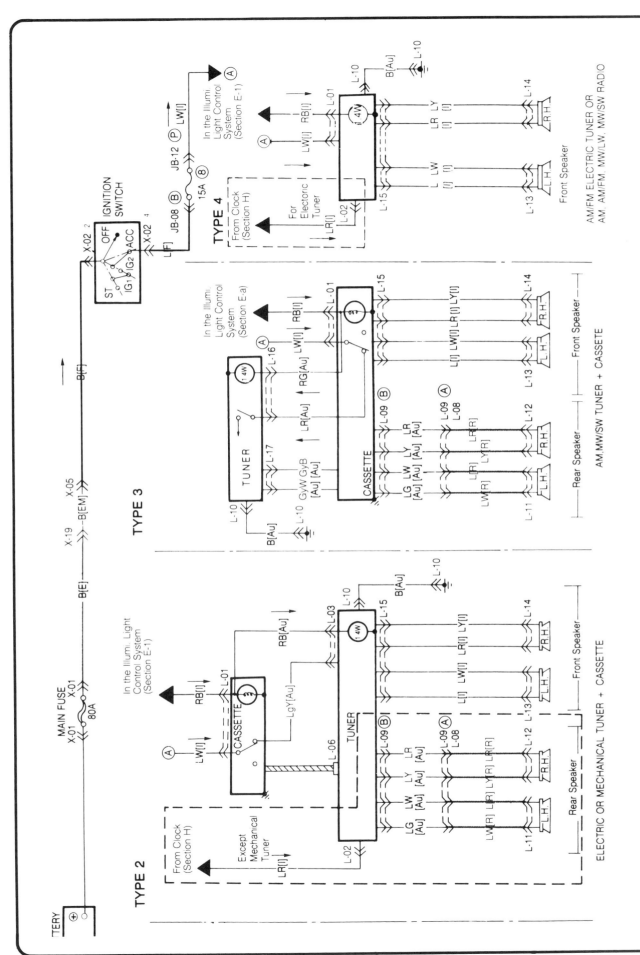

Fig. 13.123 Audio system wiring diagram (Estate model) (continued)

322

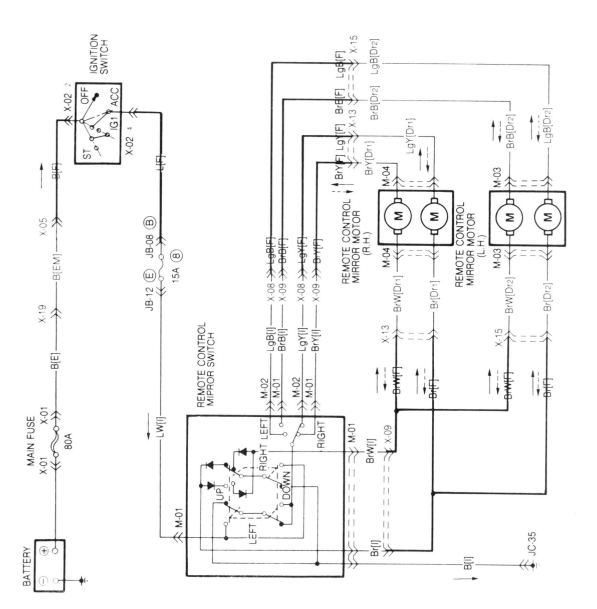

Fig. 13.124 Remote control exterior mirror wiring diagram (Estate model)

Index